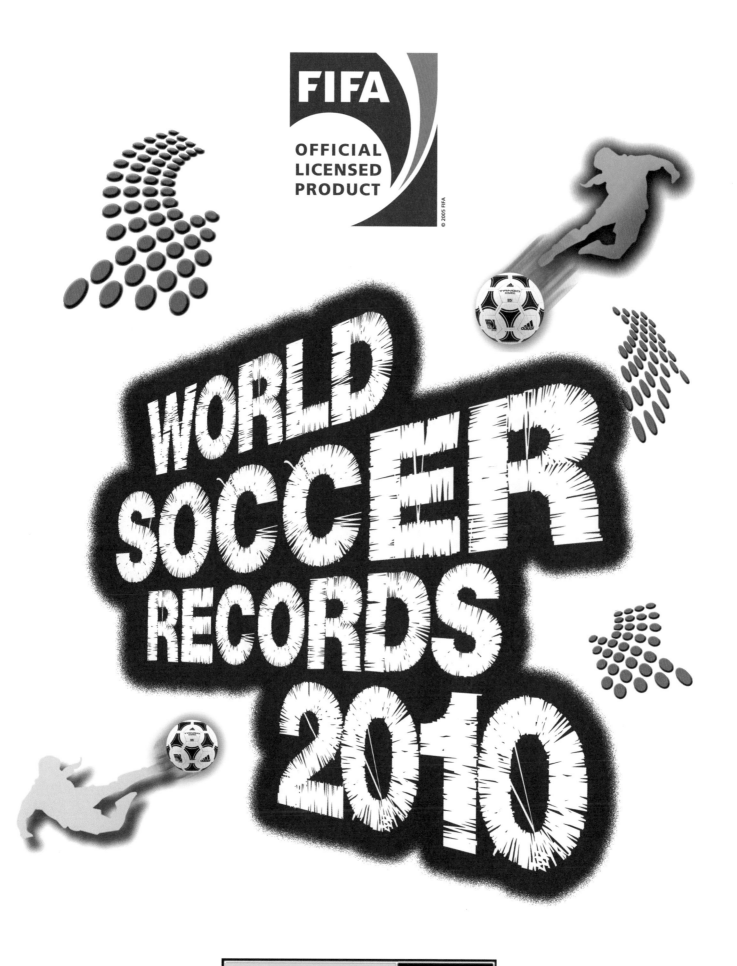

This edition published in 2009

Copyright © Carlton Books Limited 2009

Published in the UK under the title *FIFA World Football Records 2010*

Carlton Books Limited
20 Mortimer Street
London W1T 3JW

10 9 8 7 6 5 4 3 2

ISBN: 978-1-84732-564-8

Editor: Martin Corteel
Designers: Paul Chattaway & Luke Griffin
Picture Research: Paul Langan
Production: Kate Pimm

Manufactured under licence by Carlton Books Limited.

Printed in Dubai

FIFA
OFFICIAL
LICENSED
PRODUCT

© 2005 FIFA

WORLD SOCCER RECORDS 2010

KEIR RADNEDGE

CONTENTS

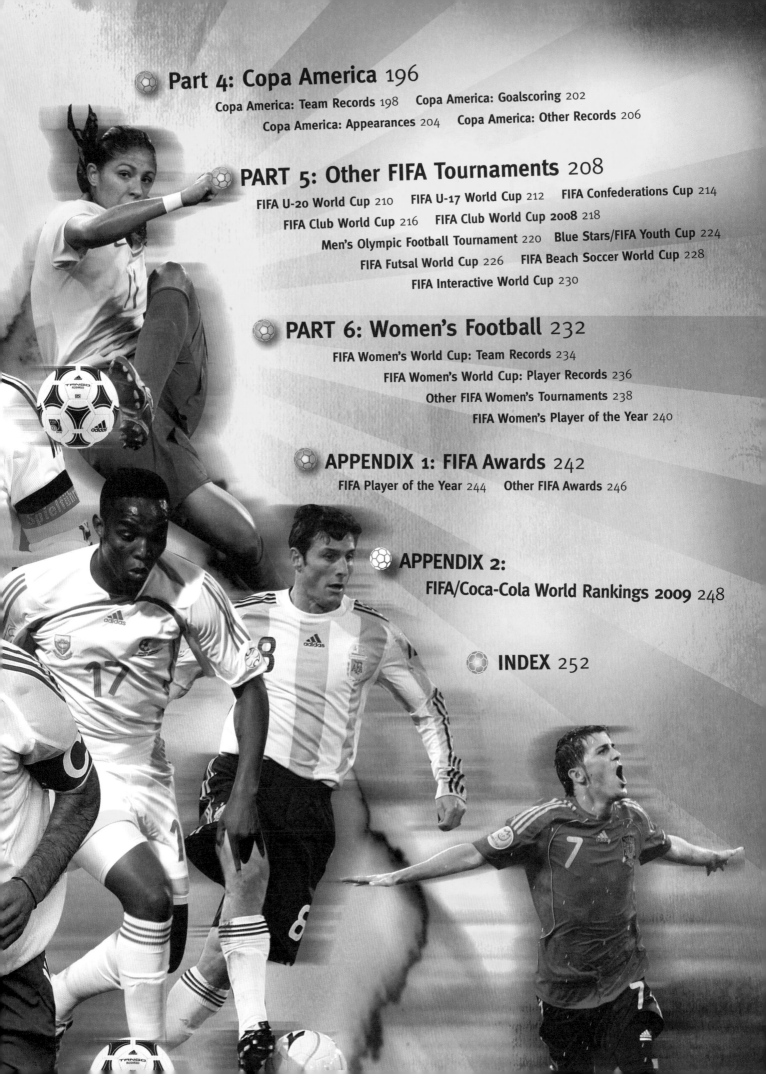

Italian team captain Fabio Cannavaro holds aloft the FIFA World Cup trophy as he is surrounded by his team-mates after the final between Italy and France in the Olympic Stadium, Berlin in 2006. Italy defeated France 5-3 in a shoot-out after a 1-1 draw.

INTRODUCTION

WELCOME to the first edition of a new venture in international football publishing – *FIFA World Football Records 2010*. Ranging across the length, breadth and depth of world football, the intention of this book is to explore, explain and intrigue the reader with the people, places and competitions that have made association football the No.1 sport around the globe.

The intention was not to create a history book relying on mere statistics, those facts and figures which enthral a focused following of their own. Rather, this book surveys key moments and crucial decisions not only in great tournaments such as the FIFA World Cup, but also all those other international events that link the football family from Albania to Zimbabwe. Of course, the pace of change and development in world football has created an enormous challenge for any statistician. The game never stands still; the appearances and goalscoring records of yesterday are being superseded year by year, even month by month. Thus a cut-off point had to be established for the statistical information contained here at the end of May 2009.

The great events of the world game link fans throughout the six geographical regions: Africa, Asia, Europe, Oceania, South America plus the Caribbean, Central and North America. Billions will be watching the next major event in the international calendar when, in 2010, the FIFA World Cup goes to Africa for the first time – to South Africa to be precise. All those viewers, whether live at matches or via television, are linked in their passion for the game with pioneers introduced here such as Charles Alcock and Lord Kinnaird. In the 19th century, they played central roles in constructing the original laws of the game that are being interpreted today by the likes of Cristiano Ronaldo and Lionel Messi.

Particular thanks are due to David O'Connor and Meike Willemsen at FIFA headquarters in Zurich, to the editorial writers and researchers, who included Kevin Connolly, Chris Hawkes, Aidan Radnedge and Andrew Warshaw, as well as Sam Ferguson and Carolina Bohorquez at Global Brands. An anomaly in football is that the game's chequered history means some of the older official records are at variance. This applied particularly in the cross-over years between amateur and professional football and the dispute over the status of some editions of early international competitions, such as the Copa America. However, the majority of fixed points have remained incontrovertible ever since the original challenge matches between Scotland and England in the late 19th century.

Here the reader will find the great countries, the great competitions, the great clubs, players and managers – from Germany to Italy, from Brazil to Argentina and on across oceans and continents echoing the spread of the game across the globe. Football owns many labels: as the simplest game, as the game of the people and as the beautiful game. It is also a game whose passion encircles the world. Hopefully, all of these things have been brought to life in these pages.

Keir Radnedge
June 2009

Argentina's Lionel Messi, left, is challenged by Nigeria's Promise Isaac during the men's football tournament final between Nigeria and Argentina in the National Stadium at the 2008 Beijing Olympics.

PART 1: THE COUNTRIES

FOOTBALL'S popularity is evident across all levels of society through all the world's continents and nations. It knows no boundaries of politics or religion or race – and at its heart is a simple structure that has worked effectively for well over a century. At the head of the world football pyramid is FIFA, the world federation. Supporting FIFA's work are the six regional geographical federations representing Africa, Asia, Europe, Oceania, South America, plus the Caribbean, Central and North America. Supporting the regions in turn are the national associations of 208 countries – and thus FIFA can boast more member countries than even the United Nations. The countries are pivotal. They field the national teams who have built sporting history through their many and varied achievements in world-focused competitions such as the FIFA World Cup. But they also oversee the growth of football in their country – from professional leagues to the game at grassroots level.

Representative teams from England and Scotland played out the first formal internationals in the late 19th century, thus laying the foundation for the four British home nations' unique independent status within a world football family otherwise comprised of nation states. The original British Home Championships was the first competition for national teams, but its demise, as a result of a congested fixture list, has left the Copa America in South America as the oldest survivor. Later came the FIFA World Cup in 1930 as well as the regional championships whose winners now compete every four years at the FIFA Confederations Cup in the country that is preparing to host the next FIFA World Cup ... the ultimate celebration of national team football.

Flags of the participating nations for the 2006 FIFA World Cup are paraded at the opening ceremony.

Europe was the cradle of modern association football. The laws were compiled in England in the middle of the nineteenth century but within only a few years they were being carried across the continent by students, engineers, sailors, soldiers and businessmen – igniting the passion evident from fans on any given day in any given country (not least the Dutch).

⚽ENGLAND

England is where football began; the country where the game was first developed, which saw the creation of the game's first Football Association and the first organized league, and which now plays host to the richest domestic league in the world. But England have not had it all their own way on the international scene. Far from it. One solitary FIFA World Cup™ win apart, as hosts in 1966, the Three Lions have found it hard to shake off the "underachievers" tag when it comes to major tournaments.

IN THE BEGINNING

The day it all began ... 30 November 1872, when England played their first official international match, against Scotland, at Hamilton Crescent, Partick. The result was a 0-0 draw in front of a then massive crowd of 4,000, who each paid an admission fee of one shilling (5p). In fact, teams representing England and Scotland had played five times before, but most of the Scottish players had been based in England and the matches are considered unofficial. England's team for the first official game was selected by Charles Alcock, the secretary of the Football Association. His one regret was that, because of injury, he could not pick himself to play. In contrast, the first rugby union international between England and Scotland had been played in 1881, but England's first Test cricket match was not played until March 1877, against Australia in Melbourne.

SHOOT-OUT SHOCKER

England have never won a shoot-out in the FIFA World Cup. In 1998 they lost to Argentina in the second round in Saint-Etienne and in 2006 they lost to Portugal in the quarter-finals in Gelsenkirchen. In each match England had a key player sent off: David Beckham in 1998 and Wayne Rooney in 2006.

THE CLASSIC

Because of England's status as being the home of modern football and Brazil's record five FIFA World Cup wins, England vs. Brazil is considered one of the game's classic rivalries. England have only won three times in 22 games – and never in major competition.

IF THE CAP FITS

England's players in the historic first game against Scotland all wore cricket-style caps while the Scots wore hoods. England's "fashion statement" sparked the use of the word "cap" to refer to any international appearance. The tradition of awarding a cap to British international footballers still survives today.

ENGLAND'S BIGGEST WINS

1882	Ireland 0 England 13
1899	England 13 Ireland 2
1908	Austria 1 England 11
1964	United States 0 England 10
1947	Portugal 0 England 10
1982	England 9 Luxembourg 0
1960	Luxembourg 0 England 9
1895	England 9 Ireland 0
1927	Belgium 1 England 9
1896	Wales 1 England 9
1890	Ireland 1 England 9

ENGLAND'S BIGGEST DEFEATS

1954	Hungary 7 England 1
1878	Scotland 7 England 2
1881	England 1 Scotland 6
1958	Yugoslavia 5 England 0
1964	Brazil 5 England 1
1928	England 1 Scotland 5
1882	Scotland 5 England 1
1953	England 3 Hungary 6
1963	France 5 England 2
1931	France 5 England 2

TELLING THE TIME

In 1961 England demolished Scotland 9-3 at Wembley. The unfortunate Scottish goalkeeper was Frank Haffey. England also had a goal disallowed. That prompted an England fan, asked the time by a sad Scottish supporter, to answer: "Almost ten past Haffey..."

THE AULD ENEMY

England have played more games – 110 – against Scotland than against any other country, even though the annual British Home Championship was scrapped after 1984. England have won 45 and lost 41 of the encounters, with 24 drawn, scoring 192 goals and conceding 169. The last time they met was on 17 November 1999, when Scotland won a European Championship qualifier 1-0 at Wembley.

TEENAGE PROMISE

Theo Walcott became England's youngest full international when he played against Hungary at Old Trafford on 30 May 2006 at the age of 17 years 75 days. On 10 September 2008, he became England's youngest scorer of a hat-trick in a 4-1 win away to Croatia in Zagreb, aged 19 years 178 days. The previous youngest international was Wayne Rooney, who was 17 years 111 days old when he played against Australia in February 2003.

FIRST DEFEAT

Hungary's 6-3 win at Wembley in 1953 was the first time England had lost at home to continental opposition. Their first home defeat by non-British opposition came against the Republic of Ireland, who beat them 2-0 at Goodison Park, Liverpool, in 1949.

RUNAWAY SUCCESS

England have hit double figures five times: beating Ireland 13-0 and 13-2 in 1882 and 1899, thrashing Austria 11-1 in 1908, crushing Portugal 10-0 in Lisbon in 1947 and then the United States 10-0 in 1964 in New York. The ten goals were scored by Roger Hunt (four), Fred Pickering (three), Terry Paine (two) and Bobby Charlton.

GAMES FOR THE BOYS

During his reign as England manager, Sven-Goran Eriksson regularly made so many changes in friendly games that the game's world federation, FIFA, created a rule to restrict the number of substitutions. Erikkson made a full 11 changes four times: against Holland (2001), Italy (2002), Australia (2003) and Iceland (2004).

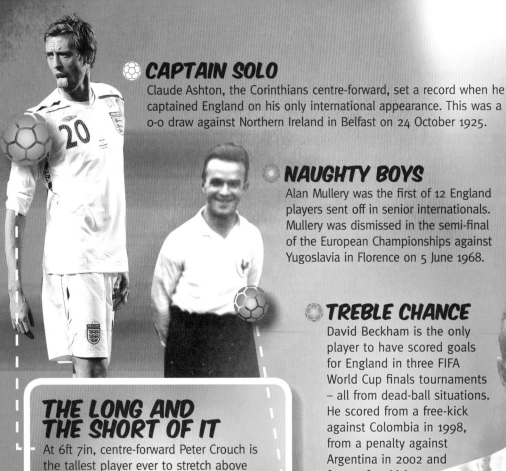

CAPTAIN SOLO

Claude Ashton, the Corinthians centre-forward, set a record when he captained England on his only international appearance. This was a 0-0 draw against Northern Ireland in Belfast on 24 October 1925.

NAUGHTY BOYS

Alan Mullery was the first of 12 England players sent off in senior internationals. Mullery was dismissed in the semi-final of the European Championships against Yugoslavia in Florence on 5 June 1968.

DOUBLING UP

Arthur Milton, the Arsenal right winger, was the last of 12 players who played full internationals for England at both football and cricket. His one England football game came against Austria in 1951. He then played six times for England's cricket team between 1958 and 1959.

TREBLE CHANCE

David Beckham is the only player to have scored goals for England in three FIFA World Cup finals tournaments – all from dead-ball situations. He scored from a free-kick against Colombia in 1998, from a penalty against Argentina in 2002 and from a free-kick against Ecuador in the second round in 2006.

THE LONG AND THE SHORT OF IT

At 6ft 7in, centre-forward Peter Crouch is the tallest player ever to stretch above opposing defences for England – while Fanny Walden, the Tottenham winger who won two caps in 1914 and 1922, was the shortest at 5ft 2. Sheffield United goalkeeper Billy "Fatty" Foulke was the heaviest England player at 18st when he played against Wales on 29 March 1897.

CAPTAINS COURAGEOUS

The international careers of Billy Wright and Bobby Moore, who both captained England a record 90 times, very nearly overlapped. Wright, from Wolves, played for England between 1946 and 1959 and Moore, from West Ham, between 1962 and 1973, including England's FIFA World Cup win in 1966.

TOP APPEARANCES

#		
1	Peter Shilton	125
2	David Beckham	112
3	Bobby Moore	108
4	Bobby Charlton	106
5	Billy Wright	105
6	Bryan Robson	90
7	Michael Owen	89
8	Kenny Sansom	86
9	Gary Neville	85
10	Ray Wilkins	84

UP THROUGH THE RANKS

Terry Venables was the only player to represent England at all levels – schoolboy, youth, amateur, under-23 [as it was] and full. He only played twice for the senior side but went on to manage them from 1994 to 1996 – guiding hosts England to within a penalty shoot-out of the European Championship final.

WRONG WAY!

Though the goal is sometimes credited to Scottish striker John Smith, it is believed that Edgar Field was the first English player to score an "own goal" as Scotland crushed England 6-1 in 1881. By the time Field put the ball in his own net, Scotland were already 4-1 up (final score 6-1). The full-back, who was an FA Cup winner and loser with Clapham Rovers, is in good company. Manchester United's Gary Neville has scored two own goals "against" England.

CLOSE BUT NO CIGAR

Jimmy Greaves is possibly the greatest goalscorer ever to play for England, with a phenomenal record of 44 goals in just 57 appearances – including six hat-tricks – making him England's best established goals-to-game striker. But Greaves missed out on a career highlight when he was injured in the final group game of the 1966 FIFA World Cup. His replacement, Geoff Hurst, scored in the second round, kept his place and went on to make history. Greaves and the other unused reserves of World Cup-winning sides were finally awarded medals by FIFA in 2007.

BECKHAM'S RECORD

David Beckham played for England for the 109th time when he appeared as a second-half substitute in the 4-0 win over Slovakia in a friendly international on 28 March 2009. That overtook the record number of England games for an outfield player, which had been set by Bobby Moore, England's 1966 FIFA World Cup-winning captain. Beckham, born on 2 May 1975, in Leytonstone, London, made his first appearance for his country on 1 September 1996, in a FIFA World Cup qualifying match against Moldova. He was appointed full-time England captain in 2001 by the then new manager Sven-Goran Eriksson – stepping down after England's quarter-final defeat by Portugal in the 2006 FIFA World Cup.

GRAND OLD MAN

Stanley Matthews became England's oldest-ever player when he lined up at outside-right against Denmark on 15 May 1957 at the age of 42 years 104 days. That was 22 years and 229 days after his first appearance. Matthews was also England's oldest marksman. He was 41 years eight months old when he scored against Northern Ireland on 10 October 1956.

TOP GOALSCORERS

1	Bobby Charlton	49
2	Gary Lineker	48
3	Jimmy Greaves	44
4	Michael Owen	40
5	Tom Finney	30
=	Nat Lofthouse	30
=	Alan Shearer	30
8	Viv Woodward	29
9	Steve Bloomer	28
10	David Platt	27

ROLL UP, ROLL UP

The highest attendance for an England game came at Hampden Park on 17 April 1937, when 149,547 spectators crushed in to see Scotland's 3-1 victory in the British Home Championships. Only 2,378 turned up in Bologna to see San Marino stun England after nine seconds in Graham Taylor's side's 7-1 victory that was not enough to secure qualification to 1994 FIFA World Cup.

THE REAL HOME OF FOOTBALL

Contrary to popular belief, myth and even most football record books, the original home of the England national football team is The Oval. It was The Oval in Kennington – now more famous for cricket – which hosted the first "unofficial" international games (five in all) between representative teams from England and Scotland between 1870 and 1872. The Oval went on to host England's first "official" home international (their second game), which also turned out to be England's first international victory (4-2 over Scotland), as well as wins against Wales and Ireland in the fledgling British Home Championship.

FIRST AND FOREMOST

England's first official international was a 0-0 draw against Scotland in Glasgow on 30 November 1872, though England and Scotland had already played a number of unofficial representative matches against each other prior to that. Given that England's only opponents for four decades were the home nations – and only Scotland for the first seven years, it is not surprising that England's first draw, win and defeat were all against their northern neighbours. After the goalless first game, the second fixture – played at The Oval on 8 March 1873 – proved a more exciting affair: England won 4-2 in a six-goal thriller. In their third game, back in Glasgow almost exactly a year later, Scotland evened things up with a 2-1 win. These fixtures completed the trio of first wins, defeats and draws for the oldest participants in international football.

YOUR COUNTRY NEEDS YOU

The first England teams were selected from open trials of Englishmen who responded to the FA's adverts for players. It was only when these proved too popular and unwieldy that, in 1887, the FA decided that it would be better to manage the process through an International Selection Committee, which continued to pick the team until Sir Alf Ramsey's appointment in 1962.

UNFINISHED BUSINESS

England's friendly, away at Argentina on 17 May 1953, was called off with the score at 0-0 due to torrential rain. Both Football Associations decided to record the "official" result as 0-0. However, when England's 1995 match against the Republic of Ireland was abandoned after 27 minutes due to crowd trouble, the 0-1 scoreline at the time was not recognized. The England players did, however, keep the caps they were awarded for the match.

WONDERFUL WALTER

Walter Winterbottom was the England national team's first full-time manager – and remains both the longest-serving (with 138 games in charge) and the youngest-ever England manager, aged just 33 when he took the job in 1946 (initially as a coach and then, from 1947, as manager). The former teacher and Manchester United player led England to four FIFA World Cups.

MANAGERIAL ROLL OF HONOUR

Name	P	W	D	L	F	A
Walter Winterbottom (1946–62)	138	77	33	28	380	195
Sir Alf Ramsey (1962–74)	113	69	27	17	224	98
Joe Mercer (1974)	7	3	3	1	9	7
Don Revie (1974–77)	29	14	7	8	49	25
Ron Greenwood (1977–82)	55	33	12	10	93	40
Bobby Robson (1982–90)	95	47	30	18	154	60
Graham Taylor (1990–93)	38	18	13	7	62	32
Terry Venables (1994–96)	24	11	11	2	35	14
Glenn Hoddle (1996–98)	28	17	6	5	42	13
Howard Wilkinson (1999–2000)	2	0	1	1	0	2
Kevin Keegan (1999–2000)	18	7	7	4	26	15
Peter Taylor (November 2000)	1	0	0	1	0	1
Sven-Goran Eriksson (2001–06)	67	40	17	10	127	60
Steve McClaren (2006–07)	18	9	4	5	32	12
Fabio Capello (2008–)	13	10	1	2	31	11

COMING OVER HERE

Argentina were the first non-UK side to play at Wembley – England won 2-1 on 9 May 1951 – while Ferenc Puskas and the "Magical Magyars" of Hungary were the first "foreign", or "continental", side to beat England at Wembley, with their famous 6-3 victory in 1953. This humiliation marked Alf Ramsey's last game as an England player. England first tasted defeat to a "foreign" side when they lost 4-3 to Spain in Madrid on 15 May 1929. Two years later England gained their revenge with a 7-1 win at Highbury.

NOT QUITE HOME...

Although synonymous with the national team, Wembley has not always been England's home. The first England international to be staged there – when it was still called the "Empire Stadium" – was a 1-1 draw with Scotland on 12 April 1924.

IRISH EYES ARE SMILING

England's first home defeat by non-United Kingdom opponents came on 21 September 1949, when they lost 2-0 to Ireland at Goodison Park.

WHO'S THE GREATEST?

Sir Alf Ramsey and Glenn Hoddle are tied as the most statistically successful England managers with win ratios of 61 per cent. Sir Alf's 1966 FIFA World Cup victory, however, puts him head and shoulders above all the rest. Technically, caretaker manager Peter Taylor has the worst record – a 100 per cent record of defeat. But then, he was only in charge for one game – a 1-0 defeat to Italy in Turin, a game that saw David Beckham making his first appearance as England captain. Steve McClaren is the only full-time manager to have failed to qualify for any international tournament, losing out to Croatia and Russia in the race to reach Euro 2008. Terry Venables was spared the need to qualify for his only tournament, Euro 1996, since England were hosts. McClaren's 16-month tenure (during which Venables served as his assistant) is also the shortest full-time reign as national team manager.

SCOTLAND

A country with a vibrant domestic league and a rich football tradition – it played host to the first-ever international football match, against England, in November 1872 – Scotland have never put in the performances on the international stage to match their lofty ambitions. There have been moments of triumph, such as an unexpected victory over Holland at the 1978 FIFA World Cup™, but far too many moments of despair. They have not qualified for the finals of a major tournament since 1998.

HOME OF THE FIRST INTERNATIONAL FIXTURE

Scotland vs. England is the oldest international rivalry in world football – their 0-0 draw, in Glasgow on 30 November 1872, was the first-ever international match. Despite England edging overall encounters 45 to 41 (with 24 draws), Scotland have recorded some famous wins, including when they became the first side to defeat England after the 1966 FIFA World Cup, claiming the "unofficial world champions" title following a 3-2 win in 1967.

REFUSING TO JOIN THE PARTY

Even though they may have faced their share of bad luck over the years, Scotland's absence from the 1950 FIFA World Cup was entirely of their own choosing. FIFA had offered the top two teams in the 1948–49 and 1949–50 British Home Championship places in the 1950 FIFA World Cup. However, Scottish Football Association (SFA) secretary George Graham announced that Scotland would not enter the FIFA World Cup unless they topped the table. When Scotland finished second to England, captain George Young pleaded with the SFA to change its mind, but Graham refused, saying the SFA had to keep its word. It is not a mistake the Scots would make again: when they finished as runners-up to England again in qualifying in 1954, they had no hesitation in taking their place in Switzerland for that year's FIFA World Cup. They should have stayed at home: the squad had only 13 players (not the 22 permitted), manager Andy Beattie resigned after the first game, and they lost their second and final match 7-0 to Uruguay.

SO CLOSE AND YET SO FAR

Scotland have made a habit of coming close to success, but then failing at the final hurdles. When they went out in the first round of the 1974 FIFA World Cup, they became the first undefeated team to exit the competition. In the qualifying stages for Euro 2008, Scotland beat 2006 FIFA World Cup runners-up France twice (both 1-0), but still failed to make the cut. In their latest game against England, the second leg of a Euro 2000 qualification playoff, they won 1-0 at Wembley – but again missed out, having already lost the first leg 2-0 at Hampden Park.

SCOTTISH LEAGUE CHAMPIONS

Club	Winners	Runners-up
Rangers	51*	29
Celtic	42	28
Heart of Midlothian	4	14
Aberdeen	4	13
Hibernian	4	6
Dumbarton	2*	0
Motherwell	1	5
Dundee	1	4
Kilmarnock	1	4
Dundee United	1	0
Third Lanark	1	0
Airdrieonians	0	4
Falkirk	0	2
Morton	0	1

* Rangers and Dumbarton shared the championship in 1891.

OLD FIRM TWO-HORSE RACE

Glasgow clubs Rangers and Celtic have dominated the history of Scottish football. Between them, they have topped the table in 93 out of 111 Scottish top-division seasons. Rangers hold the record for the most titles won, with 51 (including one shared with Dumbarton), while Celtic have won the most Scottish Cups – 34. They have both won nine titles in a row – Rangers from 1988–89 to 1996–97 and Celtic from 1965–66 to 1973–74. Of their head-to-head matches, perhaps none was more fiercely contested than Celtic's 2-1 victory in the 1904–05 playoff to decide the title after both sides had finished level on 41 points. An English referee had to be brought in for the 6 May match at Hampden Park to avoid even the slightest hint of bias. In addition to their individual records, the "Old Firm" derby holds the record for the highest-ever UK league match attendance: in 1939, 118,567 spectators crammed into Ibrox to see Rangers beat Celtic 2-1, thanks to goals from Dave Kinnear and Alex Venters.

THE TARTAN ARMY

Despite not reaching a major finals since 1998, Scotland are famous for their noisy, friendly, kilt-clad "Tartan Army" of followers. Scottish fans received awards for their exemplary behaviour at the 1998 FIFA World Cup and the 1992 European Championship. The Army lived up to its name in 1977, however, when they tore up the Wembley turf following Scotland's 2-1 victory over England.

DON'T COME HOME TOO SOON

Scotland have never made it past the initial stages of the finals of an international tournament. They've gone out of the FIFA World Cup on goal difference three times: to Brazil in 1974, to eventual runners-up Holland (on goals scored) in 1978 and to the Soviet Union in 1982.

MAJOR TOURNAMENTS

FIFA WORLD CUP™: 8 appearances – First-round exits every time.
EUROPEAN CHAMPIONSHIP: 2 appearances – First-round exits in 1992 and 1996.
FIRST INTERNATIONAL: Scotland 0 England 0 (Glasgow, 30 November 1872)
BIGGEST WIN: Scotland 11 Ireland 0 (Glasgow, 23 February 1921)
BIGGEST DEFEAT: Uruguay 7 Scotland 0 (Basel, Switzerland, 19 June 1954)

ROOM FOR ONE MORE?

Hampden Park, Scotland's national stadium, boasts the record for the highest-ever football attendance in Europe. The crowd was so huge no one can be quite sure how many squeezed in to watch Scotland vs. England in 1937, though the official figure is usually quoted as 149,415. Scotland won the British Home Championship tie 3-1, though they ended runners-up to Wales in the overall tournament.

THE UNBEATABLE "LISBON LIONS"

The year 1967 was an exciting one for Scottish sides in Europe: Kilmarnock reached the semi-finals of the Inter-Cities Fairs Cup and Rangers were runners-up in the European Cup-Winners' Cup, but most memorably Celtic became the first British side to win the European Cup when they beat the favourites Inter Milan 2-1 in Lisbon. At the final whistle, a pitch invasion by jubilant – but not violent – Celtic fans meant that the trophy could not be presented on the pitch, as planned. Captain Billy McNeill had to be escorted under armed guard to a special presentation podium. The Celtic side, all of whom were born within a 30-mile radius of the club, won every tournament they entered in the 1966–67 season, a record that remains unmatched in Scottish football.

KING KENNY

Kenny Dalglish is Scotland's joint-top international goalscorer (with Denis Law) and remains the only player to have won more than a century of caps for the national side, with 102 in total – 11 more than the next highest cap-winner, goalkeeper Jim Leighton. Despite growing up a Rangers fan (he was born in Glasgow on 4 March 1951), Dalglish made his name spearheading Celtic's domestic dominance in the 1970s, winning four league titles, four Scottish Cups and one League Cup. He then went on to become a legend at Liverpool, winning a hat-trick of European Cups (1978, 1981 and 1984) and leading the side as player-manager to their first-ever league and cup double in 1986. He later joined Herbert Chapman and Brian Clough as one of the few managers to lead two different sides to the league title – guiding Blackburn Rovers to the summit of English football in 1994–95. For Scotland, Dalglish scored in both the 1978 and 1982 FIFA World Cup finals, netting the first goal in the famous 3-2 victory over eventual runners-up Holland in the 1978 group stages. He played his last international in 1986.

OTHER SHORT REIGNS

Then-Aberdeen manager Alex Ferguson took charge of Scotland for the 1986 FIFA World Cup finals after the tragic death of manager Jock Stein following the 1-1 draw with Wales that secured a playoff place. Ferguson led Scotland to victory over Australia, but could not steer the side past the first round in Mexico, exiting with only one point and one goal. At least Ferguson lasted the whole tournament – Scotland's first full-time manager, Andy Beattie, resigned after his side's first match in the 1954 FIFA World Cup (a 1-0 defeat to Austria) after he had been given only 13 of a possible maximum 22 players to work with.

GONE TOO SOON

The late Celtic legend Tommy Burns (16 December 1956–15 May 2008), in addition to a clean sweep of winners' medals from the domestic Scottish game and eight caps, holds the dubious honour of being Scotland's shortest-reigning manager. Taking over as caretaker after Berti Vogts resigned, his single game in charge was a dispiriting 4-1 defeat to Sweden. Burns went on to help chart the national team's mini-revival as assistant to Walter Smith from 2004–07.

HOW DO THEY MANAGE IT?

Scotland has produced arguably the greatest British managers, including Matt Busby, Bill Shankly, Jock Stein and Alex Ferguson. Between them, they have in excess of 109 years of management experience, taking in more than 5,000 games and winning 35 league titles, 24 FA Cups and six European trophies, including four European Cups – the continent's ultimate club prize. Stein's Celtic became the first British side to win the European Cup in 1967, while Busby led Manchester United to the same honour in 1968 – a decade after the devastating Munich air crash that killed eight of the "Busby Babes" and which left Busby in a hospital for two months. Stein went on to lead the Scottish national side, where he was succeeded by Ferguson. Shankly took Liverpool from second division mediocrity to promotion, three league titles, two FA Cups and the UEFA Cup, while Ferguson continues to lead Manchester United as they dominate the English league and Europe – he has collected 11 league titles, five FA Cups, two European Champions Cups and two World Club Championships.

SCOTLAND – PEOPLE

Tommy Burns – shortest reign as manager
Berti Vogts – only foreign manager
Kenny Dalglish – most international caps
Denis Law – shares goalscoring record with Dalglish
Hampden Park – record attendance (1937)
John McDougall – first Scotland hat-trick, vs. England in 1878

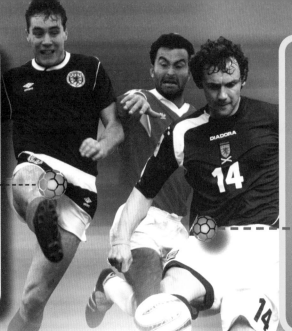

TOP SCORERS

1	Kenny Dalglish	30
=	Denis Law	30
3	Hughie Gallacher	24
4	Lawrie Reilly	22
5	Ally McCoist	19
6	Bob Hamilton	15
7	Andy Wilson	14
=	Maurice Johnston	14
9	Bob McColl	13
=	James McFadden	13

TOP APPEARANCES

1	Kenny Dalglish	102
2	Jim Leighton	91
3	Alex McGleish	77
4	Paul McStay	76
5	Tom Boyd	72
6	Christian Dailly	67
7	Willie Miller	65
8	Danny McGrain	62
9	Richard Gough	61
=	Ally McCoist	61

THAT'S ALL, VOGTS

Berti Vogts was the first foreigner to take charge of the Scottish national team – and probably ensured the Scotland manager's job would be held by a Scot for the foreseeable future. Vogts lost 16 of his 31 games in charge – including 5-0, 6-0 and 4-0 drubbings at the hands of France, Holland and Wales respectively. He resigned after just two years, citing negative media pressure.

ROUGH HANDS

Alan Rough was the only goalkeeper not to wear gloves at the 1978 World Cup. It was not the most successful of decisions: he conceded six goals as Scotland failed to qualify for the second round – though this was better than the glove-wearing Mexican goalkeepers Jose Reyes and Pedro Soto, who conceded 12 goals in just three games between them.

HAT-TRICK HERO

John McDougall became the first Scottish international to score a hat-trick – in a 7-2 victory over England in a friendly at Hampden Park on 2 March 1878. McDougall started the scoring after just seven minutes, and Scotland were 4-0 up by half-time. He played five games for Scotland, scoring four goals in total, and he also played for Vale of Leven in the domestic league.

THE LAWMAN

Denis Law is joint top scorer for Scotland with Kenny Dalglish, scoring 30 goals in only 55 games compared with the 102 it took Dalglish to do the same. Law twice scored four goals in a match for Scotland. First against Northern Ireland on 7 November 1962, helping win the British Home Championships. He repeated the feat against Norway in a friendly on 7 November 1963. Law clearly enjoyed playing against Norway, having grabbed a hat-trick in Bergen just five months earlier.

I HAVEN'T FELT THIS GOOD SINCE ARCHIE GEMMILL SCORED AGAINST HOLLAND

Archie Gemmill scored Scotland's greatest goal on the world stage in the surprise 3-2 victory over Holland at the 1978 FIFA World Cup. He jinked past three defenders before chipping the ball neatly over Dutch goalkeeper Jan Jongbloed. Amazingly, in 2008, this magical moment was turned into a dance in the English National Ballet's "The Beautiful Game".

WALES

In a land where rugby union remains the national obsession, Wales have struggled to impose themselves on the world of international football. Despite having produced a number of hugely talented players, Wales have only ever played once in the finals of a major tournament – at the 1958 FIFA World Cup™ finals in Sweden.

CAUGHT ON CAMERA

Pioneer movie-makers Sagar Mitchell and James Kenyon captured Wales vs. Ireland in March 1906, making it the first filmed international match.

LUCK ON THEIR SIDE

Wales's one and only appearance at the finals of a major tournament owes something to luck. They had finished second in their group, behind Czechoslovakia, with only the winners going through. But then FIFA ordered Israel, who due to political problems in the Middle East had won their group without playing a game, to play one of the second-place teams. Belgium were drawn out of the hat, but refused to travel to Israel. Wales were next. They accepted, and went on to beat Israel 4-0 on aggregate (played over two legs) to win a place in Sweden.

YOUNG DRAGON

Gareth Bale became the youngest player to play for Wales when he came on as sub against Trinidad and Tobago on 27 May 2006 aged just 16 years and 315 days.

SHUT OUT

On 3 March 1902, Leigh Roose became the first Welsh keeper in 21 games to keep a clean sheet against England. Roose went on to captain the national side.

BILLY MEREDITH

Born in Chirk, Wales, on 30 July 1874, Billy Meredith was an early superstar of football, and a controversial figure at that. A star for both Manchester clubs, the outside-right – and former pit-pony driver – played for Wales on 48 occasions, scoring 11 goals.

BRICKS TO BRILLIANCE

Goalkeeper Neville Southall made the first of his record 92 appearances for Wales in a 3-2 win over Northern Ireland on 27 May 1982. The former hod-carrier and bin man kept 34 clean sheets in 15 years playing for Wales and won the English Football Writers' Player of the Year in 1985 thanks to his performances alongside Welsh captain Kevin Ratcliffe at Everton. In his final match for Wales on 20 August 1997, he was substituted halfway through a 6-4 defeat against Turkey in Istanbul.

TOP CAPS

1	Neville Southall	92
2	Gary Speed	85
3	Dean Saunders	75
4	Peter Nicholas	73
=	Ian Rush	73
6	Mark Hughes	72
=	Joey Jones	72
8	Ivor Allchurch	68
9	Brian Flynn	66
10	Andy Melville	65

GIGANTE BUONO

Welsh legend John Charles, who was never booked or sent off, was nicknamed "The Gentle Giant" by fans at Juventus, where he won three league titles and two Italian cups. In 1958, he capped off a Player-of-the-Year season with Juve by playing with Wales at the FIFA World Cup. However, he missed the 1-0 quarter-final defeat to Brazil through injury.

⚽ MATCH RECORDS

Wales's record victory is an 11-0 win over Ireland at Wrexham on 3 March 1888; their 9-0 defeat to Scotland on 23 March 1878 remains their worst loss.

⚽ WHERE'S OUR GOLDEN BOY?

One of the most skilful and successful players never to appear at the FIFA World Cup, Ryan Giggs somehow missed 18 consecutive friendlies for Wales.

⚽ MANAGING

Dave Bowen followed up captaining Wales in their one and only appearance in the FIFA World Cup finals in 1958, by becoming their longest-serving manager from 1964–74.

⚽ RUSH FOR GOAL

Ian Rush is Wales's leading goalscorer, with 28 goals in 73 games. His first came in a 3-0 win over Northern Ireland on 27 May 1982; he scored the 28th and final goal in a 2-1 win over Estonia in Tallinn in 1994.

⚽ HOME CHAMPIONS

Wales won the Home Championship (an annual competition played between England, Ireland, Scotland and Wales between 1883 and 1984) on 12 occasions, seven outright and five shared.

TOP GOALS

1	Ian Rush	28
2	Trevor Ford	23
=	Ivor Allchurch	23
4	Dean Saunders	22
5	Mark Hughes	16
=	Cliff Jones	16
=	Craig Bellamy	16
8	John Charles	15
9	John Hartson	14
10	Robert Earnshaw	13

⚽ HAT-TRICK HERO

Welsh striker Robert Earnshaw holds the remarkable record of having scored hat-tricks in all four divisions of English football, the FA Cup, the League Cup, as well as scoring three for the national team against Scotland on 18 February 2004.

NORTHERN IRELAND

Northern Ireland have played as a separate country since 1921 (before that there had been an all-Ireland side). They have qualified for the FIFA World Cup™ finals on three occasions: in 1958 (when they became the smallest country to reach the quarter-final stage), 1982 (when they reached the second round) and 1986.

YOUNG GUN

Norman Whiteside became the then-youngest player at a FIFA World Cup finals (beating Pele's record) when he represented Northern Ireland in Spain in 1982 aged 17 years and 41 days. He went on to win 38 caps, scoring nine goals – before injury forced his retirement aged just 26.

AGE OLD QUESTION

Sam Johnston is the youngest player to have played for any Ireland national team. He was 15 years and 154 days old when he turned out for the old combined team (before the founding of the Irish Free State) in 1882. He also scored in his second game, making him Ireland's youngest-ever goalscorer, too.

HERO HEALY

Northern Ireland's record goalscorer has scored more than double the amount of international goals than the next highest player on the list. He scored two goals on his debut against Luxembourg on 23 February 2000, and scored all three as Northern Ireland stunned Spain 3-2 in a qualifier for Euro 2008 on 6 September 2006.

"PETER THE GREAT"

Former Manchester City and Derby County striker Peter Doherty, one of the most expensive players of his era, won the English league and FA Cup as a player, and earned 19 caps for Northern Ireland in a career interrupted by World War Two. His late goal to earn a 2-2 draw in 1947 ensured Northern Ireland avoided defeat against England for the first time. As manager, he led Northern Ireland to the quarter-finals of the 1958 FIFA World Cup – Northern Ireland remain the smallest country ever to reach that stage of the competition. They were defeated 4-0 by France, who went on to finish third.

TOP CAPS

1	Pat Jennings	119
2	Mal Donaghy	91
3	Sammy McIlroy	88
4	Keith Gillespie	83
5	Jimmy Nicholl	73
6	Michael Hughes	71
=	Maik Taylor	71
8	David McCreery	67
9	Nigel Worthington	66
=	David Healy	66

GEORGE BEST

One of the greatest players never to grace a FIFA World Cup, Best (capped 37 times by Northern Ireland) nevertheless won domestic and European honours with Manchester United – including both a European Champions Cup medal and the European Footballer of the Year award in 1968. He also played in the United States, Hong Kong and Australia before his "final" retirement in 1984.

TOP GOALS

1	David Healy	35
2	Billy Gillespie	13
=	Colin Clarke	13
4	Joe Bambrick	12
=	Gerry Armstrong	12
=	Jimmy Quinn	12
=	Iain Dowie	12
8	Billy Bingham	10
=	Jimmy McIlroy	10
=	Peter McParland	10
=	Johnny Crossan	10

AWARD-WINNING FANS

The Amalgamation of Northern Ireland Football Supporters' Clubs was awarded the 2006 Brussels International Supporters' Award for its work with the Irish Football Association to tackle sectarianism in football.

GIANT JENNINGS

Pat Jennings's record 119 appearances for Northern Ireland also stood at one stage as an international record. The former Tottenham Hotspur and Arsenal goalkeeper made his international debut – aged just 18 – against Wales on 15 April 1964, and played his final game in the 1986 FIFA World Cup, against Brazil, on his 41st birthday.

BINGHAM'S DOUBLE

Billy Bingham was a key player on the right wing in Northern Ireland's 1958 FIFA World Cup run, and managed the national side to FIFA World Cup qualification in 1982 and 1986 – the only time the country has made it to consecutive tournaments.

REP. OF IRELAND

It took a combination of astute management and endless searching through ancestral records before the Republic of Ireland finally qualified for the finals of a major tournament, at the 20th time of asking. But ever since Jack Charlton took the team to Euro '88, Ireland have remained one of Europe's most dangerous opponents.

COME ONE COME ALL

Jack Charlton's Irish team of the late 1980s and early '90s made the most of family connections to widen the talent pool. Goalscoring hero Tony Cascarino qualified through a grandfather who, it turned out, was not actually a blood relative.

ED BROOKES

Bohemians striker Ed Brookes scored Ireland's first hat-trick just one year after the Football Association of Ireland's recognition from FIFA in a 3-1 win over the United States in June 1924.

MORE FOR MOORE

Paddy Moore was the first player ever to score four goals in a FIFA World Cup qualifier when Ireland came from behind to draw 4-4 with Belgium on 25 February 1934. Don Givens became the only Irishman to equal Moore's feat when he scored all four as Ireland beat Turkey in October 1975.

CAPTAIN ALL-ROUND

Johnny Carey not only captained Matt Busby's Manchester United to the English league title in 1952, he also captained both Northern Ireland (nine caps) and later the Republic of Ireland (27 caps). He went on to manage the Republic of Ireland between 1955 and 1967.

CROSSING THE CODES

Cornelius "Con" Martin was a Gaelic footballer whose passion for soccer resulted in his expulsion from the Gaelic Athletic Association. His versatility meant he was as good at centre-half as he was in goal, both for club (Aston Villa) and country. He played both in goal and outfield for the fledgling Irish national team, scoring a penalty in the 2-0 victory over England at Goodison Park in 1949 – in what was England's first home defeat to a non-British opponent.

⚽ STEVE STAUNTON

Ireland's record cap holder was made captain for the 2002 FIFA World Cup after Roy Keane's sensational walkout. Staunton went on to manage Ireland from 2006–07 but was replaced after he failed to guide the team to the finals of the 2008 European Championships.

⚽ CHAMPION CHARLTON

Jack Charlton became a hero after he took Ireland to their first major finals in 1988, defeating England 1-0 in their first game at the European Championship. Even better was their first FIFA World Cup finals two years later, where the unfancied Irish lost out only to hosts Italy in the quarter-finals.

TOP GOALS

1	Robbie Keane	37
2	Niall Quinn	21
3	Frank Stapleton	20
4	Don Givens	19
=	Tony Cascarino	19
=	John Aldridge	19
7	Noel Cantwell	14
8	Gerry Daly	13
=	Jimmy Dunne	13
10	Ian Harte	11

⚽ CROKE PARK

Croke Park is the traditional Dublin home of the Gaelic Athletic Association and banned "foreign" sports ... until Ireland were given special permission to play their qualifiers for Euro 2008 there while their traditional home, Lansdowne Road, was being renovated.

KEANE CARRY-ON

Roy Keane stormed out of Ireland's preparation for the 2002 FIFA World Cup in Japan and Korea, heading home before the tournament had even started. Keane's career with Ireland began against Chile on 22 May 1991. He played in every game of Ireland's remarkable run to the quarter-finals in the 1990 FIFA World Cup in Italy. Originally appointed captain by Mick McCarthy, Keane returned to the Irish set-up after McCarthy resigned – but announced his international retirement after Ireland failed to qualify for the 2006 FIFA World Cup. His final game was a 1-0 defeat to France on 7 September 2005.

TOP CAPS

1	Steve Staunton	102
2	Kevin Kilbane	93
3	Shay Given	92
4	Niall Quinn	91
5	Tony Cascarino	88
6	Robbie Keane	86
7	Paul McGrath	83
8	Packie Bonner	80
9	Ray Houghton	73
10	Kenny Cunningham	72
=	Liam Brady	72
=	Damien Duff	72

FRANCE

France – nicknamed "Les Bleus" – are one of the most successful teams in the history of international football. They are one of only two countries to be World and European champions at the same time. They won the FIFA World Cup™ in 1998 as tournament hosts, routing Brazil 3-0 in the final. Two years later, they staged a sensational, last-gasp recovery to overhaul Italy in the Euro 2000 final. The French equalized in the fifth minute of stoppage time, then went on to win 2-1 on a golden goal. France had previously won the European Championship in 1984, beating Spain 2-0 in the final in Paris. They reached the 2006 FIFA World Cup™ final too, but lost to Italy in a penalty shoot-out. France also won FIFA's Confederations Cup in 2001 and 2003 and took the Olympic football gold medal in 1984.

PIONEERS

France were one of only four European teams to take part in the first FIFA World Cup finals, in Uruguay in 1930. They were also one of only 17 countries to take part in the first-ever European Championship in 1958.

PARTYING IN PARIS

France's 1998 FIFA World Cup victory led to the greatest scenes of celebration in Paris since the French capital was liberated from German occupation in 1944. According to police estimates, around two million people burst on to the streets; with nearly a million dancing along the Champs-Elysées in the centre of Paris. The supporters' favourite chant was for Zinedine Zidane: "Zidane – president!"

FRANCE STARS SEE RED

France have had a player sent off in each of their FIFA World Cup final appearances. Marcel Desailly was dismissed for a foul on Cafu in their 1998 win over Brazil, and Zinedine Zidane was sent off in the 2006 final for a head butt on Italy defender Marco Materazzi.

KOPA – FRANCE'S FIRST SUPERSTAR

Raymond Kopa (born on 13 October 1931) was France's first international superstar. Born into a family of Polish immigrants (the family name was Kopaszewski), he was instrumental in Reims's championship successes of the mid-1950s. He later joined Real Madrid and became the first French player to win a European Cup winner's medal. He was the playmaker of the France team that finished third in the 1958 FIFA World Cup finals. His performances for his country that year earned him the European Footballer of the Year award.

BEST AND WORST

France's first full international match was a 3-3 draw against Belgium in Brussels on 1 May 1904. They scored their biggest-ever international win when they beat Azerbaijan 10-0 in a Euro 2006 qualifier at Auxerre on 6 September 1995. They suffered their biggest defeat, 17-1 to Denmark, in the London Olympics on 22 October 1908.

FRANCE AND FIFA

France were one of the founder members of FIFA in 1904. Frenchman Robert Guerin became the first president of the governing body. Another Frenchman, Jules Rimet, was president from 1921 to 1954. Rimet was the driving force behind the creation of the FIFA World Cup and football's most coveted trophy is named in his honour.

CROSSING THE BARRIERS

France's teams have usually included a high proportion of players from immigrant backgrounds or ethnic minorities. Three of France's greatest players – Raymond Kopa, Michel Platini and Zinedine Zidane – were the sons or grandsons of immigrants. In 2006, 17 of France's 23-man FIFA World Cup squad had links to the country's former colonies.

KISSING COLLEAGUES

Marseille colleagues centre-back Laurent Blanc and goalkeeper Fabien Barthez had a special ritual during France's run to the 1998 FIFA World Cup crown. Before the game, Blanc would always kiss Barthez's shaven head, even when the veteran defender was suspended for the final.

PLATINI'S CAREER
(LEAGUE APPEARANCES):

Year	Club	Appearances	Goals
1972–79	Nancy	181	98
1979–82	Saint-Etienne	104	58
1982–87	Juventus	147	68

TARNISHED CROWN

Marseille are the only French club to win the European Cup. They beat Milan 1-0 in the 1993 final. But they were not allowed to defend the trophy. Club president Bernard Tapie was found guilty of trying to fix a league match at Valenciennes.

PLATINI'S GLITTERING CAREER

Michel Platini (born in Joeuf on 21 June 1955) has enjoyed a glittering career, rising from a youngster at Nancy to become one of France's greatest-ever players, a hero in Italy, and now the president of UEFA. He was also joint organizing president (along with Fernand Sastre) of the 1998 FIFA World Cup finals in France. Platini was the grandson of an Italian immigrant who ran a café in Joeuf, Lorraine. He began with the local club, Nancy, before starring for Saint-Etienne, Juventus and France. He was instrumental in France's progress to the 1982 FIFA World Cup semi-finals and was the undisputed star of the European Championships two years later, when France won the tournament on home soil.

BARTHEZ 16

THE FULL SET

Four France stars have a full set of top international medals – FIFA World Cup, European Championship and European Cup winners. Marcel Desailly, Bixente Lizarazu, Didier Deschamps and Zinedine Zidane all played in France's winning teams of 1998 and 2000. In addition, Desailly won the European Cup with Marseille in 1993 and Milan the following year. Deschamps won with Marseille in 1993 and Juventus in 1996; Lizarazu with Bayern Munich in 2001; and Zidane with Real Madrid in 2002.

FONTAINE'S FEAT

France's Just Fontaine still holds the record for the most goals scored in a FIFA World Cup finals tournament. He stepped in when Rene Bliard was injured – and scored 13 goals in only six appearances at the 1958 finals as France took third place. He netted 30 goals in just 21 games for his country. He also scored 121 league goals in 131 league games for Reims and helped them reach the 1959 European Cup final, where they lost 2-0 to Real Madrid.

KOPA'PREMIER

In 1958, Raymond Kopa was the first French player to be voted European Footballer of the Year. Michel Platini was the next, in 1983, 1984 and 1985. Striker Jean-Pierre Papin received the honour in 1991. Zinedine Zidane won the award in 1998, after France's FIFA World Cup victory.

HENRY BENCHED

France's record scorer Thierry Henry missed out on an appearance in the 1998 FIFA World Cup final because of Marcel Desailly's red card. Henry was France's leading scorer in the competition with three goals in the group games. Coach Aime Jacquet planned to use him as a substitute in the final, but midfielder Desailly's sending-off forced a re-think. Jacquet decided to reinforce the midfield and Henry spent the full 90 minutes of the final on the bench.

BITTER-SWEET FOR TREZEGUET

Striker David Trezeguet has bitter-sweet memories of France's clashes with Italy in major finals. He scored the "golden goal" that beat the Italians in extra-time in the Euro 2000 final, but six years later, he was the man who missed as France lost the FIFA World Cup final on penalties. Trezeguet's shot bounced off the bar and failed to cross the line.

LILIAN IN THE PINK

Defender Lilian Thuram made his 142nd and final appearance for France in their defeat by Italy at Euro 2008. His international career had spanned nearly 14 years, since his debut against the Czech Republic on 17 August 1994. Thuram was born in Pointe a Pitre, Guadeloupe on 1 January 1972. He played club football for Monaco, Parma, Juventus and Barcelona before retiring in the summer of 2008 because of a heart problem. He was one of the stars of France's 1998 FIFA World Cup-winning side and scored both goals in the semi-final victory over Croatia – the only international goals of his career. He gained another winner's medal at Euro 2000. He first retired from international football after France's elimination at Euro 2004, but was persuaded by coach Raymond Domenech to return for the 2006 FIFA World Cup campaign and made his second appearance in a FIFA World Cup final. He broke Marcel Desailly's record of 116 caps in the group game against Togo.

TOP CAPS

1	Lilian Thuram	142
2	Marcel Desailly	116
3	Thierry Henry	111
4	Zinedine Zidane	108
5	Patrick Vieira	106
6	Didier Deschamps	103
7	Laurent Blanc	97
=	Bixente Lizarazu	97
9	Sylvain Wiltord	92
10	Fabien Barthez	87

TOP GOALS

1	Thierry Henry	48
2	Michel Platini	41
3	David Trezeguet	34
4	Zinedine Zidane	31
5	Just Fontaine	30
=	Jean-Pierre Papin	30
7	Youri Djorkaeff	28
8	Sylvain Wiltord	26
9	Jean Vincent	22
10	Jean Nicolas	21

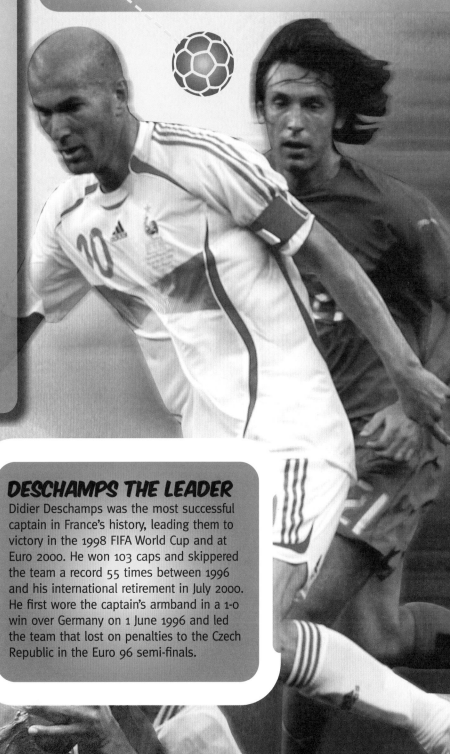

ZIDANE AND SAINT-DENIS

The Stade de France, at Saint-Denis in Paris, was the scene of Zinedine Zidane's greatest triumph, in the 1998 FIFA World Cup final. There was another family connection. Zidane's father Smail had settled in Saint-Denis after emigrating to France from Algeria. He later moved to Marseille, where Zinedine was born.

DESCHAMPS THE LEADER

Didier Deschamps was the most successful captain in France's history, leading them to victory in the 1998 FIFA World Cup and at Euro 2000. He won 103 caps and skippered the team a record 55 times between 1996 and his international retirement in July 2000. He first wore the captain's armband in a 1-0 win over Germany on 1 June 1996 and led the team that lost on penalties to the Czech Republic in the Euro 96 semi-finals.

⚽ WINNING WITH YOUTH

In the early 1990s, France became the first European country to institute a national youth development programme. The best young players were picked to attend the national youth academy at Clairefontaine. Then they went on to the top clubs' academies throughout the nation. The scheme has produced a rich harvest of stars. FIFA World Cup winners Didier Deschamps, Marcel Desailly and Christian Karembeu started at Nantes. Lilian Thuram, Thierry Henry, Manu Petit and David Trezeguet began with Monaco and Zinedine Zidane and Patrick Vieira were graduates from Cannes.

⚽ ALBERT THE FIRST

Albert Batteux (1919–2003) was France's first national manager. Before his appointment in 1955, a selection committee had picked the team. Batteux was also the most successful coach in the history of French football. He combined managing France with his club job at Reims. His biggest achievement was guiding the national team to third place in the 1958 FIFA World Cup finals. The team's two big stars, Raymond Kopa and Just Fontaine, had both played under his charge at Reims.

⚽ JACQUET'S TRIUMPH

Aime Jacquet, who guided France to FIFA World Cup victory in 1998, was also their most controversial national coach. He was criticized for alleged defensive tactics despite France's run to the semi-finals of Euro 96 and a record of only three defeats in four years. A month before the 1998 finals, the sports daily *L'Equipe* claimed he was not capable of building a successful team!

PLATINI THE YOUNGEST

Michel Platini became France's youngest-ever manager when he was appointed on 1 November 1988 aged just 33 years and 133 days. The previous youngest manager was Just Fontaine, who was 33 years and 217 days when he took charge in 1967. Platini stepped down after France's elimination at the group stage of Euro 92 and was replaced by Gerard Houllier.

NO TIME FOR FONTAINE

Former striker Just Fontaine spent the shortest-ever spell in charge of the France team. He took over on 22 March 1967 and left on 3 June after two defeats in friendlies.

HIDALGO REIGNS LONGEST

The longest-serving France manager was Michel Hidalgo, another who played under Batteux at Reims. He was appointed on 27 March 1976 and stayed for more than eight years. Hidalgo was also the first France coach to win a major trophy – the European Championship in 1984. He retired straight after France's victory on 27 June. He had also steered France to the FIFA World Cup semi-finals in 1982, when they lost to West Germany in highly controversial circumstances.

SECOND IS BEST

The site for the world-renowned Stade de France, the venue for France's big matches in Saint-Denis in the north of Paris, was the French football authorities' second choice. Original favourite was Melun-Senart, to the east of the capital, but the site in Saint-Denis, with a touch of presidential intervention, won out. Its construction began in 1995. The stadium was opened in January 1998 after two years and seven months of building work, at a cost of approximately 280 million Euros. It has a capacity of 80,000.

OVAL BALL

Fabien Barthez's father, Alain, was a fine rugby union player who won one cap for France.

ROUX SETS THE PACE

Former Auxerre coach Guy Roux holds the record for the most Ligue 1 games in charge. Roux (born on 18 October 1938) guided his team through 890 matches during a 44-year spell. He took over as player/coach in 1961 and only retired as coach in 2005. He led Auxerre from languishing in the old third division to becoming French champions in 1996. They also won the French Cup four times, in 1994, 1996, 2003 and 2005. Roux knew that an unfashionable provincial club like Auxerre could not compete financially with the big clubs, so he developed a youth policy that produced a succession of stars, such as Eric Cantona and Basile Boli. Roux's success was one of the catalysts for the now highly successful French Federation's national youth development programme.

FRANCE MANAGERS

Albert Batteux	1955–62
Henri Guerin	1962–66
Jose Arribas/Jean Snella	1966
Just Fontaine	1967
Louis Dugauguez	1967–68
Georges Boulogne	1969–73
Stefan Kovacs	1973–75
Michel Hidalgo	1976–84
Henri Michel	1984–88
Michel Platini	1988–92
Gerard Houllier	1992–93
Aime Jacquet	1993–98
Roger Lemerre	1998–2002
Jacques Santini	2002–04
Raymond Domenech	2004–

GERMANY

Politics may have divided the country in two for over 40 years, but few countries can match Germany's record in international football. Three-time winners of the FIFA World Cup™ (1954, 1974 and 1990) and three-time European Championships winners (1972, 1980 and 1996), in 1974 they became the first country in history to hold the World and European titles at the same time – and have remained a fearsome opponent in top-level football matches ever since.

ALWAYS A THREAT

Germany has been reunified since October 1990 and won its first trophy as one nation in the 1996 European Championships. Since then, the Germans have reached the last four of the FIFA World Cup in 2002 (runners-up) and 2006 (third as hosts) as well as Euro 2008 (runners-up). Germany had finished third in the 1934 FIFA World Cup finals, but that was their last glimpse of honours before the country was divided into West and East Germany after World War II. West Germany became one of the strongest and most consistent teams in world football, winning the FIFA World Cup in 1954, 1974 and 1990, and the European Championships in 1972 and 1980. They also finished FIFA World Cup runners-up in 1966, 1982 and 1986, and were European runners-up in 1976. By contrast, their eastern cousins qualified for the FIFA World Cup finals only once, in 1974.

DIAMOND STUDS

The Germans have always been in the forefront of technical innovation – as they showed in the 1954 FIFA World Cup final. The pitch in Bern was wet and rain was falling. West Germany were one of the first teams to wear removable studs, so were able to change them at half-time. Their Hungarian opponents wore traditional fixed-studded boots – and Hungary's goalkeeper, Gyula Grosics, slipped on the wet turf as Helmut Rahn scored West Germany's winning goal.

SHOOT-OUT SURE-SHOTS

German teams have always put in hours of preparation for penalty shoot-outs. Their last two major successes – the 1990 FIFA World Cup and Euro 96 successes – both came after shoot-out victories in the semi-finals. England were the Germans' victims on both occasions.

DOUBLING UP

West Germany were the first side to hold the European Championship and the FIFA World Cup at the same time. They beat the Soviet Union 3-0 in the 1972 European final, then surprised Holland 2-1 in the FIFA World Cup final two years later.

HISTORY MAN

East and West Germany met only once at senior national team level. That was on 22 June 1974, in the FIFA World Cup finals for which the West played hosts. Drawn in the same group, East Germany produced a shock 1-0 win in Hamburg. Both teams progressed to the second round.

GOLDEN WONDER

Germany became the first team to win a major title thanks to the now-discarded golden goal system when they beat the Czech Republic in the Euro 96 final at Wembley. Oliver Bierhoff's equalizer forced extra-time after Patrik Berger scored a penalty for the Czechs. Bierhoff grabbed Germany's winner five minutes into extra-time to end the game and the championship.

EAST GERMANY –
TOP APPEARANCES AND GOALS

APPEARANCES

1	Joachim Streich	98
2	Hans-Jurgen Dorner	96
3	Jurgen Croy	86
4	Konrad Weise	78
5	Eberhard Vogel	69

GOALS

1	Joachim Streich	53
2	Eberhard Vogel	24
3	Hans-Jurgen Kreische	22
4	Rainer Ernst	20
5	Henning Frenzel	19

GERMAN REUNIFICATION

Political reunification of the two Germanys was finalized on 3 October 1990 and former East German clubs had joined western leagues for the 1990–91 season. However, FIFA ruled that former East German internationals could not play for their new country until political reunification had been completed. So Germany's first truly combined team, which contained former eastern players – Matthias Sammer and Andreas Thom (substitute) – took to the field against Switzerland on 19 December 1990.

BOTH SIDES NOW

Eight players appeared for both the old East Germany and then Germany after reunification in October 1990.

Player	East German	Germany
Ulf Kirsten	49	51
Matthias Sammer	23	51
Andreas Thom	51	10
Thomas Doll	29	18
Dariusz Wosz	7	17
Olaf Marschall	4	13
Heiko Scholz	7	1
Dirk Schuster	4	3

THE 1954 "MIRACLE OF BERN"

West Germany's FIFA World Cup victory in 1954 was considered crucial to the country's unity and future economic success. Winning coach Sepp Herberger's biographer wrote: "That was the real founding day of the West German state." The victory was portrayed again by the movie-maker Sonke Wortmann more than 50 years later in a film called *Das Wunder von Bern* ("The Miracle of Bern").

AUSTRIAN CONNECTION

Germany's squad for the 1938 FIFA World Cup finals in France contained several Austrian players. After Germany had swallowed up Austria in 1938, Adolf Hitler and his Nazi regime insisted that, for political reasons, the Germany squad should include several Austrians. However, it caused friction in the camp, coach Sepp Herberger could not unite the contrasting styles and they were knocked out in the first round by Switzerland, 4-2 in a replay.

THE B TEAMS

The 1970–76 period was a golden time for West German football. The national team profited from the emergence of two top-class club sides, Bayern Munich and Borussia Monchengladbach. Bayern won the European Cup three years in a row between 1974 and 1976, while Borussia were UEFA Cup winners in 1975 and European Cup finalists two years later. Bayern contributed Sepp Maier, Paul Breitner, Franz Beckenbauer, Georg Schwarzenbeck, Uli Hoeness and Gerd Muller to the 1974 FIFA World Cup-winning squad, while Borussia supplied Berti Vogts, Herbert Wimmer, Rainer Bonhof, Gunter Netzer and Jupp Heynckes.

MAGICAL MATTHAUS

Lothar Matthaus is Germany's most-capped player. He appeared in five FIFA World Cup finals – 1982, 1986, 1990, 1994 and 1998 – a record for an outfield player. Versatile Matthaus could operate as a defensive midfielder, an attacking midfielder, or as a sweeper. He was a FIFA World Cup winner in 1990, a finalist in 1982 and 1986 and a European Championship winner in 1980. His record 150 appearances – spread over a 20-year international career – were split 87 for West Germany and 63 for Germany. He also scored 23 goals and was voted top player at the 1990 FIFA World Cup.

"DER BOMBER"

Gerd Muller was the most prolific scorer of the modern era. Neither tall nor graceful, he was quick, strong and had a predator's eye for the net. He also had the temperament to score decisive goals in big games, including the winner in the 1974 FIFA World Cup final, the winner in the semi-final against Poland and two goals in West Germany's 1972 European Championship final victory over the USSR. He netted 68 goals in 62 appearances for West Germany and remains the leading scorer in the Bundesliga and all-time record scorer for his club, Bayern Munich.

⚽ FAMOUS FRITZ

A Kaiserslautern stalwart – he remained with the club for 31 years after joining the youth team aged eight in 1928 – few players captured the heart of fledgling post-war West Germany like Fritz Walter. A former prisoner of war in Russia, during which he contracted malaria, Walter first played for the national team in 1940. Appointed captain by Sepp Herberger in 1951, he led the side – including his younger brother Ottmar – to a shock victory over firm favourites Hungary at the 1954 FIFA World Cup and became the first German in history to lift the famous Jules Rimet trophy.

⚽ GOLDEN GLOVES

Sepp Maier was at the heart of West Germany's triumphs of the early 1970s, including the 1972 European Championships and the 1974 FIFA World Cup. He remains West Germany's most-capped goalkeeper, winning 95 caps in an international career lasting from 1965 to 1979. He played his whole club career for Bayern Munich and helped them win the European Cup three times. A car crash in 1979, in which he received life-threatening injuries, ended his playing days, but he went on to become a goalkeeping coach for both Germany and his old club.

TOP CAPS

1	Lothar Matthaus	150
2	Jurgen Klinsmann	108
3	Jurgen Kohler	105
4	Franz Beckenbauer	103
5	Thomas Hassler	101
6	Berti Vogts	96
7	Sepp Maier	95
=	Karl-Heinz Rummenigge	95
9	Michael Ballack	92
10	Rudi Voller	90

STREICH BY NAME...

Joachim Streich was the greatest star of East German football. The striker held the record for both caps and goals in an international career running from 1969 to 1984. He netted 53 times in 98 appearances for his country and was also the record scorer in the old East German league, with 229 goals for Hansa Rostock and Magdeburg.

EURO GLORIES

Five German players have been voted European Player of the Year. Gerd Muller was the first West German winner in 1970. He was followed by Franz Beckenbauer in 1972 and 1976, Karl-Heinz Rummenigge in 1980 and 1981 and Lothar Matthaus in 1990. Matthias Sammer, who began his career in East Germany, was the first winner from the reunified Germany, picking up the award in 1996.

SUPER SEELER

All-action centre-forward Uwe Seeler was the top German player of the late 1950s and early '60s. He scored 43 goals in 72 appearances and played, and scored, in four FIFA World Cup finals tournaments (1958, 1962, 1966 and 1970). He also skippered West Germany to the 1966 FIFA World Cup final in England. He scored more than 400 league goals in a 19-year career with his home club, Hamburg.

DER KAISER

Franz Beckenbauer is widely regarded as the greatest player in German football history. He has also made a huge mark as a FIFA World Cup-winning coach, administrator and organizer. Beckenbauer (born on 11 September 1945) was a 20-year-old attacking wing-half when West Germany reached the 1966 FIFA World Cup final. He later defined the role of attacking sweeper, first in the 1970 FIFA World Cup finals, and then as West Germany won the 1972 European Championships and the 1974 FIFA World Cup. When West Germany needed a coach in the mid-1980s, they turned to Beckenbauer, despite his lack of experience. He delivered a FIFA World Cup final appearance in 1986, a Euro 88 semi-final and 1990 FIFA World Cup triumph in his final game in charge. He later became president of Bayern Munich, the club he captained to three consecutive European Cup victories between 1974 and 1976. He also led Germany's successful bid for the 2006 FIFA World Cup finals and headed the organizing committee. No wonder he is known as the "Kaiser" (the "Emperor") for his enormous influence on German football.

KINGS OF KAISERSLAUTERN

Four of the West German team that won the FIFA World Cup in 1954 had grown up together in the Pfalz town of Kaiserslautern. Fritz Walter, the greatest German player of the time, and his brother Ottmar, were childhood friends with the Liebrich brothers, Ernst and Werner. Ernst in turn went to school with Werner Kohlmeyer. All five played for Kaiserslautern. Four of the old friends – Werner Kohlmeyer, Werner Liebrich, Ottmar Walter and captain Fritz Walter – all played against Hungary in the 1954 FIFA World Cup final.

VOGTS THE "GUARD DOG"

Berti Vogts was known as "the guard dog" because of his tigerish marking jobs on some of the world's top players. The high point of Vogts's playing career came in West Germany's FIFA World Cup victory over Holland, when he marked Johan Cruyff out of the match. Vogts later went on to coach the reunified Germany to victory at Euro 96.

TOP SCORERS

1	Gerd Muller	68
2	Rudi Voller	47
=	Jurgen Klinsmann	47
4	Karl-Heinz Rummenigge	45
5	Miroslav Klose	44
6	Uwe Seeler	43
7	Michael Ballack	41
8	Oliver Bierhoff	37
9	Fritz Walter	33
10	Klaus Fischer	32

OTTO THE FIRST

Germany's first international manager was Otto Nerz, a qualified doctor who played for Mannheim and Tennis Borussia Berlin as an amateur. He was a strict disciplinarian and an admirer of English football who led Germany to third place in the 1934 FIFA World Cup finals. They lost 3-1 to Czechoslovakia in the semi-finals, but beat Austria 3-2 in the third-place play-off. The Nazi government sacked Nerz in 1936 after Germany's shock defeat by Norway in the football tournament at the Nazi showcase Berlin Olympics.

 ## CHANGE OF DIRECTION

Germany has a tradition for continuity in team management. Helmut Schon took over in 1964 after being Sepp Herberger's assistant; Jupp Derwall, who took over from Schon, had been his No.2. But that policy changed after West Germany's exit from the 1984 European Championships. Instead of replacing Derwall with his assistant, Erich Ribbeck, the DFB preferred the star quality of Franz Beckenbauer instead. Later managerial "outsiders" included Rudi Voller and Jurgen Klinsmann.

GERMANY'S HOME VENUES

Ground	Capacity
Dortmund	80,708
Berlin (Olympic Stadium)	74,500
Munich	69,000
Gelsenkirchen	61,524
Stuttgart	57,000
Hamburg	57,000
Frankfurt	50,300
Cologne	50,000
Hanover	49,000
Kaiserslautern	46,615

SEPP'S SURPRISE

Sepp Herberger (1897–1977) was one of the most influential figures in Germany's football history. He was their longest-serving coach (28 years at the helm) and his legendary status was assured after West Germany surprised odds-on favourites Hungary to win the 1954 FIFA World Cup final – a result credited with dragging the country out of a post-war slump. Herberger took charge in 1936 and led the team into the 1938 FIFA World Cup finals. During the war years he used his influence to try to keep his best players away from the heavy fighting. When organized football resumed in 1949, the federation decided to advertise for a national coach, but Herberger persuaded DFB chief Peco Bauwens to give him back his old job. He had a clause in his contract guaranteeing him a totally free hand in organization and selection policy. Among Herberger's favourite sayings was: "The ball is round and the match lasts 90 minutes. Everything else is just theory."

BAYERN BRILLIANCE

Bayern Munich are Germany's record champions. They have won the title on 21 occasions – 20 since the creation of the unified national league (the Bundesliga) in 1963. Until then the championship had been decided by end-of-season play-offs between the top teams of the country's regional leagues. Bayern's only championship under the old system came in 1932 when they beat Eintracht Frankfurt 2-0 in the final.

GOAL RUSH

Germany's biggest win was 16-0 against Russia in the 1912 Olympic Games in Stockholm. Gottfried Fuchs of Karlsruhe scored ten of the goals, which remains a national team record to this day.

QUICK START

Wing-back Arne Friedrich had made only two Bundesliga appearances when he was selected for his Germany senior debut in a 2-2 draw against Bulgaria in 2002.

SCHON IN SAARLAND

Helmut Schon is remembered as one of Germany's most successful managers. He started his international coaching career with Saarland, now part of Germany, but which had been made a separate state (with a population of 970,000) after the country's post-war division. Saarland's greatest moment came in the 1954 FIFA World Cup qualifiers, when they beat Norway 3-2 in Oslo to top their qualifying group. They were eventually eliminated by Sepp Herberger's West Germany.

BONUS BATTLE

Helmut Schon's 1974 FIFA World Cup winners came close to walking out before the finals started. Schon was prepared to send his squad home in a row over bonuses. A last-minute deal was brokered between Franz Beckenbauer and federation vice-president Hermann Neuberger. The vote among the squad went 11-11, but Beckenbauer persuaded the players to accept the DFB's offer. It was a great decision: they beat Holland 2-1 in the final.

GERMANY'S MANAGERS

Otto Nerz	1928–36
Sepp Herberger	1936–64
Helmut Schoen	1964–78
Jupp Derwall	1978–84
Franz Beckenbauer	1984–90
Berti Vogts	1990–08
Erich Ribbeck	1998–2000
Rudi Voller	2000–04
Jurgen Klinsmann	2004–06
Joachim Low	2006–

HOLLAND

The walled banks of orange-shirted Holland fans may have become a regular feature at the world's major football tournaments, but that has not always been the case. It wasn't until the 1970s, with Johan Cruyff and his team's spectacular brand of Total Football, that the country possessed a side worthy of the modern legend. They won the European Championship in 1988 and have regularly challenged for the game's major honours.

LUCKY RINUS

In 1974, Rinus Michels succeeded Frantisek Fadrhonc, the Czech who had steered Holland through the FIFA World Cup qualifiers, as Holland manager with Fadrhonc becoming his assistant. Holland were fortunate to qualify on goal difference. Belgium's Jan Verheyen had a "winner" disallowed for offside in the final qualifier in Amsterdam. TV replays showed the Russian referee had made a mistake. Had the goal stood, Belgium would have gone through at Holland's expense.

HERO HAPPEL

Ernst Happel is second only to Rinus Michels for his coaching achievements with Dutch teams. The former Austria defender made history by steering Feyenoord to the European Cup in 1970 – the first Dutch side to win the trophy. He was drafted in to coach Holland at the 1978 FIFA World Cup finals after guiding Belgian side Brugge to the European Cup final. In Johan Cruyff's absence, Happel drew the best from Ruud Krol, Johan Neeskens and Arie Haan as Holland reached the final before losing in extra-time to Argentina in Buenos Aires.

CAUGHT SHORT

Three Holland coaches have guided club sides to European Cup victories, but have never been as successful with the national team. Guus Hiddink, a 1988 winner with PSV Eindhoven, steered Holland to within a penalty shoot-out of the 1998 FIFA World Cup final. Frank Rijkaard, Barcelona's winning coach in 2006, quit after Holland's Euro 2000 semi-final shoot-out defeat to Italy. Louis van Gaal – Ajax coach in 1995 – was the least successful of the trio. His Holland squad failed to qualify for the 2002 FIFA World Cup finals.

MICHELS THE MASTER

Rinus Michels (1928–2005) was named FIFA's Coach of the Century in 1999 for his achievements with Holland and Ajax. The former Ajax and Holland striker took over the manager's job at his old club in 1965 and began creating the side that would go on to dominate European football in the early 1970s. Michels built the team around Johan Cruyff – as he later did with the national side – and introduced the concept known as "Total Football". He moved to Barcelona after Ajax's 1971 European Cup victory, but he was called back to mastermind Holland's 1974 FIFA World Cup bid. Nicknamed "The General", he was known as a disciplinarian who could impose order on the many different factions within the Dutch dressing room. Michels used that skill to great effect after taking over the national team again for their 1988 European Championship campaign. In the finals, Holland beat England and the Republic of Ireland to reach the last four. Then they knocked out hosts West Germany, before beating the Soviet Union 2-0 in the final. Michels had taken charge for a third spell as manager when Holland reached the semi-finals of Euro 92. He retired straight after the tournament.

PATIENT VAN BASTEN

The Holland manager's job is one of the most precarious in world football. The longest-serving manager in the modern era is Marco van Basten. He was appointed on 29 July 2004 and quit in June 2008 after Holland's quarter-final elimination from Euro 2008.

VAN BASTEN'S TOURNAMENT

Marco van Basten was the hero of Holland's 1988 European Championship success. He netted a hat-trick to see off England in the group games, scored a semi-final winner against West Germany, and then cracked a spectacular flying volley to clinch a 2-0 victory over the Soviet Union in the final. The Holland forward also starred in Italy's Serie A with AC Milan, and was twice the league's top scorer before persistent ankle trouble ended his career prematurely.

THE MISSING LINK

Johan Cruyff remains one of the most influential figures in Dutch football. His negotiations with the Dutch Federation before the 1994 FIFA World Cup finals broke down and he twice refused offers by Van Basten to step down and become Cruyff's assistant.

HOLLAND SUPPORTERS

Holland have one of the biggest groups of travelling supporters in world football. According to police, some 100,000 made the trip to Switzerland for Euro 2008. The fans nearly all wear Holland's orange shirt, creating a colourful scene wherever they go, but that caused problems for the Swiss authorities, whose police and railway staff wear orange reflective jackets. They had to change to yellow during Euro 2008 because the Dutch kept mistaking them for fellow fans!

HOLLAND MANAGERS (SINCE 1980)

Jan Zwartkruis	1978–81
Rob Baan	1981
Kees Rijvers	1981–84
Rinus Michels	1984–85
Leo Beenhakker	1985–86
Rinus Michels	1986–88
Thijs Libregts	1988–90
Nol de Ruiter	1990
Leo Beenhakker	1990
Rinus Michels	1990–92
Dick Advocaat	1992–95
Guus Hiddink	1995–98
Frank Rijkaard	1998–2000
Louis van Gaal	2000–02
Dick Advocaat	2002–04
Marco van Basten	2004–08
Bert van Marwijk	2008–

AMSTERDAM ARENA

Construction work on Holland's major venue, the Amsterdam ArenA, started in 1993. The project cost £100m and the stadium was opened on 14 August 1996. It has been Ajax's home ground ever since and was also one of the leading venues when Holland co-hosted Euro 2000. The unusual spelling was adopted after a complaint by a nightclub of the same name.

HOLLAND'S TABLOID WOES

Holland were drawn into a tabloid "scandal" the day before the 1974 FIFA World Cup final against West Germany. The German newspaper *Bild* claimed that four Dutch players and four German girls had taken part in a "naked party" at the team hotel before the semi-final win over Brazil that clinched Holland's final place. Coach Rinus Michels simply accused the German media of trying to stir up trouble.

HOLLAND'S DOUBLE LOSERS

Nine Holland players were on the losing side in both the 1974 (2-1 to West Germany) and 1978 (3-1 to Argentina) FIFA World Cup finals. Jan Jongbloed, Ruud Krol, Wim Jansen, Arie Haan, Johan Neeskens, Johnny Rep and Rob Rensenbrink started both games. Wim Suurbier started in 1974 and was a substitute in 1978. Rene Van der Kerhof was a sub in 1974 and started in 1978.

GOING DUTCH FULL-TIME

Professionalism was not introduced into Dutch football until 1954. Holland's emergence as a major power came even later, after Ajax and Feyenoord decided to go full-time professional in the early 1960s. Until then, even stars such as Ajax left winger Piet Keizer – who worked in a tailor's – had part-time jobs outside the game.

CRUYFF'S CONVERSION

Johan Cruyff used to smoke 20 cigarettes a day before undergoing heart bypass surgery in 1991 while he was coach of Barcelona. He gave up smoking after the operation and later fronted an anti-smoking campaign on behalf of the Catalan regional government.

FLYING FEAR DENIED BERGKAMP MORE CAPS

Dennis Bergkamp would have won many more than 79 caps, but for his fear of flying. Bergkamp refused to board aircraft after the Holland squad were involved in a bomb hoax incident during the 1994 FIFA World Cup in the United States. He missed away games for Holland and his clubs unless he could reach them by road, rail or boat.

TOP GOALS

1	Patrick Kluivert	40
2	Dennis Bergkamp	37
3	Faas Wilkes	35
4	Abe Lenstra	33
=	Johann Cruyff	33
=	Ruud van Nistelrooy	33
7	Bep Bakhuys	28
8	Kick Smit	26
9	Marco van Basten	24
10	Leen Vente	19

THE WINNING CAPTAIN

With his distinctive dreadlocks, Ruud Gullit cut a swathe through world football through the 1980s and '90s. Twice a European Cup winner with AC Milan and a former European Footballer of the Year, he will always be remembered fondly by the Dutch fans as being the first man in a Holland shirt to lift a major trophy – the 1988 European Championship.

HOLLAND'S EURO STARS

Three Dutch players have won the European Footballer of the Year award – Johan Cruyff, Ruud Gullit and Marco Van Basten. Cruyff picked up the award in 1971, 1973 and 1974. Gullit was the next Holland star honoured, in 1987. Van Basten was chosen in 1988, 1989 and 1992.

"HOLLAND ON TOUR"

The great Milan side of the late 1980s were often known as "Holland on tour" because of their Dutch stars – Ruud Gullit, Marco van Basten and Frank Rijkaard. They had been key figures in Holland's 1988 European Championship victory and were equally important in Milan's 1989 and 1990 European Cup wins. Gullit and van Basten both scored twice in the 1989 victory over Steaua Bucharest. Rijkaard scored the only goal against Benfica a year later.

DE BOER BOYS SET RECORD

Twins Frank and Ronald De Boer hold the record for the most games played by brothers together for Holland. Frank won 112 caps, while Ronald won 67.

THE PITBULL

Midfielder Edgar Davids was so tough in the tackle that his nickname was "The Pitbull".

CRUYFF THE MAGICIAN

Johan Cruyff's footballing achievements have made him the most famous living Dutchman. Cruyff (born in Amsterdam on 25 April 1947) was the catalyst for the rise of both Ajax and the national team. As one Dutch paper wrote before the 1974 FIFA World Cup final: "Cruyff woke up Holland and took us to a world-class level." His great opponent, Franz Beckenbauer, said: "He is the best player to have come from Europe." Cruyff joined Ajax as a ten-year-old and made his league debut at 17. He led them to eight championships and the European Cup three years in a row. He and coach Rinus Michels also developed the style of playing known as "Total Football", which became a trademark for club and country. Cruyff made his international debut, against Hungary, on 7 September 1966. He scored 33 goals in 48 appearances and captained his country 33 times. He was named Player of the Tournament in the 1974 FIFA World Cup finals and was voted European Player of the Year three times.

TOP CAPS

1	Edwin Van der Sar	130
2	Frank De Boer	112
3	Philip Cocu	101
4	Clarence Seedorf	87
5	Marc Overmars	86
=	Gio Van Bronckhorst	86
7	Aaron Winter	84
8	Rud Krol	83
9	Dennis Bergkamp	79
=	Patrick Kluivert	79

⚽ DUTCH DESPAIR

Holland's most painful defeat in recent years came on 1 September 2001. Their 1-0 loss to the Republic of Ireland in Dublin ended their hopes of reaching the 2002 FIFA World Cup finals. The Dutch conceded a shock 68th-minute goal, even though they were playing against ten men after Gary Kelly was sent off. It was the result that forced the resignation of coach Louis van Gaal.

⚽ ALL-TIME LEADING SCORER

Born in Amsterdam on 1 July 1976, centre-forward Patrick Kluivert made his debut for Holland in 1994. In the following ten years he made 79 appearances for the national side, scoring an all-time Dutch record 40 goals.

⚽ EARLY DAYS

Holland played their first international against Belgium in Brussels on 30 April 1905. Eddy de Neve scored all the goals in Holland's 4-1 win. The Dutch and their Belgian neighbours have been arch-rivals ever since.

⚽ HOLLAND'S RISE

Holland were eliminated in the early stages of the 1934 and 1938 FIFA World Cups and they did not qualify for the World Cup finals again until 1974, after narrowly pipping Belgium in their group. The rise of Dutch football coincided with a move to full-time professionalism by the leading clubs in the early 1960s.

VAN DER SAR TOPS THE LOT

Goalkeeper Edwin van der Sar (born in Voorhout on 29 October 1970) is Holland's most-capped player, having made 130 appearances for the national side. He joined Ajax in 1990 and helped them win the European Cup five years later. He made his Holland debut on 7 June 1995, against Belarus, and was their first-choice keeper for 13 years. He quit international football after Holland's elimination at Euro 2008, but new coach Bert van Marwijk persuaded him to return briefly after injuries to his successors, Maarten Stekelenburg and Henk Timmer. Van der Sar has also won the European Cup with Manchester United, as well as spending spells with Juventus and Fulham.

HOLLAND – MODERN GREATS

Holland have been one of the strongest nations in world football for the past 35 years. The Dutch "Total Football" team – led by Johan Cruyff – reached the 1974 FIFA World Cup final, only to lose 2-1 to West Germany. Four years later, the Dutch lost the final against Argentina, 3-1 in extra-time in Buenos Aires. In between, they reached the European Championship semi-finals in 1976. Coach Rinus Michels steered Holland to their one major honour, in 1988, when they beat the Soviet Union 2-0 in the European Championship final. They had gained revenge over West Germany for the 1974 defeat by winning 2-1 in the semi-finals. The Dutch have never reached another final, though they have frequently challenged in major tournaments. They lost the 1998 FIFA World Cup semi-final to Brazil and were quarter-finalists in 1994. They also lost European Championship semi-finals in 1992, 2000 and 2004.

HOLLAND SO CLOSE

Holland came within a post's width of winning the 1978 FIFA World Cup final. Rob Rensenbrink's shot bounced off an upright in the last minute of normal time. The game finished 1-1 after 90 minutes and Argentina went on to win the game 3-1 in extra-time, enough to shatter Dutch final dreams for the second FIFA World Cup in a row.

BEST AND WORST

Holland's record win is 9-0, which they have achieved twice. The first time came against Finland at the Stockholm Olympics on 4 July 1912. The second time was when they thrashed Norway in a FIFA World Cup qualifier in Rotterdam on 1 November 1972. The Dutch suffered their worst defeat on 21 December 1907, when they lost 12-2 to England's amateurs at Darlington!

PENALTY PLAGUE

Missed penalties have become a nightmare for Holland, causing their downfall in several major tournaments. The jinx started in the Euro '92 semi-final when Peter Schmeichel saved Marco van Basten's kick, enabling Denmark to win the penalty shoot-out. Holland lost their Euro 96 quarter-final to France 5-4 on penalties and, two years later, went down 4-2 to Brazil in a FIFA World Cup semi-final shoot-out. Worse followed when Holland co-hosted Euro 2000. They missed two penalties in normal time in the semi-final against Italy. Then Italy keeper Francesco Toldo saved two spot-kicks to eliminate the Dutch in the shoot-out.

TROUBLE IN THE CAMP

The Dutch are famous for arguing among themselves at major tournaments. Critics claim that trouble in the dressing room caused their failures at the European Championship in both 1976 and 1996. Holland playmaker Wim Van Hanegem confirmed a nation's concern when he said: "It happens so often that we think there's a problem if we don't have a problem!"

NEESKENS'S EARLY GOAL

Holland took a first-minute lead in the 1974 FIFA World Cup before a West German player had even touched the ball. The Dutch put together a move of 14 passes from the kick-off before Johan Cruyff was tripped in the box by Uli Hoeness. Johan Neeskens converted the first ever penalty in a World Cup final ... but they still went on to lose.

"TOTAL FOOTBALL"

Holland's 1974 FIFA World Cup finalists played a revolutionary style of football described as "Total Football" ("totaalvoetbal"), which Rinus Michels and Johan Cruyff had pioneered at Ajax. The game was based on quick passing and fluid movement, with players frequently interchanging positions. Hence full-backs Wim Suurbier and Ruud Krol often appeared in attack and midfielder Johan Neeskens was a frequent scorer with well-timed breaks from midfield.

ITALY

Only Brazil (with five victories) can claim to have won the FIFA World Cup™ more times than Italy. The Azzurri became the first nation to retain the trophy (through back-to-back successes in 1934 and 1938), snatched a surprise win in Spain in 1982, and collected football's most coveted trophy for a fourth time in 2006 following a dramatic penalty shoot-out win over France. Add the 1968 European Championship success to the mix and few nations can boast a better record. The success story does not end there. Italian clubs have won the European Cup on 11 occasions and the country's domestic league, Serie A, is considered among the strongest in the game. Italy are a true powerhouse of world football.

FLYING HIGH

Vittorio Pozzo is the only man to have won the FIFA World Cup twice as manager – both times with Italy, in 1934 and 1938 (only two players, Giuseppe Meazza and Giovanni Ferrari, were selected in both finals). Pozzo also led Italy to the 1936 Olympics title. Born in Turin on 2 March 1886, Pozzo learned to love football as a student in England, watching Manchester United. He returned home reluctantly when his family bought him a return ticket for his sister's wedding – and then refused to let him leave Italy again. Pozzo fired up his Italian team ahead of their 1938 semi-final against Brazil by revealing their opponents had already booked their plane to Paris for the final – Italy won 2-1.

RETURNING HERO

Marcello Lippi resigned as Italy coach immediately after leading them to glory at the 2006 FIFA World Cup, but returned to the job two years later after the sacking of Roberto Donadoni following a disappointing showing at Euro 2008. Either side of Donadoni's reign, Lippi managed a run of 31 consecutive matches unbeaten as Italy boss – equalling a world record set by Javier Clemente with Spain and Alfio Basile with Argentina.

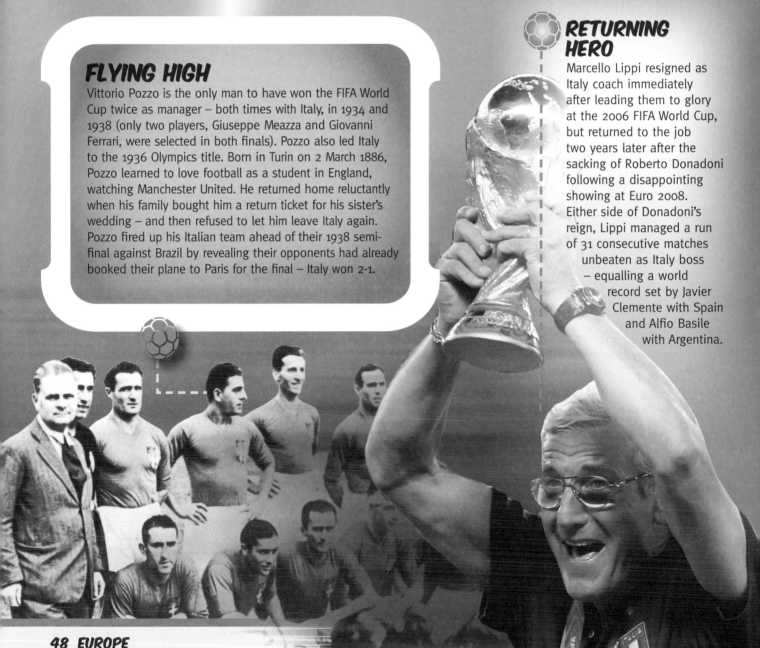

IN SAFE KEEPING

During World War Two, Italy's Jules Rimet FIFA World Cup trophy – won in 1938 – was hidden in a shoebox under the bed of football official Ottorino Barassi. He preferred to keep it there, rather than its previous home – a bank in Rome. The trophy was handed back to FIFA, safe and untouched, only when the FIFA World Cup resumed in 1950.

ROTTEN RETURN

Italy's players were pelted with tomatoes by angry fans when they returned home after crashing out of the 1966 FIFA World Cup at the group stages. After a nervy and unconvincing 2-0 opening victory over Chile, they slumped to a 1-0 defeat to the Soviet Union – and then crashed to a humiliating reverse against North Korea, by the same scoreline.

SECOND TIME LUCKY

The only time a major international tournament has been settled by a replay was Italy's win over Yugoslavia in the 1968 European Championship. To the delight of their fans, hosts Italy won the second game 2-0, two days after a 1-1 draw in the same Stadio Olimpico in Rome.

WE'LL MEET AGAIN

Italy and Argentina are the only two countries to have met each other in five successive FIFA World Cups. They drew in 1974, Italy won in 1978 and 1982, they drew again in 1986, and Argentina dramatically won on penalties in their FIFA World Cup semi-final clash in Naples in 1990.

SLOW STARTERS

Italy are the only country to have won the FIFA World Cup despite failing to win a first-round game. They drew all three group matches against Peru, Poland and Cameroon at the 1982 tournament in Spain. The Azzurri ("The Blues") only sneaked through to the second round by dint of having scored one more goal in the group stages than Cameroon, who had been unlucky not to have beaten the Italians in the two sides' final group-game encounter, which ended in a 1-1 draw. The Italians made the most of their luck, progressing to the final, where they beat West Germany 3-1 to win the trophy for the third time.

TOURNAMENT SPECIALISTS

FIFA WORLD CUP™: 16 appearances – winners 1934, 1938, 1982, 2006
EUROPEAN CHAMPIONSHIP: 7 appearances – winners 1968
FIRST INTERNATIONAL: Italy 6 France 2 (Milan, May 1910)
BIGGEST WIN: Italy 9 US 0 (Brentford, England, August 1948)
BIGGEST DEFEAT: Hungary 7 Italy 1 (Budapest, April 1924)

THE MANAGERS:

Vittorio Pozzo	1912, 1924
Augusto Rangone	1925–28
Carlo Carcano	1928–29
Vittorio Pozzo	1929–48
Ferruccio Novo	1949–50
Carlino Beretta	1952–53
Giuseppe Viani	1960
Giovanni Ferrari	1960–61
Giovanni Ferrari/Paolo Mazza	1962
Edmondo Fabbri	1962–66
Helenio Herrera/Ferruccio Valcareggi	1966–67
Ferruccio Valcareggi	1967–74
Fulvio Bernardini	1974–75
Enzo Bearzot	1975–86
Azeglio Vicini	1986–91
Arrigo Sacchi	1991–96
Cesare Maldini	1997–98
Dino Zoff	1998–2000
Giovanni Trapattoni	2000–04
Marcello Lippi	2004–06
Roberto Donadoni	2006–08
Marcello Lippi	2008–

OFF THE SPOT

Only England have lost as many FIFA World Cup penalty shoot-outs as Italy – three apiece. Roberto Baggio, nicknamed "The Divine Ponytail", was involved in all three of Italy's spot-kick defeats, in 1990, 1994 and 1998. Left-back Antonio Cabrini is the only man to have missed a penalty during normal time in a FIFA World Cup final – the score was 0-0 at the time but, fortunately for him, Italy still beat West Germany 3-1 in 1982.

⚽ COMEBACK KID

Paolo Rossi was the unlikely hero of Italy's 1982 FIFA World Cup triumph, winning the Golden Boot with six goals – including a memorable hat-trick against Brazil in the second round, and the first of Italy's three goals in their final win over West Germany. But he only just made it to the tournament at all, having completed a two-year ban for his alleged involvement in a betting scandal only six weeks before the start of the tournament.

⚽ GLOVE CONQUERS ALL

Goalkeeper Walter Zenga went 517 minutes without conceding a goal at the 1990 FIFA World Cup – a tournament record – while the only two goals conceded by Gianluigi Buffon during the 2002 FIFA World Cup were an own goal and a penalty. Buffon became the world's most expensive goalkeeper when he joined Juventus from Parma for €52 million in 2001. He always wears a black scarf around his neck during games, to protect him from catching a cold.

⚽ HAND OF HISTORY

Silvio Piola is the domestic Serie A league's all-time leading scorer, with 274 goals in 537 games between 1929 and 1954 for Pro Vercelli, Lazio, Torino, Juventus and Novara. Piola, born in Robbio on 29 September 1913, also scored twice when Italy beat Hungary 4-2 in the 1938 FIFA World Cup final. Another notable goal was his equalizer in a 2-2 draw with England in 1939 – although he later admitted to having punched the ball into the back of the net, simultaneously giving an England defender a black eye.

ROLLING RIVA

Italy's all-time top scorer is Luigi, or "Gigi", Riva, who scored 35 goals in 42 appearances for his country. One of his most important strikes was the opening goal in the 1968 European Championship final win over Yugoslavia. Despite his prolific form after having switched from left winger to striker, he never played for one of Italy's traditional club giants. Instead, Riva – born in Leggiuno on 7 November 1944 – spent his entire league career with unfashionable Sardinian club Cagliari, and at one point turned down a move to the mighty Juventus. His goals (21 of them) fired the club to their one and only league championship in 1970. Riva suffered his fair share of bad luck with injuries, breaking his left leg while playing for Italy in 1966, then his right leg in 1970, again when he was away on international duty.

RIGHT CALL

Italy captain Giacinto Facchetti called correctly when their 1968 European Championships semi-final against Russia ended in a draw after extra-time (in the days before penalties) and had to be settled by tossing a coin. The attacking left-back had luck on his side that time, then lifted the trophy after a 2-0 replay victory in the final against Yugoslavia. Facchetti, who also won the European Cup with Internazionale in 1964 and 1965, had an impressive scoring record for a defender, ending his career with 59 goals in 476 league appearances. He played on the left flank, even though he was a naturally right-footed player.

TOP APPEARANCES

1	Paolo Maldini	126
2	Fabio Cannavaro	122
3	Dino Zoff	112
4	Giacinto Facchetti	94
5	Alessandro Del Piero	91
6	Gianluigi Buffon	90
7	Gianluca Zambrotta	81
=	Franco Baresi	81
=	Giuseppe Bergomi	81
=	Marco Tardelli	81

TOP SCORERS

1	Luigi Riva	35
2	Giuseppe Meazza	33
3	Silvio Piola	30
4	Roberto Baggio	27
=	Alessandro Del Piero	27
6	Adolfo Baloncieri	25
=	Filippo Inzaghi	25
=	Alessandro Altobelli	25
9	Christian Vieri	23
=	Francesco Graziani	23

HAPPY CENTENARY

After captaining Italy to the 2006 FIFA World Cup title, Fabio Cannavaro was named FIFA World Player of the Year – at 33, the oldest winner of the prize, as well as the first defender. Cannavaro, born in Naples in 1973, played every minute of the 2006 tournament and the final triumph against France was the ideal way to celebrate his 100th international appearance.

HELPING HANDS

Future international goalkeeper Angelo Peruzzi was a 14-year-old ballboy at the 1984 European Cup final between Roma and Liverpool. He later made 16 appearances for Roma before playing for Juventus, Internazionale and Lazio.

ZOFF THE SCALE

Goalkeeper Dino Zoff set an international record by going 1,142 minutes without conceding a goal between September 1972 and June 1974. Zoff was Italy's captain when they won the 1982 FIFA World Cup – emulating the feat of another Juventus goalkeeper, Gianpiero Combi, who had been the victorious skipper in 1934. Zoff coached Italy to the final of the 2000 European Championship, which they lost 2-1 to France thanks to an extra-time "golden goal" – then quit a few days later, unhappy following the criticism levelled at him by Italy's prime minister, Silvio Berlusconi.

QUICK CHANGE

The FIFA World Cup's fastest substitution came in 1998, when Italy's Alessandro Nesta was replaced by Giuseppe Bergomi in the match against Austria after just four minutes. That record was equalled when England's Michael Owen was replaced by Peter Crouch against Sweden in 2006.

RIVAL REIGNS

Internazionale won 17 games in a row in the 2006–07 season – a record for any of Europe's top five leagues. They ended that victorious campaign with two more Serie A records – 97 points and 30 wins. But Inter's cross-city rivals AC Milan remain the only champions to have completed an entire Serie A season unbeaten, in 1991–92. They went 58 games without defeat between May 1991 and March 1993 – the run began with a goalless draw against Parma, the same team who finally ended the streak after beating them 1-0. AC Milan have kept the English spelling of the city's name, rather than the Italian Milano, in tribute to Alfred Edwards and Herbert Kilpin – the two Britons who founded the club in 1899.

MEDAL COLLECTORS

Giovanni Ferrari not only enjoys the status of having won both the 1934 and 1938 FIFA World Cups with Italy, he also holds the record for most Serie A titles, with eight triumphs. Five were with Juventus, two with Internazionale and one with Bologna. He is not the only man to win eight league championship medals – the record is shared with Virginio Rosetta, twice with Pro Vercelli and six times with Juventus, and Giuseppe Furino, all with Juventus.

CONTINENTAL CROWNS

Italian clubs have won 36 European trophies, after the 2008–09 season, more than those from any other nation. English and Spanish clubs have both won 33.

TEACHING AN OLD DOG NEW TRICKS

Goalkeeper Marco Ballotta became the oldest Serie A player when turning out for Lazio for the last time at the age of 44 years and 38 days, in May 2008. He retired later that year, before returning to the game as a striker with eighth-division team Calcara Samoggia.

SECONDS OUT

The world's fastest red card after kick-off was shown to Bologna's Giuseppe Lorenzo when he hit a Parma player in a Serie A match in December 1990 – he was sent off just ten seconds into the match.

BEEFING UP

The stadium shared by AC Milan and Internazionale is popularly known as San Siro, after the district in which it is located. Its official title, however, is Stadio Giuseppe Meazza, named after the star inside-forward on the pitch and dance enthusiast off it who played for both clubs as well as Italy's 1934 and 1938 FIFA World Cup-winning sides. Meazza, born in Milan on 23 August 1910, was first spotted by an Inter scout while playing keepy-uppy in the street with a ball made of rags – but was so thin he had to be fattened up with plenty of steaks. His last goal for Italy was a penalty in the 1938 World Cup semi-final against Brazil – taken while trying to pull up his shorts, whose elastic had broken.

KEEPING IT IN THE FAMILY

Cesare and Paolo Maldini are the only father and son to have hoisted the European Cup as winning captains – both with AC Milan, and both for the first time in England. Cesare lifted the trophy after his team beat Benfica at Wembley, London, in 1963. Paolo repeated the feat 40 years later, when Milan defeated Juventus at Old Trafford, Manchester.
Cesare was Italy coach and Paolo Italy captain at the 1998 FIFA World Cup, and they both featured at the 2002 tournament – though by now Cesare was in charge of Paraguay. The Maldini dynasty may not end there – Paolo's son, Christian, is emerging through the youth ranks at Milan. If he makes it into the first team, Christian will be the only player allowed to wear Paolo's famous No.3 jersey. Although he remains Italy's most-capped player, Paolo narrowly failed to win an international tournament – he played for Italy sides that finished third and runners-up in both FIFA World Cup and European Championships tournaments.

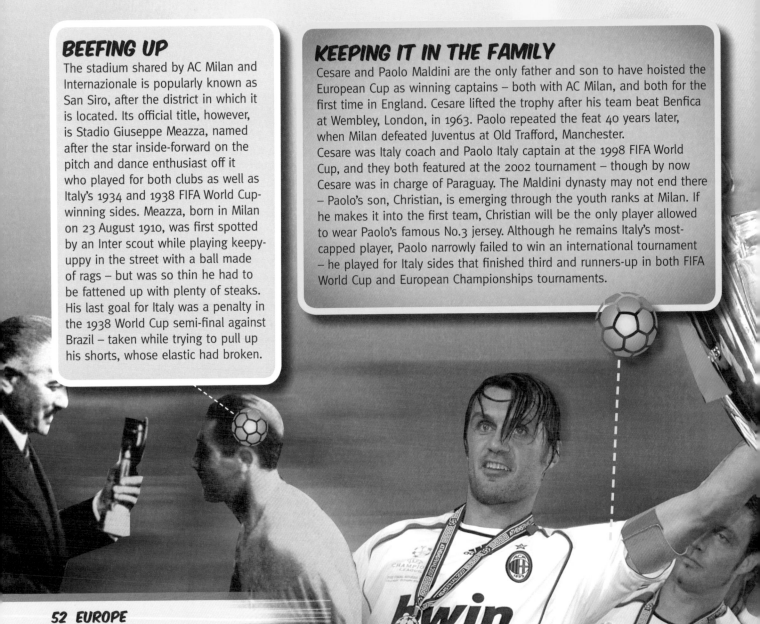

CLEAN SWEEP

Italian clubs won all three UEFA trophies in the 1989–90 season, a unique treble. AC Milan took the European Cup (beating Benfica 1-0 in the final), Juventus the UEFA Cup (beating Fiorentina 3-1) and Sampdoria the Cup-Winners' Cup (beating Anderlecht 2-0 in the final).

ITALIAN LEAGUE TITLES

Juventus	27
AC Milan	17
Internazionale	17
Genoa	9
Torino	7
Bologna	7
Pro Vercelli	7
Roma	3
Lazio	2
Fiorentina	2
Napoli	2
Cagliari	1
Casale	1
Novese	1
Sampdoria	1
Hellas Verona	1
Spezia	1

TRAGIC TORINO

Torino were Italy's most successful club side when their first-team squad was wiped out in an air crash at Superga, above Turin, on 4 May 1949. The club has only won the Serie A title once since then, in the 1976–77 season. Among the victims was star forward Valentino Mazzola, who had gone along on the trip despite being ill. His son Sandro, only six at the time of the disaster, went on to star in the Italy teams that won the 1968 European Championships and finished as FIFA World Cup runners-up two years later.

GRAND OLD TEAM TO PLAY FOR

Every Italian FIFA World Cup squad has featured at least one Juventus player. The Turin team, known as the "Grand Old Lady" of Italian club football, were relegated a division in 2006 after being found guilty of match-fixing – and, as a result, were forced to endure their first season outside the top division since the club's foundation in 1897. Their 51 trophies are an Italian club record – and, in 1985, they became the first team to have won the European, UEFA and Cup-Winners' Cups.

TRAVELLING TRAPATTONI

Italian Giovanni Trapattoni has won domestic league titles as a coach in Italy, Germany, Portugal and Austria – with Juventus, Bayern Munich, Benfica and Salzburg. Only the German Udo Lattek has also coached teams in four different countries to league title success. Trapattoni is the only manager to have won all three UEFA club competitions as well as the World Club Cup, all with the great Juventus sides of the 1980s.

ITALY'S GREATEST PLAYERS

(as chosen by the Italian football association)

1 Giuseppe Meazza
2 Luigi Riva
3 Roberto Baggio
4 Paolo Maldini
5 Giacinto Facchetti
6 Sandro Mazzola
7 Giuseppe Bergomi
8 Valentino Mazzola

SPAIN

Spain is home to some of the strongest club sides in Europe (boasting a total of 11 European Cups between them) and has produced some of the biggest names in the sport, but for years, as major tournament failures became the depressing norm (the 1964 European Championship triumph apart), La Roja were labelled as the major underachievers of the world game. But that all changed on 29 June 2008 in the final of the European Championship, when Fernando Torres's 33rd-minute goal was enough to hand Spain a 1-0 victory over Germany and the country's first taste of international success for 44 years. The victory propelled Spain to the No.1 spot in the FIFA world rankings for the first time in history.

WISE HEAD, OLD SHOULDERS

Luis Aragones became the oldest coach to win the European Championships when Spain won the 2008 tournament, a month short of his 70th birthday. Aragones, a former centre-forward and known only as "Luis" during his playing days, had lined up for Spain in the run-up to the 1964 finals, but had to watch the team win the competition from the sidelines after being left out of the squad. During his time as national coach between 2004 and 2008, the so-called "Wise Man Of Hortaleza" won more matches than any other Spanish boss – 38. Aragones, born in Hortaleza, Madrid on 28 July 1938, spent most of his playing career with Atletico Madrid, where he was surprisingly appointed a youthful coach (aged 36) immediately after retiring in 1974.

SAINT CLEMENTE

Javier Clemente is one of only three managers to go 31 international games in a row without losing – and Italian Marcello Lippi only managed his feat in two separate reigns. Clemente's success as an international manager must have been all the more rewarding as injury forced him to retire as a player at the age of just 21.

RED ALERT

Spain refused to play in the first European Championship in 1960, in protest at having to travel to the Soviet Union, a Communist country. But they changed their minds four years later, not only hosting the tournament but also winning it – by beating the visiting Soviets 2-1 in the final. Spain were captained by Fernando Olivella and managed by Jose Villalonga, who had been the first coach to win the European Cup, with Real Madrid in 1956.

SWOON IN JUNE

The date 22 June has been an unfortunate one for Spain, especially when it comes to penalty shoot-outs. They lost on spot-kicks on this date to Belgium in the 1986 FIFA World Cup, England in the 1996 European Championship and South Korea in the 2002 World Cup. But their luck changed on 22 June 2008, when they beat Italy on penalties in the quarter-finals of the European Championship, after the game had ended in a 0-0 draw. The win also marked Spain's first victory over Italy in a competitive match since 1920.

GROUNDS FOR APPEAL

No single country has provided more venues when hosting a FIFA World Cup finals than the 17 stadiums – in 14 cities – used by Spain in 1982. The 2002 tournament was played at 20 different venues but ten were in Japan and ten in South Korea. The 1982 competition was the first FIFA World Cup to be expanded from 16 to 24 teams. The final was played in Madrid's Estadio Santiago Bernabeu.

THREE AND EASY

Only three Spaniards have scored in three separate FIFA World Cup final tournaments – Raul, Julio Salinas and Fernando Hierro, who is the country's second top scorer despite largely spending his career playing as a defender.

RIGHT SAID FRED

When Spain came back from 2-0 and then 3-2 down to win 4-3 in Madrid in May 1929, they became the first non-British team to beat England. Spain's victory, in the Estadio Metropolitano, came with the help of their English coach Fred Pentland, who had moved to Spain in 1920. He had most success with Athletic Bilbao, leading them to league and cup doubles in 1930 and 1931 – and inflicting Barcelona's worst-ever defeat, a 12-1 rout in 1931.

OUT-CLASSED

Salvador Artigas, in 1969, was the last manager of Spain's national team who had not been an international player. Three of his ten successors were defenders, four midfielders and only two forwards:

Miguel Muñoz (midfield)	1969 & 1982–88
Ladislav Kubala (forward)	1969–1980
Jose Santamaria (defender)	1980–1982
Luis Suarez (midfield)	1988–91
Vicente Miera (defender)	1991–92
Javier Clemente (midfield)	1992–98
Jose Antonio Camacho (defender)	1998–2002
Inaki Saez (defender)	2002–04
Luis Aragones (centre-forward)	2004–08
Vicente Del Bosque (midfield)	2008–

VILLA ROSY

Spain went unbeaten throughout 2008, winning 15 of the 16 games they played and drawing the other against Italy – albeit winning on penalties. With 12 goals, David Villa broke the Spanish international scoring record for a calendar year. The previous record-holder had been Raul, who netted on ten occasions in 1999. Villa's goal against England in a February 2009 friendly meant he had scored in six consecutive internationals – another Spanish record.

TOP CATALAN

A team representing the region of Catalonia has been playing friendly matches, sometimes against international sides, since 1904, but is not recognized by either FIFA or UEFA. Spanish internationals who have recently played for the Catalan XI include Barcelona's Carles Puyol (above), Gerard Pique and Bojan Krkic.

MAJOR TOURNAMENTS

FIFA WORLD CUP™: 12 appearances – fourth-place 1950

EUROPEAN CHAMPIONSHIPS: Eight appearances – winners 1964, 2008

FIRST INTERNATIONAL: Spain 1 Denmark 0 (Brussels, Belgium, 28 August 1920)

BIGGEST WIN: Spain 13 Bulgaria 0 (Madrid, 21 May 1933)

BIGGEST DEFEAT: Italy 7 Spain 1 (Amsterdam, Netherlands, 4 June 1928); England 7 Spain 1 (Highbury, London, England, 9 December 1931)

YELLOW PERIL

Julio Alberto was booked after just six minutes of Spain's game against Brazil at the 1986 FIFA World Cup – though his record for the quickest FIFA World Cup yellow card was broken eight years later, when Russia's Sergei Gorlukovich was cautioned inside the first minute against Sweden.

FIT FOR PURPOSE

Luis Suarez played through injury for Spain in the 1964 European Championship final – luckily for his team-mates, since he set up both goals in a 2-1 triumph. He was named European Footballer of the Year in 1960 – the only Spanish-born player to have taken the prize.

HEAVEN SCENT

First-choice goalkeeper Santiago Canizares was forced to miss the 2002 FIFA World Cup finals after dropping a bottle of after-shave lotion on his foot and severing a tendon.

TRI-NATIONS

Ladislav Kubala is the only man to have played for not one, not two, but three different countries – though he never played in the finals of a major international tournament. Despite being born in Budapest on 10 June 1927, he made his international debut for Czechoslovakia in 1946 – winning five more caps for the country of his parents' birth. He then appeared three times for birthplace Hungary after moving back to the country in 1948, before playing 19 games for Spain after leaving Hungary as a refugee and securing a transfer to Barcelona in 1951.

THE RAUL THING

Real Madrid striker Raul Gonzalez Blanco – known as Raul – is not only Spain's most prolific international goalscorer, with 44 goals in 102 games, he also tops the scoring charts for both the European Cup, with 66 goals, and Real Madrid – after passing Alfredo Di Stefano's tally of 309 club goals during the 2008–09 season. Raul scored seven Spain goals in just four days in March 1999 – four in a 9-0 thrashing of Austria, followed by three as San Marino were crushed 6-0, but he was controversially left out of Spain's Euro 2008-winning squad by coach Luis Aragones, who condemned the player's lack of success in big international tournaments. Football and family are closely entwined for the man born in Madrid on 27 June 1977 – he celebrates each goal by kissing his wedding ring, a gesture reserved for his wife, Mamen Sanz.

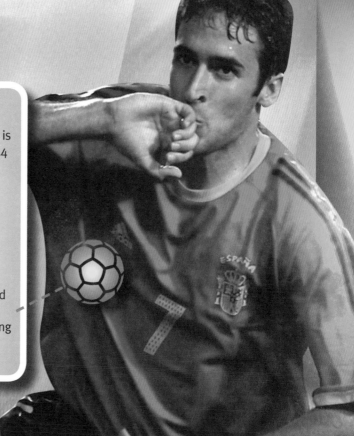

ZUBI PRIZE

Goalkeeper Andoni Zubizarreta won more caps for Spain than any other player, 126 from 1985 to 1998 – and his 622 La Liga appearances is also a Spanish league record. He played in four FIFA World Cups, although his last tournament was a disaster as he fumbled the ball into his own net during a defeat to Nigeria in 1998, as Spain crashed out of the tournament in the first round.

TORRES! TORRES!

Fernando Torres originally wanted to be a goalkeeper as a child, before becoming a striker. Torres, born in Madrid on 20 March 1984, was only 19 when he was made captain of his boyhood heroes Atletico Madrid. He has a knack for scoring the only goal in tournament finals – most famously in the 2008 European Championship, for Spain against Germany in Vienna. He had already achieved the feat in the Under-16 European Championships in 2001 and for the Under-19s the following year.

TOP CAPS

1	Andoni Zubizarreta	126
2	Raul	102
3	Iker Casillas	89
=	Fernando Hierro	89
5	Jose Antonio Camacho	81
6	Rafael Gordillo	75
7	Carles Puyol	72
8	Emilio Butragueno	69
=	Xavi Hernandez	69
10	Luis Arconada	68

TOP SCORERS

1	Raul	44
2	Fernando Hierro	29
3	Fernando Morientes	27
4	Emilio Butragueno	26
5	David Villa	25
6	Alfredo Di Stefano	23
=	Julio Salinas	23
8	Michel	21
9	Telmo Zarra	20
10	Fernando Torres	18

GIFT OF THE FAB

Arsenal's Cesc Fabregas became Spain's youngest ever FIFA World Cup player – and the country's youngest international for 70 years – when he came on as a substitute against Ukraine at the 2006 FIFA World Cup aged 19 years 41 days. Despite wearing the name "Fabregas" on the back of his Arsenal shirt, he is better known in Spain as simply "Cesc".

WHO CAN TELMO

Telmo Zarraonaindia, commonly known as "Zarra", scored a Spanish championship record of 251 goals in 277 games for Athletic Bilbao between 1940 and 1955 – and 20 goals in 20 games for Spain, between 1945 and 1951. He was nicknamed the "finest head in Europe after Churchill".

FIFA FIRST

Real Madrid were the only club formally represented at FIFA's first meeting in Paris in 1904 – though the club was then known simply as Madrid FC. Spanish clubs, such as Real Madrid and Real Betis, dropped the word "Real" – meaning "Royal" – from their names during the Second Spanish Republic, between 1931 and 1939.

PERFECT PICHICHI

The annual award for top scorer in La Liga is called the "Pichichi" – the nickname of Rafael Moreno, a striker for Athletic Bilbao between 1911 and 1921. He scored 200 goals in 170 games for the club, and once in five matches for Spain. Pichichi, who often took the field wearing a large white cap, died suddenly in 1922, aged just 29.

MORE THAN JUST A CLUB

Barcelona, founded in 1899 by a Swiss businessman Hans Gamper, prides itself on being "more than a club". The club's famous blue and purple resisted the march of commercialism for more than a century until 2006, when the club signed a deal with (and gave money to) the United Nations Children's Fund (UNICEF) in exchange for using the charity's logo on its shirts.

FEELING SUPERSONIC

Francisco "Paco" Gento holds the record for European Cup winners' medals, playing in all five triumphant finals from 1956 to 1960 and another in 1966 – all for Real Madrid. The left winger was so fast, he was nicknamed "El Supersonico" and "The Storm Of Cantabria". At the height of Beatlemania, he and a couple of team-mates posed for publicity photos in Beatle wigs – winning the team the nickname of "Ye-ye".

MAD FOR MADRID

Real Madrid have won the European Cup more often than any other club, with a total of nine wins – including five in a row when the competition was first introduced in 1956. After the fifth triumph, they were allowed to keep the original trophy. The most memorable victory was the 7-3 triumph over Eintracht Frankfurt in 1960, when Ferenc Puskas scored four goals for Real and Alfredo Di Stefano grabbed the other three. The club's celebrity supporters include former dictator Generalissimo Franco, actor Antonio Banderas and crooner Julio Iglesias – who played as a teenage goalkeeper for a Real Madrid youth team before being injured in a car crash. The club can also count Rafael Nadal among its fans, despite the fact the tennis star has former Barcelona defender Miguel Angel Nadal as an uncle.

THE VULTURE

Born in the Spanish capital and a star for Real for over a decade, Emilio Butragueno was a man made in Madrid. Nicknamed The Vulture for his predatory instincts in the penalty area, he made 69 appearances for the Spanish national side, scoring on 26 occasions.

HEROES AND SEVILLANS

Just three of the ten founder members of the Spanish league in 1928 have never been relegated – Athletic Bilbao, Barcelona and Real Madrid. Despite being one of Spain's oldest clubs, Sevilla, formed in 1905, were denied a place in the first season after being defeated in a qualifying tournament by Racing Santander. Despite having won only one Liga title since then, in 1946, Sevilla have beaten Real Madrid 72 times in the league – more than any other club in Spanish league history.

SPANISH STREAKS

Only two clubs have gone through an entire top division season unbeaten – Athletic Bilbao in 1929–30 and Real Madrid two years later. This was the first of Real Madrid's record 31 Spanish league titles.

TOP OF THE WORLD

Spain rose to the top of the FIFA world rankings for the first time in July 2008, after winning the European Championship co-hosted by Austria and Switzerland. They became only the sixth team to reach the No.1 spot and the first to do so without ever winning the FIFA World Cup.

SPANISH LEAGUE CHAMPIONSHIPS

Real Madrid	31
Barcelona	19
Atletico Madrid	9
Athletic Bilbao	8
Valencia	6
Real Sociedad	2
Deportivo de la Coruna	1
Sevilla	1
Betis	1

TREASURE CHEST

The Spanish first division goalkeeper who concedes the fewest goals per game each season is awarded the Zamora Trophy. This is named after legendary keeper Ricardo Zamora, who played 46 times for Spain between 1920 and 1936 – including the legendary 4-3 win over England in Madrid in 1929. Zamora was the first Spanish star to play for both Barcelona and Real Madrid. Later he was league title-winning coach of ... Atletico Madrid.

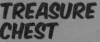

MAIN STADIUMS: (CAPACITY)

Camp Nou, Barcelona: 98,772
Santiago Bernabeu, Madrid: 80,354
Estadio de la Cartuja, Seville: 72,000
Vicente Calderon, Madrid: 57,200
Lluis Companys, Barcelona: 56,000
Mestalla, Valencia: 55,000
Manuel Ruiz de Lopera, Seville: 52,500
Ramon Sanchez Pizjuan, Seville: 45,500
San Mames, Bilbao: 40,000
Manuel Martinez Valero, Elche: 38,750

BELGIUM

For eight decades Belgium failed to produce a side capable of challenging for the game's greatest prizes. Then came the golden period: runners-up at the 1980 European Championship; semi-finalists at the 1986 FIFA World Cup™; and regular qualifiers – and even contenders – for major tournaments. Recent times have been tougher, and a nation hopes that failure to qualify for Euros 2004 and 2008 and the 2006 FIFA World Cup™ does not signal a slide back into darker times.

MOTHER'S BOY

Not many footballers turn down a move to AC Milan, but Jan Ceulemans did just that, after seeking the advice of his mum. Belgium's most-capped player (he played 96 times for his country) spent the bulk of his career with Club Brugge, but is best remembered by fans for his contributions to three consecutive FIFA World Cup campaigns. Belgium's finest performance came in finishing fourth at the 1986 tournament in Mexico, when midfielder and captain Ceulemans scored three goals. Born in Lier on 28 February 1957, he retired from international football after the 1990 FIFA World Cup – and later, between 2005 and 2006, returned to Club Brugge as manager.

VAN DRIVEN OUT

Rene Vandereycken scored the first penalty during normal play of a European Championship final in 1980, when Belgium lost 2-1 to West Germany. However, the midfielder did not make it to the end of Belgium's run to the FIFA World Cup semi-finals in 1986; he was sent home early following a clash with coach Guy Thys.

HOME ALONE

In 2000, when they co-hosted the tournament with Holland, Belgium became the first European Championship hosts not to make it through the first round of the finals.

SPECS APPEAL

Many footballers wear contact lenses, but Belgium captain Jef Jurion was notable in the late 1950s and early 1960s for wearing a pair of specially made glasses during the matches he played.

LIMITED KOMPANY

Belgium won Olympic bronze in 1900 and gold 20 years later, but they just missed out on a medal at the 2008 Beijing Games, when they lost to Brazil in the bronze medal play-off. Star player Vincent Kompany missed the match after being summoned back to Europe by his German club Hamburg.

TOP CAPS

1	Jan Ceulemans	96
2	Eric Gerets	86
=	Franky Van der Elst	86
4	Enzo Scifo	84
5	Paul van Himst	81
6	Bart Goor	78
7	Georges Grun	77
8	Timmy Simons	71
9	Lorenzo Staelens	70
=	Marc Wilmots	70

TOP GOALSCORERS

1	Paul Van Himst	30
=	Bernard Voorhoof	30
3	Marc Wilmots	28
4	Joseph Mermans	27
5	Raymond Braine	26
=	Robert De Veen	26
7	Jan Ceulemans	23
=	Marc Degryse	23
=	Wesley Sonck	23
10	Henri Coppens	21

CLUB MATES

Belgium ended a 1964 match against Holland with a team entirely made up of Anderlecht players, after Liege goalkeeper Guy Delhasse was substituted by Anderlecht's own Jean Trappeniers. Up-front that day was Paul Van Himst, who went on to score 30 goals for Belgium – a tally matched only by pre-war striker Bernard Voorhoof, who scored his 30 goals in 61 international appearances (compared to Van Himst's 81). Voorhoof is one of only four footballers to have played in all three pre-war FIFA World Cups – 1930, 1934 and 1938. The others were Romanian Nicolae Kovacs and Frenchmen Edmund Delfour and Etienne Mattler.

GOLDEN NOT-SO-OLDIE

Fernand Nisot held the record for being the youngest ever international footballer for 60 years. He made his Belgium debut in 1911 aged 16 years and 19 days.

DOUBLING UP

Belgian goalkeeper Jean-Marie Pfaff scored the decisive penalty for Bayern Munich in a 1983–84 UEFA Cup shoot-out win over PAOK Salonika – having just saved a penalty himself.

HE'S OUR GUY

Belgium's longest-serving, and most successful, coach was Guy Thys, who led them to the final of the 1980 European Championships and to the semi-finals of the FIFA World Cup six years later. He served 13 years in the job – from 1976 to 1989 – then returned to the role just eight months after stepping down, to take his country to the 1990 FIFA World Cup.

CONSOLATION FOR KEEPER

The Lev Yashin Award (for the best goalkeeper at a FIFA World Cup) was introduced in 1994. The first recipient was Belgium goalkeeper Michel Preud'homme, despite his country only making it as far as the second round.

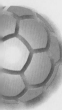

BULGARIA

The glory days of the "golden generation" apart – when Bulgaria finished fourth at the 1994 FIFA World Cup™ in the United States, sensationally beating defending champions Germany 2-1 in the quarter-finals – a consistent pattern emerges with Bulgarian football. Regular qualifiers for the game's major competitions, and the birthplace of some of the sport's biggest names (such as Hristo Stoichkov and Dimitar Berbatov), the country has too often failed to deliver on the big occasions and make its mark on world football.

WAITING GAME

Bulgaria qualified for five of the seven FIFA World Cups staged between 1962 and 1986, but failed to win a game, going 16 matches without success. They only made it to the finals of the European Championship for the first time in 1996, but were knocked out in the first round. Hristo Stoichkov scored all of Bulgaria's three goals, including the only free-kick to hit the back of the net at Euro '96.

GO FOURTH AND MULTIPLY

The so-called "Golden Generation" of 1994 was the only Bulgarian side to win a match at a FIFA World Cup finals – finishing fourth after beating Greece, Argentina, Mexico and Germany. Bulgaria had only just qualified for the tournament, thanks to Emil Kostadinov's last-minute goal in Paris that knocked out Gerard Houllier's France.

HRISTO'S HISTORY

Hristo Stoichkov, born in Plovdiv, Bulgaria, on 8 February 1968, shared the 1994 FIFA World Cup Golden Boot, awarded to the tournament's top scorer, with Russia's Oleg Salenko. Both scored six times, though Stoichkov became the sole winner of that year's European Footballer of the Year award. Earlier that same year, he had combined up-front with Brazilian Romario to help Barcelona reach the final of the UEFA Champions League. Earlier in his career he was banned for a year after a brawl during the 1985 Bulgarian cup final between CSKA Sofia and Levski Sofia. Stoichkov won trophies with clubs in Bulgaria, Spain, Saudi Arabia and the United States before retiring as a player in 2003.

MAYOR WITH NO HAIR

Balding Yordan Letchkov headed the winning goal against holders and defending champions Germany in the 1994 FIFA World Cup quarter-final in the United States. At the time, he played for German club Hamburg. He later became mayor of Sliven, the Bulgarian town where he was born in July 1967.

MOB RULES

Manchester United and Bulgaria centre-forward Dimitar Berbatov claims to have learned English by watching the Godfather movies. Berbatov joined United from Tottenham in 2008 for a club and Bulgarian record fee of £30.75m. Before joining Spurs, he had been a member of the Bayer Leverkusen side who narrowly missed out on a treble in 2002. They finished runners-up in the Champions League, German Bundesliga and the German cup.

TOP SCORERS

1	Hristo Bonev	47
2	Dimitar Berbatov	41
3	Hristo Stoichkov	37
4	Emil Kostadinov	26
5	Petar Zhekov	25
=	Ivan Kolev	25
7	Nasko Sirakov	23
8	Dimitar Milanov	20
9	Georgi Asparuhov	19
=	Dinko Dermendzhiev	19

A NATION MOURNS

Bulgaria lost two of its most popular footballing talents in a June 1971 car crash that killed strikers Georgi Asparuhov, aged 28, and Nikola Kotkov, aged 32. Asparuhov scored 19 goals in 50 internationals, including Bulgaria's only goal of the 1966 FIFA World Cup finals in a 3-1 defeat by Hungary.

TOP CAPS

1	Borislav Mikhailov	102
2	Hristo Bonev	96
3	Krasimir Balakov	92
4	Dimitar Penev	90
5	Stiliyan Petrov	84
=	Hristo Stoichkov	84
7	Naska Sirakov	81
8	Ayan Sadakov	80
=	Radostin Kishishev	80
10	Zlatko Yankov	79

SAINT STEFAN

Bulgaria's best football performances at the Olympics were a bronze medal in Melbourne in 1956 and a silver in Mexico City 12 years later. Stefan Bozhkov was a playing member of the Melbourne team and the coach of the Mexico City side.

ALL-ROUNDER ALEKSANDAR

Defender Aleksandar Shalamanov played for Bulgaria at the 1966 FIFA World Cup, six years after representing his country as an alpine skier at the Winter Olympics. He also went to the 1964 Olympics as an unused member of the volleyball squad. Shalamanov was voted Bulgaria's best sportsman in 1967 and 1973.

HEAD BOY

Bulgaria's most-capped player is Borislav Mikhailov, born in Sofia on 12 February 1963, who sometimes wore a wig while playing and later had a hair transplant. After retiring in 2005, he was appointed president of the Bulgarian Football Union. His father Bisser was also a goalkeeper and Boris's own son, Nikolay, signed for Liverpool in 2007. All three have played for Levski Sofia.

CROATIA

Croatia's distinctive red-and-white chequered jersey has become one of the most recognized in world football – just ask England. Croatia broke English hearts not once but twice in the Euro 2008 qualifying tournament, beating them 2–0 in Zagreb and shocking them 3–2 at Wembley to secure qualification. Croatia's subsequent march to the quarter-finals at Euro 2008 confirmed their status as a football power.

GOOD AND BAD

Croatia's joint highest-scoring victories were the 7-0 wins over Andorra in 2006 and Australia in 1998. Croatia's worst defeat in the modern era was a 4-1 loss to Slovakia in a 1994 friendly, a 3-0 defeat to Portugal at Euro 96 and the 4-1 home trouncing by England.

HAPPY OPENINGS

Few national teams have been as successful in their infancy as Croatia. Having previously been part of Yugoslavia, in their very first senior competition as an independent country, Euro 96, Croatia reached the quarter-finals, then came third at the 1998 FIFA World Cup, where they became known as the "golden generation". Since becoming eligible to participate in 1993, Croatia have qualified for every FIFA World Cup and have missed only one European Championship.

EXPORT SPECIALISTS

Nearly all of Croatia's national team squad play for overseas clubs. Of the 23 selected against Romania in February 2009, only five of the squad were home-based.

TOP CAP

Dario Simic, with 100 appearances before his 2008 retirement, is Croatia's most capped international player, surpassing Robert Jarni's 81.

BEST BOSSES

Slaven Bilic lost only three of his first 30 matches in charge as Croatia manager. Statistically, however, that is not the best percentage record. Drazan Jerkovic (above) and Vlatko Markovic joint-managed the national side for only four games but won them all. Jerkovic, Croatia's first coach after the split from Yugoslavia, died in 2008 aged 72. He was top scorer in the 1960 European Championship, playing for a Yugoslavia squad that finished runners-up. He was also one of four joint top scorers at the 1962 FIFA World Cup in Chile, with four goals.

DINAMO THE POWER

Dinamo Zagreb is the most popular club in the country, claiming between 33 and 36 per cent of the population supporting them. The club controversially changed its name to HAK-Gradanski in 1992 and another name change was made the following year to Croatia Zagreb. These were widely seen as political moves and were never accepted by the club's true fans, who kept calling it Dinamo in their chants and on banners.

TOP GOALS

1	Davor Suker	45
2	Darijo Srna	17
3	Goran Vlaovic	16
4	Nico Kovac	15
5	Eduardo da Silva	13

FAMILY AFFAIR

Nico Kranjcar is the son of former Croatian coach Zlatko Kranjcar, but it wasn't always an easy affiliation. "Two days before he became Croatia's head coach everyone said I should get a call-up," Nico once said. "Then when Dad picked me for Euro 2004 suddenly it was because I was his son."
No such problems for the Kovac brothers, Robert and Nico, both of whom are part of Croatian footballing folklore. The siblings were born in Berlin but are proud Croats. Nico has now hung up his boots at international level, but Robert still plays on after having won more than 80 caps.

BILIC BEAT

Shortly after becoming Croatia manager, the guitar-playing Slaven Bilic and his rock band released a single, "Vatreno Ludilo" ("Fiery Madness"), which recalled the team's progress during the 1998 FIFA World Cup and went to No.1 in the Croatian charts. Fashion-conscious Bilic also sports a diamond-studded earring.

CZECH REPUBLIC

The most successful of the former Eastern Bloc countries, as Czechoslovakia they finished as runners-up in the 1934 and 1938 FIFA World Cup™ competitions, and then shocked West Germany in a penalty shoot-out to claim the European Championship in 1976. Playing as the Czech Republic since 1994, they came agonizingly close to victory at Euro 96, and lost out in the semi-finals at Euro 2004. Recent times have been tougher, but the Czech Republic remains one of Europe's stronger footballing nations.

UNLUCKY SEVEN?

Karel Bruckner steered the Czech Republic to the semi-finals of Euro 2004 in Portugal and retired after the 2008 finals. He had been in charge for seven years. His subsequent comeback as Austria coach was short-lived, however: he lasted only seven months.

THE CANNON COLLECTS

Pavel Nedved's election as European Footballer of the Year in 2003 ended an impatient wait for fans in the Czech Republic who had seen a string of outstanding players overlooked since Josef Masopust had been honoured back in 1962. Masopust, a midfield general, had scored the opening goal in the FIFA World Cup final that year before Brazil hit back to win 3-1 in the Chilean capital of Santiago. Years later, Masopust was remembered by Pele and nominated as one of his 125 greatest living footballers. At club level, Masopust won eight Czechoslovak league titles with Dukla Prague, the army club. He was also the winner, in 1962, of the first Czech Golden Ball as domestic footballer of the year. It was another day and in another age. Masopust was presented with his award before the kick-off of a European Cup quarter-final with Benfica – with a minimum of fuss. Years later, Masopust said: "Eusebio just shook hands with me, I put the trophy in my sports bag and went home on the tram."

JOZEF THE FIRST

Jozef Venglos was one of the great characters of Czech football. He managed Czechoslovakia to the final of the 1980 European Championship, where they lost to West Germany and, eight years later, in a second stint, to the quarter-finals. In 1990 he took over at Aston Villa, becoming the first foreign manager of an English top division club. Known as "The Doctor", he returned to Britain in 1998 for a brief stint at Celtic.

LATE WINNER

For years, Oldrich Nejedly was honoured "only" as joint top scorer at the 1934 FIFA World Cup, with four for runners-up Czechoslovakia. In 2006, 16 years after his death, FIFA revised the tally, awarding him a previously disputed goal, which brought his total to five goals, making him top scorer. He also netted twice at the 1938 tournament, in which the Czechs reached the quarter-finals.

TOP APPEARANCES
(CZECHOSLOVAKIA AND CZECH REPUBLIC)

1	Karel Poborsky	118
2	Pavel Nedved	91
3	Jan Koller	90
=	Zdenek Nehoda	90
5	Pavel Kuka	87
6	Jiri Nemec	84
7	Vladimir Smicer	81
8	Tomas Ujfalusi	77
9	Marian Masny	76
10	Ladislav Novak	75

TEN OUT OF TEN

Giant striker Jan Koller is Czech football's all-time leading marksman with 55 goals in 90 appearances. Koller scored on his senior debut against Belgium and struck ten goals in ten successive internationals. He scored six goals in each of the 2000, 2004 and 2008 European Championship qualifying campaigns. He began his career with Sparta Prague, who converted him from goalkeeper to goalscorer. Then, in Belgium, he was top scorer with Lokeren, before scoring 42 goals in two league title-winning campaigns with Anderlecht. Later, with Borussia Dortmund in Germany, he once went in goal after Jens Lehmann was sent off and kept a clean sheet – having scored in the first half.

TOP SCORERS

1	Jan Koller	55
2	Antonin Puc	35
3	Milan Baros	32
4	Zdenek Nehoda	31
=	Pavel Kuka	31
6	Oldrich Nejedly	29
7	Josef Silny	28
8	Vladimir Smicer	27
=	Adolf Scherer	27
10	Frantisek Svoboda	22

LOST HERO

Striker Rudolf Kucera was one of the finest young players of his era in Europe in the early 1960s. But his talent and potential were lost to football after he suffered a head injury in a European Cup tie against Polish outfit Gornik Zarbrze.

GOING FOR A SONG

Army club Dukla Prague were immortalized by British rock band Half Man Half Biscuit with their song: "All I Want For Christmas Is A Dukla Prague Away Kit".

WALK-OUT

Belgium's 1920 victory in the Olympic Games was overshadowed when Czechoslovakia walked off the pitch after half an hour in protest following what they saw as biased refereeing. Czechoslovakia are the only team to have been disqualified in the history of Olympic football.

POPULAR KAREL

Euro 96 gave the frizzy-haired Karel Poborsky the perfect platform to take his career to new heights as he helped the Czech Republic reach the final and then sealed a dream move to Manchester United. His lob against Portugal in the quarter-finals was rated as one of the finest opportunist goals in the tournament's history. His 118 appearances is a record for his country.

CECH CAP

Goalkeeper Petr Cech has worn a protective cap while playing ever since suffering a fractured skull during an English Premier League match in October 2006. He later added a chin protector after a facial operation following a training accident.

DENMARK

Denmark have been playing international football since 1908, but it was not until the mid-1980s that they became competitive at the game's major tournaments. The country's crowning moment came in 1992 when, after being called up as a replacement just ten days before the start of the tournament, they walked away with the European Championship crown, shocking defending world champions West Germany 2-0 in the final. They may not have been able to repeat that success, but remain a significant player in the world game.

EXPLOSIVE STUFF

Three weeks before Denmark beat England at Wembley in September 1983, a Danish newspaper arranged a competition for football songs. The winning chorus: "We are red, we are white, we are Danish dynamite!" was to accompany the team's success during the following decade. The Danish fans' passionate, but peaceful, behaviour earned the accolade of receiving UNESCO's "Fair Play Trophy" in 1984.

MARKED MAN

Danish international and Liverpool defender Daniel Agger has numerous tattoos, including a viking on his upper right arm, tribal symbols across his upper back and an intricate band around his left elbow.

THE UNEXPECTED IN 1992

Few football fans are ever likely to forget June 1992, Denmark's finest hour, when their team managed to win the European Championship. Denmark had not qualified for the final round in Sweden, but ten days before the opening match UEFA asked them to take the place of Yugoslavia, who were thrown out of the tournament in the wake of international sanctions over the Balkan War. The Danes had come second in their qualifying group, behind Yugoslavia, and they took over their spot at the tournament proper. Expectations were minimal, but then the inconceivable happened. Relying heavily on goalkeeper Peter Schmeichel, his defence, and the creative spark of Brian Laudrup, Denmark crafted one of the biggest shocks in modern football history by winning the tournament, culminating in a 2-0 victory over world champions Germany. Their victory was all the more remarkable in that Brian's brother Michael, their finest player, quit during the qualifying competition after falling out with coach Richard Moller Nielsen. He revived his international career in 1993, only for Denmark to fail to qualify for the subsequent FIFA World Cup in the United States.

TOP CAPS

1	Peter Schmeichel	129
2	Thomas Helveg	108
3	Michael Laudrup	104
4	Morten Olsen	102
=	Jon Dahl Tomasson	102
6	John Sivebaek	87
7	Jan Heintze	86
8	Martin Jorgensen,	85
9	Lars Olsen	84
=	Dennis Rommedahl	84

TREND-SETTER

Nils Middleboe, who represented Denmark at three different Olympic Games, was the first ever goalscorer for the national football team. Then, in 1913, he moved abroad to play for Chelsea, becoming Denmark's first player to play in England and the first of many foreign players with the West London club.

SLICED AND CURED

Denmark's 6-1 victory over Uruguay in the 1986 FIFA World Cup finals in Neza, Mexico City, ranks among the country's greatest matches. Sadly, Denmark's adventure was ended by Spain in the last 16.

QUICK-DRAW

Ebbe Sand scored the fastest FIFA World Cup goal ever scored by a substitute, when he netted a mere 16 seconds after coming on to the pitch in Denmark's clash against Nigeria at the 1998 FIFA World Cup.

HISTORY MAN

Poul Nielsen died nearly half a century ago, but the 52 goals he scored in 38 appearances still stands as a Danish record. Sadly, he never played in the FIFA World Cup finals.

LEADERSHIP STYLE

Morten Olsen captained Denmark at the 1986 FIFA World Cup. After he retired from playing in 1989, he switched to coaching, first at Brondby, then FC Koln, before moving on to Ajax Amsterdam ... and then taking on the job as Danish national coach in 2000.

BROTHERS IN ARMS

Michael and Brian Laudrup are among the most successful footballing brothers of modern times. Michael played in Italy with Lazio and Juventus and in Spain with Barcelona and Real Madrid, representing his country in three European Championship and two FIFA World Cups. Brian starred in Germany with Bayer Urdingen and Bayern Munich (1990–92), in Italy with Fiorentina and Milan, in Scotland for Rangers and in London for Chelsea.

EXPORT SPECIALISTS

Danish footballers have long been coveted by foreign clubs. The first player to sign a professional contract abroad was Carl "Skomar" (Shoemaker) Hansen, who was bought by Rangers in 1921. Later Danish players were mainly sold to clubs in England, Germany, Holland and Belgium. Allan Simonsen became internationally known while playing for Borussia Monchengladbach in the 1970s. He won the UEFA Cup in 1975 and 1979, and was voted 1977 European Footballer of the Year.

TOP GUNS

In November 2006, following a national poll, the Danish FA named the following eight players as the country's best of all time.

Morten Olsen	(1970–89)
Henning Jensen	(1972–80)
Allan Simonsen	(1972–86)
Preben Elkjær	(1977–88)
Michael Laudrup	(1982–98)
Brian Laudrup	(1987–98)
Peter Schmeichel	(1987–2001)
Jon Dahl Tomasson	(1997–present)

GOLDEN GLOVES

Peter Schmeichel was rated as the world's best goalkeeper in the early 1990s, winning the English title with Manchester United and, famously, the European Championship with his national team.

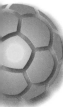

HUNGARY

For a period in the early 1950s, Hungary possessed the most talented football team on the planet. They claimed Olympic gold in Helsinki in 1952, inflicted a crushing first-ever Wembley defeat on England the following year, and entered the 1954 FIFA World Cup™, unbeaten in three years, as firm favourites to win the crown. They lost to West Germany in the final and Hungary's footballing fortunes on the world stage have never been the same again.

GLORIOUS FAILURE

Hungary were runaway favourites to win the 1954 FIFA World Cup in Switzerland. They arrived for the finals having been unbeaten for four years. In the first round they thrashed West Germany 8-3, despite finishing with ten men after skipper Ferenc Puskas injured an ankle.

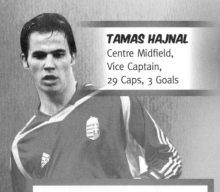

TAMAS HAJNAL
Centre Midfield,
Vice Captain,
29 Caps, 3 Goals

TURNING POINT

The turning point in Hungary's football history came with the futile 1956 revolt against Communist rule, which saw captain Ferenc Puskas and many of his national team-mates flee the country. He was only allowed to return from his Spanish self-exile to visit his family long after his retirement from playing.

HUNGARY'S GOLDEN BOY

Florian Albert remains the only Hungarian player to have been voted European Footballer of the Year, in 1967. Born on 15 September 1941 in the small town of Hercegszanto, near to the border with the former Yugoslavia, Albert spent his entire career (1958–74) playing for the Budapest club Ferencvaros. Joint top-scorer, with four goals, at the 1962 FIFA World Cup, in which Hungary reached the quarter-finals, Albert emerged as the new golden boy of Hungarian football during the national team's rebuilding years following the events of the 1956 revolution. He went on to score 32 goals in 75 matches for the national team.

GOODISON LESSON

In the 1966 FIFA World Cup, Hungary gave Brazil a footballing lesson at Goodison Park, running out 3-1 winners before their progress was stopped by the Soviet Union in the quarter-finals. It was Brazil's first defeat in the FIFA World Cup since the 1954 quarter-finals, when they had lost 4-2 to ... Hungary.

HUNGARY FOR IT

Hungary's 6-3 win over England at Wembley in 1953 remains one of the most significant international results of all time. Hungary became the first team from outside the British Isles to beat England at home, a record that had stood since 1901. The Hungarians had been undefeated for three years and had won the Olympic tournament the year before, while England were the so-called "inventors" of football. The British press dubbed it "The Match of the Century". In the event, the match revolutionized the game in England, Hungary's unequivocal victory exposing the naivete of English football tactics. England captain Billy Wright later summed up the humiliation by saying: "We completely underestimated the advances that Hungary had made, and not only tactically. When we walked out at Wembley ... I looked down and noticed that the Hungarians had on these strange, lightweight boots, cut away like slippers under the ankle bone. I turned to big Stan Mortensen and said: 'We should be all right here, Stan, they haven't got the proper kit.'"

LEADING APPEARANCES

1	Jozsef Bozsik	101
2	Laszlo Fazekas	92
3	Gyula Grosics	86
4	Ferenc Puskas	85
5	Imre Garaba	82

HIGH FLYERS

1938 – Hungary reach the FIFA World Cup final in France, losing 4-2 to Italy.

1953 – Hungary become the first team from outside the British Isles to beat England at home, winning 6-3 at Wembley.

1954 – Hungary reach the FIFA World Cup final in Switzerland and, despite being odds-on favourites, lose 3-2 to West Germany.

1964 – Hungary reach the semi-finals of European Championship in Spain.

1965 – Ferencvaros become Hungary's first, and to date only, European club winner, lifting the Inter-Cities Fairs (UEFA) Cup.

1972 – Hungary reach the semi-finals of European Championships in Belgium, before losing 1-0 to the Soviet Union.

1986 – The last time Hungary qualify for the FIFA World Cup finals – in Mexico.

ZOLTAN GERA
Striker, Captain,
59 Caps 17 Goals

⚽ BLACKPOOL

When Hungary met England in 1953, the *Daily Mirror* newspaper declared that "Blackpool FC were playing the Hungarians" – due to the inclusion of four of the FA Cup holders' players (including centre-half Harry Johnston and outside-right Stanley Matthews) in England's team. Not that their inclusion in the side did much good: they crashed to a 6-3 defeat.

LOWEST OF THE LOW

When things in Hungary are bad, they are said to be "béka segge alatt" ("under the belly of a frog"). Football was held to have reached that point when the national team, in the 1980s, began a long sad sequence of failing to qualify for all the major tournament finals.

GALLOPING MAJOR

Ferenc Puskas was one of the greatest footballers of all time, scoring a remarkable 84 goals in 85 international matches for Hungary and 514 goals in 529 matches in the Hungarian and Spanish leagues. Possessing the most lethal left-foot shot in the history of football, he was known as the "Galloping Major" – by virtue of his playing for the army team Honved before joining Real Madrid and going on to play for Spain. During the 1950s he was top scorer and captain of the legendary "Mighty Magyars" (the nickname given to the Hungarian national team), as well as of the army club Honved.

GOLDEN HEAD

Sandor Kocsis, top scorer in the 1954 FIFA World Cup finals with 11 goals, was so good in the air he was known as "The Man With The Golden Head". In 68 internationals he scored an incredible 75 goals, including a record seven hat-tricks. His tally included two decisive extra-time goals in the 1954 FIFA World Cup semi-final against Uruguay, when Hungary had appeared to be on the brink of defeat.

⚽ GOING FOREIGN

Englishman Jimmy Hogan was a hero in Hungary for coaching the virtues of pure football in the 1920s. He was even the Hungarian Federation's guest of honour following the 1953 victory over England. The value of new ideas from abroad was still being maintained into the new century under Erwin Koeman, one of Holland's European champions in 1988.

NORWAY

Although they played their first international, against Sweden, in 1908 and qualified for the 1938 FIFA World Cup™, it would take a further 56 years, and the introduction of a direct brand of football, before Norway reappeared at a major international tournament. Success in such competitions has been rare, they have never progressed beyond the second round, but Norway retains the distinction of being the only nation in history never to have lost to Brazil.

DRILLO'S PAD

Known by the nickname "Drillo", Egil Olsen was renowned for knowing the precise height of every significant mountain on earth. An aggressive anti-smoker, he never drove anywhere while manager at Wimbledon, always walking to the training ground, often in his boots.

BIG JOHN

Centre-forward John Carew has an un-Norwegian-sounding name because he is half-Gambian. The number seven figures prominently in his career. He has had seven clubs (including loan deals) and was the seventh Aston Villa player to score a league hat-trick – in a 4-1 win over Newcastle United in 2007–08. He was also Norway's first black player.

BOOT CAMPER

Egil Olsen, one of Europe's most eccentric coaches, was signed up for a surprise second spell as national manager when Norway put their faith in the direct-football specialist along the road towards the 2010 FIFA World Cup finals in South Africa – 15 years after he had led the unfancied Scandinavians to the 1994 finals. That had been Norway's first finals appearance since 1938 and they followed it up by beating Brazil in the first round in France in 1998, making a hero out of the man in Wellington boots who guided his country to an impressive No.2 in FIFA's official rankings. Before answering his country's call for a second stint as manager, Olsen's last job had been as manager of Iraq but he left after only three months in charge. Remarkably, in his first match back at the helm for Norway, he masterminded a 1-0 win away to Germany with his route-one tactics. But life was not quite as happy for Olsen during his time at Wimbledon in the 1999–2000 Premier League season. The Norwegian, a firm believer in sports science, imposed a zonal marking system, which he was convinced would work. Critics held it responsible for Wimbledon's collapse in the second half of the season.

WINNING STREAK

Rosenborg are by far the most successful club in Norway. They have won the league title 20 times in total, including 13 straight successes between 1992 and 2004 – a figure second in the world only to the 14-year streak of Skonto Riga of Latvia. Both sides' runs ended in 2005.

LEADING APPEARANCES

1	Thorbjorn Svenssen	104
2	Henning Berg	100
3	Erik Thorstvedt	97
4	Oyvind Leonhardsen	86
5	Kjetil Rekdal	83
6	Erik Mykland	78
7	Svein Grondalen	77
8	Tore Andre Flo	76
9	Steffen Iversen	76
10	John Arne Riise	76

1936 AND ALL THAT

Norway's victory over Germany in the 1936 Olympic Games in Berlin, three years after Adolf Hitler came to power, was a political as well as a sporting milestone. The crowd, Hitler among its number, also included his henchmen Goebbels, Goering and Hess. Germany lost 2-0 and Hitler, who had never seen an international match before, left early in a huff.

ERIK THE VIKING

Erik Thorstvedt's career at Tottenham Hotspur could not have got off to a worse possible start. Less than five minutes into his debut against Nottingham Forest, he dropped the ball to gift Nigel Clough the opening goal. Despite the blunder, Thorstvedt became hugely popular and earned himself the nickname "Erik The Viking".

WIN OF THE YEAR

Norway's defeat of Germany in February 2009 was their first since the 1936 Olympic success. All the more remarkable was that Germany had only recently finished as Euro 2008 runners-up, while Norway had not won a competitive game for a year. The historic winner was scored in the 63rd minute by Christian Grindheim from a low cross from Morten Gamst Pedersen.

YOUR BOYS TOOK A HELL OF A BEATING

Bjorge Lillelien's famous commentary after Norway beat England 2-1 in a qualifier for the 1982 FIFA World Cup remains one of the iconic moments of European football. A commentator from 1957 until just before his death from cancer in 1987, he concentrated on winter sports and football. Roughly translated, it sounded as follows: "Lord Nelson, Lord Beaverbrook, Sir Winston Churchill, Sir Anthony Eden, Clement Attlee, Henry Cooper, Lady Diana, Maggie Thatcher, can you hear me? Your boys took a hell of a beating." Although the commentary was for Norwegian radio, it soon made its way to an English audience and has achieved cliché status. In 2002, Lillelien's words were designated the greatest piece of sports commentary ever by the *Observer* newspaper's sports supplement. Such is its place in British sporting culture, parodies of the commentary have been written to celebrate a vast array of domestic sporting victories.

OLE THE GUNNER

Ole Gunnar Solskjaer will always be considered a Manchester United hero for his decisive role in helping the club win the 1999 Champions League in such dramatic fashion against Bayern Munich in Barcelona. Yet he turned down the chance of taking charge of Norway after he retired from the game. The goal-grabber from Kristiansand, on the west coast of Norway, preferred to concentrate on his work as a UNICEF ambassador as well as a reserve-team coach back at Old Trafford.

LEADING SCORERS

Jorgen Juve	33
Einar Gundersen	26
Harald Hennum	25
Tore Andre Flo	23
Ole Gunnar Solskjaer	23
Gunnar Thoresen	22
John Carew	21
Steffen Iversen	21
Jan Age Fjortoft	20
Odd Iversen	19

POLAND

The history of Polish football is littered with tremendous highs and depressing lows. Olympic gold-medal success in 1972, and back-to-back third-place finishes in the 1982 and 1986 FIFA World Cup™ competitions were followed by failure to qualify for any tournament until 1992. Poland made it to the European Championship for the first time in 2008 and will co-host the tournament (with Ukraine) in 2012.

SUPER ERNEST

Ernest Wilimowski wrote his name into FIFA World Cup history in 1938 when he scored a hat-trick but still finished on the losing side against Brazil in the finals in France. Later, after Poland had been overrun by the Nazi army in 1939, Wilimowski transferred to Germany. He even played for Greater Germany. For years, his name and fame were erased from Poland's football records.

POLE DANCING

Three is Poland's lucky football number. The years 1974 and 1982 stand out in the annals of the country's sport because, on both occasions, the Poles came third at the FIFA World Cup. In 1974, with their lightning speed and team chemistry, they were almost unstoppable after upsetting England in qualifying. Memorably, when they played hosts West Germany, the pitch was half-flooded and the Poles, who needed a win to reach the final, wanted the game postponed. Instead, in miserably wet conditions, Gerd Muller scored a late German winner. In 1982, in Spain, only Grzegorz Lato, Andrzej Szarmach, Marek Kusto and Wladyslaw Zmuda remained from the 1974 squad. But the exciting mix of veterans and youngsters were no match for Italy in the semi-finals, losing 2-0.

CLOWNING AROUND

The late, great Brian Clough famously described Poland goalkeeper Jan Tomaszewski as "a clown" after a series of inept displays for his country. But the comment came back to haunt both Clough and England when Tomaszewski had the last laugh. On an extraordinary night on 17 October 1973, he produced the most incredible performance of his life at a rain-sodden Wembley – almost single-handedly guiding his team to the FIFA World Cup finals, at the expense of England.

LATO'S MISSION

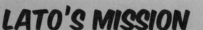

Grzegorz Lato, one of Poland's finest ever players, became president of the country's football federation in 2008, promising to clean up the sport as Poland gears up to co-host the 2012 European Championships with Ukraine. "I am determined to change the image of Polish football, to make it transparent and pure," said Lato, a legend in the 1970s and '80s and the top scorer at the 1974 FIFA World Cup (with seven goals).

OLD FIRM EXCESS

In 2006, Celtic goalkeeper Artur Boruc was cautioned for making the Catholic sign of the cross before a game with Rangers, their arch Protestant rivals. Celtic fans have since given Boruc the nickname "The Holy Goalie".

LEADING APPEARANCES

1	Grzegorz Lato	100
2	Kazimierz Deyna	97
3	Jacek Bak	96
4	Wladyslaw Zmuda	91
5	Jacek Krzynowek	89
6	Michael Zewlakow	85
7	Antoni Szymanowski	82
8	Zbigniew Boniek	80
9	Wlodzimierz Lubanski	75
10	Tomasz Waldoch	74

LEADING SCORERS

1	Wlodzimierz Lubanski	48
2	Grzegorz Lato	45
3	Kazimierz Deyna	41
4	Ernest Pol	39
5	Andrzej Szarmach	32
6	Gerard Cieslik	27
7	Zbigniew Boniek	24
8	Ernest Wilimowski	21
9	Dariusz Dziekanowski	20
10	Roman Kosecki	19

⚽ STAR SIGN LEO

Leo Beenhakker became the first foreigner to coach Poland when he took charge in July 2006. In a career spanning more than 30 years, Beenhakker has coached Holland and Saudi Arabia, as well as Trinidad and Tobago. He also won three Spanish league titles with Real Madrid from 1987–89 and two Dutch league titles with Ajax in 1980 and 1990. The silver-haired Dutchman underlined his workaholic reputation in the spring of 2009 by taking up an extra role as consultant back home with Feyenoord.

COOL KEEPER

What is it with Polish goalkeepers? The country's outfield players may not be household names worldwide, but Jerzy Dudek (Liverpool), Artur Boruc (Celtic), Lukasz Fabianski (Arsenal) and Tomasz Kuszczak (Manchester United) have all played significant roles at four of Britain's most successful clubs. Lukasz Zaluska, heading from Dundee United to Celtic, may prove the next in line.

⚽ BLACK HISTORY

Poland has long been rocked by a string of corruption scandals involving referees, players, club officials and federation members. The crisis was exacerbated by the appalling condition of many stadiums, financial problems and hooliganism. In 2001 the government intervened and Poland were very nearly banned from international competition by FIFA, which forbids any form of governmental intervention.

BONIEK

Zbigniew Boniek, arguably the best player Poland has ever produced, earned a place among football's legends for his role in the country's progress to third place at the 1982 FIFA World Cup. However, his absence from the tournament's semi-final will go down as one of the great "what ifs" of the competition. Robbed of their star forward through suspension, could Poland have upset both Italy and the odds and reached the final? Instead they lost 2-0.

PORTUGAL

Portugal's first experience of international competition almost ended in triumph. Inspired by Eusebio, they marched through to the semi-finals of the 1966 FIFA World Cup™, only to lose to eventual champions England. A standout performance in the 1984 European Championship apart, more than 30 years would pass before Portugal enjoyed such giddy heights again. A "golden" generation of players arrived on the scene and since the turn of the century Portugal have become a consistent force on the world football stage.

THE BLACK PANTHER

Born in Mozambique, Eusebio da Silva Ferreira was named Portugal's "Golden Player" to mark UEFA's 50th anniversary in 2004. Signed by Benfica in 1960 at the age of 18, he scored a hat-trick in only his second game – against Santos in a friendly tournament in Paris – outshining the opponents' young star, Pele. He helped Benfica win the second of their European Cups in 1962, was named European Footballer of the Year in 1965, and led Portugal to third place in the 1966 FIFA World Cup, finishing the tournament as top scorer with nine goals. A phenomenal striker, Eusebio scored 320 goals in 313 appearances in the Portuguese league, won the first European Golden Boot in 1968 (repeating the feat in 1973), and his 41 goals for Portugal has been bettered only by Pauleta, who took 24 more games to score just six more goals.

RED MIST

The record for the most red cards shown in a FIFA World Cup match is four: the second-round clash between Portugal and Holland in 2006. Costinho and Deco saw red for Portugal; Khalid Boulahrouz and Geovanni van Bronckhurst for the Dutch.

TOP APPEARANCES

1	Luis Filipe Madeira FIGO	127
2	FERNANDO Manuel Silva COUTO	110
3	RUI Manuel Cesar COSTA	94
4	Pedro Miguel Resendes "PAULETA"	88
5	JOAO Manuel VIEIRA PINTO	81
6	VITOR Manuel Martins BAIA	80
7	RICARDO Alexandre Martins PEREIRA	79
8	Nuno Miguel Soares "NUNO GOMES"	72
9	JOAO Domingos Silva PINTO	70
10	SIMAO Pedro Fonseca SABROSA	68

THE FAMOUS FIVE

Eusebio, Mario Coluna, Jose Augusto, Antonio Simoes, and Jose Torres were the "Fabulous Five" in Benfica's 1960s Dream Team, who made up the spine of the Portuguese national side at the 1966 FIFA World Cup. Coluna (the "Sacred Monster"), scored the vital third goal in the 1961 European Cup final and captained the national side in 1966. Jose Augusto, who scored two goals in the opening game against Hungary, went on to manage the national side and later the Portuguese women's team. Antonio Simoes (the "Giant Gnome" – just 1.58 metres/5ft 3in tall) made his debut for Portugal and Benfica in 1962, aged just 18. Jose Torres – the only one of the five not to win the European Cup (he played in the 1963 final defeat to Milan) – scored the winner against Russia in the 1966 third-place match, and went on to manage the national side to their next appearance at the FIFA World Cup finals in 1986.

CRISTIANO RONALDO

Cristiano Ronaldo dos Santos Aveiro got his second name because his father was a great fan of US President Ronald Reagan. Despite growing up a Benfica fan, Ronaldo began his career with local rivals Sporting before moving to Manchester United in 2003. He enjoyed a fantastic season in 2008, winning the Premier League, the Champions League, the Golden Boot in the Premier League and Europe, and capping it all by becoming the second Portuguese player (after Luis Figo) to win the FIFA World Player of the Year award.

GOLDEN OLDIE

Nene, who scored the only goal in Portugal's 1-0 European Championship victory over Romania in 1984, is the oldest goalscorer in the history of the FIFA World Cup finals competition at 34 years and 213 days.

CLOUD NINE

Scoring nine goals in one match against Leca, eight goals in one match against Boavista, six goals in a game three times, five goals in a game 12 times and four goals in a game 17 times, Fernando Baptista Peyroteo is one of the most prolific goalscorers in world football history. He scored an astonishing 330 goals in 197 Portuguese league games (1.68 goals a game) between 1937 and 1949, and 15 goals in just 20 games for the national side.

MOST-CAPPED KEEPER

Vitor Baia, one of only two goalkeepers to have won a clean sweep of the European Cup, the UEFA Cup and the now-defunct European Cup-Winners' Cup, played in goal for Portugal a record 80 times. When he returned to Porto from Barcelona in 1999 to find his old No.1 jersey taken, he chose No.99, and went on to use the name for his charity foundation "Vitor Baia 99".

TOP GOALSCORERS

1	Pedro Miguel Resendes "PAULETA"	47
2	EUSEBIO da Silva Ferreira	41
3	Luis Filipe Madeira FIGO	32
4	Nuno Miguel Soares "NUNO GOMES"	29
5	RUI Manuel Cesar COSTA	26
6	JOAO Manuel VIEIRA PINTO	23
7	Tamagnini Baptista "NENE"	22
8	CRISTIANO RONALDO dos Santos Aveiro	21
9	SIMAO Pedro Fonseca SABROSA	18
10	Rui Manuel Trinidade JORDAO	15

BRIGHT YOUNG THING

Jose Manuel Soares, known as "Pepe", was a small, but incredibly gifted, young striker who scored twice in Portugal's first Olympics appearance in 1928 when he was just 20 years old. Sadly, Pepe died three years later from food poisoning, but his impact at Belenenses was so great that a statue of him stands at the entrance to their Restelo Stadium in Lisbon.

THE "GOLDEN GENERATION"

So-called for winning the FIFA U-20 World Cup twice in a row, in 1989 and 1991, Portugal's "Golden Generation", featuring Luis Figo, Fenando Couto, Rui Costa, Nuno Gomes and Sergio Conceicao, never managed to repeat their success at the top level, despite reaching the semi-finals of Euro 96, the final of Euro 2004 and the semi-finals of the 2006 FIFA World Cup.

GOODISON GLORY

At the 1966 FIFA World Cup Portugal defeated North Korea 5-3 in an incredible quarter-final at Everton's Goodison Park. The sensational Eusebio spurred an amazing comeback after the Koreans had gone 3-0 ahead in the first 25 minutes. He scored four goals to take Portugal to the semi-finals in their first-ever FIFA World Cup appearance. Despite the tears that flowed after defeat to eventual winners England, Portugal rallied to claim third place with a 2-1 victory over Russia. The winner came from a penalty, converted by ... Eusebio.

ROMANIA

The history of Romanian football is littered with a series of bright moments – they were one of four countries (with Brazil, France and Belgium) to appear in the first three editions of the FIFA World Cup™ – followed by significant spells in the doldrums – since 1938 they have only qualified for the finals of the tournament four times in 14 attempts. The country's football highlight came in 1994 when, inspired by Gheorghe Hagi, they reached the quarter-finals of the FIFA World Cup™.

WIN SOME, LOSE SOME...

Romania enjoyed a great start to their first-ever game in the first-ever FIFA World Cup when Adalbert Desu scored in the first minute. Romania won 3-1 in the match, which saw Peru's Placido Galindo become the first player to be sent off in a FIFA World Cup on 54 minutes. Only 3,000 spectators – the lowest recorded attendance for a FIFA World Cup finals match – witnessed the drama.

THE "HERO OF SEVILLE"

Helmuth Duckadam, the "Hero of Seville", will always be remembered for saving four consecutive penalties as Steaua Bucharest became the first Eastern European side to win the European Cup, beating Barcelona in a shoot-out in 1986. A rare blood disease forced him to retire from the game in 1991, after which he became a stopper of a different kind as a major in the Romanian Border Police.

CENTURY MAN

Gheorghe Hagi, Romania's "Player of the [20th] Century", scored three goals and was named in the Team of the Tournament in the 1994 FIFA World Cup in the United States, where Romania lost out on penalties to Sweden after a 2-2 draw in the quarter-finals. Hagi made his international debut in 1983, aged just 18, scored his first goal aged 19 (in a 3-2 defeat by Northern Ireland) and remains Romania's top goalscorer with 35 goals in 125 games. Despite retiring from international football after the 1998 FIFA World Cup, Hagi couldn't resist answering his country's call to play in Euro 2000. Sadly, two yellow-card offences in six minutes in the quarter-final against Italy meant Hagi's final bow on the international stage saw him receive a red card – and leave the field to take an early bath. Farul Constanta, in Hagi's hometown, named their stadium after him in 2000 – but fans stopped referring to it as such after he took the manager's job at rivals Timisoara.

TERRIFIC TRIO

Gheorghe Hagi, Ilie Dumitrescu and Florin Raducioiu lit up the FIFA World Cup in the United States in 1994. Together they scored nine of Romania's ten goals (Raducioiu four, Hagi three, Dumitrescu two). All three successfully converted their penalties in the quarter-final shoot-out against Sweden, but misses from Dan Petrescu and Miodrag Belodedici sent the Romanians crashing out. All three made big-money moves for the following 1994–95 season: Hagi went from Brescia to Barcelona, Dumitrescu from Steaua Bucharest to Tottenham Hotspur, and Raducioiu went from warming the bench at Milan to the first team at Espanyol.

TOP APPEARANCES

1	Dorinel Munteanu	134
2	Gheorghe Hagi	125
3	Gheorghe Popescu	115
4	Ladislau Boloni	108
5	Dan Petrescu	95
6	Bogdan Stelea	91
7	Michael Klein	90
8	Marius Lacatus	84
9	Mircea Rednic	83
10	Silviu Lung	77

HARD TO SAY GOODBYE

Dorinel Munteanu is another Romanian international who found it hard to give up the national side – he originally retired in 2004, but ended up playing for Romania until 2007. He became Romania's most-capped player, playing 134 games (scoring 16 goals). Munteanu made his debut in a 1-0 defeat in Norway on 23 May 1991, and made his final appearance (again) in a 3-1 defeat to Germany on 12 September 2007. He was an ever-present in the Romania side who played at the 1994 and 1998 FIFA World Cups.

HOW MANY?

Striker Rodion Camataru may have scored 22 goals in 75 games for Romania, but he is best remembered for controversially winning the European Golden Boot in the 1986–87 season. Camataru's impressive tally of 44 goals remains the second highest total ever for the Romanian league, but suspicions were raised when it emerged that 18 of these goals came in the final six games of the season. The competition was later suspended and resurfaced only a decade later with a complex new formula for rating the difficulty level of different European leagues.

PAYING THE PENALTY

Romania were knocked out of consecutive FIFA World Cup finals on penalties. In 1990, after a dull 0-0 draw, they lost out 5-4 on penalties to the Republic of Ireland. They went one better in 1994, reaching the quarter-finals, but lost 5-4 on penalties again – this time to Sweden. Their only penalty shoot-out victories have come against lowly opposition in minor tournaments – 5-3 against China in the "Great Wall Cup" in 1985 and 4-2 against Georgia in the 2000 Cyprus Cup.

HIGH FIVE

On 25 May 1930, Rudolf Wetzer scored five goals (a Romanian record) as Romania destroyed Greece 8-1 in a pre-FIFA World Cup friendly match. Wetzer played in the 1924 Olympics and went on to captain the side at the 1930 FIFA World Cup, though he failed to find the net in Romania's three games in Uruguay. In total, Wetzer scored 12 goals in 17 appearances for Romania, playing his final game – still as captain – in a 2-0 defeat to Bulgaria in 1932.

A GOOD NAME

Gheorghe Popescu was a Romanian international defender, born in 1918, who went on to great success as manager of Steaua Bucharest before becoming president of the Romanian Football Association. Gheorghe "Gica" Popescu – no relation – was also a Romanian international defender, born in 1967, who won 115 caps and a string of European club titles, including the now-defunct Cup-Winners' Cup, the UEFA Cup, as well as domestic leagues and cups in Holland, Spain, Romania and Turkey.

TOP GOALS

1	Gheorghe Hagi	35
2	Iuliu Bodola	31
3	Adrian Mutu	29
4	Anghel Iordanescu	26
5	Viorel Moldovan	25
6	Ladislau Boloni	23
7	Rodion Camataru	22
8	Dudu Georgescu	21
=	Florin Raducioiu	21
10	Stefan Dobay	20

MAJOR TOURNAMENTS

FIFA WORLD CUP™: 7 appearances – quarter-finals 1994
EUROPEAN CHAMPIONSHIP: 4 appearances – quarter-finals 2000
FIRST INTERNATIONAL: Yugoslavia 1 Romania 2 (Belgrade, Yugoslavia, 8 June 1922)
BIGGEST WIN: Romania 9 Finland 0 (Bucharest, Romania, 14 October 1973)
BIGGEST DEFEAT: Hungary 9 Romania 0 (Budapest, Hungary, 6 June 1948)

RUSSIA

Before the break-up of the Soviet Union in 1992, the USSR were among the powerhouses of world football, winning the inaugural European Championship in 1960, striking gold at the 1956 and 1988 Olympic Games, and qualifying for the FIFA World Cup™ on all but two occasions (1974 and 1978). Playing as Russia since August 1992, the good times have eluded them, although a fourth-place finish at the 2008 European Championship could signal a return to former glories.

WHAT'S IN A NAME?

The current Russian national team is recognized as the official successor to both the CIS (Commonwealth of Independent States) side and the USSR. Of the three, the USSR had the longest, and most successful, record, including a victory in the inaugural European Championships in 1960 and Olympic gold-medal success in 1956 (Melbourne) and 1988 (Seoul). The 1960 success was made slightly more straightforward by Spain's refusal to travel to the Soviet Union for the quarter-finals. This walkover, however, was followed by an impressive 3-0 semi-final win over Czechoslovakia, followed by a much tighter 2-1 extra-time victory over Yugoslavia in the final in France. The side's next best result also came in the European Championship when they lost the 1988 final 2-0 to Holland in Germany. The CIS evolved out of the political compromise that arose following the break-up of the Soviet Union in 1991, after the Soviet team had already qualified for Euro 1992. It was the only tournament the CIS, comprising 12 former Soviet states, played in, and it was a tournament to forget: they finished bottom of their group following a 3-0 defeat to Scotland.

GOLDEN BOY

Igor Netto captained the USSR national side to their greatest successes: gold at the 1956 Olympics in Melbourne and victory in the first-ever European Championship in France in 1960. Born in Moscow in 1930, Netto was awarded the Order of Lenin in 1957, and became an ice hockey coach after retiring from football.

SUPER STOPPER

FIFA declared Lev Yashin to be the finest goalkeeper of the 20th century – naturally, he made it into their Century XI team, too. In a career spanning 20 years, Yashin played 326 league games for Dynamo Moscow – the only club side he ever played for – and won 78 caps for the Soviet Union, conceding on average less than a goal a game (only 70 in total). With Dynamo, he won five Soviet championships and three Soviet cups, the last of which came in his final full season in 1970. He saved around 150 penalties in his long career, and kept four clean sheets in his 12 World Cup matches. Such was Yashin's worldwide reputation, Chilean international Eladio Rojas was so excited at scoring past the legendary Yashin in the 1962 FIFA World Cup that he gave the surprised keeper a big hug with the ball still sitting in the back of the net. Yashin was nicknamed the "Black Spider" for his distinctive black jersey and his uncanny ability to get a hand, arm, leg or foot in the way of shots and headers of all kinds. In 1963, Yashin became the first, and so far only, keeper to be named European Footballer of the Year, the same year in which he won his fifth Soviet championship and starred for the Rest of the World XI in the English FA's Centenary Match at Wembley.

TOP APPEARANCES

(Russia only)

1	Viktor Onopko	109
2	Valeriy Karpin	72
3	Vladimir Beschastnykh	71
4	Dimitri Alenichev	55
=	Yuri Nikiforov	55
=	Sergei Semak	55
=	Alexi Smertin	55
8	Dimitri Khokhlov	53
9	Yuri Kovtun	50
=	Aleksandr Mostovoi	50

TOP GOALS

(Russia only)

1	Vladimir Beschastnykh	26
2	Valeriy Karpin	17
3	Dmitriy Sychov	15
4	Andrei Arshavin	14
5	Aleksandr Kerzhakov	13
6	Igor Kolyvanov	12
7	Pavel Pavlyuchenko	10
=	Sergei Kiryakov	10
=	Aleksandr Mostovoi	10
10	Igor Simutenkov	9

MAJOR TOURNAMENTS

FIFA WORLD CUP™: 9 appearances (7 as USSR, 2 as Russia) – fourth, 1966
EUROPEAN CHAMPIONSHIP: 9 appearances (5 as USSR, 1 as CIS 1992, 3 as Russia) – winners 1960 (USSR), semi-finals 2008 (Russia)
FIRST INTERNATIONAL:
Russian Empire: Finland 2 Russian Empire 1 (Stockholm, Sweden, 30 June 1912)
USSR: USSR 3 Turkey 0 (Moscow, 16 November 1924) (final international: Cyprus 0 USSR 3, Larnaca, 13 November 1991)
CIS: USA 0 CIS 1 (Miami, USA, 25 January 1992) (final international: Scotland 3 CIS 0, Norrkoping, Sweden, 18 June 1992)
Russia: Russia 2 Mexico 0 (Moscow, 16 August 1992)
BIGGEST WIN:
USSR: USSR 11 India 1 (Moscow, 16 September 1955); Finland 0 USSR 10 (Helsinki, 15 August 1957)
CIS: El Salvador 0 CIS 3 (San Salvador, 29 January 1992)
Russia: San Marino 0 Russia 7 (San Marino, 7 June 1995)
BIGGEST DEFEAT:
Russian Empire: Germany 16 Russian Empire 0 (Stockholm, Sweden, 1 July 1912)
USSR: England 5 USSR 0 (London, 22 October 1958)
CIS: Mexico 4 CIS 0 (Mexico City, 8 March 1992)
Russia: Portugal 7 Russia 1 (Lisbon, 13 October 2004)

⊙ HARDER TIMES

In the modern era, Vladimir Beschastnykh is Russia's leading international goalscorer, with 26 goals in 71 games, though this is only a little over half of Oleg Blokhin's 42-goal haul (in 112 games) for the Soviet national side. Beschastnykh scored his first goal in a 3-0 friendly win against Austria in 1994, and went on to play in the final game of Russia's disappointing FIFA World Cup campaign in the USA the same year. He played all three games in a similarly disappointing 2002 FIFA World Cup, scoring in the final game against Belgium in Shizuoka. Russia lost the game 3-2 and crashed out of the tournament in the first round, having already lost to Japan.

CAPPING IT ALL

Viktor Onopko, despite being born in the Ukraine, played all his career for the Soviet Union, CIS and Russian national football teams. The first of Onopko's 113 international caps (including four for the CIS) came in a 2-2 draw against England in Moscow on 29 April 1992. He played in the 1994 and 1998 FIFA World Cups, as well as the European Championship in 1996. He was due to join the squad for the European Championship in 2004 but missed out through injury. Onopko's club career, spanning 19 years, took him from Shakhtar Donetsk, Spartak Moscow, Real Oviedo, Rayo Vallecano, Alania Vladikavkaz and FC Saturn. He was Russian footballer of the year in 1993 and 1994.

MONEY MAN

Roman Abramovich, the commodities billionaire behind Chelsea's 21st-century success, has also been instrumental in the resurgence of Russian football at all levels – including the key step of importing Dutchman Guus Hiddink to manage the national side. In 2008, Hiddink took Russia to the semi-finals of the European Championship (their best post-Soviet performance), where they lost 3-0 to eventual winners Spain. Abramovich also sponsors the "National Academy of Football" in Russia, which helps build training facilities and pitches to support youth football throughout the country.

SERBIA

The former Yugoslavia was one of the strongest football nations in eastern Europe. They reached the FIFA World Cup™ semi-finals in 1930 and 1962, they were also runners-up in the European Championships of 1960 and 1968. In addition, Yugoslavia's leading club, Red Star Belgrade, remain the only team from eastern Europe to win the European Cup, when they beat Marseille on penalties in the 1991 final.

BOYCOTT HITS YUGOSLAV HOPES

The rivalry between Serbia and Croatia was apparent even in the early days of the old federation. Yugoslavia reached the last four of the inaugural FIFA World Cup in 1930. But they did so without any Croat players, who boycotted the squad for the finals in protest at the new federal association headquarters being located in the Serb capital, Belgrade.

BOBEK'S GOAL GREED

Stjepan Bobek was the undisputed top scorer for the former Yugoslavia. He netted 38 times in 63 appearances, between 1946 and 1956. Bobek was a Croat, born in Zagreb, but he spent virtually his entire career with Partizan Belgrade (in Serbia), netting a record 403 goals in 468 league appearances for the club.

TOP GOALS

1	Savo Milosevic	37
2	Predrag Mijatovic	28
3	Dejan Savicevic	19
4	Mateja Kezman	17
5	Dragan Stojkovic	15
6	Dejan Stankovic	13
7	Nikola Zigic	13
8	Darko Kovacevic	10
=	Slavisa Jokanovic	10
10	Sinisa Mihailjovic	9

MILJANIC THE PICK

Miljan Miljanic was Yugoslavia's most famous coach, who steered Red Star to success, then did the same for Real Madrid. He made his name guiding Red Star to four championships and the semi-finals of the European Cup in 1971. He then coached Yugoslavia to the last eight of the FIFA World Cup finals in 1974, and later guided Real Madrid to back-to-back La Liga titles in 1975 and 1976.

SANTRAC LASTS LONGEST

Slobodan Santrac was the first manager of the "new" Yugoslavia. He served the longest term too, between 1994 and 1998, winning 26 of his 43 games in charge. Since Santrac's departure, Serbia have employed Milan Zivadinovic, Vujadin Boskov (twice), Ilija Petkovic (twice), Milovan Doric, Ivan Curkovic, Dejan Savicevic (twice), Spanish coach Javier Clemente, Miroslav Dukic and current manager Radi Antic.

THE WHITE EAGLES

The national team of former Yugoslavia were nicknamed "Plavni" ("Blues") because of their shirt colour. However, Serbia decided to change their colours after Montenegro voted to become independent. They went for red, not blue. The team asked supporters for a new nickname. The broadcaster B92 proposed "Beli Orlovi" ("White Eagles"), taken from the double-headed white eagle on Serbia's national flag. The name was adopted by both the Serb fans and the national association. The national team is now known as "Beli Orlovi" and the Under-21 side is called "Orlici" ("Eaglets").

MAGIC DRAGAN

Yugoslavia's greatest player was Red Star left winger Dragan Dzajic, who later went on to become the club's president. He made his international debut at 18, won a national record 85 caps and scored 23 goals. The most important was his last-minute winner against world champions England in the 1968 European Championship semi-final in Florence, which took Yugoslavia to the final against Italy. Pele said of Dzajic: "He's a real wizard. I'm sorry he's not Brazilian."

SAVICEVIC STRIKES

Dejan Savicevic is Serbia's greatest player of the modern era. The attacking midfielder was a key member of Red Star's 1991 European Cup-winning team. He also inspired them to three consecutive championships. He moved on to Milan and starred as his new club beat Barcelona 4-0 in the 1994 European Cup final. He created the opening goal, then crashed home a 35-yard volley. Savicevic later became a prominent supporter of the drive for Montenegrin independence from Serbia and has been credited with playing an influential role in the referendum vote on 21 May 2006 that led to the establishment of a separate Montenegrin state.

TOP CAPS

1	Savo Milosevic	102
2	Dragan Stojkovic	84
3	Dejan Stankovic	78
4	Predrag Mijatovic	73
5	Slavisa Jokanovic	64
=	Sinisa Mihailjovic	64
7	Darko Kovacevic	59
=	Mladen Krstajic	59
=	Zoran Mirkovic	59
10	Dejan Savicevic	56

SWEDEN

Eleven appearances at the FIFA World Cup™ finals (with a best result of second, as tournament hosts, in 1958) and three Olympic medals (including gold in London in 1948), bear testament to Sweden's rich history on the world football stage. Recent success has been hard to find, however, with a semi-final appearance at the 1992 European Championship (again as hosts) the country's best performance in recent years.

TIME TO GIVE UP THE DAY JOB

The Swedish federation allowed only amateur, home-based players to be called up to the squad for the 1950 FIFA World Cup, despite being the only side without any professional players. However, Sweden still finished third, beating Spain 3-1 in their decisive last game. With professionals allowed in the squad for the 1958 finals, Sweden – as hosts – lost 5-2 in the final to Brazil.

AGE SHALL NOT WEARY THEM

Aged 33 years and 159 days, Tore Keller is the oldest hat-trick scorer in FIFA World Cup finals history – scoring three of Sweden's eight without reply against Cuba in the first round of the 1938 tournament. Nils Liedholm, part of Sweden's 1948 Olympic gold-medal winning team, became the oldest player, at 35, to score in a FIFA World Cup final itself, as Sweden lost 5-2 to Brazil in 1958.

ZLATAN IBRAHIMOVIC
Striker, 56 caps, 20 goals

GRE-NO-LI OLYMPIC AND ITALIAN GLORY

Having conquered the world by leading Sweden to gold in the 1948 Olympics in London, Gunnar Gren, Gunnar Nordahl and Nils Liedholm were snapped up by AC Milan. Their three-pronged "Gre-No-Li" forward line led the Italian giants to their 1951 scudetto win. Nordahl, who topped the Serie A scoring charts five times between 1950 and 1955, remains Milan's all-time top scorer with 221 goals in 268 games. Gren and Liedholm went on to appear for the Swedish national team in the 1958 FIFA World Cup – where they finished runners-up.

RAVELLI'S REF RAGE

Swedish goalkeeping hero Thomas Ravelli was banned for six games while playing for MLS side Tampa Bay in 1998 for kicking the ball at a referee who had just awarded a penalty against him. Ravelli kept goal for Sweden a record 143 times – conceding 143 goals. He saved two penalties, including the crucial sudden-death strike from Miodrag Belodedici, in the 1994 FIFA World Cup quarter-final to send Sweden to the semi-finals, where they lost 1-0 to Brazil.

LOSING LOSERS

Despite losing to Nottingham Forest in the final of the 1979 European Cup, Malmo contested the World Club Cup in 1979 after the English side declined the invitation. Sadly, Malmo ended as runners-up again, losing out on away goals to Olimpia Asuncion from Paraguay.

AS LONG AS WE BEAT THE DANES

In 1931, Sweden's record goalscorer, Sven Rydell, became the first footballer to be awarded the prestigious Svenska Dagbladet gold medal for scoring two goals in a 3-1 victory over Denmark in the Nordic Championship. Rydell scored 49 goals in 43 games for Sweden (1.14 per match) – including seven hat-tricks and two four-goal hauls – and his tournament tally of six goals was instrumental in Sweden winning the bronze medal in the 1924 Olympics in Paris. His daughter, Ewa Rydell, carried on the family's Olympic tradition when she competed as a gymnast in 1960 and 1964.

BROTHERS IN ARMS

The Nordahl brothers – Bertil, Knut and Gunnar – all won gold medals with Sweden in the 1948 Olympics football tournament. All three went on to play in Italy: Bertil with Atalanta, Knut with Roma, while Gunnar became a goalscoring legend at AC Milan before also turning out for Roma. Twins Thomas and Andreas Ravelli continued the brotherly tradition, winning 143 and 41 caps for Sweden respectively.

MANAGER SWAP

The most successful manager Sweden ever had was Englishman George Raynor, who led them to Olympic gold in London in 1948 and steered Sweden to third place and the runners-up spot in the 1950 and 1958 FIFA World Cups respectively. Raynor got one over on the country of his birth when Sweden became only the second foreign side to win at Wembley, with a 3-2 victory over England in 1959. Working in the opposite direction, in 2001 Sven-Goran Eriksson left Serie A side Lazio to become England's first foreign coach. He led the side to three consecutive quarter-finals – in the FIFA World Cups of 2002 and 2006 and the 2004 European Championship in between. Eriksson, however, failed to lead England to a win over his home country, recording three draws (1-1 in a friendly, 2001; 1-1 in a 2002 FIFA World Cup group game; 2-2 in a 2006 FIFA World Cup group game) and one defeat (0-1 in a friendly, 2004).

NOT YOU AGAIN...

Anyone who has ever thought their side has been cursed by the luck of the draw, should spare a thought for Sweden, who have been drawn against Brazil a record seven times in the FIFA World Cup: in 1938, 1950, 1958 (the final), 1978, 1990 and twice in 1994 (a group match and the semi-final). Sweden have won none of these encounters, racking up five defeats (six goals for, 19 against) and two 1-1 draws (in 1978 and in the group match in 1994).

EMERGENCY MAN

Goalkeeper Karl-Oskar "Rio-Kalle" Svensson, who played in the bronze and silver medal-winning sides at the 1950 and 1958 FIFA World Cups, held down a job as a fire fighter in Helsingborg. He holds the unenviable record of having conceded the most goals in the Swedish top division – 575 in 349 games.

GOTHENBURG FLY THE FLAG

Under Sven-Goran Eriksson, IFK Gothenburg became the first Swedish team to win a European tournament when, in 1982, they crushed Hamburg 4-0 on aggregate in the UEFA Cup final.

ONE MORE ENCORE, AGAIN!

One of the most famous and decorated Swedish footballers of modern times, Henrik Larsson (a star on the club scene with both Celtic and Barcelona) quit international football after the 2002 FIFA World Cup ... and again after the 2006 FIFA World Cup in Germany. He then made a further comeback in the 2010 FIFA World Cup qualifiers. With 37 goals in his 104 appearances, including five in his three FIFA World Cups, fans and officials clamoured for his return each time he tried to walk away. Sweden's failure to qualify for the tournament in 1998 meant that a record-equalling 12 years elapsed between Larsson's first FIFA World Cup finals goal against Bulgaria in 1994 and his last – so far! – with his dramatic equalizer in the 2-2 group-round draw with England in 2006.

SWITZERLAND

Switzerland set a record in 2006 when they became the first side in FIFA World Cup™ finals history to depart the tournament without conceding a goal. It sums up the country's football history: three FIFA World Cup™ quarter-final appearances apart (in 1934, 1938 and 1954 – the latter as tournament hosts), Switzerland has failed to establish itself on the international football stage. The country co-hosted the 2008 European Championship with Austria, and is better known as being the home of both FIFA and UEFA.

SWITZERLAND: HEART OF WORLD FOOTBALL...

Both the Fédération Internationale de Football Association (FIFA) and the Union des Associations Européennes de Football (UEFA) are based in Switzerland. UEFA was formed in Basel and its administrative base is in Nyon. Along with France, Belgium, Denmark, Holland, Spain (represented by Madrid FC, who later became Real Madrid) and Sweden, the Swiss federation was one of FIFA's founding members, signing the foundation act in Paris on 21 March 1904 – a full year before the Swiss team's first international match. FIFA is based in Zurich, and celebrated its 50th birthday in 1954 by choosing to host its showpiece FIFA World Cup in its home country, Switzerland.

HOT STUFF

Switzerland's 7-5 defeat by Austria in the quarter-finals of the 1954 FIFA World Cup remains the highest-scoring game in the finals tournament. In the so-called "Hitzeschlacht von Lausanne" (the "Heat Battle in Lausanne"), Switzerland, with the Austrian keeper suffering sunstroke, were 3-0 up after just 20 minutes. With an amazing nine goals in the first half (Austria 5 Switzerland 4), the final score could have been even worse for the Swiss – Austria also missed a penalty.

LLAMA FARMER FREI-ING HIGH

After being compared to a llama by an angry Swiss sports press for spitting at Steven Gerrard at Euro 2004, Alexander Frei, Switzerland's all-time top scorer, adopted a llama at Basel zoo as part of his apology to the nation.

ONE MAN LEAGUE

Heinz Hermann, in addition to being Switzerland's most-capped player, won the Swiss player of the year trophy an incredible five seasons in a row between 1984 and 1988.

"MERCI KOBI"

Former Swiss international player and manager, Jakob "Kobi" Kuhn, was left close to tears as his players unfurled a "thank you" banner at the end of his final game as Swiss national manager – the 2-0 victory over Portugal in the final group game of Euro 2008. How times have changed for Kuhn: while now a much-loved elder statesmen of the Swiss game, when Kuhn was just 22 years old, he was sent home from the 1966 FIFA World Cup for missing a curfew. He was then banned from the national side for a year. The shoe was on the other foot when Kuhn had to send Alexander Frei home from Euro 2004 after the centre-forward spat at England's Steven Gerrard. Kuhn spent most of his playing career, where he was described as playing "with honey in his boots", with FC Zurich, winning six league titles and five Swiss Cups. He played 63 times for the national side, scoring five goals. He then worked his way up through the ranks of the Swiss national team, leading first the Under-18s, then the Under-21s and finally the senior national team.

THE ORIGINAL BOLT

Karl Rappan did so much for Swiss football – including founding its first national football fan club – that it is often forgotten that he was Austrian. After a moderately successful career as a player and coach in Austria, Rappan achieved lasting fame as an innovative manager in Switzerland, leading the national side in the 1938 and 1954 FIFA World Cups, as well as securing league titles and cups as manager of Grasshopper-Club, FC Servette and FC Zurich. He developed a flexible tactical system – which allowed players to switch positions depending on the situation and putting greater pressure on their opponents. This revolutionary new idea became known as the "Swiss bolt", and helped the unfancied hosts defeat Italy on the way to the quarter-finals of the 1954 FIFA World Cup, before losing out to Rappan's home country, Austria. An early advocate of a European league, Rappan eventually settled for the simpler knock-out tournament, the Intertoto Cup, which he helped devise and launch in 1961. Rappan is Switzerland's longest-serving and statistically most successful manager, with 29 victories in 77 games in charge.

CLEAN SHEET WIPE-OUT

The Swiss national team made history in 2006 by becoming the first – and to date only – team to exit the FIFA World Cup without conceding a single goal in regulation time. However, in the shoot-out defeat to Ukraine in the second round, following a goalless 120 minutes, they failed to score a single penalty and lost 3-0. Despite being beaten three times in the shoot-out, goalkeeper Pascal Zuberbuhler's performances in Germany earned him the record for consecutive clean sheets at an international football tournament.

LOST IN TRANSLATION

When FC St Gallen was established as the first Swiss football club in 1879, something must have got lost in translation – in their first competitive game 20 years later, they realized they had made their goals twice the size specified by the original English laws of the game.

ONE MAN('S) TEAM

The kind of brash confidence that inspired Max "Xam" Abegglen to name the football club he helped found "FC Xamax" after himself led him through a stunning debut and career in arguably Switzerland's finest performances on the world football stage. Aged just 20 when he won his first cap on 19 November 1922, Abegglen scored a hat-trick as Switzerland hammered the Netherlands 5-0 in Bern.

TOP SCORERS

1	Alexander Frei	39
2	Kubilay Turkyilmaz	34
3	Max Abegglen III	34
4	Andre Abegglen II	29
=	Jacques Fatton	29
6	Adrian Knup	26
7	Josef Hugi II	23
8	Charles Antenen	22
9	Lauro Amado	21
=	Stephane Chapuisat	21

CHAMPION CHAPPI

Stephane "Chappi" Chapuisat was the first Swiss player to win the UEFA Champions League when he led the line for Borussia Dortmund in their 3-1 victory over Juventus in 1997. Chapuisat's significant contribution in the final was to make way for Lars Ricken, whose goal with his first touch put the game – at 3-1 – beyond Juventus. Stephane's father, Pierre-Albert Chapuisat, was also a successful Swiss international – earning 34 caps for the national side in the 1970s and 1980s – but he failed to reach the heights of his son, Stephane, who would later add both the Club World Cup and the Swiss super league (while playing for Grasshoppers) to his winners' medal collection.

TOP APPEARANCES

1. Heinz Hermann 117 (15 goals)
2. Alain Geiger 112 (2 goals)
3. Stephane Chapuisat 103 (21 goals)
4. Johann Vogel 94 (2 goals)
5. Patrick Muller 81 (3 goals)
6. Severino Minelli 80
7. Andre Egli (Andy) 79 (8 goals)
8. Ciriaco Sforza 79 (6 goals)
9. Raphael Wicky 75 (1 goal)
10. Hakan Yakin 75 (20 goals)

TURKEY

Galatasaray's penalty shoot-out success over Arsenal in the 2000 UEFA Cup final signalled a change in fortune for Turkish football. Prior to that night in Copenhagen, Turkey had qualified for the FIFA World Cup™ only twice (in 1950, when they withdrew, and 1954), and had consistently underachieved on the world stage. Since 2000, however, Turkish fans have had plenty to cheer about, including a third-place finish at the 2002 FIFA World Cup™ in Japan and South Korea, and a semi-final appearance at the 2008 European Championship.

FATIH TERIM

Having coached Galatasaray to their UEFA Cup triumph in 2000, Fatih Terim put a disappointing year and a half in Italy with Fiorentina behind him to lead Turkey in their amazing run to the 2008 European Championship semi-finals. Defeat to Portugal in the opening game left the Turks with an uphill task, but stunning successive comebacks against Switzerland and the Czech Republic took them through to the quarter-finals. A 119th-minute goal seemed to have clinched the tie for Croatia, but, as the Croatian players celebrated, "Emperor" Fatih urged his players to get up, pick the ball out of the net and fight on to the very end. They did just that, and Semih Senturk's improbable equalizer took the match to penalties. The semi-final against Germany provided yet another rollercoaster ride, but this time there was no answer to the Germans' last-minute winner. When Fatih said "there is something special about this team" few could disagree.

ANGRY ALPAY

Never a shrinking violet, midfielder Alpay Ozalan caused an international stir when he taunted David Beckham nose-to-nose after the England star missed a penalty in a qualifying match for the 2004 European Championships in Instanbul. This incident – among others – contributed to Aston Villa cancelling Alpay's contract. The fiery defender went to play in Korea and Japan, but was fired by Urawa Reds after being sent off three times in just seven matches.

QUICK OFF THE MARK

Hakan Sukur scored the fastest-ever FIFA World Cup finals goal – taking only 11 seconds to score Turkey's first goal in their third-place playoff match against South Korea at the 2002 FIFA World Cup. Turkey went on to win the game 3-2 to claim third place, their finest-ever performance in the competition. His total of 51 goals (in 112 games) is more than double his nearest competitor in the national team ranking. His first goal came in only his second appearance, as Turkey beat Denmark 2-1 on 8 April 1992. He went on to score four goals in a single game twice – in the 6-4 win over Wales on 20 August 1997 and in the 5-0 crushing of Moldova on 11 October 2006.

THE FATHER OF TURKISH FOOTBALL

Ali Semi Yen not only founded Galatasaray and served as its president, he was also president of the Turkish National Olympic Committee and coached the Turkish football team in their first-ever international against Romania in 1923. Born Ali Semi, he took the additional name "Yen" (meaning "beat!") after a change in Turkish law required everyone to carry a family name.

⚽ TOP APPEARANCES

1	Rustu Recber	119
2	Hakan Sukur	112
3	Bulent Korkmaz	102
4	Tugay Kerimoglu	94
5	Alpay Ozalan	90
6	Ogun Temizkanoglu	76
7	Abdullah Ercan	71
8	Oguz Cetin	70
9	Fatih Akyel	64
10	Tuncay Sanli	62

⚽ TOP GOALS

1	Hakan Sukur	51
2	Lefter Kucukandonyadis	20
3	Metin Oktay	19
=	Cemil Turan	19
=	Tuncay Sanli	19
6	Nihat Kahveci	17
7	Zeki Riza Sporel	15
8	Arif Erdem	11
=	Ertugrul Saglam	11
10	Burhan Sargun	8
=	Hami Mandirali	8

⚽ THREE'S THE CHARM

Turkey's record victory is 7-0 – a winning margin they've managed three times: against Syria (1949), South Korea (1954) and San Marino (1996). However, they've also lost 8-0 on three separate occasions – to Poland in 1968, and twice to England: in 1984, when Bryan Robson scored a hat-trick, and again at Wembley in 1987, when Gary Lineker claimed three.

⚽ HAT-TRICK HERO

Turkey captain Tuncay Sanli became the first Turkish player to score a hat-trick in the UEFA Champions League when he scored all of Fenerbahce's goals in their 3-0 defeat of Manchester United in Istanbul in 2004. He has also notched up two hat-tricks for the national side, against Switzerland on 16 November 2005 (final score 4-2) and in another 4-2 victory, this time over Austria, on 19 November 2008.

⚽ GUESS WHO'S BACK?

Rustu Recber doesn't know the meaning of the word "quit". Less than a year after retiring from international football after Euro 2008, Turkey's highest-capped player came out of retirement to join the national team once more in the qualifying campaign for the 2010 FIFA World Cup in South Africa. This was not his first international comeback – for Euro 2008, Rustu had been relegated to the bench, but played in the quarter-final against Croatia after first-choice keeper Volkan Demirel was sent off in the final group game. Rustu was the hero of the penalty shoot-out, saving from Mladen Petric to send Turkey through to their first-ever European Championship semi-final, where they lost to Germany. Back in 1993, Rustu came back from an even more devastating set-back after he was seriously injured in a car crash that resulted in the death of a friend. The accident also scuppered a potential move to Besiktas, although he went on to star for Fenerbahce, winning five Turkish league titles in 12 years with them. With his distinctive pony-tail and charcoal-black war paint, Rustu has always stood out, but perhaps never more so than as a star performer in Turkey's third-place performance at the 2002 FIFA World Cup finals. He was elected into the Team of the Tournament and was named FIFA's Goalkeeper of the Year.

⚽ ALL ABOUT THE MONEY...

Turkey qualified for the 1950 FIFA World Cup with ease, crushing Syria 7-0 in their highest-ever victory. However, financial difficulties forced them to withdraw. They were not the only ones: France also refused to travel all the way to Brazil, while India declined to attend after being informed they would not be allowed to play barefoot. Scotland stayed away for reasons of domestic pride.

MAJOR TOURNAMENTS

FIFA WORLD CUP™: 2 appearances – 3rd place 2002
EUROPEAN CHAMPIONSHIP: 3 appearances – semi-finals 2008
FIRST INTERNATIONAL: Turkey 2 Romania 2 (Istanbul, 26 October 1923)
BIGGEST WIN: Turkey 7 Syria 0 (Ankara, 20 November 1949)
Turkey 7 Korea Republic 0 (Geneva, Switzerland, 20 June, 1954)
Turkey 7 San Marino 0 (Istanbul, 10 November 1996)
BIGGEST DEFEAT: Poland 8 Turkey 0 (Chorzow 24 April 1968)
Turkey 0 England 8 (Istanbul, 14 November 1984)
England 8 Turkey 0 (London, 14 October 1987)

UKRAINE

Ukraine has been a stronghold of football in Eastern Europe for many years. A steady flow of talent from Ukrainian clubs with a rich European pedigree, such as Dynamo Kiev, provided the Soviet national team with many standout players in the years before independence. Since separating from the Soviet Union in 1991, Ukraine has become a football force in its own right, qualifying for the FIFA World Cup™ for the first time in 2006, reaching the quarter-finals.

SUPER SHEVA

In 2004, Andrei Shevchenko became the third Ukrainian to win the Ballon D'Or – the first to do so was his 2006 FIFA World Cup coach Oleg Blokhin. Shevchenko was the first to win the award since Ukraine's independence from the Soviet Union. Born on 29 September 1976, he was a promising boxer as a youngster, before deciding to focus on football full-time. He has won trophies at every club he's played for, including five titles in a row with Dynamo Kiev, the Serie A and the Champions League with AC Milan, and even two cups in his "disappointing" time at Chelsea. Shevchenko is Ukraine's highest-capped player and leading goalscorer, with 40 goals in 86 games. This includes two at the 2006 FIFA World Cup, where Shevchenko captained his country in their first-ever appearance at a major finals.

SCIENTIFIC SOCCER SUPREMO

"Footballers should be able to do everything on the pitch," said Ukrainian coach Valeri Lobanovsky, who professed not to believe in such definitions as "defenders", "strikers" and "midfielders". Having retired as a player at 29, Lobanovsky (born on 6 January 1939) went on to become a successful manager of his hometown club, Dynamo Kiev, as well as the national teams of the Soviet Union and Ukraine. Perhaps his greatest achievement was managing Dynamo Kiev to become the first side from the USSR to win a major European trophy – the European Cup-Winners' Cup in 1975, a feat he repeated in 1986. Famed for his pioneering, scientific approach to football, he was among the first to use computer-aided analysis and cutting-edge diet techniques and monitoring to get the best out of his players. Over the decades, he nurtured many of the finest talents in Soviet and Ukrainian football, from Oleg Blokhin in the 1970s, through Igor Belanov in the 1980s, and Andrei Shevchenko in the 1990s.

HARD START

With the newly independent Ukraine unable to register with FIFA in time for the qualifying rounds for the 1994 FIFA World Cup, many of their stars opted to play for the Commonwealth of Independent States team, which had briefly succeeded the Soviet Union. Andrei Kanchelskis, Viktor Onopko, Sergei Yuran and Oleg Salenko could all have played for the new Ukraine side, but decided not to. Ukraine then failed to qualify for an international tournament until the 2006 FIFA World Cup in Germany, where they lost 3-0 in the quarter-finals to eventual winners Italy.

PENALTY KING

Oleksandr Skovkovskyi, who holds Dynamo Kiev's appearance record (with more than 300), is the second highest-capped player (with 85, behind only Andrei Shevchenko) for the Ukraine national side. He is best remembered for two saves in the penalty shoot-out against Switzerland that took Ukraine to the FIFA World Cup quarter-finals in Germany in 2006. It had all looked very different at the start of 2006: he broke his collarbone in a friendly before the start of the Ukrainian season and feared he might not be able to make it to the finals at all. In the event, he made a full recovery in just two months to make his mark in Ukraine's biggest result to date on the international stage.

LEADING FROM THE FRONT

Oleg Blokhin, Ukraine's manager on their first appearance at the FIFA World Cup finals in 2006, made his name as a star striker with his hometown club Dynamo Kiev. Born on 5 November 1952, in the days when Ukraine was part of the Soviet Union, Blokhin scored a record 211 goals in another record 432 appearances in the USSR national league. He also holds the caps and goals records for the USSR, with 42 goals in 112 games. He led Kiev to two triumphs in the European Cup-Winners' Cup in 1975 and 1986, scoring in both finals, and winning the European Footballer of the Year trophy for his exploits in 1975. Always an over-achiever, Blokhin became the first manager to lead Ukraine to the finals of an international tournament, at the 2006 FIFA World Cup in Germany, where they lost out to eventual winners Italy 3-0 in the quarter-finals after knocking out Switzerland in the second round – also on penalties. Blokhin was renowned for his speed – when Olympic gold medallist Valeriy Borzov trained the Kiev squad in the 1970s, Blokhin recorded a 100 metres time of 11 seconds, just 0.46 seconds slower than Borzov's own 1972 medal-winning run.

CUP-WINNING KIEV

The Soviet Union might have made a big impression at the 1974 FIFA World Cup – after all, the nucleus came from the Dynamo Kiev side who would win both the European Cup-Winners' Cup (against Ferencvaros) and then the European Supercup (against Bayern Munich) the following year. However, the Soviet government refused to send the team to Chile for the second leg of a Europe/South America qualifying playoff because the match was due to be played in the Estadio Nacional in Santiago ... which had been used as a concentration camp during the military coup that saw the overthrow of communist president Salvador Allende.

MAJOR TOURNAMENTS

FIFA WORLD CUP™: 1 appearance – quarter-finals (2006)
FIRST INTERNATIONAL: Ukraine 1 Hungary 3 (Uzhhorod, Ukraine, 29 April 1992)
BIGGEST WIN: Ukraine 6 Azerbaijan 0 (Kiev, Ukraine, 15 August 2006)
BIGGEST DEFEAT: Croatia 4 Ukraine 0 (Zagreb, Croatia, 25 March 1995); Spain 4 Ukraine 0 (Leipzig, Germany, 14 June 2006)

OTHER TEAMS EUROPE

For the major European football powers, a qualifying campaign for one of the game's major international tournaments would not be the same without an awkward trip to one of the former Eastern Bloc countries or the chance of a goal-fest against the likes of San Marino or Luxembourg. For these countries' players, the thrill of representing their nation is more important than harbouring dreams of world domination.

BEYOND THE IRON CURTAIN

The break-up of the Soviet Union in 1990 led to 15 new footballing nations, though initially Russia played on at the 1992 European Championship as CIS, or the Commonwealth of Independent States – without the involvement of Estonia, Latvia and Lithuania. In the coming years, UEFA and FIFA approved the creation of separate teams for Russia, Armenia, Azerbaijan, Belarus, Estonia, Georgia, Kazakhstan, Kyrgyzstan, Latvia, Lithuania, Moldova, Tajikstan, Turkmenistan, Ukraine and Uzbekistan. Upheavals in the early 1990s would also fragment the former Yugoslavia into Croatia, Serbia, Bosnia-Herzegovina, Macedonia, Slovenia and Montenegro, while Czechoslovakia split into Slovakia and the Czech Republic.

SLO STARTERS

The only team to beat Italy on their way to winning the 2006 FIFA World Cup were Slovenia, who triumphed 1-0 in an October 2004 qualifier, thanks to a late goal by centre-back Bostjan Cesar. However, Slovenia still missed out on the finals.

THE FULL MONTE

Montenegro became the 208th and latest country to be recognized by FIFA, not long after Serbia and Montenegro had competed in the 2006 FIFA World Cup. But the new nation did not become a FIFA or UEFA member in time to compete in qualifiers for the 2008 European Championships and had to wait until the 2010 FIFA World Cup campaign for their first competitive match – a 2-2 draw at home to Bulgaria, in September 2008.

FORLORN BOURG

If at first you don't succeed, try and try again – but poor Luxembourg have valiantly tried and failed to qualify for 17 consecutive World Cups. The only time they were not involved was the very first in 1930, when there was no qualification tournament and Luxembourg were not invited to the finals. The country has only ever recorded three victories in FIFA World Cup qualifiers: 4-2 at home to Portugal in October 1961, 2-0 at home to Turkey in October 1972, and 2-1 away to Switzerland in September 2008, when Alphonse Leweck scored a late winner.

YEAR AFFILIATED TO FIFA

Albania: 1932
Andorra: 1996
Austria: 1905
Belarus: 1992
Bosnia-Herzegovina: 1996
Cyprus: 1948
Estonia: 1923
Faroe Islands: 1988
Finland: 1908
Georgia: 1992
Greece: 1927
Iceland: 1947
Israel: 1929
Kazakhstan: 1994
Latvia: 1922
Liechtenstein: 1974
Luxembourg: 1910
Macedonia: 1994
Malta: 1959
Moldova: 1994
Montenegro: 2007
San Marino: 1988
Slovakia: 1994
Slovenia: 1992

SELVA SERVICE

San Marino, with a population of under 30,000, is the smallest country to be a member of UEFA. Striker Andy Selva is not only San Marino's top scorer, with eight goals, but also the only players to score more than once in recorded senior internationals for the country.

TRAVELLING MEN

Israel looked like qualifying for the 1958 FIFA World Cup without kicking a ball, because scheduled opponents Turkey, Indonesia and Sudan refused to play them. But FIFA ordered them into a two-legged playoff against a European side – which Israel lost 4-0 on aggregate to Wales. Israel were unfortunate again in the 2006 FIFA World Cup qualifiers, ending the campaign unbeaten – yet failing even to make the playoffs, finishing third in their group behind France and Switzerland. Coach Avram Grant later went on to manage Chelsea, losing the 2008 Champions League final on penalties to Manchester United. Israel hosted, and won, the 1964 Asian Nations Cup, qualified for the 1970 FIFA World Cup through Oceania's qualifying competition, but are now members of the European Federation.

GIVING IT UP

Lithuania and Estonia did not bother playing their final group game against each other in the 1934 FIFA World Cup qualifying competition. Sweden had already guaranteed themselves top spot, and the sole finals place available, by beating Lithuania 2-0 and Estonia 6-2.

PARTY CRASHERS

Surprise Euro 2004 winners Greece became the first team to beat both the holders and the hosts on the way to winning either a European Championship or FIFA World Cup. In fact, they beat hosts Portugal twice – in both the tournament's opening game and the final, with a quarter-final victory over defending champions France in between.

SEVEN SECONDS AWAY

San Marino football fans have never had much to cheer about, suffering trouncing after trouncing, but Davide Gualtieri startled Graham Taylor's England in a November 1993 FIFA World Cup qualifier at Wembley. The winger raced on to a backpass by Stuart Pearce to give San Marino the lead, after just 8.3 seconds – the fastest goal ever scored in a FIFA World Cup tie. San Marino stayed in front for another 20 minutes, before capitulating 7-1 – though both teams failed to qualify for the 1994 FIFA World Cup.

BALKANS ON THE BALL

Yugoslavia's players shared the goals during their 9-0 thrashing of Zaire at the 1974 FIFA World Cup – seven different players got on the scoresheet: Bosnian Dusan Bajevic (who scored a hat-trick), Serbian Dragan Dzajic, Croatian Ivica Surjak, Bosnian Josip Katalinski, Serbian Vladislav Bogicevic, Slovenian Branko Oblak and Serbian Ilija Petkovic.

REIM AND REASON

Estonian midfielder Martin Reim is not only the most-capped European footballer of all time, but also the player who has made the most international appearances without ever appearing in a FIFA World Cup finals. Reim, born in Tallinn on 14 May 1971, made his international debut in 1992 and retired from international football 15 years, 156 matches and 14 goals later. He spent almost his entire career playing in his homeland, save for a season-long spell with Finnish side FC KooTeePee of Kotka in 1999–2000. Only five men have won more international caps in football history. Another long-serving Estonian is midfielder Marko Kristal, who scored nine goals in 143 games for his country between 1992 and 2005. He became the youngest European to reach a century of caps when, aged 27, he played in a 2-2 draw against Cyprus in a March 2001 FIFA World Cup qualifier. The second most-capped European footballer is Latvian midfielder Vitalijs Astafjevs, who has made 152 appearances.

MOST INTERNATIONAL GOALS

Albania: Riza Lushta 30
Andorra: Ildefons Lima 5
Austria: Toni Polster 44
Belarus: Maxim Romaschenko 20
Bosnia-Herzegovina: Elvir Boli 24
Cyprus: Michalis Konstantinou 26
Estonia: Andres Oper 35
Faroe Islands: Rogvi Jacobsen 10
Finland: Jari Litmanen 30
Georgia: Shota Arveladze 26
Greece: Nikos Anastopoulos 29
Iceland: Eidur Gudjohnsen 23
Israel: Mordechai Spiegler 25
Kazakhstan: Viktor Zubarev 12
Latvia: Maris Verpakovskis 24
Liechtenstein: Mario Frick 13
Luxembourg: Leon Mart 16
Macedonia: Gjorgji Hristov 17
Malta: Carmel Busuttil 23
Moldova: Serghei Clescenco 11
Montenegro: Mirko Vucinic 6
San Marino: Andy Selva 8
Slovakia: Szilard Nemeth 22
Slovenia: Zlatko Zahovic 35

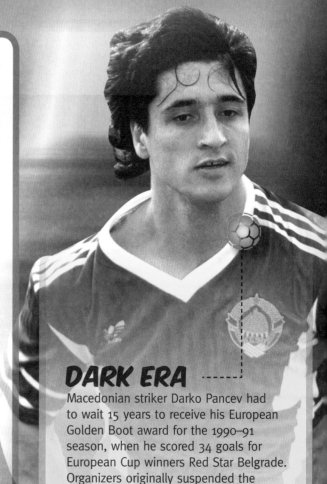

DARK ERA

Macedonian striker Darko Pancev had to wait 15 years to receive his European Golden Boot award for the 1990–91 season, when he scored 34 goals for European Cup winners Red Star Belgrade. Organizers originally suspended the competition between 1991 and 1996, due to disagreements about goal tallies in Cyprus – but eventually agreed to hand Pancev his prize in August 2006. The unlucky European top scorers from 1992 to 1996 were Scotland's Ally McCoist (twice), Welshman David Taylor, Armenian Arsen Avetisyan and Georgian Zviad Endeladze.

MALTESE POSSE

Malta midfielder Andre Schembri followed in not only his father's, but also his grandfather's footsteps, when he made his debut for his country in 2006. He scored his first goal against Hungary on 11 October 2006.

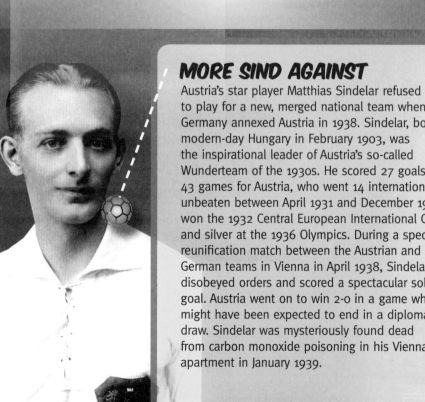

THE GUD SON

Iceland striker Eidur Gudjohnsen made history on his international debut away to Estonia in April 1996, by coming on as a substitute for his own father, Arnor Gudjohnsen. Eidur was 17 at the time, his father 34 – though both were disappointed they did not get to play on the pitch at the same time. The Icelandic Football Association thought they would get a chance to do so in Iceland's next home game, but Eidur was ruled out by an ankle injury and the opportunity never arose again.

HAPPY ELVIR

Elvir Bolic holds the caps and goals record for Bosnia-Herzegovina, scoring 24 times in 52 games since the country began playing internationals in 1996. His was also the strike that ended Manchester United's 40-year unbeaten record at home in European competition: it was the only goal of the game for Turkish side Fenerbahce during a Champions League tie at Old Trafford in October 1996.

MOST INTERNATIONAL APPEARANCES

Albania: Foto Trashoka 73
Andorra: Oscar Sonejee 76
Austria: Andreas Herzog 103
Belarus: Sergei Gurenko 80
Bosnia-Herzegovina: Elvir Boli 52
Cyprus: Ioannis Okkas 88
Estonia: Martin Reim 156
Faroe Islands: Oli Johannesen 83
Finland: Jari Litmanen 122
Georgia: Levan Kobiashvili 79
Greece: Theo Zagorakis 120
Iceland: Runar Kristinsson 106
Israel: Arik Benado 95
Kazakhstan: Ruslan Baltiev 67
Latvia: Vitalijs Astafjevs 152
Liechtenstein: Mario Frick 81
Luxembourg: Jeff Strasser 88
Macedonia: Goce Sedloski 88
Malta: David Carabott 122
Moldova: Serghei Clescenco 69
Montenegro: Vladimir Bozovic 15
San Marino: Mirco Gennari, Federico Gasperoni 48
Slovakia: Miroslav Karhan 90
Slovenia: Zlatko Zahovi 80

TOP KAT

Srecko Katanec has twice quit as an international coach after falling out with his star player. In 2002, he led Slovenia to their first FIFA World Cup finals, where temperamental captain and playmaker Zlatko Zahovic was sent home in disgrace after a tantrum. Tearful Katanec quit after his country's first-round elimination, allowing Zahovic to return to the side. Katanec later took over as Macedonia coach, but resigned in April 2008 after falling out with skipper Goran Pandev.

MORE SIND AGAINST

Austria's star player Matthias Sindelar refused to play for a new, merged national team when Germany annexed Austria in 1938. Sindelar, born in modern-day Hungary in February 1903, was the inspirational leader of Austria's so-called Wunderteam of the 1930s. He scored 27 goals in 43 games for Austria, who went 14 internationals unbeaten between April 1931 and December 1932, won the 1932 Central European International Cup and silver at the 1936 Olympics. During a special reunification match between the Austrian and German teams in Vienna in April 1938, Sindelar disobeyed orders and scored a spectacular solo goal. Austria went on to win 2-0 in a game which might have been expected to end in a diplomatic draw. Sindelar was mysteriously found dead from carbon monoxide poisoning in his Vienna apartment in January 1939.

TU-WHIT TWO-NIL

Finland's adopted lucky mascot is an eagle-owl called "Bubi" that occasionally swoops down on the Helsinki Olympic Stadium during international matches – making his debut during a 2-0 European Championship qualifier win over Belgium in June 2007 and holding up the game for several minutes as he flew about the pitch and perched on goalposts. The eagle owl was later voted the Finnish capital's "Resident of the Year".

HIGH LIFE

At 64°09'N, Reykjavik, in Iceland, is the northernmost city to host a FIFA World Cup match – though so far only in qualifiers. The northernmost FIFA World Cup finals venue is Sandviken in Sweden, at 60°37'N – while Christchurch in New Zealand (43°32'S) holds the record for southernmost FIFA World Cup venue, with the finals record held by Mar del Plata in Argentina (38°01'S).

LAT'S ENTERTAINMENT

After Austria, who had finished top of their qualifying group, were annexed by Germany prior to the 1938 FIFA World Cup, Latvia – who had finished as runners-up behind the Austrians – hoped to take their place, but were overlooked and the tournament went ahead with 15 teams instead of 16. After spending the years between 1940 to 1991 as part of the Soviet Union, Latvia finally qualified for their first major finals in 2004, defeating Turkey in a playoff to reach the European Championship finals.

BARREN SPELLS

Seven European teams have failed to score a single goal during a FIFA World Cup qualifying campaign: Liechtenstein (across eight games ahead of the 2002 tournament), San Marino (eight games in 1998), Malta (six games in 1978), Cyprus (four games in 1966), Israel (four games in 1954), Finland (three games in 1938) and Lithuania (one game in 1934).

WAKING THE DEAD

Slovenia's current main venue is the Ljudski vrt stadium, in the city of Maribor. It has a capacity of 12,435 and, creepily, was built on the site of a former cemetery.

NO-SCORE ANDORRA

Since playing their first international on New Year's Day 1996 – a 6-1 home defeat to Estonia – Andorra have only won three matches, two of them friendlies. Their only competitive triumph was a 1-0 success over Macedonia in an October 2004 FIFA World Cup qualifying match, when left-back Marc Bernaus struck the only goal of the game. Perhaps their lack of strength should come as no surprise – the principality is the sixth smallest country in Europe, with a population of just 71,822 and they have played their most high-profile games, against England, across the Spanish border in Barcelona.

HANDS OFF

Gordon Banks only touched the ball four times during England's 5-0 victory over Malta in a May 1971 FIFA World Cup qualifying match at Wembley – each time from a backpass.

RECORD WIN

Albania: 5-0 vs. Vietnam (A, December 2003)
Andorra: 2-0 vs. Belarus (H, April 2000); 2-0 vs. Albania (H, April 2002)
Austria: 9-0 vs. Malta (H, April 1977)
Belarus: 5-0 vs. Lithuania (H, June 1998)
Bosnia-Herzegovina: 7-0 vs. Estonia (H, September 2008)
Cyprus: 5-0 vs. Andorra (H, November 2000)
Estonia: 6-0 vs. Lithuana (H, July 1928)
Faroe Islands: 3-0 vs. San Marino (H, May 1995)
Finland: 10-2 vs. Estonia (H, August 1922)
Georgia: 7-0 vs. Armenia (H, March 1997)
Greece: 8-0 vs. Syria (H, November 1949)
Iceland: 9-0 vs. Faroe Islands (H, July 1985)
Israel: 9-0 vs. Chinese Taipei (A, March 1988)
Kazakhstan: 7-0 vs. Pakistan (H, June 1997)
Latvia: 8-1 vs. Estonia (A, August 1942)
Liechtenstein: 4-0 vs. Luxembourg (A, October 2004)
Luxembourg: 6-0 vs. Afghanistan (A, July 1948)
Macedonia: 11-1 vs. Liechtenstein (A, November 1996)
Malta: 7-1 vs. Liechtenstein (H, March 2008)
Moldova: 5-0 vs. Pakistan (A, August 1992)
Montenegro: 3-0 vs. Kazakhstan (H, May 2008)
San Marino: 1-0 vs. Liechtenstein (H, April 2004)
Slovakia: 7-0 vs. Liechtenstein (H, September 2004); 7-0 vs. San Marino (H, October 2007)
Slovenia: 7-0 vs. Oman (A, February 1999)

RECORD DEFEAT

Albania: 0-12 vs. Hungary (A, September 1950)
Andorra: 1-8 vs. Czech Republic (A, June 2005); 0-7 vs. Croatia (A, October 2006)
Austria: 1-11 vs. England (H, June 1908)
Belarus: 0-5 vs. Austria (A, June 2003)
Bosnia-Herzegovina: 0-5 vs. Argentina (A, May 1998)
Cyprus: 0-12 vs. West Germany (A, May 1969)
Estonia: 2-10 vs. Finland (A, August 1922)
Faroe Islands: 0-7 vs. Yugoslavia (A, May 1991); 0-7 vs. Romania (A, May 1992); 0-7 vs. Norway (H, August 1993);
Finland: 0-13 vs. Germany (A, September 1940)
Georgia: 0-5 vs. Romania (A, April 1996); 1-6 vs. Denmark (A, September 2005)
Greece: 1-11 vs. Hungary (A, March 1938)
Iceland: 2-14 vs. Denmark (A, August 1967)
Israel*: 1-7 vs. Egypt (A, March 1934)
Kazakhstan: 0-6 vs. Turkey (H, June 2006); 0-6 vs. Russia (A, May 2008)
Latvia: 0-12 vs. Sweden (A, May 1927)
Liechtenstein: 1-11 vs. Macedonia (H, November 1996)
Luxembourg: 0-9 vs. England (H, October 1960); 0-9 vs. England (A, December 1982)
Macedonia: 0-5 vs. Belgium (H, June 1995)
Malta: 1-12 vs. Spain (A, December 1983)
Moldova: 0-6 vs. Sweden (A, June 2001)
Montenegro: 0-4 vs. Romania (A, May 2008)
San Marino: 0-13 vs. Germany (H, September 2006)
Slovakia: 0-6 vs. Argentina (A, June 1995)
Slovenia: 0-5 vs. France (A, October 2002)

* Played under the British Mandate of Palestine.

BACK DOWN TO EARTH

Three countries have failed to qualify for the FIFA World Cup two years after winning the European Championship – Czechoslovakia (who took the title in 1976), Denmark (1992) and Greece (2004). Otto Rehhagel's Greece team got their 2006 FIFA World Cup qualification campaign off to the worst possible start, losing 2-1 to minnows Albania just two months after being crowned shock European champions.

GEORGIA ON MY MIND

Dynamo Tbilisi, from Georgia, and Zalgiris Vilnius, from Lithuania, played out a 2-2 draw in May 1990 in a game later categorized as an international match between the clubs' two countries. The fixture is now regarded as Georgia's first international, even though the country did not become independent from Russia for another 11 months.

SEVEN UP

Austria and Switzerland played out the highest-scoring game of any FIFA World Cup finals, when Austria eventually triumphed 7-5 in their 1954 quarter-final. The Swiss hosts were 3-0 up after just 19 minutes of the match in Lausanne, but were 5-4 down by half-time. Apart from Austria, for whom Theodor Wagner scored a first-half hat-trick, only one other team has won a FIFA World Cup finals match from three goals down – Portugal, against North Korea, in another quarter-final 12 years later, with Eusebio netting four goals as the Portuguese ran out 5-3 winners. Austria were involved in another goal-packed game in their 1954 semi-final – though were on the wrong end of a rout this time, losing 6-1 to eventual champions West Germany.

SOUTH AMERICA

South America provided the first hosts of the FIFA World Cup™ and the first winners in the shape of Uruguay and claims nine successes in total (Brazil five, Argentina and Uruguay two each). It also boasts fans with a unique cultural tradition whose magic can turn a football match into a carnival.

ARGENTINA

Copa America champions on 14 occasions, FIFA Confederations Cup winners in 1992, Olympic gold medallists in 2004 and 2008 and, most treasured of all, FIFA World Cup™ winners in 1978 and 1986: no country has won as many international titles as Argentina. The country has a long and rich football history (the first Argentine league was contested in 1891) and has produced some of the greatest footballers ever to have played the game.

MAIN STADIUMS: (CAPACITY)

El Monumental, Buenos Aires: 65,645

Estadio Juan Domingo Peron, Avellaneda: 64,161

Estadio Alberto J Armando/La Bombonera, Buenos Aires: 57,395

Estadio José Amalfitani, Buenos Aires: 49,540

Estadio Tomas Adolfo Duco, Buenos Aires: 48,314

Estadio Malvinas Argentinas, Mendoza: 48,000

Estadio Olímpico Chateau Carreras, Córdoba: 46,083

Estadio Pedro Bidegain, Buenos Aires: 43,494

Estadio Gigante de Arroyito, Rosario: 41,654

Estadio Lanús, Lanús: 40,320

CHILD'S PLAY

This kid could have quite a future, if his bloodline is anything to go by – Benjamin Aguero Maradona, born in February 2009, is the son of Atletico Madrid and Argentina young sensation Sergio "Kun" Aguero and partner Giannina Maradona, whose father just happens to be the legendary Diego. Aguero was given his nickname by friends who thought his hairstyle made him resemble a Japanese cartoon character.

DO YOU COME HERE OFTEN?

Argentina and Uruguay have played each other more often than any other two nations – 161 matches, including the first international played outside the UK, in 1902. Argentina won that one, 6-0, in the Uruguayan capital Montevideo and have led the way ever since – winning 80 games, compared to Uruguay's 53, with 43 draws.

RESULTS GAME

Alfio Basile had two spells as manager of Argentina and set a joint world record with 31 games unbeaten. But poor results in the 2010 FIFA World Cup qualifying campaign saw him replaced by Diego Maradona. Predecessors included Humberto Maschio and Omar Sivori, who had, as players, lined up for both Argentina and Italy. Argentina won their first FIFA World Cup in 1978 under Cesar Luis Menotti, whose captain, Daniel Passarella, managed Argentina to the quarter-finals 20 years later in France.

THE GOOD DOCTOR?

Carlos Bilardo was a double world champion – he won the Intercontinental Cup as a player, when his Estudiantes de La Plata team beat Manchester United in 1968, and the FIFA World Cup as Argentina coach ten years later. Bilardo was also a qualified doctor and helped run his father's furniture business – and was notorious for his mischievous tricks to irritate opponents on the pitch. As Estudiantes manager in 2003–04, he was pictured swigging from a bottle of Champagne on the bench, but insisted it merely contained a soft drink. After winning the FIFA World Cup as Argentina coach in 1986, he led them to the final again in 1990, once more against West Germany, but this time his team lost. He returned to the national set-up in 2008 as an adviser to new coach Diego Maradona, the player who had been his captain in 1986.

MAJOR TOURNAMENTS

FIFA WORLD CUP™: 14 appearances – winners 1978, '86

COPA AMERICA: 38 appearances – winners 1921, 1925, 1927, 1929, 1937, 1941, 1945, 1946, 1947, 1955, 1957, 1959, 1991, 1993

CONFEDERATIONS CUP:
Three appearances – winners 1993

FIRST INTERNATIONAL: Uruguay 2 Argentina 3 (Montevideo, Uruguay, 16 May 1901)

BIGGEST WIN: Argentina 12 Ecuador 0 (Montevideo, Uruguay, 22 January 1942)

BIGGEST DEFEAT: Czechoslovakia 6 Argentina 1 (Helsingborg, Sweden, 15 June 1958); Bolivia 6 Argentina 1, La Paz, Bolivia, 1 April 2009

THE KIDS ARE ALL RIGHT

Argentina's youngsters have won the FIFA World Under-20 Championship a record six times, most recently in 2005 and 2007. Sergio Aguero and Mauro Zarate scored the goals in a 2-1 final win over the Czech Republic, when Canada hosted the tournament in 2007.

CHINA IN YOUR HAND

In an unusual move, the two 2008 Olympics football finalists Argentina and Nigeria were allowed to take two drinks breaks during the match, which was watched by 89,102 spectators. The game was played in stifling heat in Chinese host city Beijing. Angel Di Maria scored the only goal for Argentina, allowing them to retain the title they won in Athens – for the first time – four years earlier.

BEGINNER'S LUCK

The youngest FIFA World Cup coach was Juan Jose Tramutola, just 27 years and 267 days old when Argentina opened their 1930 campaign by beating France 1-0. Argentina went on to reach the final, only to lose 4-2 to Uruguay – with both sides providing their own choice of ball for each of the halves.

NUMBERS GAME

Argentina's FIFA World Cup squads of 1978 and 1982 were given numbers based on alphabetical order, rather than positions, which meant the No.1 shirt was worn by midfielders Norberto Alonso in 1978 and Osvaldo Ardiles in 1982. The only member of the 1982 squad whose shirt number broke the alphabetical order was No.10, Diego Maradona.

WORTH WAITING FOR

Argentina's national stadium, "El Monumental" in Buenos Aires, hosted its first game in 1938. But the original design was not completed until 20 years later – largely thanks to the £97,000 River Plate received for a transfer fee from Juventus for Omar Sivori. The stadium is a must-see stop on the itinerary of many global football tourists, for the "Superclásico" derby between hosts River Plate and cross-city rivals Boca Juniors.

A ROUND DOZEN

Argentina were responsible for the biggest win in Copa America history, when five goals by Jose Manuel Moreno helped them thrash Ecuador 12-0 in 1942. Moreno won league titles in Argentina, Mexico, Chile and Colombia.

FRINGE PLAYERS

Daniel Passarella was a demanding captain when he led his country to glory at the 1978 World Cup. He was the same as coach. After taking over the national side in 1994, he refused to pick anyone unless they had their hair cut short – and ordered striker Claudio Caniggia to get rid of his "girl's hair".

GLOBAL GLORY

The old Intercontinental Cup, contested by the club champions of Europe and South America until 2004, was won most often by Argentine sides, who triumphed nine times. Boca Juniors took three titles, Independiente two, with single successes for Estudiantes, Racing Club, River Plate and Vélez Sársfield.

TOP CAPS

#	Player	Caps
1	Javier Zanetti	129
2	Roberto Ayala	115
3	Diego Simeone	106
4	Oscar Ruggeri	97
5	Diego Maradona	91
6	Ariel Ortega	86
7	Gabriel Batistuta	78
8	Juan Pablo Sorin	76
9	Americo Gallego	73
10	Daniel Passarella	70

STRENGTH IN RESERVE

In 1990, Argentina became the first country to reach a FIFA World Cup final by winning both their quarter-final and semi-final on penalties. The hero both times was reserve goalkeeper Sergio Goycochea, who was thrust into action during the group stage when first-choice Nery Pumpido broke his leg. A year earlier, Pumpido had nearly lost a finger during a training-ground accident, but surgeons managed to secure it.

SPOT-KICK FLOP

If at first you don't succeed, try and try again – unfortunately Martin Palermo missed all three penalties he took during Argentina's 1999 Copa America clash with Colombia. The first hit the crossbar, the second flew over the bar, and the third was saved. Colombia won the match 3-0.

WINNING TOUCH

Midfielder Marcelo Trobbiani played just two minutes of FIFA World Cup football – the last two minutes of the 1986 final, after replacing winning goalscorer Jorge Burruchaga. Trobbiani touched the ball once, a backheel. The former Boca star ended his international career with 15 caps and one goal to his name.

FITTER, JAVIER

Javier Zanetti is Argentina's most-capped player, with 129 international appearances and counting – despite being surprisingly left out of Jose Pekerman's squad for the 2006 FIFA World Cup finals. He returned to the team under Alfio Basile, to overtake Roberto Ayala's record caps tally. Zanetti, who can play at full-back or in midfield, has also played more Serie A matches than any other non-Italian.

SECOND TIME LUCKY

Luisito Monti is the only man to play in the FIFA World Cup finals for two different countries. The centre-half, born in Buenos Aires on 15 May 1901 but with Italian family origins, was highly influential in Argentina's run to the 1930 final. They lost the game 4-2 to Uruguay – after Monti allegedly received mysterious pre-match death threats. Following a transfer to Juventus the following year, he was allowed to play for Italy and was on the winning side when they beat Czechoslovakia in the 1934 final. Another member of the 1934 team was Raimundo Orsi, who had also played for Argentina before switching sides in 1929.

SUPER MARIO

Valencia's Mario Kempes, who scored twice in the 1978 FIFA World Cup final and won the Golden Boot, was the only member of Cesar Menotti's squad who played for a non-Argentine club. Playing for Valencia, he had been the Spanish league's top scorer for the previous two seasons.

DIVINE DIEGO

To many people Diego Armando Maradona is the greatest footballer the world has ever seen, better even than Pele. The Argentine legend, born in Lanus on 30 October 1960, first became famous as a ball-juggling child during half-time intervals at Argentinos Juniors matches. He was distraught to be left out of Argentina's 1978 FIFA World Cup squad and was then sent off for retaliation at the 1982 tournament. Maradona, as triumphant Argentina captain in Mexico in 1986, scored the notorious "Hand of God" goal and then a spectacular individual strike within five minutes of each other in a quarter-final win over England. He again captained Argentina to the final in 1990, in Italy – the country where he inspired Napoli to Serie A and UEFA Cup success. He was thrown out of the 1994 FIFA World Cup finals in disgrace after failing a drugs test. Maradona captained Argentina 16 times in FIFA World Cup matches, a record, and was surprisingly appointed national coach in 2008, despite scant previous experience as a manager.

A FINE MESSI

Lionel Messi is now recognized as being among the world's most talented players, but his international debut was one to forget. He was sent off just 40 seconds after coming on as a substitute in August 2005. Messi has been at Spanish club Barcelona since the age of 13, after staff there agreed to pay for growth hormone treatment – allowing him to reach the heady heights of 5ft 6in (1.69m). Anointed by the man himself as "the new Maradona", he scored against Getafe in April 2007 after a solo run from the halfway line that bore an uncanny similarity to Maradona's famous goal against England in 1986.

IN THE CUP FOR TOTTINGHAM

After Argentina won the FIFA World Cup for the first time in 1978, Osvaldo Ardiles and Ricardo Villa crossed the Atlantic to Europe and both joined English club Tottenham Hotspur, where they both played a major role in the club's 1981 FA Cup final appearance. Ardiles was granted a solo line in the club's Cup final song, "Ossie's Dream"; Villa went one better, scoring the spectacular solo winner against Manchester City in a replay at Wembley.

TOP SCORERS

1	Gabriel Batistuta	56
2	Hernan Crespo	36
3	Diego Maradona	34
4	Luis Artime	24
5	Leopoldo Luque	22
=	Daniel Passarella	22
7	Jose Sanfilippo	21
=	Herminio Masantonio	21
9	Mario Kempes	20
10	Norberto Mendez	19
=	Jose Manuel Moreno	19
=	Rene Pontoni	19

THE ANGEL GABRIEL

Gabriel Batistuta, nicknamed "Batigol" and Argentina's all-time leading scorer, is the only man to have scored hat-tricks in two separate FIFA World Cups. He scored the first against Greece in 1994 and the second against Jamaica four years later. Hungary's Sandor Kocsis, France's Just Fontaine and Germany's Gerd Muller each scored two hat-tricks in the same FIFA World Cup. Batistuta, born in Reconquista on 1 February 1969, also set an Italian league record during his time with Fiorentina, by scoring in 11 consecutive Serie A matches at the start of the 1994–95 season.

BRAZIL

No country has captured the soul of the game to the same extent as Brazil. The country's distinctive yellow-shirted and blue-shorted players have thrilled generations of football fans, have produced some of the game's greatest moments, and no FIFA World Cup™ tournament would be the same without them. Brazil – the nation that gave birth to Pele, Garrincha, Zico, Ronaldo and Kaka – are the only team to appeared in the finals of every FIFA World Cup™, and have won the competition a record-breaking five times.

CHANGING COLOURS

The original shirts worn by the Brazil national side were white with blue collars, but following the defeat to Uruguay in the 1950 FIFA World Cup, the colours were criticized for lacking patriotism. The newspaper *Correio da Manha* held a competition to design a kit incorporating the four colours of the Brazilian flag. The winning design was a yellow jersey with green trim, and blue shorts with white trim, drawn by 19-year-old Aldyr Garcia Schlee. The new colours were first used in March 1954 in a match against Chile, and have been used ever since.

EXTRA CONTINENTAL

Brazil is the only country to have won the FIFA World Cup outside of its own continent – which it has achieved on three occasions, in 1958 in Sweden, in the United States in 1994 and in Japan/Korea in 2002.

1966 AND ALL THAT

Brazil's preparation for the 1966 FIFA World Cup in England was affected by political influences. All the major clubs wanted their players included in the squad to increase their transfer value. In the final months of preparation, coach Vicente Feola (right) was working with a squad of 46, of whom only 22 would go to England. This caused unrest among the players and Brazil failed to progress beyond the group stages – one of their worst-ever performances.

BRAZIL'S RECORD

MATCHES PLAYED	92
WON	64
DRAWN	14
LOST	14
GOALS FOR	201
GOALS AGAINST	84
WINNERS:	1958, 1962, 1970, 1994, 2002
RUNNERS-UP:	1950, 1998
THIRD PLACE:	1938, 1978
FOURTH PLACE:	1974

FIRST INTERNATIONAL
Argentina 3 Brazil 0 (Buenos Aires, 20 September 1914)

BIGGEST WIN
Brazil 14 Nicaragua 0 (Mexico, 17 Oct 1975)

HEAVIEST DEFEAT
Uruguay 6 Brazil 0
(Chile, 18 September 1920)

⚽ FIERCEST RIVALS
Brazil's oldest club classic is Fluminense versus Botafogo in Rio de Janeiro. The clubs faced each other for the first time on 22 October 1905, when Fluminense won 6-0. One particular match stirred a controversy that lasted 89 years. The two teams disagreed on the result of the 1907 championship, whose title was disputed up to 1996 ... when they finally decided to share it.

LAND OF FOOTBALL
No country is more deeply identified with football success than Brazil, who have won the FIFA World Cup a record five times – in 1958, 1962, 1970, 1994 and 2002. They are also the only team never to have missed a FIFA World Cup finals and are favourites virtually every time the competition is staged. After winning the trophy for a third time in Mexico in 1970, Brazil kept the Jules Rimet Cup permanently. Sadly, it was stolen from the federation's headquarters in 1983 and was never recovered. Brazilians often refer to their country as "o país do futebol" ("the country of football"). It is the favourite pastime of youngsters, while general elections are often held in the same year as the FIFA World Cup, with critics arguing that political parties try to take advantage of the nationalistic surge created by football and bring it into politics. Charles Miller, the son of a Scottish engineer, is credited with bringing football to Brazil in 1894. Yet the sport would only truly become Brazilian when blacks were able to play at the top level in 1933. At first, because of the game's European origin, it was the sport of Brazil's urban white elite. However, it quickly spread among the urban poor as Brazilians realized the only thing they needed to play was a ball, which could be substituted inexpensively with a bundle of socks, an orange, or even a cloth filled with paper.

CLOSE ENCOUNTERS
Brazil have been involved in many memorable games. Their 3-2 defeat to Italy in 1982 is regarded as one of the classic games in FIFA World Cup finals history. Paolo Rossi scored all three of Italy's goals with Brazil coach Tele Santana much criticized for going all out in attack when only a 2-2 draw was needed. Brazil's 1982 squad, with players such as Socrates (above), Zico and Falcao, is considered one of the greatest teams never to win the tournament. In 1994, a 3-2 win over Holland in the quarter-finals – their first competitive meeting in 20 years – was just as thrilling, with all the goals coming in the second half.

⚽ UNMISSABLE
Brazil's devotion to football and its own FIFA World Cup achievements is on show in the Museum of Football in Sao Paulo, which boasts 17 rooms of exhibits, spread across three floors and which cost around £9.4m. The whole exhibition includes 1,442 photos and six hours of video. The museum was designed to be totally accessible to those with special needs, including the use of audio-gates, touch-sensitive signs, sound sensors, maps, colour codes and plaques – everything required to ensure visitors can interact fully with their surroundings.

THE KING

Pele is considered by many as the greatest player of all time, a sporting icon *par excellence* and not only for his exploits on the pitch. When, for instance, he scored his 1,000th goal, Pele dedicated it to the poor children of Brazil. He began playing for Santos at the age of 15 and won his first FIFA World Cup two years later, scoring twice in the final. Despite numerous offers from European clubs, the economic conditions and Brazilian football regulations at the time allowed Santos to keep hold of their prized asset for almost two decades, until 1974. All-time leading scorer of the Brazilian national team, he is the only footballer to be a member of three FIFA World Cup-winning teams. Despite being in the Brazilian squad at the start of the 1962 tournament, an injury suffered in the second match meant he was not able to play on and, initially, he missed out on a winner's medal. However, FIFA announced in November 2007 that he would be awarded a medal retrospectively. After the disastrous 1966 tournament, when Brazil fell in the first round, Pele said he did not wish to play in the FIFA World Cup again. He was finally talked round and ended up, in 1970, playing a key role in what is widely considered as one of the greatest sides ever. Since his retirement in 1977, Pele has been a worldwide ambassador for football, as well undertaking various acting roles and commercial ventures.

WHAT'S IN A NAME?

Born Edson Arantes do Nascimento, Pele is the one person who has never liked the nickname. He has admitted to having punched the classmate who came up with it, earning a two-day suspension from school. The word had no meaning in Portuguese so he presumed it was an insult, though he has since discovered the word means "miracle" in Hebrew.

BLACK DIAMOND

Leonidas da Silva, who died aged 90 in 2004, is widely credited with being the first player to perfect the bicycle kick. Top scorer at the 1938 FIFA World Cup – including four goals in a single game against Poland – he was left out of the team in the semi-finals. It turned out to be a big mistake by then Brazil manager, Ademar Pimenta, as Brazil were knocked out by Italy. Apparently, when he scored his final goal against Poland, Leonidas was shoe-less, grounds for the referee to invalidate the goal. Cleverly, Leonidas splashed his feet into the dark mud and the referee could not tell he was not wearing any shoes!

VALUABLE LEAF

Didi was the playmaker of Brazil's two FIFA World Cup-winning teams of 1958 and 1962. A genius in midfield, he was already a world star before the arrival of Garrincha and Pele. For Didi, whose real name was Valdir Pereira, football was all about making technical superiority count over physical strength. He disdained physical contact, once saying: "It's the ball that needs to run, not the player." He was also a free-kick expert. It was with a trademark, floating "dead leaf" kick that he scored the goal against Peru that sent Brazil through to the 1958 FIFA World Cup finals in Sweden.

TWO NAMES, TWO COUNTRIES

Playing for two countries is not allowed nowadays, but Jose Altafini, the third highest scorer in the history of Italy's Serie A who had dual nationality, played international football for both Brazil and Italy. In Brazil he was nicknamed "Mazzola" for his striking resemblance to the former Torino forward Valentino Mazzola. He played in the 1958 FIFA World Cup for Brazil, though not in the latter stages of the tournament, and then switched to Italy for the 1962 event. The Italians preferred to call him by his real name.

LITTLE BIRD

The names of Pele, Rivelino, Zico, Ronaldo and Ronaldinho crop up automatically as some of the greatest Brazilian players. But Garrincha, the "Little Bird", is perhaps the country's forgotten hero. The diminutive winger was prodigiously skilled, but made his name just before the advent of television. He scored a remarkable 232 club goals from the wing, as well as being perhaps the greatest dribbler in history. A brilliant practitioner of the banana kick, he helped Brazil win the FIFA World Cups of 1958 and 1962 and played the majority of his professional career for Botofogo.

MOST GOALS

1	Pele	77
2	Ronaldo	62
3	Romario	55
4	Zico	52
5	Bebeto	39
6	Rivaldo	34
7	Jairzinho	33
8	Ademir	32
=	Ronaldinho	32
=	Tostao	32

MOST APPEARANCES

1	Cafu	142
2	Roberto Carlos	125
3	Claudio Taffarel	101
4	Djalma Santos	98
5	Ronaldo	97
6	Gilmar	94
7	Pele	92
=	Rivelino	92
9	Dida	91
=	Dunga	91

WHITHER RONALDO?

Only one person knows exactly what happened to Ronaldo in the hours before the 1998 FIFA World Cup final – the man himself. The Brazilian superstar sparked one of the biggest mysteries in FIFA World Cup history when his name was left off the teamsheet before the game, only for it to reappear just in time for kick-off. It was initially reported that Ronaldo had been struggling with an ankle injury, and then that he had an upset stomach. Finally team doctor Lidio Toledo revealed the striker had been rushed to hospital after suffering a convulsion in his sleep, but that he had been cleared to play after neurological and cardiac tests. A below-par Ronaldo was subsequently eclipsed by Zinedine Zidane in a one-sided match that saw France crowned world champions for the first time. The most dramatic account came from Ronaldo's roommate Roberto Carlos. "Ronaldo was scared about what lay ahead. The pressure had got to him and he couldn't stop crying," said the legendary full-back. "At about four o'clock, he became ill. That's when I called the team doctor and told him to get over to our room as fast as he could."

LEADING BRAZILIAN FIFA WORLD CUP™ MARKSMEN

1	15	Ronaldo
2	12	Pele
3	9	Jairzinho (the only player to score in every game played at a FIFA World Cup, in 1970)
=	9	Vava
5	8	Ademir (top scorer in 1950)
=	8	Leonidas (top scorer in 1938)
7	7	Rivaldo, Careca
9	6	Bebeto, Rivelino

OTHER TEAMS SOUTH AMERICA

TIM'S TIME

Peru were coached at the 1982 FIFA World Cup by Tim, who had been waiting an unprecedented 44 years to return to the FIFA World Cup finals – after playing once as striker for his native Brazil in the 1938 tournament.

EVERYONE OUT

Nineteen players were sent off when Uruguay played Chile in June 1975 – ten Chileans and nine Uruguayans. Referee Sergio Vasquez, a Chilean, was later suspended and fined for losing control.

EMPTY VICTORY

Chile reached the 1974 FIFA World Cup finals thanks to a walkover against the Soviet Union, in a qualifying playoff. The USSR, a Communist state, refused to play in Santiago's Estadio Nacional because it had been used as a detention camp by the regime of Chilean dictator Augusto Pinochet. Despite there being no opposition, Chile's players kicked off in an empty stadium, scored in an unguarded net and were awarded the win by the referee.

A FIRST FOR ECUADOR

LDU Quito, based in the Ecuador capital, became the first and to date only team from the country to claim an international title when they won the Copa Libertadores in 2008. They beat Brazilian side Fluminense 3-1 on penalties in the final – after the two legs had ended 5-5 on aggregate. LDU went on to lose to Manchester United in the final of the FIFA Club World Cup later in the year.

DRAWING A BLANC

Paraguay were the first victims of a FIFA World Cup "golden goal", Laurent Blanc's sudden-death strike for France past goalkeeper Jose Luis Chilavert after 113 minutes of their 1998 second-round match in Lens.

HIGH LIFE

Bolivia and Ecuador play their home internationals at higher altitudes than any other teams on earth. Bolivia's showpiece Estadio Hernando Siles stadium, in the capital La Paz, is 3,637 metres (19,900ft) above sea level, while Ecuador's main Estadio Olimpico Atahualpa, in Quito, sits 2,800 metres (9,185ft) above sea level. Opposing teams have complained that the rarefied nature of the air makes it difficult to breathe, let alone play, but a FIFA ban on playing competitive internationals at least 2,500 metres (8,200ft) above sea level, first introduced in May 2007, was amended a month later – adjusting the limit to 3,000 metres (9,840ft) and allowing Estadio Hernando Siles to be used as a special case. The altitude ban was suspended entirely in May 2008. FIFA had changed its mind after protests by Bolivia, Ecuador and other affected nations Colombia and Peru. Other campaigners to overturn the law included Argentina legend Diego Maradona. He may have regretted his decision. In March 2009 Bolivia scored a shock 6-1 home win in a FIFA World Cup qualifier against an Argentina side coached by ... Maradona.

HOME SECURITY

Colombia are the only country to go through a Copa America tournament without conceding a goal, when they hosted and won the cup for the first and only time in 2001. Their striker Victor Aristazabal ended the 2001 tournament as top scorer, with six, but the only goal of the final against Mexico came from versatile defender Ivan Cordoba. Colombia almost lost the right to host the competition, due to security fears that prompted Argentina to withdraw, but after pondering a move to Venezuela, South American football's governing body, CONMEBOL, decided to keep the contest in Colombia after all.

SIX AND OUT

Bolivia and El Salvador have both played the most FIFA World Cup finals matches without managing to win even once – six each. At least Bolivia did achieve a goalless draw against South Korea in 1994. But they went a record five successive FIFA World Cup finals matches without scoring a goal, across the 1930 and 1994 tournaments, before Erwin Sanchez put an end to their barren spell in a 3-1 defeat to Spain in their final 1994 fixture.

NATIONAL STADIUMS

Bolivia:
Estadio Hernando Siles, La Paz (45,000 capacity)

Chile:
Estadio Nacional, Santiago (63,379)

Colombia:
Estadio El Campín, Bogotá (48,600)

Ecuador:
Estadio Olimpico Atahualpa, Quito (40,948)

Paraguay:
Estadio Defensores del Chaco, Asunción (36,000)

Peru:
Estadio Nacional, Lima (45,574)

Venezuela:
Estadio Polideportivo de Pueblo Nuevo, San Cristóbal (38,755)

BASKET CASE

The only South American CONMEBOL member still waiting to reach the FIFA World Cup finals for the first time is Venezuela, a country where, although being second in popularity to basketball for many years, football is fast gaining ground. Venezuela hosted its first Copa America in 2007, with the team captained by Spanish-based midfielder Juan Arango reaching the quarter-finals. Venezuela goalkeeper Rafael Dudamel scored from a free-kick in a 5-2 FIFA World Cup qualifier defeat to Argentina in October 1996.

CARDS FOR CARLOS

Chile were the first country to have one of their men shown a red card at a FIFA World Cup finals – Carlos Caszely was the culprit, 67 minutes into a 1974 first-round clash against hosts West Germany in Berlin.

LUCKY LEO

Leonel Sanchez holds the Chilean record for international appearances, scoring 23 goals in 84 games. But he was lucky to remain on the pitch for one of them – escaping a sending-off despite punching Italy's Mario David in the face during their so-called "Battle of Santiago" clash at the 1962 FIFA World Cup. Sanchez, a left winger born in Santiago on 25 April 1936, finished the tournament as one of six players sharing the Golden Boot – he, Brazilians Garrincha and Vava, Russian Valentin Ivanov, Yugoslavian Drazan Jerkovic and Hungarian Florian Albert all scored four.

MEDELLIN MURDER

Tragic Colombian defender Andres Escobar, 27, was shot dead outside a Medellin bar ten days after scoring an own goal in a 1994 FIFA World Cup first-round match against the United States. Colombia lost the game 2-1 and were eliminated from a tournament some observers – including Pele – had tipped them to win.

MARKSMAN SPENCER

Ecuadorian striker Pedro Alberto Spencer is the leading scorer in Copa Libertadores history, with 54 goals – 48 for Uruguayan club Penarol between 1960 and 1970, and six for Ecuador's Barcelona in 1971 and 1972. But he played only 11 times for Ecuador between 1959 and 1972, hitting four goals. That period included four appearances for Uruguay between 1962 and 1964, scoring once – in a 2-1 defeat to England at Wembley. He never played at a FIFA World Cup finals.

MOST INTERNATIONAL GOALS

Bolivia: Joaquin Botero 20
Chile: Marcelo Salas 37
Colombia: Adolfo Valencia 31
Ecuador: Agustin Delgado 31
Paraguay: Jose Saturnino Cardozo 25
Peru: Teofilo Cubillas 26
Venezuela: Giancarlo Maldonado 16

MOST INTERNATIONAL APPEARANCES

Bolivia: Luis Cristaldo and Marco Sandy 93
Chile: Leonel Sanchez 84
Colombia: Carlos Valderrama 111
Ecuador: Ivan Hurtado 159
Paraguay: Carlos Gamarra 110
Peru: Roberto Palacios 122
Venezuela: Jose Manuel Rey 103

ELITE CUB

Peru forward Teofilo Cubillas became the first player to twice end a FIFA World Cup finals with at least five goals – he scored five apiece in 1970 and 1978, though failed to win the Golden Boot on either occasion. Germany's Miroslav Klose emulated the achievement by scoring five in 2002 and the same tally four years later, the same year he picked up the Golden Boot award.

RENE HIGUITA

Eccentric goalkeeper Rene Higuita managed to score three goals for his country and also performed a famous, and acrobatic, "scorpion kick" save at Wembley in September 1995, hurling himself into the air and flicking away a Jamie Redknapp shot with the heels of both feet. He played for Colombia at the 1990 FIFA World Cup, but missed the 1994 FIFA World Cup finals due to a seven-month jail sentence for his involvement in a kidnapping and then tested positive for cocaine in November 2004.

BLOND AMBITION

A bronze statue of Colombia midfielder Carlos Valderrama – featuring his famous blond shock of hair – stands outside Estadio Eduardo Santos in Santa Marta. Valderrama is the only Colombian to be named South American Footballer of the Year, in 1987 and 1993. He captained his country at the 1990, 1994 and 1998 FIFA World Cups.

CRAZY KEEPER

Keeping clean sheets for Colombia all the way through the 2001 Copa America was Oscar Cordoba, who went on to become his country's most-capped goalkeeper – with 73 appearances between 1993 and 2006.

WE HAPPY THREE

The first player to be named South American Footballer of the Year three times was not Pele, Garrincha or Diego Maradona, but Chilean centre-back Elias Figeroa, who took the prize in three consecutive years between 1974 and 1976 while playing for Brazilian club Internacional. The only players to emulate such a hat-trick were Brazil's Zico, in 1977, 1981 and 1982, and Argentina forward Carlos Tevez, in 2003, 2004 and 2005. Two more Chileans have won the award: Marcelo Salas in 1997 and Matias Fernandez in 2006. Outside of Brazil and Argentina, the most winners of the prize have come from Chile and Paraguay, with five apiece – Paraguay's were Romerito (1985), Raul Vicente Amarilla (1990), Jose Luis Chilavert (1996), Jose Cardozo (2002) and Salavador Cabanas (2007).

IVAN THE ADMIRABLE

Ecuador defender Ivan Hurtado is South America's most-capped footballer, playing 159 games since making his debut in 1992 – including five goals. He was one of Ecuador's most influential players at their first FIFA World Cup finals, in 2002, and captained them as they reached the second round four years later.

CLEAN CARLOS

Carlos Gamarra, Paraguay's most-capped player with 110 appearances, went through eight games at centre-back across the 1998 and 2002 FIFA World Cups without conceding a single free-kick. He was named in FIFA's team of the tournament in 1998, but had an unhappier 2006 FIFA World Cup – scoring an own-goal in Paraguay's opening 1-0 defeat to England.

Africa has been one of the great contributors to world football with a stream of outstanding players even before nations such as Cameroon, Nigeria and later Côte d'Ivoire and Ghana began to make their mark on the international scene. The continent will also be the focus of world football attention in 2010 when its fans welcome the FIFA World Cup™ finals to the Rainbow Nation of South Africa.

AFRICA

Only recently has the world woken up to the true potential of African football. The continent's star players have shone in top-flight European domestic leagues for over a decade, but FIFA World Cup™ success has eluded the continent – only Cameroon (1990) and Senegal (2002) have reached the quarter-finals. Maybe that will all change in 2010, when the tournament will be played in Africa for the first time.

PHARAOHS REIGN

The first African Nations Cup goal was a penalty scored by Egypt's Raafat Ateya in the 21st minute of their 2-1 semi-final win over Sudan in 1957. "The Pharaohs" have won the tournament a record six times, including the last two titles (held in 2006 and 2008). Playmaker Mohamed Aboutrika struck the decisive penalty in the 2006 final shoot-out against the Côte d'Ivoire, then scored the only goal against Cameroon at the climax of the 2008 competition. Aboutrika, a philosophy graduate who was born in Giza on 7 November 1978, has won the nickname "The Smiling Assassin" for his ruthless goalscoring and cheery appearance.

UNFULFILLED PROMISE

Zambia have never qualified for a FIFA World Cup, but caused a sensation when they beat Italy 4-0 in a group game at the 1988 Olympics in Seoul. Kalusha Bwalya scored a hat-trick and later revealed the Italians had rudely snubbed his team before the game – but were pleading for autographs afterwards. Tragedy struck on 27 April 1993. Zambia were in a strong position to reach the 1994 FIFA World Cup but lost their coach and 18 of their players when the military plane carrying them crashed in Gabon on its way to a qualifier in Senegal killing everyone on board. Olympic hero Bwalya missed the flight because he was playing for Dutch team PSV Eindhoven at the time.

FASHION POINTS

Cameroon were docked six FIFA World Cup qualifing points by FIFA after wearing a forbidden one-piece kit for the 2004 African Cup of Nations. They won the points back on appeal.

WELL METSU

Senegal matched the best FIFA World Cup performance by an African team by reaching the quarter-finals in 2002 – and just as Cameroon had done 12 years earlier, they did so by beating the defending champions 1-0 in the opening game. Papa Bouba Diop's goal was enough to beat France, who had Senegalese-born Patrick Vieira in their midfield. Senegal's coach that day was Bruno Metsu, a Frenchman.

TEST OF ENDURANCE

Ivory Coast won the two highest-scoring penalty shoot-outs in full international history – they beat Ghana 11-10 over 24 penalties in the 1992 African Cup of Nations, and Cameroon 12-11 over the same number of kicks at the same tournament 14 years later.

EAGLETS SOAR

The first African country to win an official FIFA tournament was Nigeria, when their "Golden Eaglets" beat Germany 2-0 in the final of the 1985 World Under-17 Championships.

DRAMATIC TURNAROUNDS

Ghana managed to concede three goals in a minute to world champions Germany in an April 1993 friendly. Ghana had been 1-0 up with 20 minutes left, before losing the game 6-1. In the 1989 FIFA World Youth Championship, Nigeria were 4-0 down with 25 minutes left in their quarter-final against the Soviet Union – but hit back to draw 4-4 before winning 5-3 on penalties.

FINALS FIRSTS

Tunisia became the first African team to win a match at a FIFA World Cup finals, when they beat Mexico 3-1 in Argentina in 1978. Morocco were the first African team to top a FIFA World Cup group, finishing above England, Poland and Portugal in Mexico in 1986.

ANGOLAN GOALS

Angola lost their first match against former colonial masters Portugal 6-0 in 1989. Their second meeting, 12 years later, was abandoned as Portugal led 5-1 after Angola had four players sent off and another, Helder Vicente, carried off injured.

AFRICAN CUP OF NATIONS TITLES

Egypt 6
(1957, 1959, 1986, 1998, 2006, 2008)
Ghana 4
(1963, 1965, 1978, 1982)
Cameroon 4
(1984, 1988, 2000, 2002)
Zaire/Congo DR 2
(1968, 1974)
Nigeria 2 (1980, 1994)
Algeria 1 (1990)
Congo 1 (1972)
Ethiopia 1 (1962)
Ivory Coast 1 (1992)
Morocco 1 (1976)
South Africa 1 (1996)
Sudan 1 (1970)
Tunisia 1 (2004)

SPRINGBOKS BACK

An 82nd-minute penalty by Theophilus "Doctor" Khumalo was the only goal in South Africa's win over Cameroon on 7 July 1992, the country's first recognized international after the end of apartheid. Four years later they both hosted, and won, the African Cup of Nations for the first time, with a 2-0 final win over Tunisia. The country's president, Nelson Mandela, presented the trophy to captain Neil Tovey.

AFRICAN CUP OF NATIONS TOP SCORERS

1	Samuel Eto'o (Cameroon)	16
2	Laurent Pokou (Ivory Coast)	14
3	Rashidi Yekini (Nigeria)	13
4	Hassan El-Shazly (Egypt)	12
5	Hossam Hassan (Egypt)	11
=	Patrick Mboma (Cameroon)	11
7	Kalusha Bwalya (Zambia)	10
=	Mulamba Ndaye (Zaire)	10
=	Francileudo Santos (Tunisia)	10
=	Joel Tiehi (Ivory Coast)	10
=	Mengistu Worku (Ethiopia)	10

HEAD OVER HEELS

Augustine "Jay Jay" Okocha was famous not only for his dazzling free-kicks but also for the acrobatic somersaults he performed when celebrating goals – a skill he shared with Nigerian team-mates Julius Aghahowa and Obafemi Martins. Okocha, whose clubs included Fenerbahce, Paris Saint-Germain and Bolton Wanderers, was a member of his country's 1996 Olympic gold medal-winning team.

REVOLUTION #9

No player has scored more goals in one African Cup of Nations than Zaire's Ndaya Mulamba's nine during the 1974 tournament. Three months later he was sent off at the FIFA World Cup in West Germany, as his team crashed to a 9-0 defeat to Yugoslavia.

GOAL RUSH RASHIDI

Rashidi Yekini is Nigeria's all-time leading scorer, with 37 goals in 70 games between 1984 and 1998. Perhaps his most significant strike came against Bulgaria in 1994, Nigeria's first-ever goal at a FIFA World Cup. They won 3-0 and reached the second round. Yekini was top scorer when Nigeria won the 1994 African Cup of Nations, 14 years after their only previous triumph in the tournament.

AFRICA – SELECTED TOP APPEARANCES

ALGERIA	Mahieddine Meftah	107
ANGOLA	Akwa	80
BOTSWANA	Dipsy Selolwane	34
CAMEROON	Rigobert Song	125
EGYPT	Hossam Hassan	169
GHANA	Abedi "Pele" Ayew	73
IVORY COAST	Didier Zokora	75
LIBYA	Tarik El Taib	48
MOROCCO	Abdel Majid Dolmi	124
MOZAMBIQUE	Tico-Tico	123
NAMIBIA	Johannes Hindjou	69
NIGERIA	Mudashiru Lawal	86
SENEGAL	Henri Camara	99
SOUTH AFRICA	Aaron Mokoena	81
SWAZILAND	Mlungisi Ngubane	91
TUNISIA	Sadok Sassi	110
ZIMBABWE	Peter Ndlovu	100

JOLLY ROGER

Cameroon striker Roger Milla, famous for dancing around corner flags after each goal, became the FIFA World Cup's oldest scorer against Russia in 1994 – aged 42 years and 39 days. He came on as a substitute during that tournament with his surname handwritten, rather than printed, on the back of his shirt. Milla, born in Yaoundé on 20 May 1952, had retired from professional football for a year before Cameroon's president, Paul Biya, persuaded him to join the 1994 FIFA World Cup squad. His goals in that tournament helped him win the African Footballer of the Year award for an unprecedented second time – 14 years after he had first been awarded the trophy. He finally ended his international career after the 1994 FIFA World Cup in the United States, finishing with 102 caps and 28 goals to his name.

SAM THE MAN

In 2005, Samuel Eto'o became the first player to be named African Footballer of the Year three years running. During the 2008 African Cup of Nations, he became the competition's highest goalscorer with a total of 16 – overtaking the Côte d'Ivoire's Laurent Pokou, who managed 14 across the 1968 and 1970 tournaments.

AFRICA – SELECTED TOP GOALSCORERS

ALGERIA	Rabah Madjer	40
ANGOLA	Akwa	36
BOTSWANA	Dipsy Selolwane	11
CAMEROON	Samuel Eto'o	37
EGYPT	Hossam Hassan	69
GHANA	Abedi "Pele" Ayew	33
IVORY COAST	Didier Drogba	34
LIBYA	Tarik El Taib	11
MOROCCO	Salaheddine Bassir	25
MOZAMBIQUE	Tico-Tico	24
NAMIBIA	Gervatius Uri Khob	12
NIGERIA	Rashidi Yekini	37
SENEGAL	Henri Camara	29
SOUTH AFRICA	Benni McCarthy	31
SWAZILAND	Sibusiso Dlamini	26
TUNISIA	Francileudo Santos	22
ZIMBABWE	Peter Ndlovu	38

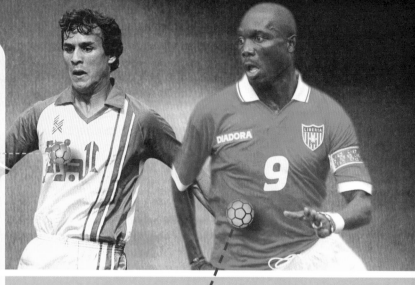

GENEROUS GEORGE

Liberia's George Weah became the first African to be named FIFA World Player of the Year in 1995, an award that recognized his prolific goalscoring exploits for Paris Saint-Germain and AC Milan. That same year he added the European Footballer of the Year and African Footballer of the Year prizes to his collection. Weah not only captained his country, but often funded the team's travels – though he remains the only FIFA World Player of the Year whose country has never qualified for a FIFA World Cup. After retiring in 2003 after 60 caps and 22 international goals, he moved into politics and ran unsuccessfully for the Liberian presidency in 2005.

FIFTEEN LOVE

Fifteen-year-old Samuel Kuffour became the youngest footballer to win an Olympic medal when Ghana took bronze at the 1992 Olympics in Barcelona – 27 days before his 16th birthday.

GOING FOR A SONG

Two players have been sent off at two separate FIFA World Cups – Cameroon's Rigobert Song, against Brazil in 1994 and Chile four years later, and France's Zinedine Zidane – red-carded against Saudi Arabia in 1998 and against Italy in the 2006 final. Song's red card against Brazil made him the youngest player to be dismissed at a FIFA World Cup – he was just 17 years and 358 days old. Song, born in Nkanglikock on 1 July 1976, became Cameroon's most-capped player, with 125 appearances – including winning displays in the 2000 and 2002 finals of the African Cup of Nations. He has been joined in the national team by his nephew, Arsenal utility player Alexandre Song Billong.

EGYPTIAN TREASURES

Hossam Hassan is Africa's most-capped player, with 169 international appearances for Egypt and 69 goals from 1985 until his international retirement 11 years later. Only Mexico's Claudio Suarez has played more times for his country, with 178 caps. Hossam Hassan's time with the national team included three triumphs at the African Cup of Nations, in 1986, 1998 and 2006. His brother Ibrahim played 125 times for his country, scoring 12 goals.

AFRICA CALLING

Africa will host the FIFA World Cup for the first time in 2010, when South Africa welcomes the world. Tournament organizer Danny Jordaan had hoped South Africa would host the 2006 tournament, but FIFA chose Germany instead – by one vote. Ten venues will be used, including the revamped, 94,700-capacity Soccer City in Johannesburg, the venue for the final. Five of the stadiums will be entirely new constructions. The official tournament mascot is a yellow and green leopard named Zakumi, from the code for South Africa "ZA" and "kumi" meaning "ten".

LOCK DEFENCE

Liberia's military leader Samuel Doe threatened to jail the national team if they lost to Gambia in 1980. The players escaped punishment by achieving a 0-0 draw.

FAMILY AFFAIR

Francois Omam-Biyik scored Cameroon's shock winner against defending champions Argentina in the opening game of the 1990 FIFA World Cup, six minutes after his brother Andre Kana-Biyik had been sent off. Cameroon finished the game with nine men after Benjamin Massing was also shown a red card, but held on for a historic victory.

KNOCKED OUT ON PENALTIES

Botswana goalkeeper and captain Modiri Marumo was sent off in the middle of a penalty shoot-out against Malawi in May 2003, after punching the opposing goalkeeper Philip Nyasulu in the face. Botswana defender Michael Mogaladi had to go in goal for the rest of the shoot-out, which Malawi won 4-1.

DEFENSIVE WALL

Zaire defender Mwepu Llunga was booked for running out of the wall and kicking the ball away as Brazil prepared to take a free-kick, at the 1974 FIFA World Cup. Zaire were the first black African country to qualify for the World Cup, but have failed to make it back.

AFRICAN COUNTRIES' BEST FIFA WORLD CUP™ PERFORMANCES

ALGERIA: First round 1982, 1986
ANGOLA: First round 2006
CAMEROON: Quarter-finals 1990
EGYPT: First round 1934, 1990
GHANA: Second round 2006
IVORY COAST: First round 2006
MOROCCO: Second round 1986
NIGERIA: Second round 1994, 1998
SENEGAL: Quarter-finals 2002
SOUTH AFRICA: First round 1998, 2002
TOGO: First round 2006
TUNISIA: First round 1978, 1998, 2002, 2006
ZAIRE/CONGO DR: First round 1974

SOUTH LONDON SOUTH AFRICANS

English club Charlton Athletic featured four South African-born players in the 1950s – though Eddie Firmani would play three internationals for Italy, while John Hewie earned 19 caps for Scotland. Firmani went on to play for Sampdoria, Internazionale and Genoa, becoming the first man to score a century of league goals in both England and Italy.

TUNED IN TO SUDAN

The 1970 African Cup of Nations in Sudan was the first time the tournament was televised. Ghana reached the final for an unprecedented fourth time in a row, but lost 1-0 to the hosts.

WRONG KIND OF LUCK

Thomas Nkono, Cameroon's goalkeeper at the 1982 and 1990 FIFA World Cups, was arrested moments before his country's African Cup of Nations semi-final against Mali in 2002. Nkono, in his role as goalkeeping coach, was accused of sprinkling "black magic" charms on the pitch. Cameroon won the match 3-0, then beat Senegal 3-2 on penalties in the final after the match had ended in a 0-0 stalemate.

STAYING AWAY

South Africa were disqualified from the four-team African Cup of Nations in 1957 after refusing to pick a multi-racial squad. Sixteen African countries boycotted the 1966 FIFA World Cup in England because FIFA insisted the top African team should face a side from Asia or Oceania in a qualification play off.

2010 FIFA WORLD CUP SOUTH AFRICA™ VENUES (CAPACITY)

Soccer City, Johannesburg (94,700)
Moses Mabhida Stadium, Durban (70,000)
Green Point Stadium, Cape Town (70,000
Ellis Park Stadium, Johannesburg (62,567)
Loftus Versfeld Stadium, Pretoria (50,000)
Nelson Mandela Bay Stadium, Port Elizabeth (48,000)
Free State Stadium, Bloemfontein (48,000)
Mbombela Stadium, Nelspruit (46,000)
Peter Mokaba Stadium, Polokwane (46,000)
Royal Bafokeng Stadium, Rustenburg (42,000)

NO-GO TOGO

The Togolese Football Federation was fined 100,000 Swiss francs after the squad and manager Otto Pfister threatened to go on strike during the 2006 FIFA World Cup in a dispute over pay bonuses. Captain and star player Emmanuel Adebayor briefly threatened to walk out of the squad, but was persuaded to stay. The Arsenal striker was named 2008 African Footballer of the Year, the first Togo player in history to win the award.

ASIA & OCEANIA

South Korea made history in 2002 – sharing with Japan the first co-hosting of the first FIFA World Cup™ in Asia. Their footballers also became the first Asian team to reach the semi-finals of the FIFA World Cup™ where they lost to Germany before losing again, narrowly, to Turkey in the third-place playoff. The Koreans could truly claim to have put Asia on the world football map.

AUSTRALIA

Victims, perhaps, of an overcomplicated qualifying system that has limited the country's FIFA World Cup™ finals appearances, and hampered by its geographical isolation that, in the early years, saw other sports prosper in the country at football's expense, it has taken many years for Australia to establish itself on the world football map. However, driven by a new generation of players, many based with top European clubs, the Socceroos delivered for the first time at the 2006 FIFA World Cup™. They are the No.1 ranked team in Asia.

AUSSIES BET ON CAHILL

The first of Tim Cahill's two goals against Japan at the 2006 FIFA World Cup caused some controversy after a British newspaper claimed that the Australian players had been betting on who would score their first goal. Cahill admitted that colleagues Lucas Neill and Archie Thompson had backed him to score. Striker Mark Viduka agreed that the players had been placing bets, but said they had only done so among themselves. FIFA took no action.

AUSTRALIA'S FIRST FINALS

Australia first qualified for the FIFA World Cup finals in 1974. They eliminated Iraq, New Zealand, Indonesia and Iran, then met South Korea in a final qualifier. They drew 0-0 at home and 2-2 away. So the tie went to a playoff in Hong Kong, where Jimmy Mackay scored Australia's winner from a free-kick.

CAHILL MAKES HISTORY

Tim Cahill netted Australia's first-ever FIFA World Cup finals goal when he scored an 84th-minute equalizer against Japan in Kaiserslautern on 12 June 2006. Cahill added another five minutes later and John Aloisi struck in stoppage time to give the Socceroos a 3-1 win – their only victory in the finals. Australia later lost 2-0 to Brazil and drew 2-2 with Croatia to qualify from their group.

AUSSIE CROWD RECORD

The record crowd for an Australia home match is 95,103 against Greece at the Melbourne Cricket Ground on 25 May 2006. Australia won the FIFA World Cup warm-up game 1-0 thanks to a Josip Skoko goal.

SOCCEROOS MAKE IT AT LAST

The Australian national team – nicknamed the "Socceroos" – have been buoyed by massive support over the past decade. Their FIFA World Cup battles – culminating in a run to the last 16 in the 2006 finals – have established football among the nation's most popular sports. For many years, the game had languished behind cricket, the two rugby codes and Aussie rules football in the public imagination. Football had been kept alive by immigrants – first from Britain, then by arrivals from Italy, Greece and the former Yugoslavia. But the nation rallied round for the 1998 FIFA World Cup qualifying playoff final against Iran, which the Socceroos lost to Iran on away goals. Four years later, Australia lost another playoff, this time to Uruguay, 3-1 on aggregate.

TOP APPEARANCES

1	Alex Tobin	87
2	Paul Wade	84
3	Tony Vidmar	76
4	Brett Emerton	69
5	Mark Schwarzer	64
=	Peter Wilson	64
7	Attila Abonyi	61
8	John Kosmina	60
=	Stan Lazaridis	60
9	Scott Chipperfield	59
=	Milan Ivanovic	59

KEWELL THE TOPS

Harry Kewell (born on 22 September 1978) is widely regarded as Australia's best-ever player. The left winger has scored 13 goals in 39 international appearances, including the equalizer against Croatia that took Australia to the last 16 of the 2006 FIFA World Cup finals. Kewell has enjoyed a successful club career with Leeds United, Liverpool and Galatasaray. He is also the only Australian-born player to gain a Champions League winner's medal, with Liverpool in 2005.

TOP SCORERS

1	Damian Mori	29
2	John Aloisi	27
3	John Kosmina	25
=	Attila Abonyi	25
5	Archie Thompson	21
=	David Zdrilic	21
7	Graham Arnold	19
8	Ray Baartz	18
9	Gary Cole	17
=	Aurelio Vidmar	17

OLD ALLEGIANCES STILL MATTER

Several Australian-born players have chosen to play for their parents' countries rather than for Australia – Joey Didulica, Anthony Seric and Josip Simunic (Croatia), Sasa Ognenovski (Macedonia) and Sasa Ilic (Serbia). Simunic even played for Croatia against Australia in the 2006 FIFA World Cup finals – and was famously sent off only after being shown three yellow cards by English referee Graham Poll.

HIDDINK'S DUAL ROLE

Guus Hiddink is Australia's most successful coach, despite running the team for only 12 matches. He steered them through the qualifying playoffs, then guided them to the last 16 of the 2006 FIFA World Cup finals. The Dutch coach, who had guided South Korea to the semi-finals of the 2002 tournament, played a dual role during the 2005–06 season. He coached Dutch champions PSV Eindhoven as well as the Socceroos. He resigned after Australia's dramatic last-16 defeat by Italy to become coach of Russia.

AUSTRALIA'S SHOOT-OUT RECORD

Australia are the only team to reach the FIFA World Cup finals via a penalty shoot-out – in the final qualifying playoff in November 2005. They had lost the first leg 1-0 to Uruguay in Montevideo. Marco Bresciano's goal levelled the aggregate score, which remained 1-1 after extra-time. Goalkeeper Mark Schwarzer made two crucial saves as Australia won the shoot-out 4-2, with John Aloisi scoring the winning spot-kick.

AUSTRALIA RECORDS

HONOURS: Oceania champions 1980, 1996, 2000, 2004
FIRST INTERNATIONAL: vs. New Zealand (lost 3-1), Auckland, 17 June 1922
BIGGEST WIN: 31-0 vs. American Samoa, Sydney, 11 April 2001
BIGGEST DEFEAT: 7-0 vs. Croatia, Zagreb, 6 June 1998

OTHER ASIAN & OCEANIAN COUNTRIES

The lesser-known Asian and Oceanian footballing nations represent the true backwaters of world football. These may well be the countries in which true football obsession has yet to take hold, but competition between, and achievements by, these teams are no less vibrant. The regions are the home to many of the game's record-breakers – from the most goals in a single game to the most career appearances – some of which will never be broken.

ON THE UP

The best Asian teams have become familiar figures at recent FIFA World Cup finals tournaments. Co-hosts South Korea and Japan both gave a good account of themselves in 2002 – with the South Koreans achieving Asia's highest-ever finish. Saudi Arabia and Iran have been powerful forces, too – though these four face a strong challenge from the Asian Federation's new members, Australia. North Korea set the standard for Asian hopefuls in 1966 when they reached the quarter-finals in their only tournament appearance. They had to compete against teams from Asia, Africa and Oceania to qualify, beating Australia 9-2 on aggregate in a final playoff. Now though, Asia is guaranteed four slots at the 2010 finals in South Africa – with the chance of a fifth. The fifth-placed team in the Asian qualifiers will play off against Oceania winners New Zealand to decide the last spot.

NORTH KOREA SHOW THE WAY

North Korea were the first Asian side to reach the FIFA World Cup quarter-finals, in England in 1966. The unfancied North Koreans were described as "mystery men" by the English media. They opened with a 3-0 defeat against the Soviet Union. Pak Seung-Zin netted an 88th-minute equalizer to earn a 1-1 draw against Chile. Then North Korea pulled off one of the great shocks in FIFA World Cup history. Pak Doo-Ik scored the only goal as they eliminated Italy to reach the last eight. They threatened another surprise in the quarter-finals. Pak Seung-Zin, Li Dong-Woon and Yang Sung-Kook netted, as they raced into a 3-0 lead against Portugal by the 25th minute, before Eusebio replied with four goals and the North Koreans went down 5-3.

SYRIA'S 24-GOAL SALUTE

Syria ran up 24 goals in the space of five days against the Maldives in the qualifiers for the 1998 FIFA World Cup finals. The Syrians won 12-0 on 4 June 1997 and repeated the scoreline on 9 June.

IRAN STOP AT 19

Iran hold the record for the highest score in an Asian zone FIFA World Cup qualifier. They thrashed Guam 19-0 in Tabriz on 24 November 2000. Karim Bagheri scored six goals and Ali Karimi four. Future national coach Ali Daei and Farhad Majidi both netted three. This was two goals better than Iran's previous highest qualifying win – 17-0 against the Maldives on 2 June 1997, when Bagheri scored seven times. Two days after their 19-goal thrashing, Guam crashed 16-0 to Tajikistan.

AN UNWANTED RECORD

South Korea hold an unwanted record for the most goals conceded in one finals tournament. They let in 16 in 1954 – in just two games. They were overwhelmed by Hungary 9-0, before Turkey trounced them 7-0. No wonder their heroic goalkeeper Hong Duk-Yung looked shaken.

MOST APPEARANCES IN THE FIFA WORLD CUP™ FINALS

South Korea	7	(1954, 1986, 1990, 1994, 1998, 2002, 2006)
Saudi Arabia	4	(1994, 1998, 2002, 2006)
Iran	3	(1978, 1998, 2006)
Japan	3	(1998, 2002, 2006)
Australia	2	(1974, 2006)
China	1	(2002)
Indonesia	1	(1938)
Iraq	1	(1986)
Israel	1	(1970)
New Zealand	1	(1982)
North Korea	1	(1966)
Kuwait	1	(1982)
United Arab Emirates	1	(1990)

NEW ZEALAND'S BRIEF APPEARANCE

Australia and New Zealand are the only teams from the Oceania region to have played in the FIFA World Cup finals. New Zealand made their one appearance in 1982, after winning a final playoff 2-1 against China. They failed to gain a point. Steve Sumner and Steve Woodin scored in their opening 5-2 defeat by Scotland. They subsequently lost 3-0 to the Soviet Union and 4-0 against Brazil.

SAUDIS MAKE FLYING START

Saudi Arabia reached the last 16 in their first FIFA World Cup finals appearance in 1994. Saeed Owairan's winner against Belgium enabled them to finish level on points with Holland at the top of Group F. Sami Al-Jaber and Fuad Amin had scored in a 2-1 win over Morocco, after the Saudis lost their opening game 2-1 to Holland. They went down 3-1 to Sweden in the last 16. Substitute Fahad Al-Ghesheyan scored in the 85th minute after the Swedes led 2-0. Kennet Andersson grabbed Sweden's decisive third goal three minutes later. The Saudis have failed to advance beyond the group stages in their three subsequent appearances.

PALESTINE THE PIONEERS

Palestine, then under British rule, were the first Asian team to enter the FIFA World Cup qualifiers. They lost 7-1 away to Egypt on 16 March 1934. They lost the return match at home on 6 April, 4-1. Four years later, they were eliminated by Greece, who won 3-1 in Tel Aviv and 1-0 at home.

CHINA YET TO REALIZE POTENTIAL

China, the world's most populous nation, have qualified just once for the FIFA World Cup finals, in 2002. They topped their final qualifying group by eight points from the United Arab Emirates, but coach Bora Milutinovic's team slumped in the finals, failing to score a goal in defeats by Costa Rica (2-0), Brazil (4-0) and Turkey (3-0).

HIDDINK'S TEAM RELISH THE DRAMA

South Korea's fourth place in 2002 is the best performance by any Asian side in the FIFA World Cup finals. Their run will be remembered for two dramatic knockout games, first against Italy, then Spain. The Koreans, coached by Dutchman Guus Hiddink, had topped Group D, but they seemed on their way out when Italy led 1-0 with a few minutes left of the last-16 clash. Then Seol Ki-Hyon levelled in the 88th minute to force extra-time. Italy playmaker Francesco Totti was sent off for a second yellow card and Ahn Jung Hwan snatched the winner a minute from the end.

JAPAN RAISE FANS' HOPES

Co-hosts Japan impressed in the 2002 group stages to reach the last 16 for the first time. Takayuki Suzuki and Junichi Inamoto scored in their opening 2-2 draw against Belgium. Inamoto grabbed the only goal against Russia. Then Hiraoki Morishima and Hidetoshi Nakata netted in a 2-0 victory over Tunisia that put Japan top of Group H. Their run came to an end against Turkey. Umit Davala scored the 12th-minute winner that took the Turks to the quarter-finals.

CHA SETS GREAT EXAMPLE

Cha Bum Kun is South Korea's all-time top scorer. The former Air Force striker netted 55 times in 121 games for his country between 1972 and 1986, though he did not score in three appearances at the 1986 FIFA World Cup finals. Cha was also the first Asian star to succeed at the highest level in Europe. He made 308 appearances in the German Bundesliga between 1978 and 1989 and scored 98 goals. He gained UEFA Cup winners' medals with both Eintracht Frankfurt (1980) and Bayer Leverkusen (1988). His 17 Bundesliga goals for Leverkusen in 1985–86 remains a record for an Asian player. He also received just one yellow card in his career in West Germany. After retiring, he returned to South Korea and set up a group of soccer schools for youth players.

NAKATA BLAZES THE TRAIL

Midfielder Hidetoshi Nakata ranks among Japan's best-ever players. He made his mark by setting up all three goals in Japan's 3-2 FIFA World Cup qualifying playoff win over Iran on 16 November 1997. He moved to Italian club Perugia after the 1998 finals and became the first Japanese player to star in Europe. He won a championship medal with Roma in 2001 and later played for Parma, Bologna and Fiorentina. Nakata started in three FIFA World Cup finals tournaments. He made ten appearances and scored one goal – the second in a 2-0 win over Tunisia that took Japan to the last 16 of the 2002 finals. He won 77 caps and scored on 11 occasions.

ASIA PRESSES ON, OCEANIA STRUGGLES

The finest Asian players have become famous worldwide over the past decade. FIFA's decision to expand the World Cup finals – and allocate more places to Asian teams – has given those stars the chance to shine on an international stage. Hidetoshi Nakata, Japan's general of the 1998 finals, led the way to success in Europe, soon followed by his colleague Shinji Ono to Feyenoord, and, more recently, by midfielder Shunsuke Nakamura at Celtic. Iran's top scorer, Ali Daei, made a name for himself in Germany with Hertha Berlin while Iranian winger, or midfielder, Mehdi Mahdavikia was twice voted "Player of the Year" by Hamburg's supporters. South Korean midfielder Park Ji-Sung has been a European Champions League winner with Manchester United and a semi-finalist with PSV Eindhoven, alongside international team-mate Lee Young-Pyo. Oceania has remained the backwater of the FIFA confederations, weakened by Australia's decision to join the Asian Federation on 1 January 2006. It consists now of New Zealand and a series of Pacific islands. Christian Karembeu, born in New Caledonia, remains the last international star to come from those islands.

KAREMBEU THE FIFA WORLD CUP™ WINNER

Christian Karembeu, born in New Caledonia, is the only FIFA World Cup winner to come from the Oceania region. He started for France in their 3-0 final victory over Brazil on 12 July 1998. The defensive midfielder had earlier begun against Denmark (group), Italy (quarter-finals) and Croatia (semi-finals). He played 53 times for France, scoring one goal, and was also a double European Cup winner with Real Madrid in 1998 and 2000.

AL-DEAYEA CAPS THEM ALL

Saudi goalkeeper Mohamed Al-Deayea had to choose between football and handball as a youngster. He was persuaded by his elder brother Abdullah to pick football. He made 181 appearances for his country, the first coming against Bangladesh in 1990, the last against Belgium in May 2006. He also appeared in the FIFA World Cup finals tournaments of 1994, 1998 and 2002. He played his last finals game in a 3-0 defeat by the Republic of Ireland on 11 June 2002 and was recalled to the squad for the 2006 finals, although he did not play.

AL-JABER TO THE FORE

Sami Al-Jaber (born on 11 December 1972 in Riyadh) became only the second Asian player to appear in four FIFA World Cup finals tournaments when he started against Tunisia in Munich on 14 June 2006. He scored in a 2-2 draw, his third goal in nine appearances at the finals. Al-Jaber played only one game in 1998 before he was rushed to hospital with a burst appendix, which ruled him out of the competition. He became Saudi Arabia's record scorer, with 44 goals in 163 matches.

ASIAN FOOTBALLER OF THE YEAR

Year	Player	Country
1988	Ahmed Radhi	Iraq
1989	Kim Joo-Sung	South Korea
1990	Kim Joo-Sung	South Korea
1991	Kim Joo-Sung	South Korea
1992	not awarded	
1993	Kazuyoshi Miura	Japan
1994	Saeed Owarain	Saudi Arabia
1995	Masami Ihara	Japan
1996	Khodadad Azizi	Iran
1997	Hidetoshi Nakata	Japan
1998	Hidetoshi Nakata	Japan
1999	Ali Daei	Iran
2000	Nawaf Al Temyat	Saudi Arabia
2001	Fan Zhiyi	China
2002	Shinji Ono	Japan
2003	Mehdi Mahdavikia	Iran
2004	Ali Karimi	Iran
2005	Hamad Al-Montashari	Saudi Arabia
2006	Khalfan Ibrahim	Qatar
2007	Yasser Al-Qahtani	Saudi Arabia
2008	Server Djeparov	Uzbekistan

HONG SETS FIFA WORLD CUP™ RECORD

South Korea defender Hong Myung-Bo was the first Asian player to appear in four consecutive FIFA World Cup finals tournaments. He played all three games as South Korea lost to Belgium, Spain and Uruguay in 1990. He scored twice in three appearances in 1994 – his goal against Spain sparking a Korean fightback from 2-0 down to draw 2-2. In 1998, he started all three group games as South Korea were eliminated at the group stage. Four years later, on home soil, he captained South Korea to fourth place in the finals, the best-ever performance by an Asian team. Hong's total of 16 appearances in the FIFA World Cup finals is also a record for an Asian player. He later became coach of the South Korea Under-20 squad.

OWAIRAN'S MAGIC GOAL

Saudi Arabia forward Saeed Owairan scored the finest goal of the 1994 FIFA World Cup finals. He dribbled for more than 50 yards, beating five challenges, to hit the winner against Belgium on 29 June. Owairan's strike took the Saudis to the last 16 for the first time and has also become a massive hit on YouTube, registering more than 320,000 hits. Owairan scored 24 goals in 50 games for his country.

KIM'S TREBLE SUCCESS

South Korea midfielder Kim Joo-Sung is the only player to have won the Asian Footballer of the Year award three times – and in successive years – between 1989 and 1991. He played in three FIFA World Cup finals tournaments, but his side never advanced beyond the group stage. He won 77 caps, scoring 14 goals, and was one of the first South Korean players to move abroad, joining Bundesliga side Bochum in 1992 and staying for two seasons.

PAK STRIKE MAKES HISTORY

North Korea's Pak Doo Ik earned legend status by scoring the goal that eliminated Italy from the 1966 FIFA World Cup finals. The shockwaves caused by the victory were comparable to those caused by the United States' 1-0 win over England in 1950. Pak netted the only goal in the 42nd minute at Middlesbrough on 19 July. North Korea thus became the first Asian team to reach the quarter-finals. Pak, an army corporal, was promoted to sergeant after the victory and later became a gymnastics coach.

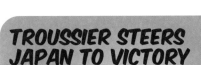

TROUSSIER STEERS JAPAN TO VICTORY

Paris-born Philippe Troussier was named Asia's Coach of the Year in 2000 after leading Japan to a 1-0 victory over Saudi Arabia in the Asian Cup final in Lebanon. He also steered the Japanese to their best-ever FIFA World Cup finish on home soil in 2002, when they lost 1-0 to Turkey in the last 16. But that achievement was overshadowed by Hiddink's success with South Korea.

SOVIET REPUBLICS FIND NEW HOME

The break-up of the former Soviet Union swelled the ranks of the Asian Confederation in the early 1990s. Former Soviet republics Kyrgyzstan, Tajikistan, Turkmenistan and Uzbekistan all joined in 1994. Uzbekistan have been the most successful, reaching the Asian Cup quarter-finals in 2007. Australia are the AFC's newest members, entering the confederation on 1 January 2006, a few months after East Timor became the 45th Asian member country.

HUGE FOLLOWING FOR FOOTBALL IN CHINA

China's national team boasts a massive fan base – as was demonstrated when they reached the FIFA World Cup finals for the only time in 2002. Between their qualification on 19 October 2001 and their opening game of the finals against Costa Rica on 4 June 2002, an estimated 170 million new TV sets were sold throughout China! TV audiences for the team's three matches regularly topped 300 million, even though China lost all three matches and failed to score a goal.

ASIAN STRENGTH GROWS AND GROWS

The Asian Football Confederation (AFC) was founded on 8 May 1954 in Manila, Philippines. There were 12 original members – Afghanistan, Burma, China, Hong Kong, India, Indonesia, Japan, Pakistan, Philippines, Singapore, South Korea and Vietnam. The AFC held its first competition – the Asian Cup for national teams – in Hong Kong in 1956. It has since made great strides, growing to embrace 45 Asian nations, plus Australia. Asian teams are well established on the world stage. The AFC now has a minimum of four places at the FIFA World Cup finals, with the chance for a fifth via the playoffs. The Asian confederation organizes annual intercontinental club tournaments for national champions and cup winners, along with the Asian Cup at four-year intervals. Asian stars – such as Iran's Ali Daei, Cha Bum-Kun and Park Ji-Sung (South Korea) and Japan's Hidetoshi Nakata – have made big impressions in Europe. Meanwhile, a new generation of Asian-born coaches is ending the reliance on managers from Europe and South America. Asian football has never been stronger.

THE ISRAEL ISSUE

Israel is, geographically, an Asian nation. It hosted – and won – the Asian Cup in 1964. However, many of the countries that later joined the Asian confederation refused to play Israel for political reasons. Israel subsequently played in the Oceania qualifiers – and reached the 1970 FIFA World Cup finals by winning a playoff against Australia. In 1989, Israel topped the Oceania group, but lost a final playoff to Colombia for a place in the 1990 finals. They switched to the European zone qualifiers in 1992 and have been a full member of the European federation, UEFA, since 1994.

HIGHEST ... AND LOWEST

The highest attendance for an Asian team in a home FIFA World Cup qualifier was the 130,000 who watched Iran draw 1-1 with Australia in the Azadi Stadium, Tehran, on 22 November 1997. The game was the first leg of a final playoff for the last place in the 1998 finals. Iran advanced on away goals after drawing the second leg 2-2 in Melbourne. The lowest attendance was the "crowd" of 20 that turned out for Turkmenistan's 1-0 win over Taiwan, played in Amman, Jordan, on 7 May 2001.

ASIAN CUP WINNERS

The Asian Cup is Asia's continental championship

Year	Winners
1956	South Korea
1960	South Korea
1964	Israel
1968	Iran
1972	Iran
1976	Iran
1980	Kuwait
1984	Saudi Arabia
1988	Saudi Arabia
1992	Japan
1996	Saudi Arabia
2000	Japan
2004	Japan
2007	Iraq

CHA LEADS THE WAY

In 1997, South Korea's Cha Bum-Kun became the first native-born national team boss to win Asia's Coach of the Year award. Cha, South Korea's all-time leading scorer, took over the national team in January 1997. He guided them through the FIFA World Cup qualifiers with nine wins and just one defeat in 12 matches. South Korea reached the finals automatically, topping Asian final group B, six points ahead of Japan.

PAK CARRIES THE FLAME

North Korea's hero of the 1966 FIFA World Cup finals, Pak Doo Ik, is still much admired by his countrymen. He was chosen as one of the 56 people to carry the Olympic torch across North Korea on its way to the 2008 Beijing Olympics. He was also the oldest – a sprightly 70.

ASIAN POWER-HOUSES

Three teams have dominated the Asian Cup since the tournament's inception in 1956: Iran, Saudi Arabia and Japan – all of whom have won Asia's premier trophy on three occasions. Iran collected three successive titles between 1968 and 1976; Saudi Arabia won the title in 1984, 1988 and 1996; while Japan have been the dominant force in recent times, winning in 1992, 2000 and 2004.

CHINA'S 4X4

Four teams carry the name of China. The China national team receives most attention, but Hong Kong (a former British colony) and Macau (a former Portuguese colony) both retain their autonomous status for football – as Hong Kong China and Macau China respectively. Meanwhile, the independent island state of Taiwan competes in the FIFA World Cup and other competitions as Chinese Taipei.

HIDDINK THE SOUTH KOREAN HERO

Dutchman Guus Hiddink is the most successful coach in Asian international football history. He had steered PSV Eindhoven to European Cup victory in 1996 and Holland to fourth place in the 1998 FIFA World Cup finals, before he took charge of the South Korea squad on 20 December 2000. He said: "When I arrived, the team was very conservative." He decided on a faster, more attacking approach, experimenting in friendlies, because South Korea had automatically qualified as co-hosts. Korean fans and media were not convinced, but hoped their team would at least reach the last 16. They did even better. Hiddink's team topped their group with wins over Poland and Portugal, eliminated Italy with a goal in the last minute of extra-time, then reached the semi-finals with a shoot-out victory over Spain. They lost 1-0 to Germany, then 3-2 in the third-place playoff to Turkey. Fourth place was still the highest-ever finish achieved by an Asian team at the finals. Hiddink became the first foreigner to be made an honorary South Korean citizen and the stadium at Gwangju was renamed in his honour.

LOCAL COACHES MAKE THEIR MARK

Three more native-born Asian national team coaches have been named Asia's Coach of the Year. The first, in 2001, was Nasser Al-Johar, who steered Saudi Arabia through to the 2002 FIFA World Cup finals, two points clear of Iran in the decisive qualifying group. Adnan Hamad followed him three years later, leading Iraq to the Asian Cup quarter-finals, little more than a year after the US invasion. The 2007 winner was Uzbekistan's Rauf Inileyev, who guided his country to the 2007 Asian Cup quarter-finals, beating China 3-0 on the way.

Football is enthusiastically followed in many parts of the Caribbean, Central and North American region of the world game. Mexican fans have long been among the most colourful followers of FIFA World Cup™ action, all the way back to the inaugural finals in 1930. Mexico was also, in 1970 and 1986, the first country to host the finals on two occasions.

MEXICO

Mexico may well be the powerhouse of the CONCACAF region and are regular qualifiers for the FIFA World Cup™ – they have failed to reach the finals of the tournament on just three occasions (1934, 1974 and 1982) – but they have always struggled to impose themselves on the international stage. Two FIFA World Cup™ quarter-final appearances (both times as tournament hosts, in 1970 and 1986) represent their best performances to date. A football-mad nation expects more.

YET TO MAKE THEIR MARK

Mexico may have played in the finals of 13 FIFA World Cup tournaments, but they have been serial underachievers, advancing to the quarter-finals only twice – both times when they were tournament hosts (in 1970 and 1986). They lost 4-1 to runners-up Italy in Toluca in 1970. Sixteen years later – after the finals were enlarged – they beat Bulgaria 2-0 in the last 16, before losing a shoot-out to West Germany in Monterrey after a 0-0 draw. Mexico have been eliminated at the last-16 stage in each of the last four World Cup finals, by Bulgaria on penalties, after a 1-1 draw (1994), 2-1 by Germany in 1998, 2-0 by the United States in 2002 and 2-1 by Argentina, after extra-time, in 2006. Mexico were among the 13 participants in the inaugural FIFA World Cup in 1930. They have since been one of the strongest teams in the CONCACAF region, qualifying for the finals on ten occasions. But they failed to progress beyond the group stage in 1930, 1950, 1954, 1958, 1962 and 1966 and once went 13 games without a win in the finals, until their 3-1 victory over Czechoslovakia in 1962.

SUAREZ SETS OUTFIELD RECORD

Mexico defender Claudio Suarez is the world's most-capped outfield player, with 178 caps. He ranks second only to Saudi Arabia goalkeeper Mohamed Al-Deayea, who has 181 caps. Suarez – nicknamed "The Emperor" – played in all of Mexico's four games in 1994 and 1998. He missed the 2002 finals because of a broken leg, but was included in the squad for the 2006 finals at the age of 37, although he did not play.

MEXICO'S FIRST GOAL

Mexico were one of the 13 nations to enter the first FIFA World Cup finals in 1930. Juan Carreno scored their first FIFA World Cup goal on 13 July, in the 70th minute of a 4-1 defeat by France in Montevideo. The Mexicans then lost 3-0 to Chile and 6-3 to Argentina.

MEXICO END LOSING STREAK

Mexico ended a FIFA World Cup finals run of 13 games without a win when they beat Czechoslovakia 3-1 in Vina del Mar (Chile) on 7 June 1962. The Czechs had already qualified from Group Three and rested four of their players, but they took the lead through Vaclav Masek after 15 seconds. Mexico replied with goals by Isidoro Diaz, Alfredo Del Aguila and Hector Hernandez. The result was a special 33rd birthday present for Mexico goalkeeper Antonio Carbajal, who was presented with a bouquet of flowers by Czech skipper Josef Masopust. However, the celebrations ended there: Mexico were still eliminated, after losing to Brazil and Spain.

AGUIRRE IN CHARGE AGAIN

Mexico coach Javier Aguirre has had two spells in charge. Aguirre, known as "The Basque" because of his ancestry, guided Mexico to the last 16 in 2002. He returned in place of Sven-Goran Eriksson on 3 April 2009, after the Swede was sacked following Mexico's 3-1 defeat by Honduras in a FIFA World Cup qualifier for South Africa 2010.

TOP APPEARANCES

1	Claudio Suarez	178
2	Pavel Pardo	147
3	Jorge Campos	130
4	Ramon Ramirez	121
5	Alberto Garcia Aspe	109
6	Oswaldo Sanchez	98
7	Cuauhtemoc Blanco	97
8	Gerardo Torrado	91
9	Carlos Hermilloso	90
10	Jared Borgetti	89

TOP SCORERS

1	Jared Borgetti	46
2	Luis Hernandez	35
=	Carlos Hermilloso	35
4	Cuauhtemoc Blanco	34
5	Enrique Borja	31
6	Zague	30
7	Hugo Sanchez	29
=	Luis Flores	29
=	Luis Garcia	29
10	Benjamin Galindo	28

UNBEATEN IN QUALIFICATION

Mexico's first taste of qualifying for a FIFA World Cup, the tournament in Brazil in 1950, raised few, if any, alarms. They breezed through the process, winning all four games in the CONCACAF preliminaries. They beat the United States 6-0 and 6-2 and defeated Cuba 2-0 and 3-0.

ROSAS NETS HISTORIC PENALTY

Mexico's Manuel Rosas scored the first penalty ever awarded in the FIFA World Cup finals when he converted a 42nd-minute spot-kick in his country's match against Argentina in 1930. Rosas scored again in the 65th minute, but it was too little too late for the Mexicans: they crashed to a 6-3 defeat.

TWO FINALS AT THE AZTECA

Mexico's main home venue, the Azteca Stadium in Mexico City, is the only stadium to have hosted a FIFA World Cup final twice – the game between Brazil and Italy in 1970 and the Argentina–West Germany clash in 1986. The stadium – built for the 1970 finals – was opened on 29 May 1966. Its original capacity was 114,600, but it was renovated in 1985, ahead of the 1986 FIFA World Cup finals, and the capacity was reduced to 105,000.

MEXICO BEATS EARTHQUAKE

Mexico stepped in to host the 1986 FIFA World Cup finals after the original choice, Colombia, pulled out in November 1982. FIFA chose Mexico as the replacement venue because of its stadiums and infrastructure, still in place from the 1970 finals. The governing body turned down rival bids from Canada and the United States. Mexico had to work overtime to be ready for the finals, after the earthquake of 19 September 1985, which killed an estimated 10,000 people in central Mexico and destroyed many buildings in Mexico City.

HERNANDEZ HEADS THE FINALS LIST

Luis Hernandez's four goals in 1998 make him Mexico's highest-ever scorer in a FIFA World Cup finals tournament. Hernandez netted twice in Mexico's 3-1 group win over South Korea. His last-minute equalizer also earned them a 2-2 draw against Holland. Hernandez, nicknamed "The Matador", gave his side the lead against Germany in the last 16, before late goals by Jurgen Klinsmann and Oliver Bierhoff eliminated the Mexicans.

CARBAJAL'S RECORD FIVE

Goalkeeper Antonio Carbajal was the first man to play in the finals of five successive FIFA World Cup finals, though he never saw his side advance beyond the group stages. He made his finals debut in a 4-0 defeat by hosts Brazil in 1950, and subsequently played in the finals of 1954, 1958 and 1962, before ending his run in England in 1966.

MEXICO RECORDS

FIRST INTERNATIONAL: won 3-2 vs. Guatemala, Guatemala City, 1 January 1923

BIGGEST WIN: 13-0 vs. Bahamas, Toluca, 28 April 1987

BIGGEST DEFEAT: 8-0 vs. England, Wembley, 10 May 1961

CONCACAF champions: 1965, 1971, 1977, 1993, 1996, 1998, 2003

CONFEDERATIONS CUP WINNERS: 1999

UNITED STATES

Some of the game's biggest names – from Pele to David Beckham – may well have graced the United States' domestic league over the years, and the country may well be one of only 15 countries to have been granted the honour of hosting a FIFA World Cup™, but football is still very much a minority sport in the world's most powerful country. However, following a series of impressive performances on the world stage, the hope is that the situation will soon change.

SUPERPOWER IN WAITING

The United States are one of the most consistent national teams of the modern era. They have played in the last five FIFA World Cup finals, qualifying four times and hosting the 1994 tournament. They were quarter-finalists in South Korea/Japan in 2002, losing 1-0 to Germany. The US have a proud FIFA World Cup history. They finished third in the inaugural competition in 1930. Twenty years later, they sprang one of the biggest shocks in the history of the finals when they beat joint favourites England 1-0 in Belo Horizonte. But soccer in the US has traditionally been overshadowed by American football, baseball and basketball. After the demise of the North American Soccer League (NASL) in 1984, the US lacked even a national professional league. The turning point was the US's 1-0 victory in Trinidad that took them to the FIFA World Cup finals in 1990 for the first time in 40 years. The 1994 finals added further impetus – and the start of Major League Soccer in 1996 led to the development of a succession of players for the national team. Many – such as Landon Donovan, Clint Dempsey and DaMarcus Beasley – have also played for European clubs.

US HERO BUT NOT A CITIZEN

Joe Gaetjens, the United States' match-winner against England, was not even a US citizen. The US Federation allowed him to play because he had applied for American nationality, but Gaetjens failed to complete the process and later played for his native Haiti in a FIFA World Cup qualifier against Mexico on 27 December 1953.

MUTED RESPONSE

There was so little domestic interest in the US's 1950 FIFA World Cup progress that only one American journalist watched them beat England – Dent McSkimming of the *St Louis Post-Dispatch*. His was the only report to appear in the US media – and he attended the game only because he was on holiday in Brazil at the time.

RECORD BREAKERS

FIFA's choice of the United States to host the 1994 finals was controversial. Critics pointed to US's poor international record, and the lack of a national professional league. But the US made it as far as the last 16, thanks to a 2-1 win over Colombia, before losing 1-0 to eventual winners Brazil. In addition, the total attendance of 3,587,538 set a record for the finals.

ENGLAND STUNNED BY GAETJENS

The US's 1-0 win over England on 29 June 1950 ranks among the biggest surprises in FIFA World Cup history. England, along with hosts Brazil, were joint favourites to win the trophy. The US had lost their last seven matches, scoring just two goals. Joe Gaetjens scored the only goal, in the 37th minute, diving to head Walter Bahr's cross past goalkeeper Bert Williams. England dominated the game, but US keeper Frank Borghi made save after save. Defeats by Chile and Spain eliminated the US at the group stage, but their victory over England remains the greatest result in the country's football history.

TOP SCORERS

1	Landon Donovan	37
2	Eric Wynalda	34
3	Brian McBride	30
4	Joe-Max Moore	24
5	Bruce Murray	21
6	DaMarcus Beasley	17
=	Earnie Stewart	17
8	Cobi Jones	15
9	Marcelo Balboa	13
=	Clint Dempsey	13
=	Hugo Perez	13

CAGLIURI'S SHOT MAKES HISTORY

The US's FIFA World Cup qualifying win in Trinidad, on 19 November 1989, is regarded as a turning point in the country's football history. The team included just one full-time professional, Paul Cagliuri, of (West) German second division club Meppen. He scored the only goal of the game with a looping shot after 31 minutes to take the US to their first finals for 40 years. The Trinidad goalkeeper Michael Maurice, claimed to have been blinded by the sun. The victory raised the profile of the team hugely, despite their first-round elimination in the 1990 finals. It also provided the impetus for the professional organization of the national squad. Cagliuri said: "It was the single most important game we ever won."

VENUE CHOICE BACKFIRES

A strange choice of venue cost the US the chance of reaching the 1986 FIFA World Cup finals. They needed only a draw against Costa Rica to join Canada and Honduras in the final qualifying group, but US Soccer decided to host the game in Torrance, California, an area full of expatriate Costa Ricans. The game was promoted enthusiastically to the Costa Rica fans and they turned the occasion into a virtual home game for their side, who won 1-0 and eliminated the US.

MEOLA SUMS UP

Goalkeeper Tony Meola, one of many part-timers in that 1989 US team, said: "Things weren't like they are today. Looking back, it's amazing that we achieved what we did. We had guys playing in semi-pro leagues and Sunday leagues. Everything the US has achieved since then is based on that win."

McGHEE OPENS THE SCORING

Bart McGhee scored the US's first goal in the FIFA World Cup finals, after 41 minutes of their opening game against Belgium in Montevideo on 13 July 1930. McGhee added a second four minutes later and Bert Patenaude completed a 3-0 win. Patenaude then scored the first hat-trick in FIFA World Cup history, against Paraguay, on 17 July. The US's run ended with a 6-1 semi-final defeat by Argentina.

TEAM AMERICA'S BRIEF EXPERIMENT

Governing body US Soccer entered the US national side in the NASL as "Team America" for one season in 1983. The experiment was soon dropped when the side finished bottom of the table. Team America struggled from the start because many of the top players preferred to stay with their own clubs. They were rarely able to field a settled side either.

TOP APPEARANCES

1	Cobi Jones	164
2	Jeff Agoos	134
3	Marcelo Balboa	128
4	Claudio Reyna	112
5	Paul Cagliuri	110
6	Landon Donovan	108
7	Eric Wynalda	106
8	Kasey Keller	102
9	Earnie Stewart	101
10	Tony Meola	100
=	Joe-Max Moore	100

ARENA'S MEN REACH LAST EIGHT

The US's best performance in the modern FIFA World Cup finals came in 2002 when they reached the last eight. Coach Bruce Arena's side beat Portugal 3-2, drew 1-1 with South Korea and lost 3-1 to qualify in second place from Group D. Brian McBride (right) and Landon Donovan scored in a 2-0 win over Mexico in the last 16. They lost 1-0 to Germany in the quarter-finals. The squad featured many players with European experience – Brad Friedel (above), Kasey Keller, Claudio Reyna, McBride, Donovan, DaMarcus Beasley and Cobi Jones. Arena was later succeeded by his assistant Bob Bradley after the US were eliminated at the group stage of the 2006 finals in Germany.

CONCACAF OTHER TEAMS

Mexico and the United States (with 21 FIFA World Cup™ finals appearances between them) are undoubtedly the powerhouses of the CONCACAF region. Of the other teams to make up the football nations in North and Central America, only two countries (Costa Rica in 1990, 2002 and 2006) and El Salvador (1970 and 1982) have managed to qualify for the FIFA World Cup™ finals on more than one occasion.

PROUD RECORD

The CONCACAF association, which covers North and Central America and the Caribbean, can proudly boast of having had at least one representative in every FIFA World Cup finals. Mexico and the United States entered the first finals in 1930 – and the US reached the semi-finals before crashing to Argentina. Since then, the region's "big two" have dominated the qualifying competition. Mexico have played in a total of 13 finals tournaments; the US have appeared in eight. In recent years, however, other countries have come forward to challenge them. Costa Rica made their third finals appearance in 2006 while Trinidad and Tobago reached the finals for the first time. CONCACAF had a record representation of four teams in 2006 – the US, Mexico, Costa Rica and Trinidad.

HIGHEST ATTENDANCE

The biggest crowd ever to watch a CONCACAF team play at home was the 119,853 people who saw Mexico lose 2-0 to Brazil in a friendly at the Aztec Stadium, Mexico City, on 7 July 1968.

COSTA RICA WIN WITHOUT A CROWD

The lowest-ever attendance for a CONCACAF FIFA World Cup qualifier was for the Costa Rica–Panama game on 26 March 2005. FIFA ordered the game, staged at the Saprissa Stadium in San Jose, to be played behind closed doors after missiles were thrown at visiting players and the match officials when Mexico won there 2-1 on 9 February. The game was known as "the ghost match". Costa Rica beat Panama 2-1, thanks to a Roy Myrie goal in the first minute of stoppage time.

COSTA RICA KEEP BATTLING

Costa Rica have been the most successful of Mexico's Central American neighbours at the FIFA World Cup finals. They qualified in 1990, 2002 and 2006, and reached the last 16 at that first attempt, beating Scotland 1-0 and Sweden 2-1 in their group. They were knocked out by Czechoslovakia, 4-1. In 2002, they beat China 2-0 and drew 1-1 with Turkey but were eliminated following a 5-2 defeat against Brazil. They departed at the group stage in 2006, losing all theee of their matches. El Salvador qualified twice, in 1970 and 1982 – but lost all six of their matches, including a 10-1 defeat by Hungary in 1982. Honduras qualified for the only time in 1982. They drew 1-1 with both Spain and Northern Ireland, but went home after losing 1-0 to Yugoslavia in their final group game.

CANADA'S SOLE APPEARANCE

Canada reached the FIFA World Cup finals for the only time in 1986, beating Honduras and Costa Rica in the final CONCACAF qualifying group, but they lost all three games and failed to score a goal. They were beaten by France (1-0), Hungary (2-0) and the Soviet Union (2-0).

REGGAE BOYZ STEP UP

In 1998, Jamaica became the first team from the English-speaking Caribbean to reach the FIFA World Cup finals. The "Reggae Boyz", as they were nicknamed, included several players based in England. They were eliminated at the group stage, despite beating Japan 2-1 in their final game with two goals by Theodore Whitmore. They had earlier lost 3-1 to Croatia and 5-0 against Argentina.

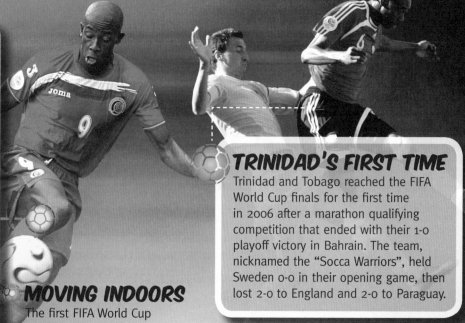

CONCACAF TEAMS IN THE FIFA WORLD CUP™ FINALS

Appearances made by teams from the CONCACAF region at the FIFA World Cup finals

1	Mexico	13
2	US	8
3	Costa Rica	3
4	El Salvador	2
5	Canada	1
=	Cuba	1
=	Haiti	1
=	Honduras	1
=	Jamaica	1
=	Trinidad & Tobago	1

MILUTINOVIC'S MAGIC TOUCH

Serb-born Bora Milutinovic has a remarkable record of guiding teams from the CONCACAF region to the FIFA World Cup finals. In 1986, he steered hosts Mexico to the quarter-finals, their best-ever performance, where they lost on penalties to eventual finalists West Germany. Four years later, he led Costa Rica to the last 16, another national record. In 1994, he steered hosts the US to the last 16. Milutinovic is the only man to have coached five different teams at the finals.

MOVING INDOORS

The first FIFA World Cup qualifier to be played indoors was the US's 2-0 win over Canada at the Seattle Seadome on 20 October 1976. This was a forerunner of events at the 1994 finals in the United States, when four matches were staged indoors at the Pontiac Silverdome in Detroit.

JEAN-JOSEPH TESTS POSITIVE

In 1974, Haiti defender Ernest Jean-Joseph became the first player to be suspended from the FIFA World Cup finals for failing a drugs test, although the authorities never specified which substance he was alleged to have taken. He was escorted home by Haitian security men after coach Antoine Tassy refused to dismiss him from the team camp.

CUBA SHOW THE WAY

In 1938, Cuba became the first team from the CONCACAF region to reach the FIFA World Cup quarter-finals. They drew 3-3 with Romania after extra-time in the first round, then won the replay 2-1 with goals by Hector Socorro and Carlos Oliveira after trailing at half-time. They were thrashed 8-0 by Sweden in the last eight. Haiti were the next Caribbean team to play in the finals, in 1974. They lost all three group games, 3-1 to Italy, 7-0 against Poland and 4-1 to Argentina.

TRINIDAD'S FIRST TIME

Trinidad and Tobago reached the FIFA World Cup finals for the first time in 2006 after a marathon qualifying competition that ended with their 1-0 playoff victory in Bahrain. The team, nicknamed the "Socca Warriors", held Sweden 0-0 in their opening game, then lost 2-0 to England and 2-0 to Paraguay.

ARTIFICIALLY FIRST

The first FIFA World Cup qualifier to be played on artificial turf was the 1-1 draw between Canada and the US in Vancouver on 24 September 1976. Artificial surfaces had been used for the previous decade in North American sports such as American football, but this was a first for soccer.

ENGLAND'S CARIBBEAN CONNECTION

England have benefited more than any other national team from their Caribbean connection. Of the 58 black players who have played for England, 55 have Caribbean roots. England's first black player, Viv Anderson (above right), who made his debut against Czechoslovakia in 1978, was the son of Jamaican parents who had arrived in England in 1954. England's most-capped black player, John Barnes, grew up in Jamaica and came to England when he was 13. Barnes won 79 caps. His father Ken captained Jamaica in the early 1960s. Other black stars have included 1990 FIFA World Cup semi-finalists Paul Parker and Des Walker. Of the present England squad, David James, Rio Ferdinand, Glen Johnson, Ashley Cole, Emile Heskey, Aaron Lennon and Theo Walcott all have Caribbean ancestry.

PART 2: FIFA WORLD CUP™

NO event magnetizes sports fans across the globe like the FIFA World Cup. Nowadays the national teams of 32 countries, compared with 16 and then 24 previously, compete every four years for the honour of being crowned champions of the world. But the power of the FIFA World Cup is that its climactic tournament also pulls fans to their television sets in all the other countries of the world to marvel at the magic of the heroes of Brazil, Italy, Argentina, Germany, England, France and their rivals. The FIFA World Cup was launched in 1930 in Uruguay, its inspiration being derived from the persuasive powers of FIFA's then-president, Frenchman Jules Rimet.

Uruguay had been Olympic champions in 1924 and 1928, but the advent of professionalism meant that the supposedly all-amateur Olympic Games could no longer claim to represent a footballing pinnacle of excellence. Only four European nations dared send teams on the long sea crossing to Montevideo for the first finals – though it was Frenchman Lucien Laurent who made history by scoring the first-ever goal in the FIFA World Cup. Since then, however, Europe has more than made amends for its initial reluctance. It equals South America with nine FIFA World Cup wins apiece and has played host to the tournament on 11 occasions – far ahead of the three held in South America (Argentina, Brazil and Uruguay all one apiece), three in Central and North America (Mexico two, United States one) and one in Asia (Japan and South Korea as co-hosts in 2002).

Nelson Mandela celebrates South Africa's victory in the 2010 FIFA World Cup hosting race.

Soccer City in Johannesburg will host the opening match and the final of the 2010 FIFA World Cup™. The remarkable stadium (pictured near completion of its construction in May 2009), next to the headquarters of the South African Football Association, will thus make history as the heart of the first finals to be staged on the African continent – by virtue of FIFA's historic decision in 2004.

2010 FIFA WORLD CUP™ PREVIEW

FIFA FOUNDED

FIFA was founded in 1904, launched the inaugural FIFA World Cup in 1930 ... and will make sporting history yet again when the finals are hosted in Africa for the first time, in South Africa, between 11 June and 11 July 2010. Remarkably, the Rainbow Nation will be celebrating "only" 18 years since being welcomed back into the world football family after Nelson Mandela helped inspire the overthrow of the Apartheid regime. Football had been always been the No.1 sport in terms of participation numbers in the country – a fact little known by the outside world, who had seen South Africa's international pride expressed largely through white-dominated cricket and rugby union. Now the world can – and will – see South Africa for the football hotbed it really is and share the thrill and excitement generated by all the nation's football fans. The South Africans' initial bid was for the 2006 finals, but they lost out narrowly to Germany. However, FIFA's insistence on an African-only solution to 2010 saw them easily head off competition from Morocco and a joint bid from Libya and Tunisia.

EXPORT VALUE

South Africa's exclusion from the world game during the Apartheid years meant many players built national team careers elsewhere in the 1950s. These included centre-forward Eddie Firmani (from Cape Town), who played three times for Italy, and defender John Hewie, who appeared 19 times for Scotland. Left winger Bill Perry not only played three times for England, but also earned even greater fame by converting a pass from Stanley Matthews to score Blackpool's winning goal in their legendary 1953 FA Cup final triumph over Bolton.

TICKET RUSH

Demand for tickets massively exceeded supply when the first sales "window" for more than 1.6m opened in spring 2009. Most applications came from South Africa, followed by the United States, United Kingdom, Germany, Italy and Australia.

STRIKING THE RIGHT NOTE

FIFA World Cup fans are being given special dispensation from standard security regulations so they can bring their vuvuzela trumpets into the stadia to create the unique atmosphere that enlivens big matches in South Africa.

ANIMAL MAGIC

Zakumi, a leopard character, is the official mascot for the 2010 FIFA World Cup – extending the theme created for the FIFA World Cup's first such mascot, World Cup Willie, in England in 1966. The mascots in between have been: Juanito (Mexico 1970), Tip and Tap (West Germany 1974), Gauchito (Argentina 1978), Naranjito (Spain 1982), Pique (Mexico 1986), Ciao (Italy 1990), Striker (United States 1994), Footix (France 1998), Kaz, Ato and Nik (Japan and Korea 2002) and Goleo (Germany 2006).

BIGGER AND BETTER

The 2010 FIFA World Cup finals will be the fourth since the expansion of the tournament to 32 national teams. For the sake of balance and geography, the teams are seeded into eight first-round groups of four. The top two teams from each group go forward into a pre-ordered knockout system comprising eight second-round ties, four quarter-finals, two semi-finals, then the third-place playoff and the final. If any of these knockout matches are level at 90 minutes, the teams will play extra-time comprising two halves of 15 minutes apiece. If they are still level, then a standard penalty shoot-out will be instituted of five spot-kicks each followed, if necessary, by "sudden death".

NATIONAL PRIDE

South Africa's first representative team was organized to play matches against the touring English club Corinthians in 1897. The first post-Apartheid game was against Cameroon in 1992 and a mere four years later South Africa both hosted and won the African Cup of Nations. They reached the 1998 and 2002 FIFA World Cup finals without progressing beyond the first group stage. The national team is nicknamed "Bafana Bafana" – "The Boys".

LONG AND WINDING ROAD

Some 204 of FIFA's 208 member nations entered the qualifying competition – including South Africa. They compete at the finals automatically as host nation but also contested the qualifiers because this "doubled up" as a qualifying competition for the 2010 African Cup of Nations. The other 31 FIFA World Cup qualifying places were allotted thus: Europe 13, Africa five, South America four or five, Asia four or five, Caribbean Central and North America three or four, Oceania one or none. The variations were due to the system of playoffs at the close of the formal worldwide preliminaries. The FIFA World Cup holders no longer have the right of direct entry to the finals.

CLUB COMMAND

Kaizer Chiefs and Orlando Pirates, both from the Johannesburg township of Soweto, are South Africa's top clubs. Chiefs, founded by Kaizer Motaung in 1970, claim a following of 16 million supporters in southern Africa. The British rock band Kaiser Chiefs (different spelling) adopted the club's name out of admiration for Lucas Radebe, a former Chiefs star who later captained the group's local club, Leeds United. Pirates, founded in 1937, were African club champions in 1995.

THE HOST CITIES

CAPE TOWN
Greenpoint Stadium
Built: new
Capacity: 70,000

DURBAN
Durban Stadium
Built: new
Capacity: 70,000

JOHANNESBURG
Ellis Park Stadium (upgrade)
Built: 1982
Capacity: 61,000

Soccer City Stadium (rebuilt)
Built: 1987
Capacity: 94,700

MANGAUNG/BLOEMFONTEIN
Free State Stadium (upgrade)
Built: 1952
Capacity: 48,000

**NELSON MANDELA BAY/
PORT ELIZABETH**
Port Elizabeth Stadium
Built: new
Capacity: 48,000

NELSPRUIT
Mbombela Stadium
Built: new
Capacity: 46,000

POLOKWANE
Peter Mokaba Stadium
Built: new
Capacity: 46,000

RUSTENBURG
Royal Bafokeng Stadium (upgrade)
Built: 1999
Capacity: 42,000

TSHWANE/PRETORIA
Loftus Versfeld Stadium (upgrade)
Built: 1906
Capacity: 50,000

ROYAL BAFOKENG SPORTS PALACE

EXIT
CAR PARKING
V.I.P. PARKING
COMPETITORS
DISABLED

FIFA
WORLD CUP™ ALL-TIME RECORDS

Brazil are five-times record winners of the FIFA World Cup™ – with Rivaldo, Ronaldo and Gilberto celebrating their most recent triumph at the finals in Japan and Korea in 2002. That was the Brazilians' fifth success in 12 tournaments since their initial triumph – with 17-year-old Pele – in Sweden in 1958.

FIFA WORLD CUP™ QUALIFIERS

FIFA OPENS WORLD CUP TO THE WORLD

FIFA has enlarged the World Cup finals twice since 1978, to take account of the rising football nations of Africa and Asia. The rise in interest is reflected in the massive number of sides entering the qualifying competition – 204 for the 2010 event. Joao Havelange, the Brazilian who was president of FIFA from 1974 to 1998, enlarged the organization both to take advantage of commercial opportunities and to give smaller nations a chance. The number of teams in the finals was first increased from 16 to 24 for the 1982 finals in Spain, with an extra place given for Africa and Asia and a chance for a nation from Oceania to reach the finals. The number of finalists was further increased to 32 for the 1998 tournament in France. This decision offered five places to African teams, four to sides from Asia and Oceania and three from North/Central America and the Caribbean. The formula for the 2010 finals in South Africa offers 13 places to Europe, four to South America, five to Africa, plus the hosts; four for Asia, with another for the winners of an Asia vs. Oceania playoff. CONCACAF (the North and Central American and Caribbean federation) has three spots. The other place will be decided by a playoff between the fifth-placed South American team and the fourth-placed team in the CONCACAF qualifiers.

THE GROWTH OF THE QUALIFYING COMPETITION

This charts the number of countries entering the qualifiers for the FIFA World Cup finals.

World Cup	Teams entering qualifiers
Uruguay 1930	
Italy 1934	32
France 1938	37
Brazil 1950	34
Switzerland 1954	45
Sweden 1958	55
Chile 1962	56
England 1966	74
Mexico 1970	75
West Germany 1974	99
Argentina 1978	107
Spain 1982	109
Mexico 1986	121
Italy 1990	116
USA 1994	147
France 1998	174
Japan/South Korea 2002	199
Germany 2006	198
South Africa 2010	205

MOVING THE FINALS AROUND

After the 1954 and 1958 finals in Europe, FIFA decided that they would be staged alternately in South America and Europe. This lasted until the award of the 1994 tournament to the United States. Things have changed since then. Japan and South Korea were the first Asian hosts in 2002 and in 2010 South Africa will become the first hosts from Africa.

ALL-TIME QUALIFIERS BY REGION

1	Europe	187
2	South America	51
3	Africa	27
4	Asia	25
5	North/Central America and Caribbean	24
6	Oceania	3

T&T AT FULL STRETCH

Trinidad and Tobago hold the record for the longest time needed to qualify for the FIFA World Cup finals. They played 1,800 minutes (20 matches) – to reach the 2006 finals. They began their marathon by beating the Dominican Republic 2-0 away and 4-0 at home in the preliminaries. They then finished second behind Mexico at the first group stage to reach the six-team final group. They finished fourth and had to play off against Bahrain. After a 1-1 home draw, they won 1-0 away, with Dennis Lawrence scoring the winning goal.

SOUTH AMERICANS STAY HOME

Argentina and Brazil both qualified for the 1934 FIFA World Cup without playing a game, because they were the only two South American entrants. Holders Uruguay refused to defend their title in Italy, because they were still angry that only four European nations had played in the 1930 finals in their homeland. Bolivia and Paraguay did not enter. Then Argentina's qualifying opponents, Chile, withdrew – as did Brazil's opponents, Peru.

EGYPT POINT THE WAY

African teams, such as Cameroon, Tunisia, South Africa and Nigeria, make frequent appearances in the modern FIFA World Cup finals, but for many years, Egypt were the only African nation to have played in the finals. They qualified in 1934, by beating Palestine 7-1 at home and 4-1 away. The next African qualifiers were Morocco, who reached the finals in Mexico 36 years later.

DUTCH EAST INDIES GIVEN FREE RIDE

The Dutch East Indies – now Indonesia – were the first Asian side to play in the finals, but they qualified in 1938 without playing a game. Their original opponents, Japan, withdrew because of its war with China. Then the United States pulled out of a final qualifier.

AUSTRIA SNUFFED OUT

Austria had qualified in 1938, but the country was absorbed by Germany in the Anschluss of the same year. So the Austrian team no longer existed and its best players played in the finals for Germany. England were invited to take Austria's place, but declined.

UAE IN A SQUEEZE

The United Arab Emirates reached the finals in 1990 by recording just one win and scoring only four goals in the Asian final round. They drew four of their five matches, but beat China 2-1 to qualify in second place behind South Korea.

THE FIRST SHOOT-OUT

The first penalty shoot-out in qualifying history came on 9 January 1977 when Tunisia beat Morocco 4-2 on spot-kicks after a 1-1 draw in Tunis. The first game, in Casablanca, had also finished 1-1. Tunisia went on to qualify for the finals.

AUSTRALIA'S INCREDIBLE GOAL SPREE

Australia set a FIFA World Cup qualifying record in 2001 that is unlikely to be beaten. They scored 53 goals in the space of two days. The details:

9 April 2001, Sydney: Australia 22, Tonga 0
Australia scorers: Scott Chipperfield 3, 83 mins; Damian Mori 13, 23, 40; John Aloisi 14, 24, 37, 45, 52, 63; Kevin Muscat 18, 30, 54, 58, 82; Tony Popovic 67; Tony Vidmar 74; David Zdrilic 78, 90; Archie Thompson 80; Con Boutsiania 87

11 April 2001, Sydney: Australia 31, American Samoa 0
Australia scorers: Boutsiania 10, 50, 84 mins; Thompson 12, 23, 27, 29, 32, 37, 42, 45, 56, 60, 65, 68, 88; Zdrilic 13, 21, 25, 33, 58, 66, 78, 89; Vidmar 14, 80; Popovic 17, 19; Simon Colosimo 51, 81; Fausto De Amicis 55

RECORD HAT-TRICK

Abdel Hamid Bassiouny of Egypt scored the fastest-ever hat-trick in qualifying history in their 8-2 win over Namibia on 13 July 2001. He netted three times in just 177 seconds between the 39th and 42nd minutes.

DAEI TOPS THE SCORERS

Iran's Ali Daei is the all-time top scorer in FIFA World Cup qualifiers. His nine goals in the 2006 qualifying campaign took his total to 30, nine ahead of the previous joint record holder, Japan's Kazu Miura. Daei also scored seven goals in the 1994 qualifiers, four in the 1998 preliminaries and ten in 2002.

SUPERGA DISASTER FOR ITALY

Italy, who qualified as holders (following their victory in 1938), decided to defend their title in 1950, despite the Superga air disaster of 4 May 1949. The crash killed all 31 passengers, including all of the Torino squad – "Il Grande Torino" – which provided up to ten of Italy's starting line-up. Midfielder Valentino Mazzola, Italy's captain, was killed along with David and Aldo Ballarin, Eusebio Castigliano, Rubens Fadini, Giuseppe Grezar, Ezio Loik, Virgilio Maroso, Danilo Martelli, Pietro Operto, Franco Ossola, Mario Rigamonti and Gyula Schubert.

MUNICH DISASTER HITS ENGLAND

England's 1958 FIFA World Cup hopes were wrecked by the Munich air disaster on 6 February 1958, which devastated champions Manchester United. Three United players – left-back Roger Byrne, left-half Duncan Edwards and centre-forward Tommy Taylor – had been outstanding in England's unbeaten qualification campaign, with each playing in all four matches. Nineteen-year-old Edwards netted twice and Taylor scored eight goals. Byrne and Taylor died in the crash; Edwards died 15 days later.

KOSTADINOV STUNS FRANCE

On 17 November 1993, in the last game of the Group Six schedule, Bulgaria's Emil Kostadinov scored one of the most dramatic goals in qualifying history to deny France a place in the 1994 finals. France seemed to be cruising with the score at 1-1 in stoppage time, but Kostadinov earned Bulgaria a shock victory after David Ginola had lost the ball. The Bulgarians reached the semi-finals of the tournament in the United States, losing 2-1 to Italy.

BAGHERI SHINES IN IRAN ROMP

Iran's Karim Bagheri scored a record seven goals as Iran beat the Maldives a record 17-0 in neutral Damascus on 2 June 1997. Amazingly, those records were beaten by Australia, Archie Thompson and David Zdrilic four years later!

HURTADO THE LEADER

Ecuador defender Ivan Hurtado has made the most appearances in FIFA World Cup qualifiers. He has played 56 games, including 16 in the 2006 preliminaries. He was Ecuador's youngest-ever international when he made his debut at 17 years 285 days.

THE FASTEST SUBSTITUTION

The quickest substitution in the history of the qualifiers came on 30 December 1980, when North Korea's Chon Byong Ju was substituted in the first minute of his country's home game against Japan.

THE FASTEST GOAL

Davide Gualtieri, of minnows San Marino, scored the fastest goal in qualifying history when he netted after just nine seconds against England on 17 November 1993. England went on to win 7-1 but still failed to qualify.

YOUNGEST AND OLDEST

The youngest player to appear in the FIFA World Cup qualifiers is Souleymane Mamam of Togo, who was 13 years 310 days when he played against Zambia on 6 May 2001. The oldest was MacDonald Taylor, who was 46 years, 180 days when he played for the Virgin Islands against St Kitts Nevis on 18 February 2004.

BWALYA LEAVES IT LATE

Zambia's Kalusha Bwalya is the oldest player to have scored a match-winning goal in a FIFA World Cup qualifying match. The 41-year-old netted the only goal against Liberia on 4 September 2004 after coming on as a substitute. He had also scored in his first qualifier, 20 years previously, in Zambia's 3-0 win over Uganda.

PALMER BEATS THE WHISTLE

Carl Erik Palmer's second goal in Sweden's 3-1 win over the Republic of Ireland in November 1949 was one of the most bizarre in qualifying history. The Irish defenders stopped, having heard a whistle, while Palmer ran on and put the ball in the net. The goal stood, because the whistle had come from someone in the crowd, not the referee. The 19-year-old forward went on to complete a hat-trick.

TOMASZEWSKI'S NO JOKE

Poland goalkeeper Jan Tomaszewski was one of the great heroes of the 1974 qualifiers. Tomaszewski was derided as a "clown" by Brian Clough before the decisive qualifier against England at Wembley, but he played the game of his life as Poland defied almost constant pressure to draw 1-1 and reach the finals at the expense of the 1966 champions.

FORWARDS ENJOY RICH PICKINGS

The rapid expansion of the qualifying competition has led to many mismatches in recent years, enabling players to set scoring records against feeble opposition. FIFA has tried to stop such mismatches by organizing preliminary qualifying tournaments for the weaker nations before they meet the stronger teams in their region. That system was further refined for the 2010 qualifiers. Ali Daei of Iran set an all-time qualifying goals record during qualification for the 2006 FIFA World Cup in Germany and Ecuador's Ivan Hurtado topped the list of all-time qualifying appearances.

THOMPSON SETS UNLIKELY MARK

Archie Thompson eased past Bagheri's record for the number of goals in a single qualifying match (seven) as Australia thrashed American Samoa 31-0 on 11 April 2001. He netted 13 goals. David Zdrilic also beat Bagheri's total with eight goals. Australia had previously smashed Iran's scoring record two days earlier with a 22-0 victory over Tonga.

QUALIFIERS GROW AND GROW

Qualifying matches were introduced for the 1934 FIFA World Cup finals. FIFA wanted 16 teams in the finals, but 32 had entered, following the initial tournament in Uruguay in 1930. Preliminary games were arranged to decide the last 16. The first-ever FIFA World Cup qualifier took place in Stockholm on 11 June 1933, when Sweden beat Estonia 6-2. The qualifying competition expanded as more and more teams entered. The numbers were first increased by the countries in Africa and Asia and the swell of newly formed national associations. In the 1990s, after the collapse of the Soviet Union and the former Yugoslavia, many new countries swelled the entrants. Only 13 teams had entered the first finals in 1930; in contrast, 205, including holders Italy, entered the qualifying campign to join hosts South Africa in the 2010 finals!

WALES IN THROUGH THE BACK DOOR

All four British teams have reached the FIFA World Cup finals only once, in 1958. England, Scotland and Northern Ireland all topped their groups, but Wales qualified by a roundabout route. They had been eliminated – then were offered a second chance. Israel had emerged unchallenged, for political reasons, from the Asian qualifying section. However, FIFA ruled that the Israelis could not qualify without playing a match and that they must play off against one of the second-placed European teams. Wales were drawn to meet them and qualified by winning both games 2-0.

UNITED STATES LEAVE IT LATE

The latest of all qualifying playoffs took place in Rome on 24 May 1934, when the USA beat Mexico 4-2 to clinch the last slot in the FIFA World Cup finals. Three days later, the Americans were knocked out 7-1 by hosts Italy in the first round of the tournament.

ITALY FORCED TO QUALIFY

Italy are the only host country who have been required to qualify for their own tournament. The 1934 hosts beat Greece 4-0 to go through. FIFA decided that, for the 1938 finals, the holders and the hosts would qualify automatically. That decision was changed for the 2006 finals. Since then, only the hosts have been exempt from qualifying.

NO INVITE, NO FIFA WORLD CUP™

The first FIFA World Cup, in 1930, staged in Uruguay, was operated on an invitation-only basis. Many countries, particularly those in Europe, declined the invite, due to economic pressures and the fear of losing their best players. Eventually 13 teams – Argentina, Belgium, Bolivia, Brazil, Chile, France, Mexico, Paraguay, Peru, Romania, United States, Uruguay and Yugoslavia – contested the first FIFA World Cup, won by Uruguay. It was a one-off affair: teams have been forced to qualify ever since.

ENGLAND IN, SCOTLAND OUT

England, led by Billy Wright (left), took part in the FIFA World Cup finals for the first time in 1950. They won their all-British group ahead of Scotland. Both teams thus qualified, but the Scots refused to go to the finals in Brazil because they had only finished second. The Scots subsequently qualified eight times, but have never advanced beyond the first round of the finals.

TURKEY THROUGH ON LUCK OF THE DRAW

Turkey were the first team to qualify for the FIFA World Cup finals after the drawing of lots. Their playoff against Spain, in Rome on 17 March 1954, ended 2-2. Qualification was decided by a 14-year-old Roman boy, Luigi Franco Gemma. He was blindfolded to draw the lots – and pulled out Turkey, instead of much-fancied Spain.

MOST SUCCESSFUL QUALIFYING ATTEMPTS

Italy	12
Germany	11
Mexico	11
Spain	11
Argentina	11
Belgium	10
Brazil	10
England	10
Sweden	10
Czech Republic	9
Hungary	9
Yugoslavia/Serbia	9

ITALY HEAD THE QUALIFYING LIST

Italy have the best qualifying record of any nation. They have qualified 12 times – in 1934, 1954, 1962, 1966, 1970, 1974, 1978, 1982, 1994, 1998, 2002 and 2006. They were exempt as holders from qualifying in 1938, 1950 and 1986. They were hosts in 1990. They have only once been eliminated in the qualifiers, when they were knocked out by Northern Ireland in 1958.

THE "FOOTBALL WAR"

War broke out between El Salvador and Honduras after El Salvador beat Honduras 3-2 in a playoff on 26 June 1969 to qualify for the 1970 finals. Tension had been running high between the neighbours over a border dispute and there had been rioting at the match. On 14 July, the Salvador army invaded Honduras.

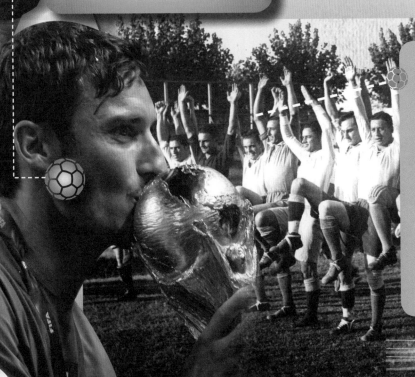

ARGENTINA'S LONG BOYCOTT

Argentina boycotted the FIFA World Cup for nearly 20 years. They were Copa America holders in 1938, but refused to travel to France because they were upset at being passed over to host the finals. They were also unhappy at being paired with Brazil in a qualifier. They did not take part in the 1950 or 1954 competitions either, after Brazil were chosen to host the 1950 finals. Argentina did not return to FIFA World Cup competition until the qualifiers for the 1958 finals.

FIFA WORLD CUP™ TEAM RECORDS

BRAZIL PROFIT FROM RIMET'S VISION

Jules Rimet, president of FIFA from 1921 to 1954, was the driving force behind the first World Cup, in 1930. The tournament in Uruguay was not the high-profile event it is now, with only 13 nations taking part. The long sea journey kept most European teams away. Only four – Belgium, France, Romania and Yugoslavia – made the trip. Regardless, Rimet's dream had been realized and the FIFA World Cup grew and grew in popularity. Brazil have been the most successful team in the competition's history, winning the trophy five times. They have won more games in the FIFA World Cup finals (64) than any other country and share with Germany/West Germany the record for the most number of games played (92). Italy have won the FIFA World Cup four times and West Germany three. The original finalists, Uruguay and Argentina, have both lifted the trophy twice. England, in 1966, and France, in 1998, have been the other winners, both as hosts.

WHY THE BRITISH TEAMS STAYED OUT

England and Scotland are considered the homelands of football, but neither country entered the FIFA World Cup until the qualifiers for the 1950 finals. The four British associations – England, Scotland, Wales and Northern Ireland – quit FIFA in the 1920s over a row over broken-time (employment compensation) payments to amateurs. The British associations did not rejoin FIFA until 1946.

ITALY KEEP IT TIGHT

Italy set the record for the longest run without conceding a goal at the FIFA World Cup finals. They went five games without conceding at the 1990 finals, starting with their 1-0 group win over Austria. Goalkeeper Walter Zenga was not beaten until Claudio Caniggia scored Argentina's equalizer in the semi-final. And a watertight defence did not bring Italy the glory it craved: Argentina reached the final by winning the penalty shoot-out 4-3.

OUT BUT UNBEATEN

Brazil were eliminated on goal difference in the 1978 semi-finals despite a seven-game unbeaten run. Since then, the expansion of the tournament and the arrival of penalty shoot-outs have meant that several more teams have been eliminated without losing a game in 90 and/or 120 minutes. Italy (1990) and France (2006) were knocked out, despite going seven games unbeaten. England (1990) and Holland (1998) went home after six-match unbeaten runs. England (twice), Brazil, Italy, Spain and Argentina have also been eliminated after going five games unbeaten.

BRAZIL COLOUR UP

Brazil's yellow shirts are famous throughout the world. But the national team wore white shirts for each of the first four World Cup tournaments. Brazil's 2-1 defeat by Uruguay, which cost them the 1950 World Cup, came as such a shock to the population that the national association decided to change the team's shirt colours, to try and wipe out the bitter memory.

MOST APPEARANCES IN THE FIFA WORLD CUP™ FINAL

1	Brazil	7
=	Germany/West Germany	7
3	Italy	6
4	Argentina	4
5	Uruguay	2
=	France	2
=	Czechoslovakia	2
=	Holland	2
=	Hungary	2
10	England	1
=	Sweden	1

MOST APPEARANCES IN FIFA WORLD CUP™ FINALS TOURNAMENTS

1	Brazil	18
2	Germany/West Germany	16
=	Italy	16
4	Argentina	14
5	Mexico	12

ONE-TIME WONDERS

Indonesia, then known as the Dutch East Indies, made one appearance in the finals, in the days when the tournament was a strictly knockout affair. On 5 June 1938, they lost 6-0 to Hungary in the first round, and have never qualified for the tournament since.

THE FIRST SHOOT-OUT FINAL

Brazil's 1994 FIFA World Cup victory in Pasadena was the first final to be decided by a penalty shoot-out. The game finished 0-0 after extra-time before Brazil beat Italy 3-2 on penalties, with goals by Romario, Branco and Dunga. Demtrio Albertini and Alberigo Evani scored for Italy, but Daniele Massaro and Roberto Baggio both missed.

BRAZIL'S WINNING STREAK

Brazil hold the record for the most consecutive wins at the World Cup finals. Their 2-1 win over Turkey on 3 June 2002 started an 11-match winning run that lasted until their 1-0 quarter-final defeat by France on 1 July 2006.

SHARING THE GOALS

France in 1982 and winners Italy, in 2006, supplied the most individual goalscorers during a FIFA World Cup finals tournament – ten. Gerard Soler, Bernard Genghini, Michel Platini, Didier Six, Maxime Bossis, Alain Giresse, Dominque Rocheteau, Marius Tresor, Rene Girard and Alain Couriol netted for France. Alessandro Del Piero, Alberto Gilardino, Fabio Grosso, Vincenzo Iaquinta, Luca Toni, Pippo Inzaghi, Marco Materazzi, Andrea Pirlo, Francesco Totti and Gianluca Zambrotta all scored for Italy, who went on to win the tournament.

A FIFA WORLD CUP™ STOPS THE WORLD

The FIFA World Cup finals are the biggest sporting event in history. Television was in its infancy when the first finals were held in Uruguay in 1930. The tournament has since become the most popular TV sporting event of all. The 2006 finals in Germany were watched by a gigantic worldwide audience of 26.3 biillion. That may have been 0.1 billion fewer than the 2002 finals, but the 2006 figures do not include the huge numbers who watched the games on public TV screenings throughout the world.

ENGLAND'S SUCCESS SETS VIEWING RECORD

England's 1966 FIFA World Cup win over West Germany was the most-watched TV programme ever in Britain. According to data released by the British Film Institute, a record 32.3 million people viewed as England won 4-2 in extra-time. The nearest rival to that figure was the 32.1 million who watched the funeral of Princess Diana in 1997.

THE QUICKEST SENDING OFF

The quickest sending off in the FIFA World Cup finals came in 1986 when Uruguay's Jose Batista was sent off after 56 seconds for a lunge at Scotland's Gordon Strachan. The latest expulsion was of Argentina's Leando Cufre, who was dismissed after the final whistle of extra-time in the 2002 quarter-final against Germany.

SPONSORS MAKE THE FINALS PAY

The 2010 FIFA World Cup finals are set to be the most lucrative ever. FIFA reportedly negotiated sponsorship and commercial backing worth around $770 million. Commercial revenue from the 2006 finals in Germany amounted to $600 million. FIFA president Sepp Blatter said: "The contracts signed for 2010 are already about 25 per cent up [on 2006]."

GERMANY'S GOAL BONANZA

West Germany conceded 14 goals in the 1954 finals, the most ever conceded by the FIFA World Cup winners. But they scored 25 – second in FIFA World Cup history only to their final victims, Hungary, who netted 27.

THE FEWEST GOALS CONCEDED

FIFA World Cup winners France (1998) and Italy (2006) hold the record for the fewest goals conceded on their way to victory. Both let in just two. Italy are also joint holders of the record for the fewest goals scored by FIFA World Cup winners. They netted just 11 in 1938, a total matched by England in 1966 and Brazil in 1994.

BRAZIL LEAD THE WAY

Brazil scored the most victories in finals tournaments when they won all their seven games in 2002. They began with a 2-1 group win over Turkey and ended with a 2-0 final triumph over Germany. They scored 18 goals in their unbeaten run and conceded on only four occasions.

MOST CONSECUTIVE MATCHES SCORING A GOAL AT FIFA WORLD CUP™ FINALS

18	Brazil	1930–58
18	Germany	1934–58, 1986–98
17	Hungary	1934–62
16	Uruguay	1930–62
15	Brazil	1978–90
15	France	1978–86

FEWEST GOALS CONCEDED IN ONE TOURNAMENT:

Switzerland: 0, 2006

THE FASTEST GOAL

Holland midfielder Johan Neeskens scored the quickest goal in FIFA World Cup final history. He netted a penalty after 90 seconds of the 1974 match after West Germany's Uli Hoeness tripped John Cruyff, but the Germans went on to win 2-1 with a decisive goal coming from Gerd Muller.

PERFORMANCES BY HOST NATION AT FIFA WORLD CUP™ FINALS

1930	Uruguay	Champions
1934	Italy	Champions
1938	France	Quarter-finals
1950	Brazil	Runners-up
1954	Switzerland	Quarter-finals
1958	Sweden	Runners-up
1962	Chile	Third place
1966	England	Champions
1970	Mexico	Quarter-finals
1974	West Germany	Champions
1978	Argentina	Champions
1982	Spain	Second round
1986	Mexico	Quarter-finals
1990	Italy	Third place
1994	United States	Second round
1998	France	Champions
2002	South Korea	Fourth place
	Japan	Second round
2006	Germany	Third place

MOST GOALS SCORED IN ONE TOURNAMENT
Hungary: 27, 1954

MOST WINS IN ONE TOURNAMENT
Brazil: 7, 2002

MOST GOALS SCORED IN ONE TOURNAMENT
Just Fontaine (France); 13, 1958

FONTAINE AND JAIRZINHO HIT HOT STREAK

France's Just Fontaine and Brazil forward Jairzinho are the only players to score in every match round of a FIFA World Cup finals. Fontaine netted 13 goals in six appearances in 1958 – still a FIFA World Cup record – while Jairzinho scored seven in six matches as Brazil won the trophy in 1970.

FRANCE STRUGGLE

France gave the worst performance of any defending FIFA World Cup holders in 2002. They lost their opening game 1-0 to Senegal, drew 0-0 with Uruguay, and were then eliminated after losing 1-0 to Denmark. They were the first defending champions to be eliminated without scoring a goal.

FIFA WORLD CUP™ GOALSCORING

KEEP ON SCORING

Brazil and Germany/West Germany hold the record for scoring in consecutive games in FIFA World Cup finals matches, with 18. Brazil's run lasted from their 2-1 defeat by Yugoslavia in 1930 until a 0-0 draw with England in the 1958 group stages. The Germans have achieved the feat twice. Their opening 5-2 win over Belgium in 1934 started a sequence that lasted until a 0-0 draw with Italy in the opening group game in 1962. The Germans' second run started with a 1-1 group-stage draw against Uruguay in 1986 and ended with a 3-0 defeat by Croatia in the 1998 quarter-finals.

THE FASTEST GOAL

Turkey's Hakan Sukur holds the record for the quickest goal scored in the FIFA World Cup finals. He netted after 11 seconds against South Korea in the 2002 third-place playoff. Turkey went on to win 3-2. The previous record was held by Vaclav Masek of Czechoslovakia, who struck after 15 seconds against Mexico in 1962.

BIGGEST FIFA WORLD CUP™ FINALS WINS

Hungary 10, El Salvador 1 (15 June 1982)
Hungary 9, South Korea 0 (17 June 1954)
Yugoslavia 9, Zaire 0 (18 June 1974)
Sweden 8, Cuba 0 (12 June 1938)
Uruguay 8, Bolivia 0 (2 July 1950)
Germany 8, Saudi Arabia 0 (1 June 2002)

HIGHEST SCORES

The highest-scoring game in the FIFA World Cup finals was the quarter-final between Austria and Switzerland on 26 June 1954. Austria staged a remarkable comeback to win 7-5, with centre-forward Theodor Wagner scoring a hat-trick, after trailing 3-0 in the 19th minute. Three other games have produced 11 goals – Brazil's 6-5 win over Poland in the 1938 first round, Hungary's 8-3 win over West Germany in their 1954 group game and the Hungarians' 10-1 rout of El Salvador at the group stage in 1982.

YOUNGEST AND OLDEST

Pele (above right) became the youngest-ever scorer in the FIFA World Cup finals – at 17 years and 239 days – when he scored Brazil's winner against Wales in the 1958 quarter-finals. Cameroon's Roger Milla (above left) – 42 years, 39 days – became the oldest scorer when he scored Cameroon's only goal in their 6-1 defeat by Russia in 1994.

MOST GOALS IN ONE FIFA WORLD CUP™

27	Hungary	(1954)
25	West Germany	(1954)
23	France	(1958)
22	Brazil	(1950)
19	Brazil	(1970)

MOST GOALS IN ALL FIFA WORLD CUP™ FINALS (100 PLUS)

1	Brazil	201
2	Germany/W Germany	190
3	Italy	122
4	Argentina	113

A STRIKING TRIO

Three players have scored in every match they have played in a FIFA World Cup finals tournament. Alcides Ghiggia (above), of winners Uruguay, was the first, netting four in four games in 1950. Just Fontaine followed eight years later, scoring 13 times in six matches as France took third place. Brazil forward Jairzinho hit seven in six games as his side won the FIFA World Cup for the third time in 1970.

MOST AND LEAST

The most goals scored in a single FIFA World Cup finals tournament is 171, in France in 1998, after FIFA extended the competition to 32 teams for the first time. The highest number of goals per match was recorded in the 1954 finals, with 140 goals in just 26 games at an average of 5.38 goals per game. The lowest average per game came in Italy in 1990, when 115 goals were scored in 52 matches, an average of 2.21 goals per game.

HARD WORK

Scoring goals in the FIFA World Cup finals has become harder than ever over the years. The great days of high-scoring matches came in the finals of the 1950s, when Brazil, Hungary, West Germany and France all netted more than 20 goals in one tournament. Austria's 7-5 win over Switzerland in 1954 (below) remains a FIFA World Cup match aggregate record, and the average of 5.38 goals scored per match a tournament record. Since then, defences have become ever more organized and harder to break down. Changes in formation have not helped attackers either, with many coaches at the 2006 FIFA World Cup finals in Germany using only one striker. The 2006 winners, Italy, demonstrated the modern trend by scoring only 12 goals in seven matches – and conceding just two.

MOST IN ONE GAME

Russia's forward Igor Salenko (above) holds the record for the most goals scored in one game at the FIFA World Cup finals – five, in his country's 6-1 win over Cameroon on 28 June 1994. Salenko finished as joint top scorer in the tournament with six goals.

FONTAINE'S LUCKY BREAK

Just Fontaine is the record top scorer in a single FIFA World Cup finals tournament, with 13 goals in 1958. But Fontaine never expected to play. He was only called up because of Rene Bliard's ankle injury and was so surprised that he borrowed Reims colleague Stephane Bruey's boots for the tournament. He netted three times against Paraguay, two more against Yugoslavia, one against Scotland, two against Northern Ireland, one in the semi-final against Brazil and four in France's 6-3 win over West Germany in the third-place match.

NO GUARANTEES FOR TOP SCORERS

Topping the FIFA World Cup finals scoring chart is a great honour for all strikers, but few have achieved the ultimate prize and helped their teams lift the trophy. Argentina's Guillermo Stabile started the luckless trend in 1930. He led the scoring charts but ended up finishing on the losing side in the final. The list of top scorers who have played in the winning side is small: Garrincha and Vava (joint top scorers in 1962), Mario Kempes (top scorer in 1978), Paolo Rossi (1982) and Ronaldo (2002). Gerd Muller, top scorer in 1970, gained his reward as West Germany's trophy winner four years later. Other top scorers, such as Just Fontaine, Sandor Kocsis and Gary Lineker, have been disappointed in the final stages. Kocsis was the only one to appear in a final – and that ended in Hungary's defeat in 1954.

ROSSI THE ITALY HERO

Paolo Rossi turned from villain to hero as Italy won the 1982 FIFA World Cup. Coach Enzo Bearzot had picked Rossi even though he had only just completed a two-year suspension after a match-fixing scandal. Rossi was criticized for a lack of fitness in the early matches, but he scored a hat-trick against Brazil, two goals as Italy beat Poland in the semi-final, and the opener in their FIFA World Cup final victory over West Germany.

HURST MAKES HISTORY

England's Geoff Hurst became the first and to date only player to score a hat-trick in a FIFA World Cup final when he netted three in the hosts' 4-2 victory over West Germany in 1966. Hurst headed England level after the Germans took an early lead, then scored the decisive third goal with a shot that bounced down off the crossbar and just over the line, according to the Soviet linesman. Hurst hit his third in the last minute. The British TV commentator Kenneth Wolstenholme described Hurst's strike famously with the words: "Some people are on the pitch. They think it's all over. It is now!"

GOLDEN, SILVER AND BRONZE

The top scorer at the FIFA World Cup is traditionally rewarded with the Golden Shoe. FIFA initiated two more scoring awards at the 2006 finals – a Silver Shoe and a Bronze Shoe for the second and third highest scorers. Argentina's Hernan Crespo finished second, behind Germany's Miroslav Klose. Brazil striker Ronaldo took bronze.

FIFA WORLD CUP™ FINALS TOP SCORERS (1930–78)

Maximum 16 teams in finals

Year	Venue	Top scorer/country	Goals
1930	Uruguay	**Guillermo Stabile** (Argentina)	8
1934	Italy	**Oldrich Nejedly** (Czechoslovakia)	5
1938	France	**Leonidas** (Brazil)	7
1950	Brazil	**Ademir** (Brazil)	9
1954	Switzerland	**Sandor Kocsis** (Hungary)	11
1958	Sweden	**Just Fontaine** (France)	13
1962	Chile	**Garrincha** (Brazil)	4
		Vava (Brazil)	
		Leonel Sanchez (Chile)	
		Florian Albert (Hungary)	
		Valentin Ivanov (Soviet Union)	
		Drazen Jerkovic (Yugoslavia)	
1966	England	**Eusebio** (Portugal)	9
1970	Mexico	**Gerd Muller** (West Germany)	10
1974	West Germany	**Grzegorz Lato** (Poland)	7
1978	Argentina	**Mario Kempes** (Argentina)	6

LINEKER LEADS ENGLAND'S LIST

Gary Lineker is England's leading FIFA World Cup scorer, and second only to FIFA World Cup winner Bobby Charlton in England's list of all-time marksmen. He netted 48 goals in 80 appearances. The high point of his FIFA World Cup career came in the 1990 semi-final, when he struck England's equalizer against West Germany. He retired from international football after the 1992 European Championships finals.

KOCSIS HEADS THEM ALL

Hungary's Sandor Kocsis was one of the finest headers of the ball who ever played. He was known as the "man with the golden head". He scored 11 goals in the 1954 FIFA World Cup finals, including three against South Korea and four in Hungary's 8-3 group win over West Germany.

KEMPES MAKES HIS MARK

Mario Kempes was Argentina's only foreign-based player in the hosts' squad at the 1978 finals. Twice top scorer in the Spanish league, Valencia's Kempes was crucial to Argentina's success. Coach Luis Cesar Menotti told him to shave off his moustache after he failed to score in the group games. Kempes then netted two against Peru, two more against Poland, and two decisive goals in the final against Holland.

STABILE MAKES AN IMPACT

Guillermo Stabile, top scorer in the 1930 FIFA World Cup finals, had never played for Argentina before the tournament. He made his debut – as a 25-year-old – against Mexico because first-choice Roberto Cherro had suffered a panic attack. He netted a hat-trick then scored twice against both Chile and the United States as Argentina reached the final. He struck one of his side's goals in the 4-2 defeat by Uruguay in the final.

EUSEBIO THE STRIKE FORCE

Portugal's Eusebio was the striking star of the 1966 FIFA World Cup finals. Ironically, he would not be eligible to play for Portugal now. He was born in Mozambique, then a Portuguese colony, but now an independent country. He finished top scorer with nine goals, including two as Portugal eliminated champions Brazil and four as they beat North Korea 5-3 in the semi-finals after trailing 3-0.

RONALDO SO CONSISTENT

Ronaldo has been a consistent scorer in each of the three FIFA World Cup finals tournaments he has played in. He netted four times in 1998, eight as Brazil won the tournament in 2002, and three more in 2006. He became the all-time top scorer when he netted Brazil's opener in a 3-0 win over Ghana in the last-16 round at Dortmund on 27 June 2006. As a teenager, Ronaldo had been a member of Brazil's winning squad in the United States in 1994, but did not play.

MULLER'S SCORING HABIT

West Germany's Gerd Muller had the knack of scoring in important games. He struck the winner against England in the 1970 quarter-final and his two goals in extra-time against Italy almost carried his side to the final. Four years later, Muller's goal against Poland ensured that West Germany reached the final on home soil. Then he scored the winning goal against Holland in the FIFA World Cup final. He also had a goal disallowed for offside – wrongly, as TV replays proved.

FIFA WORLD CUP™ FINALS ALL-TIME TOP-TEN SCORERS

	Name/country	Tournaments	Total Goals
1	Ronaldo (Brazil)	1998, 2002, 2006	15
2	Gerd Muller (W Germany)	1970, 1974	14
3	Just Fontaine (France)	1958	13
4	Pele (Brazil)	1958, 1962, 1966, 1970	12
5	Sandor Kocsis (Hungary)	1954	11
	Jurgen Klinsmann (W Germany/Germany)	1990, 1994	11
7	Gabriel Batistuta (Argentina)	1994, 1998, 2002	10
	Teofilo Cubillas (Peru)	1970, 1978	10
	Miroslav Klose (Germany	2002, 2006	10
	Gregorz Lato (Poland)	1974, 1978	10
	Gary Lineker (England)	1986, 1990	10
	Helmut Rahn (W Germany)	1954, 1958	10

Jurgen Klinsmann has been an influential force at the FIFA World Cup both as a player and a coach. He scored three goals when West Germany won the FIFA World Cup in 1990, five more – for a unified Germany – in the 1994 finals, and three in 1998. He then coached Germany to the semi-finals in 2006.

WHO SCORED THE FIRST HAT-TRICK?

For many years, Argentina's Guillermo Stabile was considered the first hat-trick scorer in the FIFA World Cup finals. He netted three in Argentina's 6-3 win over Mexico on 19 July 1930, but has since been superseded by Bert Patenaude of the United States. FIFA changed its records in November 2006, to acknowledge that Patenaude's treble two days earlier, in the Americans' 3-0 win over Paraguay, had been the tournament's first hat-trick.

PELE SO UNLUCKY

Pele would surely have been the all-time FIFA World Cup top scorer but for injuries. He was sidelined early in the 1962 finals, and again four years later. He scored six goals in Brazil's 1958 triumph, including two in the 5-2 final victory over Sweden. He also netted Brazil's 100th FIFA World Cup goal as they beat Italy 4-1 in the 1970 final.

RAHN MAKES AN IMPACT

Helmut Rahn was West Germany's top FIFA World Cup scorer until the arrival of Gerd Muller. He hit the winner in the 1954 final with a trademark goal, drifting in from the right to strike with a left-foot shot. He had started the tournament as a reserve and did not establish his starting place until the quarter-finals, when his goal settled the game against Yugoslavia.

LEONIDAS RIDES HIS LUCK

Controversy surrounded Leonidas's claim to be top scorer in the 1938 FIFA World Cup finals. FIFA initially credited the Brazil forward with eight goals, but he was later deducted a goal, from the quarter-final against Czechoslovakia. However, his four against Poland in the first round ensured he finished as the tournament's leading scorer, with seven.

FIFA WORLD CUP™ APPEARANCES

Two players, Mexico's Antonio Carbajal and Germany's Lothar Matthaus, have appeared in a record five FIFA World Cup™ final tournaments, but for many players, appearing just once in football's ultimate event is cause enough for dreams. The following pages chart individual appearance records at football's premier competition, from the longest to the shortest, to the greatest time elapsed between FIFA World Cup™ appearances.

BRANDTS SCORED FOR BOTH SIDES

Holland defender Ernie Brandts is the only player to have scored for both sides in a FIFA World Cup finals match. Brandts's 18th-minute own goal gave Italy the lead in their decisive second group-stage game in 1978, but he then started Holland's revival with a 50th-minute equalizer before Arie Haan scored the winner to take the Dutch to the final.

PROSINECKI'S SCORING RECORD

Robert Prosinecki is the only player to have scored for different countries in FIFA World Cup finals tournaments. He netted for Yugoslavia in their 4-1 win over the United Arab Emirates in the 1990 tournament. Eight years later, following the break-up of the old Yugoslavia, he scored for Croatia in their 3-0 group-game win over Jamaica, and then netted the first goal in his side's 2-1 third-place playoff victory over Holland.

MONTI AND THE "ORIUNDI"

Luisito Monti is the only man to have played in two FIFA World Cup final matches for different countries. He was on the losing side for Argentina in 1930, then gained a winner's medal for Italy in 1934. Monti was one of the "oriundi" – Argentines of Italian descent. The Italian government awarded him dual citizenship when he moved to Italy with Juventus, so he could play for the national team.

YOUNGEST AND OLDEST

Northern Ireland forward Norman Whiteside became the then youngest player to appear in the FIFA World Cup finals when he started against Yugoslavia in 1982, aged just 17 years and 41 days. The oldest player to feature in the tournament was Cameroon forward Roger Milla, who faced Russia in 1994 aged 42 years and 39 days.

BICKEL'S LONG WAIT

Switzerland's Alfred "Fredy" Bickel endured the longest wait between FIFA World Cup appearances – 12 years and 13 days. He was on the losing side against Hungary in the 1938 quarter-finals before World War Two forced the abandonment of subsequent FIFA World Cups. Bickel had to wait until 25 June 1950 before he made his next appearance, in Switzerland's 3-0 defeat by Yugoslavia.

QUICKEST SUBSTITUTIONS

The three fastest substitutions in the history of the FIFA World Cup finals have all come in the fourth minute. In each case the player substituted was so seriously injured that he took no further part in the tournament: Steve Hodge came on for Bryan Robson in England's 0-0 draw with Morocco in 1986; Giuseppe Bergomi replaced Alessandro Nesta in Italy's 2-1 win over Austria in 1998; and Peter Crouch subbed for Michael Owen in England's 2-2 draw with Sweden in 2006.

MOST APPEARANCES IN FIFA WORLD CUP™ FINALS

25 Lothar Matthaus (West Germany/ Germany)
23 Paolo Maldini (Italy)
21 Diego Maradona (Argentina)
 Uwe Seeler (West Germany)
 Wladyslaw Zmuda (Poland)

MOST FIFA WORLD CUP™ FINALS TOURNAMENTS

These players all played in at least four FIFA World Cup finals tournaments.

5 **Antonio Carbajal** (Mexico) 1950, 1954, 1958, 1962, 1966;
 Lothar Matthaus (West Germany/Germany) 1982, 1986, 1990, 1994, 1998

4 **Djalma Santos** (Brazil) 1954, 1958, 1962, 1966;
 Pele (Brazil) 1958, 1962, 1966, 1970;
 Uwe Seeler (West Germany) 1958, 1962, 1966, 1970;
 Karl-Heinz Schnellinger (West Germany) 1958, 1962, 1966, 1970;
 Gianni Rivera (Italy) 1962, 1966, 1970, 1974;
 Pedro Rocha (Uruguay) 1962, 1966, 1970, 1974;
 Wladyslaw Zmuda (Poland) 1974, 1978, 1982, 1986;
 Giuseppe Bergomi (Italy) 1982, 1986, 1990, 1998;
 Diego Maradona (Argentina) 1982, 1986, 1990, 1994;
 Enzo Scifo (Belgium) 1986, 1990, 1994, 1998;
 Franky van der Elst (Belgium) 1986, 1990, 1994, 1998;
 Andoni Zubizarreta (Spain) 1986, 1990, 1994, 1998;
 Paolo Maldini (Italy) 1990, 1994, 1998, 2002;
 Hong Myung-Bo (South Korea) 1990, 1994, 1998, 2002;
 Cafu (Brazil) 1994, 1998, 2002, 2006;
 Sami Al-Jaber (Saudi Arabia) 1994, 1998, 2002, 2006.

THE "DOUBLE" CHAMPIONS

Franz Beckenbauer and Mario Zagallo comprise a unique duo. They have both won the FIFA World Cup as a player and a coach. Attacking sweeper Beckenbauer also had the distinction of captaining West Germany to victory on home soil in 1974. As coach, he steered them to the final in Mexico in 1986 and to victory over Argentina in Italy four years later. He was nicknamed "Der Kaiser" (The Emperor) both for his style and his achievements. Zagallo gained two winners' medals as a player. He was the left winger in Brazil's triumphant march to the 1958 championship, before playing a deeper role in their 1962 victory. He took over from the controversial Joao Saldanha as Brazil coach three months before the 1970 finals and guided the side to victory in all six of its games, scoring 19 goals and routing Italy 4-1 in the final. Zagallo later filled the role of technical director when Brazil won the FIFA World Cup for a fourth time in 1994. His nickname is "The Professor".

MOST FIFA WORLD CUP™ FINALS MATCHES (BY POSITION)

Goalkeeper: Claudio Taffarel (Brazil, 18 matches).
Defence: Cafu (Brazil, 20); Wladyslaw Zmuda (Poland, 21); Franz Beckenbauer (Germany, 18); Paolo Maldini (Italy, 23).
Midfielders: Grzegorz Lato (Poland, 20); Lothar Matthaus (Germany, 25); Wolfgang Overath (Germany, 19); Pierre Littbarski (Germany, 18).
Forwards: Diego Maradona (Argentina, 21); Uwe Seeler (Germany, 21).

DOUBLE WINNERS

Players who have played on the winning side in two FIFA World Cup finals:

Giovanni Ferrari (Italy), 1934, 1938
Giuseppe Meazza (Italy), 1934, 1938
Pele (Brazil), 1958, 1970
Didi (Brazil), 1958, 1962
Djalma Santos (Brazil), 1958, 1962
Garrincha (Brazil), 1958, 1962
Gilmar (Brazil), 1958, 1962
Nilton Santos (Brazil), 1958, 1962
Vava (Brazil), 1958, 1962
Zagallo (Brazil), 1958, 1962
Zito (Brazil), 1958, 1962
Cafu (Brazil), 1994, 2002

CAFU'S TREBLE CHANCE

Brazil right-back Cafu holds the record for appearing in most FIFA World Cup finals – three. He was a 21st-minute substitute for Jorginho when Brazil beat Italy on penalties in 1994; he played the whole game when they lost 3-0 to France in 1998; and he then captained Brazil to their 2-0 win over Germany in 2002. Cafu holds another record, too. He has collected more yellow cards – six – than any other player in the history of the finals tournament.

CAFU ENJOYS MOST WINS

Brazil right-back Cafu has been on the winning side more times than any other player in the FIFA World Cup finals. He first appeared as a 69th-minute substitute against the United States in 1994. In his 20 matches, Brazil won 16 – including the 2002 final – drew one (the 1994 final, which they won on a penalty shoot-out) and lost three. The three defeats came against Norway, 2-1 in a 1998 group game; France, 3-0 in the 1998 final; and France again, 1-0 in the 2006 quarter-finals.

PUZACH THE FIRST SUB

The first substitute in FIFA World Cup finals history was Anatoli Puzach of the Soviet Union. He replaced Viktor Serebrianikov at half-time of the Soviets' 0-0 draw with hosts Mexico on 31 May 1970. The 1970 tournament was the first in which substitutes were allowed, with two permitted for each side. FIFA increased this to three per team for the 1998 finals.

LEADING CAPTAINS

Three players have each captained their teams in two FIFA World Cup finals – Diego Maradona of Argentina, Dunga of Brazil and West Germany's Karl-Heinz Rummenigge. Maradona lifted the trophy in 1986, but was a loser four years later. Dunga was the winning skipper in 1994, but was on the losing side in 1998. Rummenigge was a loser on both occasions, in 1982 and 1986. Maradona has made the most appearances as captain at the FIFA World Cup finals, leading out Argentina 16 times between 1986 and 1994.

FIRSTS FOR EARLY DISMISSALS

Red and yellow cards – for sendings-off and cautions – were introduced at the 1970 finals. The first player to receive a red card was Chile's Carlos Caszely, against hosts West Germany in 1974. The first goalkeeper to be sent off was Italy's Gianluca Pagliuca, for handling outside his area against Norway in 1994. The first player ever to be sent off in the FIFA World Cup finals was Peru captain Mario de los Casas against Romania in 1930.

FASTEST RED CARDS IN THE FIFA WORLD CUP™ FINALS

1 min	Jose Batista (Uruguay) vs. Scotland, 1986
3 min	Marco Etcheverry (Bolivia) vs. Germany, 1994
	Ion Vladoiu (Romania) vs. Switzerland, 1994
	Morten Wieghorst (Denmark) vs. South Africa, 1998
6 min	Lauren (Cameroon) vs. Chile, 1998
8 min	Giorgio Ferrini (Italy) vs. Chile, 1962
	Miklos Molnar (Denmark) vs. South Africa, 1998

FASTEST YELLOW CARDS

1 min	Sergei Gorlukovich (Russia) vs. Sweden, 1994
	Giampiero Marini (Italy) vs. Poland, 1982
2 min	Jesus Arellano (Mexico) vs. Italy, 2002
	Henri Camara (Senegal) vs. Uruguay, 2002
	Michael Emenalo (Nigeria) vs. Italy, 1994

SIMUNIC'S THREE-CARD MATCH

Croatia's Josip Simunic holds the record for collecting the most yellow cards in one match at the FIFA World Cup finals – three against Australia in 2006. He received three yellows before he was finally sent off after a blunder by English referee Graham Poll. When Poll showed Simunic his second yellow, he clearly forgot he had already booked him.

THE LONGEST SUSPENSIONS

The longest ban imposed in FIFA World Cup finals history was the 15-month suspension of Argentina's Diego Maradona. He had tested positive for the banned drug ephedrine after Argentina's 2-1 group-game win over Nigeria in 1994. The longest suspension for on-field misconduct was the eight-match ban handed to Italy's Mauro Tassotti, also in 1994, after his elbow smashed Spain midfielder Luis Enrique's nose in the quarter-finals.

MALDINI'S MINUTES RECORD

Lothar Matthaus of West Germany/Germany has started the most FIFA World Cup finals matches – 25. But Italy defender Paolo Maldini has stayed on the field for longer, despite starting two games fewer. Maldini played for 2,220 minutes, Matthaus for 2,052. According to the stopwatch, the top four are completed by Uwe Seeler of West Germany, who played for 1,980 minutes, and Argentina's Diego Maradona, who played for 1,938.

YOUNGEST PLAYERS IN FIFA WORLD CUP™ FINAL

Pele (Brazil) – 17 years, 249 days, in 1958
Giuseppe Bergomi (Italy) – 18 years, 201 days, in 1982
Ruben Moran (Uruguay) – 19 years, 344 days, in 1950

OLDEST PLAYERS IN FIFA WORLD CUP™ FINAL

Dino Zoff (Italy) – 40 years, 133 days, in 1982
Gunnar Gren (Sweden) – 37 years, 241 days, in 1958
Jan Jongbloed (Holland) – 37 years, 212 days, in 1974
Nilton Santos (Brazil) – 37 years, 32 days, in 1962

FOUR AND OUT

The most players sent off in one FIFA World Cup finals game is four. Costinha and Deco of Portugal and Khalid Boulahrouz and Gio van Bronckhorst of Holland were sent off by Russian referee Valentin Ivanov in their second-round match in Germany in 2006.

ARGENTINA'S DISCIPLINE RECORD

Argentina lead the list of players sent off in the FIFA World Cup finals. They have had ten players dismissed, including two – Pedro Monzon and Gustavo Dezotti – in the 1990 final.

CANIGGIA – SENT OFF, WHILE ON THE BENCH...

Claudio Caniggia of Argentina became the first player to be sent off from the substitutes' bench, during the match against Sweden in 2002. Caniggia was dismissed in first-half stoppage time for dissent towards UAE referee Ali Bujsaim. Caniggia carried on protesting after the referee warned him to keep quiet, so Bujsaim showed him a red card.

SHOOT-OUT SAVIOURS

West Germany's Harald "Toni" Schumacher and Sergio Goycochea of Argentina hold the record for the most penalty shoot-out saves in the finals – four each. Schumacher's saves came over two tournaments – in 1982 and 1986, including the decisive stop in the 1982 semi-final against France. Goycochea made his crucial saves in 1990, first in Argentina's quarter-final win over Yugoslavia and then against Italy to take his team to the final. His four shoot-out saves in one tournament is also a record. The record for the most shoot-out saves in one game is held by Portugal goalkeeper Ricardo. He saved three times to knock out England in the quarter-finals of the 2006 FIFA World Cup.

BALLACK'S BITTER-SWEET SEMI-FINAL

Germany star Michael Ballack will never forget the 2002 FIFA World Cup semi-final against co-hosts South Korea in Seoul. The midfielder was yellow-carded by referee Urs Meier in the 71st minute for bringing down Lee Cun-Soo. Four minutes later, Ballack drove home a rebound to win the game for Germany, even though the yellow card he had received moments before meant he was suspended for the final.

DENILSON STEPS UP FROM THE BENCH

Brazil winger Denilson has made the most substitute appearances at the FIFA World Cup finals – 11. He was involved in 12 of Brazil's games at the 1998 and 2002 finals, but started only one, against Norway in 1998. He was a half-time substitute for Leonardo in the 1998 final and came on for Ronaldo in stoppage time of the 2002 final (his last appearance in the finals), when Brazil beat Germany 2-0.

UNBEATEN GOALKEEPERS IN THE FIFA WORLD CUP™ FINALS

Walter Zenga (Italy)	517 minutes without conceding a goal, 1990
Peter Shilton (England)	502 minutes, 1986–90
Sepp Maier (W Germany)	475 minutes, 1974–78
Gianluigi Buffon (Italy)	460 minutes, 2006
Emerson Leao (Brazil)	458 minutes, 1978
Gordon Banks (England)	442 minutes, 1966

FIFA WORLD CUP™ GOALKEEPING

NUMBER ONE NUMBER ONES

The Lev Yashin Award was introduced in 1994 for the man voted best goalkeeper of the FIFA World Cup – though a goalkeeper has been picked for an all-star team at the end of every tournament dating back to 1930. The all-star team was expanded from 11 to 23 players in 1998, allowing room for more than one goalkeeper. Players who have been picked for the all-star teams but who have missed out on the Lev Yashin Award were Paraguay's Jose Luis Chilavert in 1998, Turkey's Rutu Recber in 2002, and Germany's Jens Lehmann and Portugal's Ricardo in 2006. The first Lev Yashin Award was presented to Belgium's Michel Preud'homme, even though he only played four games, conceding four goals, at the 1994 competition – his side were edged out 3-2 by Germany in the second round. Legendary Soviet goalkeeper Lev Yashin, after whom the trophy is named, played in the 1958, 1962 and 1966 FIFA World Cups and was a member of his country's 1970 squad as third-choice keeper and assistant coach – although he was never chosen for a FIFA World Cup team of the tournament. Yashin conceded the only FIFA World Cup finals goal scored directly from a corner-kick, taken by Colombia's Marcos Coll during a 4-4 draw in 1962.

BROTHERS IN ARMS

Brothers Viktor and Vyacheslav Chanov were two of the three goalkeepers in the Soviet Union's 1982 FIFA World Cup squad, but first-choice Rinat Dasayev was preferred to them both throughout. Viktor, eight years younger than Vyacheslav, did make one appearance at the 1986 FIFA World Cup four years later and ended his career with 21 caps. Vyacheslav had to wait until 1984 for his first and only international appearance.

OLIVER'S ARMS

Germany's Oliver Kahn is the only goalkeeper to have been voted FIFA's Player of the Tournament, winning the award at the 2002 FIFA World Cup – despite taking a share of the blame for Brazil's winning goals in the final.

PLAYERS VOTED BEST GOALKEEPER OF THE TOURNAMENT

1930	Enrique Ballestreros (Uruguay)
1934	Ricardo Zamora (Spain)
1938	Frantiek Planika (Czechoslovakia)
1950	Roque Maspoli (Uruguay)
1954	Gyula Grosics (Hungary)
1958	Harry Gregg (Northern Ireland)
1962	Viliam Schrojf (Czechoslovakia)
1966	Gordon Banks (England)
1970	Ladislao Mazurkiewicz (Uruguay)
1974	Jan Tomaszewski (Poland)
1978	Ubaldo Fillol (Argentina)
1982	Dino Zoff (Italy)
1986	Harald Schumacher (West Germany)
1990	Sergio Goycoechea (Argentina)
1994	Michel Preud'homme (Belgium)
1998	Fabien Barthez (France)
2002	Oliver Kahn (Germany)
2006	Gianluigi Buffon (Italy)

DEFENSIVE WALTER

Italy's Walter Zenga holds the FIFA World Cup record for the most consecutive minutes without conceding a goal. He managed 518 minutes at the 1990 tournament in his home country. Argentina's Claudio Caniggia finally put the ball past him in the semi-final. Zenga's five successive clean sheets at the tournament is also a FIFA World Cup record. Fellow Italian Gianluigi Buffon conceded only two on the way to winning the tournament in 2006 – an own goal by team-mate Cristian Zaccardo and a penalty by France's Zinedine Zidane.

FIVE-STAR CARBAJAL

Antonio Carbajal, of Mexico, is one of only two men to have appeared at five FIFA World Cup finals – the other was Germany's versatile Lothar Matthaus. Carbajal, who played in 1950, 1954, 1958, 1962 and 1966, conceded a record 25 goals in his 11 FIFA World Cup finals appearances – the same number let in by Saudi Arabia's Mohamed Al-Deayea across ten games in 1994, 1998 and 2002. Al-Deayea was a member of the Saudi squad for the 2006 tournament but did not play.

ITALY'S ELDER STATESMAN

Dino Zoff became both the oldest player and oldest captain to win the FIFA World Cup when his Italian side lifted the trophy in Spain in 1982. He was 40 years and 133 days old at the time. Alongside him in the team was defender Giuseppe Bergomi, aged 18 years and 201 days, a difference of 21 years and 297 days.

RIGHT WAY FOR RICARDO

Spain's Ricardo Zamora became the first man to save a penalty in a FIFA World Cup finals match, stopping Valdemar de Brito's spot-kick for Brazil in 1934. Spain went on to win 3-1.

UNLUCKY BREAK

Goalkeeper Frantiek Planika broke his arm during Czechoslovakia's 1938 second-round clash against Brazil, but played on, even though the game went to extra-time before ending in a 1-1 draw. Not surprisingly, given the extent of his injury, Planika missed the replay two days later, which the Czechs lost 2-1, and never added to his tally of 73 caps.

NOT SO SWEET 16

No goalkeeper had conceded more goals in one FIFA World Cup than the 16 put past South Korea's Hong Duk-Yung in Switzerland in 1954. They all came in just two games, a 9-0 trouncing by eventual finalists Hungary and a 7-0 defeat to Turkey.

BATTERING RAMON

Argentina's 6-0 win over Peru at the 1978 FIFA World Cup aroused suspicion because the hosts needed to win by four goals to reach the final at the expense of arch-rivals Brazil – and Peruvian goalkeeper Ramon Quiroga had been born in Argentina. He insisted, though, that his saves prevented the defeat from being even more embarrassingly emphatic. Earlier in the same tournament, Quiroga had been booked for a foul on Grzegorz Lato after running into the Polish half of the field.

MORE AND MORA

Luis Ricardo Guevara Mora holds the unenviable record for most goals conceded in just one FIFA World Cup finals match. The 20-year-old had to pick the ball out of the net ten times in El Salvador's thrashing by Hungary in 1982 – and his team-mates managed only one goal of their own in reply. In this game he also set the record for being the youngest goalkeeper to participate in the FIFA World Cup finals.

PLAYING THROUGH THE PAIN BARRIER

The first FIFA World Cup clean sheet was kept by Jimmy Douglas of the United States in a 3-0 win over Belgium in 1930. He followed that up with another, as Paraguay were beaten by the same scoreline – but Argentina proved too good, winning 6-1 in the semi-final. Douglas injured his knee after only four minutes, but had to play on as this occurred in the days before substitutes were allowed.

THREE'S COMPANY

Both Czechoslovakia and Belgium used all three of their goalkeepers at the 1982 FIFA World Cup in Spain – Zdenek Hruska, Stanislav Seman and Karel Stromsik for the Czechs, and Jean-Marie Pfaff, Theo Custers and Jacques Munaron for the Belgians.

THE PETER PRINCIPLE

Peter Shilton became the oldest FIFA World Cup captain when he led England for their 1990 third-place playoff against hosts Italy. He was 40 years and 292 days old as he made his 125th and final appearance for his country – though his day was spoiled by a 2-1 defeat, including a goalkeeping error that gifted Roberto Baggio Italy's opener. Shilton, born in Leicester on 18 September 1949, also played for England at the 1982 and 1986 tournaments. He became captain in Mexico in 1986 after Bryan Robson was ruled out of the tournament by injury and Ray Wilkins by suspension, and featured in one of the FIFA World Cup's all-time memorable moments, when he was out-jumped by Argentina's Diego Maradona for the infamous "Hand of God" goal. Shilton jointly holds the record for most FIFA World Cup clean sheets, with ten – along with France's Fabien Barthez, who played at the 1998, 2002 and 2006 tournaments. Both men made 17 FIFA World Cup finals appearances apiece.

SWEDISH STALEMATE

Brazil, amazingly, were involved in the first FIFA World Cup finals match to end in a 0-0 stalemate – against England, at the seventh tournament, in Sweden in 1958. Gilmar was in goal for Brazil while Colin McDonald was at the other end of the Gothenburg pitch for England. Gilmar is the only goalkeeper to have played on the winning side in a World Cup final twice.

TONY AWARD

US goalkeeper Tony Meola quit the national team after the 1994 FIFA World Cup because he wanted to switch sports and take up American football instead. He failed to make it in gridiron and returned to soccer, but did not play for his country again until 1999. He retired for a second time after reaching a century of international appearances and still holds the record for being the youngest FIFA World Cup captain, having worn the armband for a 5-1 defeat to Czechoslovakia in 1990, aged 21 years 316 days.

TRADING PLACES

The first goalkeeper to be substituted at a FIFA World Cup was Romania's Stere Adamache, who was replaced by Ric Rducanu 27 minutes into a 3-2 defeat to Brazil in 1970. Romania were 2-0 down at the time.

NOT THINKING OUTSIDE THE BOX

Italy's Gianluca Pagliuca became the first goalkeeper to be sent off at a FIFA World Cup when he was dismissed for handball outside his area after just 21 minutes of his country's group match against Norway in 1994. Coach Arrigo Sacchi responded surprisingly by replacing star player Roberto Baggio with substitute keeper Luca Marchegiani – to the obvious disgust of Baggio.

TOP GOALS

Year	Goals
1930	70 (3.89 per match)
1934	70 (4.12 per match)
1938	84 (4.67 per match)
1950	88 (4 per match)
1954	140 (5.38 per match)
1958	126 (3.6 per match)
1962	89 (2.78 per match)
1966	89 (2.78 per match)
1970	95 (2.97 per match)
1974	97 (2.55 per match)
1978	102 (2.68 per match)
1982	146 (2.81 per match)
1986	132 (2.54 per match)
1990	115 (2.21 per match)
1994	141 (2.71 per match)
1998	171 (2.67 per match)
2002	161 (2.52 per match)
2006	147 (2.3 per match)

SWISS MISS

Switzerland were eliminated from the 2006 FIFA World Cup despite their goalkeeper Pascal Zuberbuhler keeping a clean sheet in all four of their matches – three in the group stage and a goalless draw with Ukraine in the second round. But the Swiss lost the resulting penalty shoot-out 3-0, despite Zuberbuhler saving Ukraine's first kick by Andriy Shevchenko. Before 2006, Switzerland had failed to keep a single clean sheet in 22 FIFA World Cup finals matches.

SPOT ON

Excluding shoot-outs, only two goalkeepers have saved two penalties apiece at a single FIFA World Cup finals – Poland's Jan Tomaszewski, from Sweden's Staffan Tapper and West Germany's Uli Hoeness in 1974, and Brad Friedel of the US, who denied South Korea's Lee Eul-Yong and Poland's Maciej Zurawski in 2002.

FIFA WORLD CUP™ MANAGERS

PUFF DADDIES

The coaches of the two sides appearing at the 1978 FIFA World Cup final were such prolific smokers that an oversized ashtray was produced for Argentina's Cesar Luis Menotti and Holland's Ernst Happel so they could share it on the touchline.

YOUNG JUAN

Juan Jose Tramutola remains the youngest-ever FIFA World Cup coach, leading Argentina in the 1930 tournament at the age of 27 years and 267 days. Italian Cesare Maldini became the oldest in 2002, taking charge of Paraguay when aged 70 years and 131 days.

DIVIDED LOYALTIES

No country has won the FIFA World Cup with a foreign coach, but several managers have found themselves taking on their homelands in FIFA World Cup clashes. These include Brazilian 1958 FIFA World Cup-winning midfielder Didi, whose Peru side lost 4-2 to his home country in 1970. Sven-Goran Eriksson was England coach for their 1-1 draw against his native Sweden in 2002, the same year Frenchman Bruno Metsu guided Senegal to a 1-0 opening-match win over France. Former Yugoslavia goalkeeper Blagoje Vidinic endured the most bittersweet moment – he coached Zaire to their first and only FIFA World Cup in 1974, and then had to watch his adopted players lose 9-0 to Yugoslavia.

SCHON SHINES

West Germany's Helmut Schon has been a FIFA World Cup coach for more matches than any other man – 25 games across the 1970, 1974 and 1978 tournaments. He has also won the most games as a coach, 16 in all – including the 1974 final against Holland. The 1974 tournament was third time lucky for Schon. He he had taken West Germany to second place in 1966 and to third in 1970. Before taking charge of the national side, Schon had worked as an assistant to Sepp Herberger, coach of West Germany's 1954 FIFA World Cup-winning team – Schon was coach of the then-independent Saarland regional side at the time. Dog-lover Schon, born in Dresden on 15 September 1915, scored 17 goals in 16 internationals for Germany between 1937 and 1941. He succeeded Herberger in 1964 and spent 14 years in charge of his country, becoming the only coach to win both the FIFA World Cup (1974) and the European Championships (1972).

FAMOUS FIVE

Two men have gone to five FIFA World Cups as coach: Brazilian Carlos Alberto Parreira and Serbian Bora Milutinovic. Parreira's greatest moment as coach came when he helped Brazil win their fourth FIFA World Cup success in 1994, though his second stint as Brazil coach was less successful – they only reached the quarter-finals in 2006. Parreira also led Kuwait (1982), the United Arab Emirates (1990), and Saudi Arabia (1998) at the finals and was looking forward to the 2010 tournament in charge of hosts South Africa, but had to step down in April 2008 for family reasons. Parreira was once sacked midway through a FIFA World Cup. In 1998 he led Saudi Arabia for the first two of their three games – losing 1-0 to Denmark and 4-0 to France – before receiving his marching orders.

FIFA WORLD CUP™- WINNING COACHES

1930   Alberto Suppici
1934   Vittorio Pozzo
1938   Vittorio Pozzo
1950   Juan Lopez
1954   Sepp Herberger
1958   Vicente Feola
1962   Aymore Moreira
1966   Alf Ramsey
1970   Mario Zagallo
1974   Helmut Schon
1978   Cesar Luis Menotti
1982   Enzo Bearzot
1986   Carlos Bilardo
1990   Franz Beckenbauer
1994   Carlos Alberto Parreira
1998   Aime Jacquet
2002   Luiz Felipe Scolari
2006   Marcello Lippi

CRASHING BORA

Along with Carlos Alberto Parreira, Bora Milutinovic has also coached at five FIFA World Cups – with a different country each time, two of them being the hosts. As well as Mexico in 1986 and the United States in 1994, he led Costa Rica in 1990, Nigeria in 1998 and China in 2002. He reached the knockout stages with every country except China – who failed to score a single goal.

SUPER MARIO

Two men have won the FIFA World Cup as both a player and as a coach. One was Mario Zagallo, a Brazil winger in 1958 and 1962, and coach in 1970 after being drafted in as a late replacement for Joao Saldanha, an outspoken ex-journalist who once fired two pistol shots at a goalkeeper he suspected of taking bribes. Saldanha was sacked after falling out disastrously with both Pele and the country's president, Emilio Garrastazu Medici. Zagallo also qualified for the 1990 FIFA World Cup as United Arab Emirates coach, but was sacked before the tournament began and was replaced by fellow Brazilian Carlos Alberto Parreira.

DREAM ELEVEN

Luiz Felipe Scolari managed a record 11 FIFA World Cup finals wins in a row, across the 2002 tournament, when he was in charge of Brazil, and 2006, when coach of Portugal. That winning run extends to 12 games if one counts Portugal's victory over England in the 2006 quarter-final, though that was on penalties after a goalless draw.

GUUS WHO?

Dutchman Guus Hiddink is the only manager to reach the semi-finals of the FIFA World Cup with two different countries – his native Holland in 1998 and with co-hosts South Korea in 2002. His Australia side were unluckily knocked out of the 2006 FIFA World Cup in the second round by Italy.

IL DUCE DARES

Vittorio Pozzo is the only man to have won the FIFA World Cup twice as coach, leading Italy to the title on home turf in 1934, before retaining the title in France four years later. His 1938 squad allegedly received a telegram, just before the final, from the country's fascist leader Benito Mussolini, warning them to: "Win or die!"

FIFA WORLD CUP™ REFEREEING

IDENTITY PARADE

Hungarian referee Istvan Zsolt threatened to call off England's opening game of the 1966 FIFA World Cup, against Uruguay, when he demanded to see the players' identity cards – and found that seven English players had left their passports at the team hotel. A police motorcyclist was sent to collect them and bring them back to Wembley Stadium so the match could go ahead.

TIME, GENTLEMEN

Welsh referee Clive Thomas disallowed what would have potentially been a winning goal by Brazil against Sweden in the 1978 FIFA World Cup. Thomas said he had blown the final whistle seconds before Zico headed in from a corner, and the game ended in a 1-1 draw. In contrast, Israeli referee Abraham Klein tried to blow the final whistle several times when England played Brazil at the 1970 FIFA World Cup in Guadalajara, but none of the players appeared to hear him.

YEARS OF EXPERIENCE

Spain's Juan Gardeazabal was the youngest man to referee a FIFA World Cup final, when he took charge of Brazil's win over Sweden, in 1958, at the age of 24 years and 193 days. Englishman George Reader was the oldest – aged 56 years and 236 days for Uruguay's win over Brazil in 1950, a game that was effectively the tournament's final. He remains the oldest man to have refereed at any FIFA World Cup. Reader died on 13 July 1978, exactly 48 years after the very first FIFA World Cup fixture.

BAKU OF THE NET

The official who signalled that Geoff Hurst's controversial extra-time goal for England in the 1966 FIFA World Cup final did cross the line is often wrongly described as a Russian linesman. In fact, Tofik Bakhramov was from Azerbaijan, so at the time he would have been a Soviet linesman. Azerbaijan's national football stadium, in the capital Baku, is now named after him.

PROLIFIC OFFICIALS

Joel Quiniou has refereed more FIFA World Cup finals matches than any other official, eight games across the 1986, 1990 and 1994 tournaments. In 1994, he became the only man to referee four matches in one FIFA World Cup – including Italy's semi-final victory over Bulgaria. Since then others have officiated in even more matches in a single FIFA World Cup: Mexico's Benito Archundia and Argentina's Horacio Elizondo each controlled five games in 2006. Elizondo was referee for both the first and final matches of the tournament, emulating the feat of English referee George Reader in 1950. Elizondo's memorable moments included a red card for Zinedine Zidane following the French star's head-butt on Marco Materazzi, another red card for Wayne Rooney, after the Englishman had stamped on Ricardo Carvalho, and a yellow card for Ghana's Asamoah Gyan, for taking a penalty too quickly. Gyan then missed his second attempt.

ALL RIGHT, JACK

Englishman Jack Taylor became the first referee to award a penalty in a FIFA World Cup final, in the very first minute of the 1974 showdown between Holland and West Germany. He penalized Uli Hoeness's foul on Johan Cruyff before West Germany had even touched the ball, and later awarded a second penalty, this time in the West Germans' favour, after 25 minutes. Taylor, a butcher from Wolverhampton, had delayed the initial kick-off by five minutes after noticing that none of the four corner-flags was in place at Munich's Olympic Stadium.

FIFA WORLD CUP™ FINAL REFEREES

1930	Jean Langenus (Belgium)
1934	Ivan Eklind (Sweden)
1938	Georges Capdeville (France)
1950	George Reader (England)
1954	William Ling (England)
1958	Maurice Guigue (France)
1962	Nikolay Latyshev (USSR)
1966	Gottfried Dienst (Switzerland)
1970	Rudi Glockner (West Germany)
1974	Jack Taylor (England)
1978	Sergio Gonella (Italy)
1982	Arnaldo Cezar Coelho (Brazil)
1986	Romualdo Arppi Filho (Brazil)
1990	Edgardo Codesal (Mexico)
1994	Sandor Puhl (Hungary)
1998	Said Belqola (Morocco)
2002	Pierluigi Collina (Italy)
2006	Horacio Elizondo (Argentina)

RED PERIL

Arturo Brizio Carter, from Mexico, sent off seven players in six games at the 1994 and 1998 FIFA World Cups, more than any other referee. His victims included Italy's Gianfranco Zola, France's Zinedine Zidane and Argentina's Ariel Ortega.

NETTO'S NET

Soviet captain Igor Netto persuaded Italian referee Cesare Jonni to disallow a goal for his own team at the 1962 FIFA World Cup, pointing out that Igor Chislenko had shot wide – the ball entered the Uruguayan goal through a hole in the net. His side still won the first-round match, 2-1.

DOUBLE DUTY

Only two men have refereed a FIFA World Cup final and a European Championship final. Italian Sergio Gonella officiated at the 1978 World Cup final between Argentina and Holland, two years after overseeing the European Championship final between West Germany and Czechoslovakia. Swiss official Gottfried Dienst took control of the 1966 FIFA World Cup final, between England and West Germany, and the 1968 European Championship final's first leg between Italy and Yugoslavia – Spain's Jose Maria Ortiz de Mendibil was awarded the replay.

FRENCH CONNECTION

Frenchman Georges Capdeville, in charge for Italy's win over Hungary in 1938, is the only man to referee the final in a FIFA World Cup hosted by his own country.

LONG SERVICE

Sweden's Ivan Eklind is the only man to referee at FIFA World Cups staged before and after World War Two – six matches in all, across the 1934, 1938 and 1950 tournaments, including the 1934 final between Italy and Czechoslovakia.

ARGIE-BARGEY

Argentina defender Pedro Monzon became the first player to be sent off in a FIFA World Cup final when, in 1990, he was dismissed for a foul on West Germany's Jurgen Klinsmann. Monzon had been on the pitch for only 20 minutes after coming on as a half-time substitute. Mexican referee Edgardo Codesal then reduced Argentina to nine men three minutes from full-time by dismissing Gustavo Dezotti for being too aggressive in trying to grab the ball from opponent Jurgen Kohler. Argentina have the worst FIFA World Cup disciplinary record of any country. As well as seeing Diego Maradona thrown out of the 1994 tournament for failing a drugs test, the nation's footballers have been sent off a record ten times and booked on 88 occasions in 64 matches since 1930.

LUCKY ESCAPE

Brazil's FIFA World Cup history and legend could have been very different had the present system of automatic suspension for a sending-off been in place in 1962. In the absence of the injured Pele, outside-right Garrincha had emerged as the defending champions' attacking inspiration. He was sent off in the closing minutes of the semi-final win over Chile ... but was merely cautioned and went on to play against Czechoslovakia in the final, which Brazil won 3-1.

BREAKING COVER

Zaire defender Mwepu Llunga was booked for running out of the wall and kicking the ball away as Brazil prepared to take a free-kick, at the 1974 FIFA World Cup. Romanian referee Nicolae Rainea ignored Llunga's pleas of innocence.

CARDS CLOSE TO CHEST

Only one group in FIFA World Cup finals history has featured no bookings at all – Group 4 in 1970, featuring West Germany, Peru, Bulgaria and Morocco. In contrast, the 2006 FIFA World Cup in Germany was the worst for both red and yellow cards, with 28 dismissals and 345 bookings in 64 matches.

GOOD SON, BAD SON

Cameroon's Andre Kana-Biyik served two suspensions during the 1990 FIFA World Cup in Italy. The first came after he was sent off in the opening match against Argentina – six minutes before his brother Francois Omam-Biyik scored the only goal of the game.

ELBOWED OUT

Italian defender Mauro Tassotti was given an unprecedented eight-game ban for smashing Spain's Luis Enrique in the face with his elbow in 1994 – an offence missed by match referee Sandor Puhl. Spain lost 2-1 and were further enraged when the Hungarian official was then selected to referee the final.

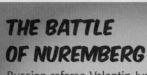

THE BATTLE OF NUREMBERG

Russian referee Valentin Ivanov sent off a record four players when Portugal beat Holland in the second round of the 2006 FIFA World Cup – two men from each side, while Portugal's Luis Figo was lucky to escape a red card for a headbutt. Ivanon showed nine yellow cards to Portugal and seven to the Netherlands during the match, though that bookings tally was matched during Cameroon's clash with Germany in 2002. Portugal's nine yellows were more than any other single team has managed – Cameroon and Germany had been given eight apiece by Spanish referee Antonio Lopez Nieto in 2002.

REPEAT OFFENDERS

France's Zinedine Zidane and Brazil's Cafu are both FIFA World Cup winners – and both notched up a record six FIFA World Cup cards, though Cafu escaped any reds, while Zidane was sent off twice. Most famously, Zidane was dismissed for headbutting Italy's Marco Materazzi in extra-time of the 2006 final in Berlin – the final match of the Frenchman's career. He had also been sent off during a first-round match against Saudi Arabia in 1998, but returned from suspension in time to help France win the trophy with a sensational two-goal performance in the final. The only other man to have been sent off twice at two different FIFA World Cups is Cameroon's Rigobert Song. When dismissed against Brazil in 1994, he became the FIFA World Cup's youngest red card offender – aged just 17 years and 358 days. He saw red for the second time against Chile in 1998.

NOT LEADING BY EXAMPLE

The first man to be sent off at a FIFA World Cup was Peru's Placido Galindo, at the first tournament in 1930 during a 3-1 defeat to Romania. Chilean referee Alberto Warnken dismissed the Peruvian captain for fighting.

SOLE CHANCE OF GLORY

India withdrew from the 1950 FIFA World Cup because some of their players wanted to play barefoot but FIFA insisted all players must wear football boots. India have not qualified for the tournament since.

FIFA WORLD CUP™ RED CARDS, BY TOURNAMENT	
1930	1
1934	1
1938	4
1950	0
1954	3
1958	3
1962	6
1966	5
1970	0
1974	5
1978	3
1982	5
1986	8
1990	16
1994	15
1998	22
2002	17
2006	28

ADVANCE BOOKING

Two players have been booked within a minute of kick-off – Italy's Giampiero Marini, against Poland, in 1982, and Russia's Sergei Gorlukovich against Sweden 12 years later. But Uruguayan Jose Batista went one worse in a 1986 first-round match against Scotland, receiving a red card after just 56 seconds for a gruesome foul on Gordon Strachan. His team-mates held on for a goalless draw.

LATE BREAKERS

Argentina goalkeeper Carlos Roa was booked after the final whistle, for time-wasting during his team's second-round penalty shoot-out against England in 1998. Brazilian defender Edinho was shown a yellow card during the quarter-final shoot-out against France in 1986. French midfielder Jacques Simon was booked after his team's 2-1 defeat to Uruguay at the 1966 FIFA World Cup had ended, for spitting at Czech referee Karol Galba. But Argentina's unused substitute Leandro Cufre outdid them all, receiving a red card for his part in a brawl minutes after his team lost on penalties to Germany in their 2006 FIFA World Cup quarter-final clash.

RIO BRAVO

The 162,764 people who watched Brazil play Colombia in Rio's Maracana in March 1977 provided the biggest crowd for a FIFA World Cup qualifying match. Sadly the game failed to live up to the occasion: it ended in a disappointing 0-0 draw.

ABSENT FRIENDS

Only 2,823 spectators turned up at the Rasunda Stadium in Stockholm to see Wales play Hungary in a first-round playoff match during the 1958 FIFA World Cup. More than 15,000 had attended the first game between the two sides, but boycotted the replay in tribute to executed Hungarian uprising leader Imre Nagy.

TWO'S COMPANY, 300'S A CROWD

The 300 people who were recorded as watching Romania beat Peru 3-1 in 1930 formed the FIFA World Cup finals' smallest attendance, with plenty of room for manoeuvre inside the Estadio Pocitos in Montevideo. A day earlier, ten times as many people are thought to have been there to watch France's 4-1 win over Mexico.

GENDER EQUALITY

Only two stadiums have hosted the finals of the FIFA World Cup for both men and women. The Rose Bowl, in Pasadena, California, was the venue for the men's final in 1994 – when Brazil beat Italy – and the women's showdown between the victorious US and China five years later, which was watched by 90,185 people. But Sweden's Rasunda Stadium, near Stockholm, just about got there first – though it endured a long wait between the men's final in 1958 and the women's in 1995. Both sets of American spectators got their money's worth, watching games that went into extra-time and which were settled on penalties.

EVERYTHING'S COMING UP ROSE BOWL

The first FIFA World Cup played in the United States, in 1994, saw a tournament-record average crowd of 68,991. The final between Brazil and Italy attracted an tournament-high attendance of 94,194. Statistics challenge critics who claim the US has yet to fall in love with soccer – the 1994 FIFA World Cup was the most-attended single-sport event in American history. Yet an even bigger crowd had been inside Pasadena's Rose Bowl for the final of the 1984 Los Angeles Olympics football tournament – 101,799 packed into the stadium to see France beat Brazil.

ROMAN EMPTY

The FIFA World Cup that saw the lowest attendances was the one held in Italy in 1934. Just 395,000 people turned out to see the matches, some 39,500 fewer than had watched the tournament four years earlier.

FIFA WORLD CUP™ FINAL ATTENDANCES

Year	Attendance	Venue
1930	93,000	(Estadio Centenario, Montevideo)
1934	45,000	(Stadio Nazionale del PNF, Rome)
1938	60,000	(Stade Olympique de Colombes, Paris)
1950	199,954	(Estádio do Maracanã, Rio de Janeiro)
1954	60,000	(Wankdorfstadion, Berne)
1958	51,800	(Rasunda Fotbollstadion, Solna)
1962	68,679	(Estadio Nacional, Santiago)
1966	98,000	(Wembley Stadium, London)
1970	107,412	(Estadio Azteca, Mexico City)
1974	75,200	(Olympiastadion, Munich)
1978	71,483	(Estadio Monumental, Buenos Aires)
1982	90,000	(Estadio Santiago Bernabéu, Madrid)
1986	114,600	(Estadio Azteca, Mexico City)
1990	73,603	(Stadio Olimpico, Rome)
1994	94,194	(Rose Bowl, Pasadena)
1998	80,000	(Stade de France, Paris)
2002	69,029	(International Stadium, Yokohama)
2006	69,000	(Olympiastadion, Berlin)

OVERALL TOURNAMENT ATTENDANCES

Year	Attendance	Average
1930	434,500	(24,139 average)
1934	358,000	(21,059)
1938	376,000	(20,889)
1950	1,043,000	(47,432)
1954	889,500	(34,212)
1958	919,580	(26,274)
1962	899,074	(28,096)
1966	1,635,000	(51,094)
1970	1,603,975	(50,124)
1974	1,768,152	(46,530)
1978	1,546,151	(40,688)
1982	2,109,723	(40,572)
1986	2,393,331	(46,026)
1990	2,516,348	(48,391)
1994	3,587,538	(68,991)
1998	2,785,100	(43,517)
2002	2,705,197	(42,269)
2006	3,359,439	(52,491)
TOTAL	30,930,108	(43,687)

MORBID MARACANA

The largest attendance for a FIFA World Cup match was at Rio de Janeiro's Maracana for the last clash of the 1950 tournament – though no one is quite sure how many were there. The final tally was officially given as 173,830, though some estimates suggest as many as 210,000 witnessed the host country's traumatic defeat. Tensions were so high at the final whistle, winning Uruguay captain Obdulio Varela was not awarded the trophy in a traditional manner, but had it surreptitiously nudged into his hands. FIFA president Jules Rimet described the crowd's overwhelming silence as "morbid, almost too difficult to bear". Uruguay's triumphant players barricaded themselves inside their dressing room for several hours before they judged it safe enough to emerge. Those spectators, however many there were, were the last to see Brazil play in an all-white kit – the unlucky colours were scrapped and, after a competition was held to find a new national strip, were replaced by the now-familiar yellow and blue.

CITY SLICKER

The capacity of South Africa's 2010 FIFA World Cup showpiece venue, Soccer City in Johannesburg, is being bumped up from 78,000 to 94,700. The design of the newly revamped stadium is being based on traditional African pottery. Soccer City will host both the opening game and the final – as well as four more first-round fixtures, a second-round clash and a quarter-final tie.

FIFA WORLD CUP™ STADIUMS & HOSTS

STAYING INDOORS

The Pontiac Silverdome in Michigan hosted the first FIFA World Cup finals match to be played indoors, at the 1994 competition. The clash between the United States and Switzerland ended 1-1. Three more first-round games were played there, including another 1-1 draw – this time between Brazil and Sweden. The teams played on grass that had been grown at Michigan State University.

OLYMPIC NAMES

The stadium hosting the opening match of the 1930 FIFA World Cup had stands named after great Uruguayan footballing triumphs: Colombes, in honour of the 1924 Paris Olympics venue; Amsterdam, after the site where that title was retained four years later; and Montevideo, even though it would be another fortnight before the home team clinched the first FIFA World Cup in their own capital city.

BERLIN CALL

Despite later becoming the capital of a united Germany, then-divided Berlin only hosted three group games at the 1974 FIFA World Cup in West Germany – the host country's surprise loss to East Germany took place in Hamburg. An unexploded World War Two bomb was discovered beneath the seats at Berlin's Olympiastadion in 2002, by workers preparing the ground for the 2006 tournament. Germany, along with Brazil, had applied to host the tournament in 1942, before it was cancelled due to the outbreak of World War Two.

TWIN PEAKS

Five stadiums have the distinction of staging both the final of a FIFA World Cup and the Summer Olympics athletics: Berlin's Olympiastadion (1936 Olympics, 2006 FIFA World Cup); London's Wembley (1948 Olympics, 1966 FIFA World Cup); Rome's Stadio Olimpico (1960 Olympics, 1990 FIFA World Cup); Mexico City's Azteca (1968 Olympics, 1970 and 1986 FIFA World Cups); and Munich's Olympiastadion (1972 Olympics, 1974 FIFA World Cup). The Rose Bowl in Pasadena, California, hosted both the final of the 1994 FIFA World Cup and the 1984 Olympics football tournament, but not the main Olympics track-and-field events.

BREAKING NEWS

A broken crossbar caused a 15-minute delay during the second-round match between Mexico and Bulgaria at the 1994 FIFA World Cup, at the Giants Stadium in New York – a venue more commonly used for NFL football. The goal collapsed after a bundle of players fell into it at once, meaning a replacement had to be erected.

RIO'S MARIO

Most people know Brazil's largest stadium as the Maracanã, named after the Rio neighbourhood and a small nearby river. But, since the mid-1960s, the official title has actually been "Estadio Jornalista Mario Filho", after a Brazilian journalist who had helped in the campaign for the stadium to be built.

WHOLE DIFFERENT BALL GAME

The Stade de France in Paris is the only stadium in the world that has staged World Cup final matches in both football (1998) and rugby union (2007). France won the first, beating Brazil, and South Africa the second, against England. The stadium's name was suggested by Michel Platini, one of the country's greatest footballers of all time and later president of UEFA. The Stade Gerland in Lyon was chosen for the 1938 FIFA World Cup but was denied any action: its only scheduled game was awarded to Sweden as a walkover after Austria's withdrawal from the tournament. Finally, 60 years later, the stadium staged six games as the FIFA World Cup returned to France.

RULES OF SELECTION

FIFA World Cup hosting rights alternated between Europe and the Americas until the 2002 tournament, which went to Asia for the first time as Japan and South Korea co-hosted the event. The first FIFA World Cup held in Africa will be hosted by South Africa in 2010, before the tournament goes to Brazil four years later – the first return to South America in 36 years. FIFA's latest rules mean no continent can apply to host more than one FIFA World Cup every eight years – and host nations for 2018 and 2022 will be named on the same day in December 2010. South Africa had only missed out on hosting the 2006 FIFA World Cup by just one solitary vote, to Germany.

UNSUCCESSFUL HOSTING BIDS

1930: Hungary, Italy, Holland, Spain, Sweden
1934: Sweden
1938: Argentina, Germany
1950: None
1954: None
1958: None
1962: Argentina, West Germany
1966: Spain, West Germany
1970: Argentina
1974: Spain
1978: Mexico
1982: West Germany
1986: Colombia (won rights, but later withdrew), Canada, USA
1990: England, Greece, USSR
1994: Brazil, Morocco
1998: Morocco, Switzerland
2002: Mexico
2006: Brazil, England, Morocco, South Africa
2010: Egypt, Libya/Tunisia, Morocco
2014: None

MEXICAN SAVE

Mexico was not the original choice to host the 1986 FIFA World Cup, but stepped in when Colombia withdrew in 1982 due to financial problems. Mexico held on to the staging rights despite suffering from an earthquake in September 1985 that left approximately 10,000 people dead, but which left the stadiums unscathed. FIFA kept faith in the country, and the Azteca Stadium went on to become the first venue to host two FIFA World Cup final matches – and Mexico the first country to stage two FIFA World Cups. The Azteca – formally named the "Estadio Guillermo Canedo", after a Mexican football official – was built in 1960 using 100,000 tonnes of concrete, four times as much as was needed for the old Wembley.

HOSTS WITH THE MOST

No other single-hosted FIFA World Cup has used as many venues as the 14 spread across Spain in 1982. The 2002 tournament was played at 20 different venues, but ten of these were in Japan and ten in co-host country South Korea.

FIFA WORLD CUP™ PENALTIES

GERMAN EFFICIENCY

Germany, or West Germany, have won all four of their FIFA World Cup penalty shoot-outs, more than any other team. Their run began with a semi-final victory over France in 1982, when goalkeeper Harald Schumacher was the matchwinner, despite being lucky to stay on the pitch for a vicious extra-time foul on France's Patrick Battiston. West Germany also reached the 1990 final thanks to their shoot-out expertise, this time proving superior to England – as they similarly did in the 1996 European Championships semi-final. Germany were better at spot-kicks than Argentina in their 2006 quarter-final, when goalkeeper Jens Lehmann consulted a note predicting the direction the Argentine players were likely to shoot towards. The vital information was scribbled on a scrap of hotel notepaper by Germany's chief scout Urs Siegenthaler. The only German national team to lose a major tournament penalty shoot-out were the West Germans, who contested the 1976 European Championships final against Czechoslovakia – their first shoot-out experience, and clearly an effective lesson, as they have not lost a shoot-out since.

⚽ NOT SO SUPREME

The 1994 tournament in the US was simply fated to end with a missed penalty. The opening ceremony featured soul-pop singer Diana Ross taking a spot-kick in Chicago's Soldier Field stadium – only for the former Supremes frontwoman (then aged 50) to toe-poke the ball wide. The goal collapsed in half, as choreographed, nevertheless.

⚽ THREE LIONS TAMED

Italy and England have lost more FIFA World Cup penalty shoot-outs than any other nation – three each. At least Italy finally managed to win one, in the 2006 final, but England have yet to triumph from 12 yards – losing to West Germany in their 1990 semi-final, Argentina in the second round in 1998 and Portugal in the quarter-finals eight years later. The penalty-missing culprits have been Stuart Pearce and Chris Waddle (1990), Paul Ince and David Batty (1998), and Frank Lampard, Steven Gerrard and Jamie Carragher (2006).

FRENCH KICKS

The first penalty shoot-out at a FIFA World Cup finals came in the 1982 semi-final in Seville between West Germany and France, when French takers Didier Six and Maxime Bossis were the unfortunate players to miss. The same two countries met in the semi-finals four years later – and West Germany again won, though this time in normal time, 2-0. But the record for most shoot-outs is shared by the 1990 and 2006 tournaments, with four apiece. Both semi-finals in 1990 went to penalties, while the 2006 final was the second to be settled that way – Italy beating France 5-3 thanks to David Trezeguet's shot hitting the crossbar.

FIFA WORLD CUP™ PENALTY SHOOT-OUTS

1982 Semi-final: West Germany 3 France 3 – West Germany won 5-4 on penalties
1986 Quarter-final: West Germany 0 Mexico 0 – West Germany won 4-1 on penalties
1986 Quarter-final: France 1 Brazil 1 – France won 4-3 on penalties
1986 Quarter-final: Belgium 1 Spain 1 – Belgium won 5-4 on penalties
1990 Second round: Republic of Ireland 0 Romania 0 – Republic of Ireland won 5-4 on penalties
1990 Quarter-final: Argentina 0 Yugoslavia 0 – Argentina won 3-2 on penalties
1990 Semi-final: Argentina 1 Italy 1 – Argentina won 4-3 on penalties
1990 Semi-final: West Germany 1 England 1 – West Germany won 4-3 on penalties
1994 Second round: Bulgaria 1 Mexico 1 – Bulgaria won 3-1 on penalties
1994 Quarter-final: Sweden 2 Romania 2 – Sweden won 5-4 on penalties
1994 Final: Brazil 0 Italy 0 – Brazil won 3-2 on penalties
1998 Second round: Argentina 2 England 2 – Argentina won 4-3 on penalties
1998 Quarter-final: France 0 Italy 0 – France won 4-3 on penalties
1998 Semi-final: Brazil 1 Netherlands 1 – Brazil won 4-2 on penalties
2002 Second round: Spain 1 Republic of Ireland 1 – Spain won 3-2 on penalties
2002 Quarter-final: South Korea 0 Spain 0 – South Korea won 5-3 on penalties
2006 Second round: Ukraine 0 Switzerland 0 – Ukraine won 3-0 on penalties
2006 Quarter-final: Germany 1 Argentina 1 – Germany won 4-2 on penalties
2006 Quarter-final: Portugal 0 England 0 – Portugal won 3-1 on penalties
2006 Final: Italy 1 France 1 – Italy won 5-3 on penalties

THE PLAYERS WHO MISSED IN SHOOT-OUTS

Argentina: Diego Maradona (1990), Pedro Troglio (1990), Hernan Crespo (1998), Roberto Ayala (2006), Esteban Cambiasso (2006)

Brazil: Socrates (1986), Julio Cesar (1986), Marcio Santos (1994)

Bulgaria: Krassimir Balakov (1994)

England: Stuart Pearce (1990), Chris Waddle (1990), Paul Ince (1998), David Batty (1998), Frank Lampard (2006), Steven Gerrard (2006), Jamie Carragher (2006)

France: Didier Six (1982), Maxime Bossis (1982), Michel Platini (1986), Bixente Lizarazu (1998), David Trezeguet (2006)

Germany/West Germany: Uli Stielike (1982)

Italy: Roberto Donadoni (1990), Aldo Serena (1990), Franco Baresi (1994), Daniele Massaro (1994), Roberto Baggio (1994), Demetrio Albertini (1998), Luigi Di Biagio (1998)

Mexico: Fernando Quirarte (1986), Raul Servin (1986), Alberto Garcia Aspe (1994), Marcelino Bernal (1994), Jorge Rodriguez (1994)

Netherlands: Phillip Cocu (1998), Ronald de Boer (1998)

Portugal: Hugo Viana (2006), Petit (2006)

Republic of Ireland: Matt Holland (2002), David Connolly (2002), Kevin Kilbane (2002)

Romania: Daniel Timofte (1990), Dan Petrescu (1994), Miodrag Belodedici (1994)

Spain: Eloy (1986), Juanfran (2002), Juan Carlos Valeron (2002), Joaquin (2002)

Sweden: Hakan Mild (1994)

Switzerland: Marco Streller (2006), Tranquillo Barnetta (2006), Ricardo Cabanas (2006)

Ukraine: Andriy Shevchenko (2006)

Yugoslavia: Dragan Stojkovic (1990), Dragoljub Brnovic (1990), Faruk Hadzibegic (1990)

THREE IN ONE

Argentina's stand-in goalkeeper Sergio Goycochea set a tournament record by saving four shoot-out penalties in 1990 – though West Germany's Harald Schumacher managed as many, across the 1982 and 1986 tournaments. Portugal's Ricardo achieved an unprecedented feat by stopping three spot-kicks in just the one shoot-out, becoming an instant hero in his side's quarter-final win over England in 2006.

BAGGIO OF DISHONOUR

Pity poor Roberto Baggio: the Italian maestro has taken part in three FIFA World Cup penalty shoot-outs, more than anyone else – and lost each and every one. Most grievously, it was his shot over the bar that gifted Brazil the trophy at the end of the 1994 final. But he also ended up on the losing side against Argentina in a 1990 semi-final and France in a quarter-final eight years later. At least on those two occasions, his own attempts did hit the back of the net.

ALL FOUR NOTHING

Switzerland exited the 2006 FIFA World Cup despite not conceding a single goal from open play during their four games, although they did miss all three of their penalties in their second-round shoot-out defeat by the Ukraine.

PART 3: EUROPEAN CHAMPIONSHIP

UEFA, the European federation, was founded during the 1954 FIFA World Cup in Switzerland and initially set itself the task of creating a championship for national teams. Many of the major European nations – such as Italy, Germany and England – refused to take part in the initial competition, launched in 1958, because their national associations feared fixture congestion. So the first finals, featuring four nations, were staged in France and saw the Soviet Union end up as first winners after defeating Yugoslavia in the final in the original Parc des Princes in the south-west of Paris. Now the map of Europe has changed so remarkably that, while UEFA's membership has more than doubled, the Soviet Union and Yugoslavia no longer exist.

The Soviets also reached the second finals in 1964, but lost their crown in the final against their Spanish hosts in the Estadio Bernabeu in Madrid. Spain's playmaker, Luis Suarez, from Italy's Internazionale, thus became the first player to win the European Championship and the European Cup in the same season. In the tournament's early years, the qualifying system was based on a simple two-legged knockout system, but this was amended to a group-based format and then, in 1980, the finals were expanded to eight nations. That year saw West Germany win for a second time, having previously triumphed in 1972. In 1996, they extended their record to three titles after beating the Czech Republic with a golden goal in extra-time at Wembley. By then the finals had been expanded again to 16 teams and history was made in 2000 when Belgium and Holland organized the first co-hosted finals. Austria and Switzerland repeated the "trick" in 2008, when Spain won their first major international trophy since their 1964 European Championship success.

Fernando Torres celebrates Spain's 2008 European Championship triumph in Vienna – after scoring the winning goal against Germany in the final.

EUROPEAN CHAMPIONSHIP QUALIFIERS

QUALIFYING COMPETITION GROWS EVER LARGER

The European Championship qualifying competition has become a huge event in its own right, with 50 teams competing for places alongside hosts Austria and Switzerland at Euro 2008. How times have changed. There were two qualifying games for the 1960 competition, to reduce the 17 entrants to 16. There were no qualifiers for the 1964 tournament, which saw teams meet each other on a home-and-away basis in the first round. A full-scale qualifying competition was first launched for the 1968 finals, with eight groups of four and one group of three. The number of qualifiers increased in size again during the 1990s as several new associations joined UEFA after the break-ups of the old Soviet Union and Yugoslavia and entered the championship for the first time.

DUTCH EDGE FIRST PLAYOFF

The first-ever qualifying playoff was held on 13 December 1995 at Liverpool when Holland beat the Republic of Ireland 2-0 to clinch the final place at Euro 96. Patrick Kluivert scored both Dutch goals.

GERMANY'S WEMBLEY WONDER NIGHT

West Germany's greatest-ever team announced their arrival at Wembley on 29 April 1972, when they beat England 3-1 in the first leg of the European Championship quarter-finals. Uli Hoeness, Gunter Netzer and Gerd Muller scored the goals. West Germany went on to win the trophy, beating the Soviet Union 3-0 in the final. Their team at Wembley was: Sepp Maier; Horst Hottges, Georg Schwarzenbeck, Franz Beckenbauer, Paul Breitner; Jurgen Grabowski, Herbert Wimmer, Gunter Netzer, Uli Hoeness; Sigi Held, Gerd Muller. Eight of them played in West Germany's 1974 FIFA World Cup final win over Holland.

IRISH STAGE FIRST QUALIFIER

The first qualifying game in European Championship history was played on 5 April 1959, when the Republic of Ireland beat Czechoslovakia 2-0 in Dublin. Seventeen teams entered the inaugural competition, so the total had to be reduced to 16 for the first round. The Czechs went through 4-2 on aggregate, after winning the second leg in Bratislava 4-0 on 10 May.

IRISH VICTORY NOT ENOUGH

West Germany's 1-0 defeat by Northern Ireland in Hamburg on 11 November 1983 was their first-ever home loss in the qualifying competition, but their 2-1 win over Albania in Saarbrucken four days later enabled them to pip Northern Ireland on goal difference for a place in the 1984 finals.

FAROES BEGIN WITH A BANG

The Faroe Islands entered the qualifiers for the first time in 1992 – and began with a shock 1-0 win over Austria at Landskrona, Sweden. Torkil Nielsen scored the only goal of the game. Austria coach Josef Hickersberger was sacked after the defeat. That was the Faroes' only win: they finished bottom of their group, which also included Yugoslavia, Denmark and Northern Ireland.

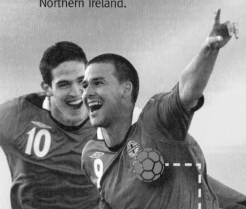

HEALY POSTS GOAL RECORD

Northern Ireland forward David Healy (born in Killyleagh on 5 August 1979) set a new scoring record with 13 goals in the Euro 2008 qualifiers. His tally included hat-tricks against Spain and Liechtenstein. Healy beat the previous record of 12 goals, netted by Croatia's Davor Suker in the qualifiers for Euro 96. Ole Madsen of Denmark scored 11 goals before the finals tournament in 1964, but qualifying groups were not introduced until two years later.

BRITS STAY HOME TO QUALIFY

The four British teams used the Home International Championship of 1966–67 and 1967–68 as a qualifying group for the 1968 finals. FIFA World Cup holders England went through but, at their own request, the British teams have been drawn separately for each subsequent qualifying competition.

EAST AND WEST COME TOGETHER

East and West Germany were originally drawn to face each other in the Group 5 qualifiers for Euro '92, but the country was officially reunified in October 1990, so a reunified team entered an international competition as "Germany" for the first time since the 1938 FIFA World Cup finals.

APPEARANCES IN THE FINALS TOURNAMENT

10	West Germany/Germany
9	Soviet Union/CIS/Russia
8	Holland
	Spain
7	Czech Republic
	Denmark
	England
	France
	Italy
5	Portugal
	Yugoslavia
4	Belgium
	Romania
	Sweden
3	Croatia
	Greece
	Switzerland
	Turkey
2	Bulgaria
	Hungary
	Scotland
1	Austria
	Latvia
	Norway
	Poland
	Republic of Ireland
	Slovenia

PANCEV FORCED TO MISS OUT

Yugoslavia's Darko Pancev (born in Skopje on 7 September 1965) was top scorer in the qualifiers for Euro 1992 with ten goals. Yugoslavia topped qualifying Group Four, but they were banned from the finals because of their country's war in Bosnia, so Pancev never had the chance to shine. After the break-up of the Yugoslav federation, he went on to become the star player for the new nation of Macedonia.

ANDORRA, SAN MARINO STRUGGLE

Minnows Andorra and San Marino each have yet to win a match in the qualifying competition. Andorra have lost all their 30 games, with a goal difference of six against 88. San Marino have lost all their 46 games, with a goal difference of six against 200!

GERMANS RUN UP 13

Germany's 13-0 win in San Marino on 6 September 2006 was the biggest victory margin in qualifying history. Lukas Podolski (4), Miroslav Klose (2), Bastian Schweinsteiger (2), Thomas Hitzlsperger (2), Michael Ballack, Manuel Friedrich and Bernd Schneider scored the goals. The previous biggest win was Spain's 12-1 rout of Malta in 1983.

FLOWERS OPENS ENGLAND'S ACCOUNT

England, Italy and West Germany did not enter the first European Championship. England and Italy entered the 1964 competition, but the West Germans stayed out until the qualifiers for the 1968 finals. England took their bow with a 1-1 draw against France at Hillsborough, Sheffield, on 3 October 1962. Ron Flowers scored their goal from a penalty. They were eliminated after France won the second leg 5-2. Italy beat Turkey, 6-0 at home and 1-0 away.

EUROPEAN CHAMPIONSHIP TEAM RECORDS

GERMANS DOMINATE AS COMPETITION TAKES OFF

In 50 years, the European Championship has grown to become the most important international football tournament, after the FIFA World Cup finals. Only 17 teams entered the first competition, won by the Soviet Union in 1960. Fifty took part in qualifying for the right to join hosts Austria and Switzerland at the 2008 finals. Germany (formerly West Germany) have dominated the tournament, even though they did not enter the first two competitions. They have won three times and finished runners-up on three more occasions. France and Spain have each triumphed twice. Denmark, in 1992, and Greece, in 2004, have been the tournament's surprise winners. Meanwhile, some of Europe's most famous teams have underachieved. Italy have only won the trophy once, on home soil in 1968; whereas England have never even reached the final – their best finish was third place in 1968.

EUROPEAN CHAMPIONSHIP WINNERS

3 **West Germany/Germany** (1972, 1980, 1996)
2 **France** (1984, 2000)
   Spain (1964, 2008)
1 **Soviet Union** (1960)
   Czechoslovakia (1976)
   Italy (1968)
   Holland (1998)
   Denmark (1992)
   Greece (2004)

FRANCE BOAST PERFECT RECORD

France, on home soil in 1984, are the only side to win all their matches since the finals expanded beyond four teams. They won them without any shoot-outs, too, beating Denmark 1-0, Belgium 5-0 and Yugoslavia 3-2 in their group, Portugal 3-2 after extra-time in the semi-finals and Spain 2-0 in the final.

GERMANS SET RECORD MARGIN

West Germany's 3-0 win over the Soviet Union in 1972 remains the biggest margin of victory in any final. Gerd Muller netted the opening goal in the 27th minute. Midfielder Herbert Wimmer added the Germans' second after 52 minutes and Muller completed the rout six minutes later. All the past four finals (1996, 2000, 2004 and 2008) have been settled by one goal.

WEST GERMANY'S THREE IN A ROW

West Germany are the only side to have reached three successive European Championship finals – in 1972 (winners), 1976 (runners-up) and 1980 (winners). They are also the only side to play in three consecutive FIFA World Cup finals, between 1982 and 1990.

SPAIN REFUSE TO MEET SOVIETS

Political rivalries wrecked the planned clash between Spain and the Soviet Union in the 1960 quarter-finals. The fascist Spanish leader, General Francisco Franco, refused to allow Spain to go to the communist Soviet Union – and banned the Soviets from entering Spain. The Soviet Union were handed a walkover on the grounds that Spain had refused to play. Franco relented four years later, allowing the Soviets to come to Spain for the finals. He was spared the embarrassment of presenting the trophy to them, however, as Spain beat the Soviet Union 2-1 in the final.

SOVIETS' TREBLE LOSS

The Soviet Union are the only team to have lost three finals – to Spain in 1964, West Germany in 1972 and Holland in 1988.

DERWALL OUT, BECKENBAUER IN

West Germany coach Jupp Derwall was sacked after his side were eliminated by Spain at the group stage of the 1984 finals – despite leading them to victory in 1980 and to the 1982 FIFA World Cup final. He was replaced by Franz Beckenbauer, who guided them to the 1986 FIFA World Cup final and FIFA World Cup victory in 1990. But Beckenbauer's squad were upset 2-1 by Holland in the Euro '88 semi-finals, despite having home advantage.

DOMENGHINI RESCUES ITALY

The most controversial goal in the history of the final came on 8 June 1968. Hosts Italy were trailing 1-0 to Yugoslavia with ten minutes left. The Yugoslavs seemed still to be organizing their wall when Angelo Domenghini curled a free-kick past goalkeeper Ilja Pantelic for the equalizer. Yugoslavia protested but the goal was allowed to stand. Italy won the only replay in finals history 2-0, two days later, with goals from Gigi Riva and Pietro Anastasi.

CZECHS WIN LONGEST SHOOT-OUT

The longest penalty shoot-out in finals history came in the 1980 third-place playoff between hosts Italy and Czechoslovakia, in Naples on 21 June. The Czechs won 9-8, following a 1-1 draw. After eight successful spot-kicks each, Czech goalkeeper Jaroslav Netolicka saved Fulvio Collovati's kick.

"NEW" TEAMS MAKE FINALS APPEARANCE

Four teams appeared in the finals for the first time at Euro 96 – Bulgaria, Croatia, Turkey and Switzerland. Two more sides appeared in new guises. The Czech Republic played for the first time after Slovakia voted in 1993 to dissolve the Czechoslovak federation. Russia competed as a separate nation for the first time too, after the break-up of the old Soviet Union.

HOLLAND END WINLESS STREAK

Holland's 2-1 semi-final win over West Germany in Hamburg on 21 June 1988 was their first over the Germans since 1956. It ended a winless streak of three draws and seven defeats against them – including the surprise defeat in the 1974 FIFA World Cup final.

PORTUGAL SPURN HOME ADVANTAGE

In 2004, Portugal became the first host nation to reach the final since France 20 years earlier. They were also the first hosts to lose the final, going down 1-0 to Greece in Lisbon on 4 July. France (1984) and Spain (1964) had previously become European champions on home soil.

ENGLAND'S SHOOT-OUT WOES

England's 4-2 shoot-out win over Spain in the Euro 96 quarter-finals remains their only penalty success in a major tournament. The game, at Wembley on 22 June, ended 0-0 after extra-time. Alan Shearer, David Platt, Stuart Pearce and Paul Gascoigne scored for England. Fernando Hierro hit the bar, then David Seaman saved Miguel Angel Nadal's kick to take the home side through. England have lost all five of their other competitive shoot-outs, including a defeat on penalties by Germany in the Euro 96 semi-finals.

FRANCE STRIKE, WITHOUT STRIKERS

France still hold the record for the most goals scored by one team in a finals tournament, 14 in 1984. Yet only one of those goals was netted by a recognized striker – Bruno Bellone, who hit the second in their 2-0 final win over Spain. France's inspirational captain, Michel Platini, supplied most of the French firepower, scoring an incredible nine goals in five appearances. He hit hat-tricks against Belgium and Denmark and a last-gasp winner in the semi-final against Portugal. Midfielders Alain Giresse and Luis Fernandez chipped in with goals in the 5-0 win over Belgium. Defender Jean-Francois Domergue gave France the lead against Portugal in the semi-finals, and added another in extra-time after Jordao had put Portugal 2-1 ahead.

DENMARK'S UNEXPECTED TRIUMPH

Denmark were unlikely winners of Euro 1992. They had not even expected to take part after finishing behind Yugoslavia in their qualifying group, but they were invited to complete the final eight when Yugoslavia were barred for security fears following the country's collapse. Goalkeeper Peter Schmeichel was their hero – in the semi-final shoot-out win over Holland and again in the final against Germany, when goals by John Jensen and Kim Vilfort earned Denmark a 2-0 win.

 BIGGEST WINS IN THE FINALS

Holland 6, Yugoslavia 1, 2000
France 5, Belgium 0, 1984
Denmark 5, Yugoslavia 0, 1984
Sweden 5, Bulgaria 0, 2004

 **FRANCE ENJOY GOLDEN GOALS**

France are the only team to have won two matches with "golden goals" in one tournament. The Euro 2000 winners owed their semi-final and final victories to extra-time deciders. Zinedine Zidane netted with a 117th-minute penalty to pip Portugal 2-1 in the semi-final in Brussels on 28 June. Four days later, David Trezeguet scored a golden goal in the 13th minute of extra-time to beat Italy 2-1 in the final.

TOP TEAM SCORERS IN THE FINALS

1960:	Yugoslavia 6
1964:	Spain, Soviet Union, Hungary 4
1968:	Italy 4
1972:	West Germany 5
1976:	West Germany 6
1980:	West Germany 6
1984:	France 14
1988:	Holland 8
1992:	Germany 7
1996:	Germany 10
2000:	France, Holland 13
2004:	Czech Republic 9
2008:	Spain 12

CIS TAKE SOVIETS' PLACE

Following the collapse of the old Soviet Union in December 1991, their team competed at Euro '92 as the Commonwealth of Independent States (CIS). This represented all the former Soviet republics, except Estonia, Latvia and Lithuania. Russia appeared in the finals for the first time as a separate nation at Euro 96.

THREE OFF AS CZECHS ADVANCE

Czechoslovakia's 3-1 semi-final win over Holland in Zagreb on 16 June 1976, featured a record three red cards. The Czechs' Jaroslav Pollak was dismissed for a second yellow card – a foul on Johan Neeskens – after an hour. Neeskens followed in the 76th minute for kicking Zdenek Nehoda. Wim van Hanegem became the second Dutchman dismissed, for dissent, after Nehoda scored the Czechs' second goal with six minutes of extra-time left.

PENALTY FAILURES COST HOLLAND

Holland missed two penalties in the match and three more in the shoot-out to lose the Euro 2000 semi-final against Italy in Amsterdam on 29 June. Italy goalkeeper Francesco Toldo saved a first-half penalty from Frank de Boer. Then Patrick Kluivert hit a 62nd-minute spot-kick against a post. The game went to a shoot-out after a 0-0 draw. De Boer and Jaap Stam missed and Toldo saved Paul Bosvelt's kick to clinch a 3-1 win for Italy – who had played most of the game with 10 men after Gianluca Zambrotta's 34th-minute sending off.

DELLAS TIMES IT RIGHT FOR GREECE

Greece scored the only "silver goal" victory in the history of the competition in the Euro 2004 semi-finals. (The silver goal rule meant that a team leading after the first period of extra-time won the match.) Traianos Dellas headed Greece's winner two seconds before the end of the first period of extra-time against the Czech Republic in Porto on 1 July. Both golden goals and silver goals were abandoned for Euro 2008. Extra-time and penalties were used to resolve drawn games in the knockout phase instead.

CROATIA ENJOY SLICE OF HISTORY

Croatia reached the finals of a major tournament for the first time as an independent nation when they qualified for Euro 96. They progressed in second place from Group D, but lost 2-1 to Germany in the quarter-finals. Centre-back Igor Stimac was sent off three minutes before the Germans' winner. Croatia had declared independence from the old federation of Yugoslavia on 25 June 1991.

TOSS FAVOURS HOSTS ITALY

Winners Italy reached the 1968 final on home soil thanks to the toss of a coin. It was the only game in finals history decided in such fashion. Italy drew 0-0 against the Soviet Union after extra-time in Naples on 5 June 1968. The Soviet captain, Albert Shesternev, made the wrong call at the toss – so Italy reached the final where they beat Yugoslavia.

EUROPEAN CHAMPIONSHIP GOALSCORING

SHEARER TALLY BOOSTS ENGLAND

Alan Shearer is the only Englishman to top the finals scoring chart. Shearer led the scorers with five goals as England went out on penalties to Germany in the Euro 96 semi-final at Wembley. He netted against Switzerland, Scotland and Holland (2) in the group and gave England a third-minute lead against the Germans. Shearer added two more goals at Euro 2000, to stand second behind Michel Platini in the all-time scorers' list.

VONLANTHEN BEATS ROONEY RECORD

The youngest scorer in finals history was Switzerland midfielder Johan Vonlanthen. He was 18 years 141 days when he netted in their 3-1 defeat by France on 21 June 2004. He beat the record set by England forward Wayne Rooney four days earlier. Rooney was 18 years 229 days when he scored the first goal in England's 3-0 win over the Swiss.

FINALS HAT-TRICK SCORERS

Dieter Muller (West Germany), West Germany 4, Yugoslavia 2, 1976
Klaus Allofs (West Germany), West Germany 3, Holland 2, 1980
Michel Platini (France), France 5, Belgium 0, 1984
Michel Platini (France), France 3, Yugoslavia 2, 1984
Marco van Basten (Holland), Holland 3, England 1, 1988
Sergio Conceicao (Portugal), Portugal 3, Germany 0, 2000
Patrick Kluivert (Holland), Holland 6, Yugoslavia 1, 2000
David Villa (Spain), Spain 4, Russia 1, 2008

ILYIN GOAL MAKES HISTORY

Anatoly Ilyin of the Soviet Union scored the first goal in European Championship history when he netted after four minutes against Hungary on 29 September 1958. A crowd of 100,572 watched the Soviets win 3-1 in the Lenin Stadium, Moscow. The Soviet Union went on to win the first final, in 1960.

KIRICHENKO NETS QUICKEST GOAL

The fastest goal in the history of the finals was scored by Russia forward Dmitri Kirichenko. He netted after just 68 seconds to give his side the lead against Greece on 20 June 2004. Russia won 2-1, but Greece still qualified for the quarter-finals – and went on to become shock winners. The fastest goal in the final was Spain midfielder Jesus Pereda's sixth-minute strike in 1964, when Spain beat the Soviet Union 2-1.

HRUBESCH GRABS HIS CHANCE

West Germany's 1980 final hero, Horst Hrubesch, grabbed his chance after first-choice Klaus Fischer was sidelined with a broken leg. Hrubesch did not win his first cap until he was 28, but he gave the Germans a tenth-minute lead against Belgium in Rome on 22 June. Then he headed the winner from Karl-Heinz Rummenigge's corner after Rene van der Eycken had levelled the scores from the penalty spot.

VAN BASTEN LEADS DUTCH CHARGE

Holland's Marco van Basten was the striking star of Euro 1988. He scored a hat-trick in the 3-1 win over England and netted a late winner to pip hosts West Germany 2-1 in the semi-finals. His strike in Holland's 2-0 win over the Soviet Union is regarded as the greatest goal ever scored in the final. He met Arnold Muhren's crossfield pass with a spectacular mid-air volley, which flew past keeper Rinat Dassayev for Holland's second goal.

RICARDO THE SHOOT-OUT DECIDER

Portugal goalkeeper Ricardo was the hero of his side's quarter-final shoot-out win against England in Lisbon on 24 June 2004. The score was 5-5 in the shoot-out – following a 2-2 draw – when Ricardo saved Darius Vassell's spot-kick. The Portugal keeper then coolly struck a penalty-kick past David James to knock England out.

TOP SCORERS IN FINALS HISTORY

1	Michel Platini (France)	9
2	Alan Shearer (England)	7
3	Nuno Gomes (Portugal)	
	Thierry Henry (France)	
	Patrick Kluivert (Holland)	
	Ruud van Nistelrooy (Holland)	6
7	Milan Baros (Czech Republic)	
	Jurgen Klinsmann (W Germany/Germany)	
	Marco van Basten (Holland)	
	Zinedine Zidane (France)	5

TOP SCORERS IN THE FINALS

1960:	2	Francois Heutte (France)
		Milan Galic (Yugoslavia)
		Valentin Ivanov (Soviet Union)
		Drazan Jerkovic (Yugoslavia)
		Slava Metreveli (Soviet Union)
		Viktor Ponedelnik (Soviet Union)
1964:	2	Ferenc Bene (Hungary)
		Dezso Novak (Hungary)
		Jesus Pereda (Spain)
1968:	2	Dragan Dzajic (Yugoslavia)
1972:	4	Gerd Muller (West Germany)
1976:	4	Dieter Muller (West Germany)
1980:	3	Klaus Allofs (West Germany)
1984:	9	Michel Platini (France)
1988:	5	Marco van Basten (Holland)
1992:	3	Dennis Bergkamp (Holland)
		Tomas Brolin (Sweden)
		Henrik Larsen (Denmark)
		Karlheinz Riedle (Germany)
1996:	5	Alan Shearer (England)
2000:	5	Patrick Kluivert (Holland)
		Savo Milosevic (Yugoslavia)
2004:	5	Milan Baros (Czech Republic)
2008:	4	David Villa (Spain)

BIERHOFF NETS FIRST "GOLDEN GOAL"

Germany's Oliver Bierhoff scored the first golden goal in the history of the tournament when he hit the winner against the Czech Republic in the Euro 96 final at Wembley on 30 June. (The golden goal rule meant the first team to score in extra-time won the match.) Bierhoff netted in the fifth minute of extra-time. His shot from 20 yards deflected off defender Michal Hornak and slipped through goalkeeper Petr Kouba's fingers.

PONEDELNIK'S MONDAY MORNING FEELING

Striker Viktor Ponedelnik headed the Soviet Union's extra-time winner to beat Yugoslavia 2-1 in the first final on 10 July 1960 – and sparked some famous headlines in the Soviet media. The game in Paris kicked off at 10pm Moscow time on Sunday. It was running into Monday morning there by the time Ponedelnik – whose name means "Monday" in Russian – scored. He said: "When I scored, all the journalists wrote the headline Ponedelnik zabivayet v Ponedelnik" – "Monday scores on Monday".

PLATINI SETS FANTASTIC STANDARD

Michael Platini towered over the 1984 finals, setting a scoring record that has yet to be beaten. France's great attacking midfielder netted nine goals as his side won the tournament on home soil. Platini opened with France's winner against Denmark, netted a hat-trick in the 5-0 win over Belgium, then scored all three in a 3-2 win over Yugoslavia. He produced his most dramatic intervention in the semi-final against Portugal, grabbing France's decider in the last minute of extra-time. He set his team on the way to a 2-0 victory over Spain in the final too, when his free-kick squirmed through goalkeeper Luis Arconada's hands. Some 24 years later, after Platini had become UEFA president, he invited Arconada to be his special guest at the 2008 final in Vienna ... on this occasion to see Spain win.

VASTIC THE OLDEST

The oldest scorer in finals history is Austria's Ivica Vastic. He was 38 years and 257 days old when he equalized in the 1-1 draw with Poland at Euro 2008.

EUROPEAN CHAMPIONSHIP APPEARANCES

BROTHERS IN ARMS

Four pairs of brothers went to Euro 2000: Gary and Phil Neville (England), Frank and Ronald de Boer (Holland), Daniel and Patrik Andersson (Sweden) and Belgium's Emile and Mbo Mpenza.

MATTHAUS MIRRORS TOURNAMENT GROWTH

The career of Lothar Matthaus straddles the growth of the European Championship. He appeared in four tournaments between 1980 and 2000. He missed Euro '92 because of injury and stayed at home for Euro 96 after falling out with coach Berti Vogts and skipper Jurgen Klinsmann. He had made his entry as a 19-year-old substitute for Bernd Dietz in West Germany's 3-2 group win over Holland in Naples on 14 June 1980. That was the first tournament which involved eight teams and two groups rather than the previous four semi-finalists. He ended his association with the championship at the age of 39 (see below), playing for a reunited Germany as they were eliminated 3-0 by Portugal at Euro 2000. By now the tournament had expanded to include 16 teams in four groups. Despite featuring in four tournaments, Matthaus only made 11 appearances in total. He did, however, enter the tournament when it was taking its first steps to expansion and left it when the European Championship had become second only to the FIFA World Cup as football's most important international competition.

PORTUGAL TRIO BANNED FOR THE LONGEST

The longest suspensions in the history of the finals were handed out to three Portugal players after their Euro 2000 semi-final defeat by France. Zinedine Zidane's "Golden Goal" penalty infuriated the Portuguese, who surrounded referee Gunter Benko and assistant Igor Sramka. The three Portuguese players – Abel Xavier, Nuno Gomes and Paulo Bento – were banned for "physically and verbally intimidating" the officials. Xavier was suspended from European football for nine months. Gomes, who was also sent off, was banned for eight months. Bento received a six-month suspension.

VAN BASTEN SPOILS SHILTON'S DAY

Goalkeeper Peter Shilton is England's most-capped player, with 125 appearances, but he will remember his 100th cap – in Dusseldorf on 15 June 1988 – for all the wrong reasons. Marco van Basten fired a second-half hat-trick past him as Holland beat England 3-1 in their second Group Two game of Euro '88.

BECKENBAUER'S 100TH ENDS IN DEFEAT

West Germany legend Franz Beckenbauer won his 100th cap in the 1976 final against Czechoslovakia. After his side's shoot-out defeat, he played only three more games for his country before retiring from international football.

MOST FINALS TOURNAMENTS PLAYED

Six players have appeared in four finals tournaments:

Lothar Matthaus (W Germany/Germany)	1980, 1984, 1988, 2000
Peter Schmeichel (Denmark)	1988, 1992, 1996, 2000
Aaron Winter (Holland)	1988, 1992, 1996, 2000
Lilian Thuram (France)	1996, 2000, 2004, 2008
Edwin van der Sar (Holland)	1996, 2000, 2004, 2008
Alessandro Del Piero (Italy)	1996, 2000, 2004, 2008

MULLERY THE FIRST TO GO

Wing-half Alan Mullery became the first England player ever to be sent off when he was dismissed in the 89th minute of their 1-0 semi-final defeat by Yugoslavia in Florence on 5 June 1968. Mullery was sent off for a foul on Dobrivoje Trivic, three minutes after Dragan Dzajic had scored Yugoslavia's winner. His dismissal came in England's 424th official international match.

HAGI'S JOURNEY ENDS IN RED

Romania's greatest player, Gheorghe Hagi won the last of his 125 caps in their 2-0 Euro 2000 quarter-final defeat by Italy on 24 June. However, his international career would end in sad circumstances: he was sent off in the 59th minute for two yellow-card offences. Hagi had previously been booked against Germany and Portugal – and had missed Romania's 3-2 group win over England through suspension.

MOST GAMES PLAYED IN THE FINALS

16	Edwin van der Sar	(Holland)
	Lilian Thuram	(France)
14	Luis Figo	(Portugal)
	Nuno Gomes	(Portugal)
	Karel Poborsky	(Czech Republic)
	Zinedine Zidane	(France)

TWO REDS END LONG RUN

After France defender Yvon Le Roux was sent off in the 1984 final, the next two finals tournaments passed without a single red card. That all changed in Spain's bad-tempered 1-1 Group B draw with Bulgaria at Leeds on 9 June 1996. Italian referee Piero Ceccarini sent off Bulgaria's Petr Houbtchev for bringing down Jose Luis Caminero, then dismissed Spain's Antonio Pizzi for a wild tackle on Radostin Kishishev.

KADLEC FATHER AND SON

Czech defenders Miroslav and Michal Kadlec are the only father and son to have played in the finals. Miroslav (born on 22 June 1964 in Uherkse Hradiste) captained the Czech Republic side that finished as runners-up to Germany at Euro 96. He also scored the winning penalty in the semi-final shoot-out against France. Michal (born on 13 December 1984 in Vyskov) made his first appearance as an 80th-minute substitute for Jaroslav Plasil in the Group A game against Turkey in Geneva on 15 June 2008.

ARAGONES THE VETERAN COACH

Luis Aragones, Spain's coach in 2008, is the oldest boss of a European champion team. Aragones (born in Madrid on 28 July 1938) was 29 days short of his 70th birthday when Spain beat Germany 1-0 in the final on 29 June. That was his last match in charge. He had taken over the national team after Euro 2004.

MATTHAUS THE OLDEST

The oldest player to appear in a game at the finals was Germany's Lothar Matthaus. He was 39 years 91 days when he played in their 3-0 defeat by Portugal on 20 June 2000.

SUAREZ GAINS UNIQUE DOUBLE

Spain's midfield general Luis Suarez is the only man to play his way to a European Championship winner's medal and a European Cup winner's medal in the same season. Suarez pulled the strings as Spain beat Hungary 2-1 in the 1964 semi-finals and the Soviet Union 2-1 in the final on 21 June 1964. Less than a month earlier, on 27 May, he was in the Internazionale team that beat Real Madrid 3-1 in the European Cup final in Vienna. Nicolas Anelka won the Champions League with Real Madrid in 2000 and was in the France squad that won Euro 2000, although he did not appear in the final.

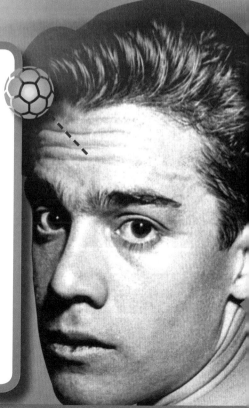

SCIFO THE YOUNGEST

The youngest player to feature in a game at the finals was Belgium midfielder Enzo Scifo. He was 18 years 115 days when he appeared in his country's 2-0 win over Yugoslavia on 13 June 1984 and started in all three of Belgium's group games.

EUROPEAN CHAMPIONSHIP OTHER RECORDS

EURO 2008 IN THE INTERNET AGE

The Internet became a massive conduit for public interest for the Euro 2008 finals. More than 105 million surfers from more than 200 countries visited the dedicated site www.Euro2008.com. The biggest volume of traffic – around 15 per cent – came from the United Kingdom. The greatest number of daily hits was 4.9 million.

SPAIN'S RECORD TV AUDIENCE

Spain's Euro 2008 final win over Germany attracted the largest TV audience in the country's history. More than 14 million homes tuned in to the game, and hundreds of thousands more watched on giant public screens in squares and parks. The final was shown live in 231 countries around the globe.

EURO 2012 UNDER WAY

Euro 2012 – which features 24 teams for the first time – will be co-hosted by Poland and Ukraine. The opening match will be staged at Poland's National Stadium in Warsaw. Ukraine will host the final, at the Olympic Stadium, Kiev. The other Polish venues are in Gdansk, Poznan and Wroclaw. The Ukrainian venues are at Lwow, Dneprpetrovsk and Donetsk.

GREEKS HAND ALBANIA WALKOVER

When Greece were drawn against Albania in the first round of the 1964 tournament, the Greeks immediately withdrew, handing Albania a 3-0 walkover win. The countries had technically been at war since 1940. The Greek government did not formally lift the state of war until 1987, although diplomatic relations were re-established in 1971.

THE "ITALIAN JOB"

The 1968 finals in Italy were used as the backdrop to a famous English-language film – *The Italian Job*, starring Michael Caine – about a British gang who use the cover of the finals to stage a daring gold robbery in Turin. The film was released in England on 2 June 1969.

NAMES ON THEIR SHIRTS

Players wore their names as well as their numbers on the back of their shirts for the first time at Euro '92. They had previously only been identified by numbers.

CHAMPIONSHIPS BECOME AN EXTRAVAGANZA

The European Championship attracts more media attention than any other football tournament except for the FIFA World Cup finals and one can only imagine the shock when TV pictures from the Euro 2008 semi-final between Germany and Turkey were disrupted by bad weather. Once the finals featured four teams and lasted for a few days; now they include 16 teams and the competition has become a three-week extravaganza. The party will last even longer in 2012 when 24 teams will contest the tournament for the first time. TV viewing figures will almost certainly set new records, while new media – such as the Internet – will play an ever-increasing role in the coverage.

FINALS HOSTS

1960 France
1964 Spain
1968 Italy
1972 Belgium
1976 Yugoslavia
1980 Italy
1984 France
1988 West Germany
1992 Sweden
1996 England
2000 Holland and Belgium
2004 Portugal
2008 Austria and Switzerland

LOW COUNTRIES START DUAL TREND

In 2000, Belgium and Holland began the trend for dual hosting the European Championship finals – it was the first time the tournament was staged in more than one country. The opening game was Belgium's 2-1 win over Sweden in Brussels on 10 June. The final was staged in Rotterdam on 2 July. Austria and Switzerland jointly hosted Euro 2008. The opening game was Switzerland's 1-0 defeat by the Czech Republic in Basel on 7 June. The final was staged in Vienna on 29 June.

TOP TEN TEAMS IN FINALS MATCHES

Team	Pld	W	D	L	F	A
West Germany/Germany	38	19	10	9	55	39
Holland	32	17	8	7	55	32
France	28	14	7	7	46	34
Spain	30	13	9	8	38	31
Portugal	23	12	4	7	34	22
Italy	27	11	12	4	27	18
Czechoslovakia/Czech Republic	25	11	5	9	36	32
Soviet Union/CIS/Russia	27	11	5	11	31	36
England	23	7	7	9	31	28
Denmark	24	6	6	12	26	38

THUNDERSTORM HAMPERS SEMI-FINAL COVERAGE

Euro 2008 TV viewers missed much of the dramatic finale to Germany's 3-2 semi-final win over Turkey because of a television blackout. A thunderstorm and high winds in Vienna – where TV operations were based – meant the loss of pictures for several minutes. TV viewers missed both Miroslav Klose's goal that gave Germany a 2-1 lead, and Semih Senturk's equalizer. But coverage was resumed just in time for Philipp Lahm's stoppage-time winner.

ELLIS BLOWS THE WHISTLE

English referee Arthur Ellis took charge of the first European Championship final between the Soviet Union and Yugoslavia in 1960. Ellis had also refereed the first-ever European Cup final, between Real Madrid and Reims, four years earlier. After he retired from football, he became the "referee" on the British version of the Europe-wide game show "It's a Knock-out."

ITALY HOSTS TWICE

Italy were the first country to host the finals twice – in 1968 and again in 1980. They were awarded the finals in 1968 in recognition of the 60th anniversary of the Italian football federation. Belgium have also hosted the finals twice: first, alone, in 1972, and then in partnership with Holland for Euro 2000.

RECORD FINAL CROWD AT THE BERNABEU

The record attendance for a European Championship final was the 120,000 who saw Spain beat the Soviet Union 2-1 at the Bernabeu in Madrid on 21 June 1964.

DUTCH TAKE TO THE WATER

Holland celebrated their 1988 triumph in unusual style. The team paraded on a barge through the canals of Amsterdam. A crowd estimated at more than one million greeted them – and many houseboats moored on the canals were damaged by happy fans dancing on their roofs!

PART 4: COPA AMERICA

JET travel has had a revolutionary effect on international sports competition over the past 50 years, but the difficulties of organizing major events in the first half of the 20th century also had positive effects. FIFA's founding membership in 1904 was entirely European, and though South American nations – such as Brazil, Argentina and Uruguay – were not slow in signing up, the opportunities available to them to play against their European cousins were scarce. Occasional European teams, usually clubs, made occasional tours to South America, but the time taken and disruption caused by long steamer crossings meant that, for example, only four European national teams went to Uruguay to play in the inaugural FIFA World Cup in 1930.

The South Americans, then, had to organize their own international competitions – which led directly to the creation in 1916 of the South American Championship, which is now known as the Copa America. Communications not being what they are today, even then organization was a far from simple matter – hence many of the initial championships are now considered "unofficial". Further problems arose over competition scheduling which, in later years, often meant that countries were unable to secure the release of their finest players who were contracted to clubs in Europe. The issue of such a player exodus was a particular problem for Argentina in the late 1950s. They won the South American title in 1957 and were considered favourites to win the FIFA World Cup the following year. By then, however, they had lost all their inspirational inside-forward trio – Humberto Maschio, Antonio Valentin Angelillo and Enrique Omar Sivori – to Italian clubs. Eventually the club versus country issue was resolved by FIFA's enforcement of a unified international calendar, which recognized the priority status of the Copa America.

Brazil celebrate victory at the 2007 Copa America – with their minds also fixed on their role as FIFA World Cup hosts in 2014.

VISITING TIME

Since 1993, two national teams from other confederations – usually from northern neighbours CONCACAF (Central and North America) – have also been invited to take part in the Copa America. Visitors have included Costa Rica (1997, 2001, 2004), Honduras (right 2001), Japan (1999), Mexico (1993, 1995, 1997, 1999, 2001, 2004, 2007) and the United States (1993, 1995, 2007). The US has been invited regularly since 1997, but has often been forced to turn down the invitation due to scheduling conflicts with Major League Soccer. However, in 2007, the US competed for the first time in 12 years. Canada was an invitee in 2001, but withdrew due to security concerns in the host country, Colombia.

TRIUMPHS BY COUNTRY

Uruguay 14 (1916, 1917, 1920, 1923, 1924, 1926, 1935, 1942, 1956, 1959, 1967, 1983, 1987, 1995)
Argentina 14 (1921, 1925, 1927, 1929, 1937, 1941, 1945, 1946, 1947, 1955, 1957, 1959, 1991, 1993)
Brazil 8 (1919, 1922, 1949, 1989, 1997, 1999, 2004, 2007)
Peru 2 (1939, 1975)
Paraguay 2 (1953, 1979)
Bolivia 1 (1963)
Colombia 1 (2001)

HOW IT STARTED

The first South American "Championship of Nations", as it was then known, was held in Argentina from 2–17 July 1916, during the country's independence centenary commemorations. The tournament was won by Uruguay, who drew with Argentina in the last match of the tournament. It was an inauspicious beginning. The 16 July encounter had to be abandoned at 0-0 when fans invaded the pitch and set the wooden stands on fire. The match was continued at a different stadium the following day and still ended goalless ... but Uruguay ended up topping the mini-league table and were hailed the first champions. Isabelino Gradin was the inaugural tournament's top scorer. The event also saw the foundation of the South American federation CONMEBOL, which took place a week into the competition on 9 July 1916. From that point on the tournament was held every two years, though some tournaments are now considered to have been unofficial.

EXTRA TIME

The longest match in the history of the Copa America was the 1919 final between Brazil and Uruguay. It lasted 150 minutes, 90 minutes of regular time plus two extra-time periods of 30 minutes each.

ENDEARING/ENDURING HONDURAS

In 2001, CONCACAF guests Honduras may only have arrived as last-minute replacements for Argentina, but they stunned Luiz Felipe Scolari's Brazil 2-0 in their 2001 quarter-final, in one of the competition's greatest-ever upsets. The opening goal was turned into his own net by Brazil's Juliano Belletti, who would later play for Scolari at English Premier League club Chelsea. Many Argentina fans gleefully celebrated the humiliation of their old rivals by another team wearing blue and white stripes, but "Big Phil" and Brazil had the last laugh: they won the following year's FIFA World Cup.

FAMILIAR FACES

Uruguay have made the most appearances (40), followed by Argentina (38), Chile (35), Paraguay (33), Brazil (32) and Peru (28). Argentina has organized the Copa America the most times – nine, followed by Uruguay (seven) and Chile (six).

COPA AMERICA WINNERS

1910	(unofficial) Argentina (league format)
1916	Uruguay (league format)
1917	Uruguay (league format)
1919	Brazil 1 Uruguay 0
1920	Uruguay (league format)
1921	Argentina (league format)
1922	Brazil 3 Paraguay 1
1923	Uruguay (league format)
1924	Uruguay (league format)
1925	Argentina (league format)
1926	Uruguay (league format)
1927	Argentina (league format)
1929	Argentina (league format)
1935	Uruguay (league format)
1937	Argentina 2 Brazil 0
1939	Peru (league format)
1941	Argentina (league format)
1942	Uruguay (league format)
1945	Argentina (league format)
1946	Argentina (league format)
1947	Argentina (league format)
1949	Brazil 7 Paraguay 0
1953	Paraguay 3 Brazil 2
1955	Argentina (league format)
1956	Uruguay (league format)
1957	Argentina (league format)
1959	Argentina (league format)
1959	Uruguay (league format)
1963	Bolivia (league format)
1967	Uruguay (league format)
1975	Peru 4 Colombia 1 (on aggregate, after three games)
1979	Paraguay 3 Chile 1 (on aggregate, after three games)
1983	Uruguay 3 Brazil 1 (on aggregate, after two games)
1987	Uruguay 1 Chile 0
1989	Brazil (league format)
1991	Argentina (league format)
1993	Argentina 2 Mexico 1
1995	Uruguay 1 Brazil 1 (Uruguay won 5-3 on penalties)
1997	Brazil 3 Bolivia 1
1999	Brazil 3 Uruguay 0
2001	Colombia 1 Mexico 0
2004	Brazil 2 Argentina 2 (Brazil won 4-2 on penalties)
2007	Brazil 3 Argentina 0

HOSTING RIGHTS BY COUNTRY

Argentina 8	(1916, 1921, 1925, 1929, 1937, 1946, 1959, 1987)
Uruguay 7	(1917, 1923, 1924, 1942, 1956, 1967, 1995)
Chile 6	(1920, 1926, 1941, 1945, 1955, 1991)
Peru 6	(1927, 1935, 1939, 1953, 1957, 2004)
Brazil 4	(1919, 1922, 1949, 1989)
Ecuador 3	(1947, 1959, 1993)
Bolivia 2	(1963, 1997)
Paraguay 1	(1999)
Colombia 1	(2001)
Venezuela 1	(2007)

SUB-STANDARD

During the 1953 Copa America, Peru were awarded a walkover win when Paraguay tried to make one more substitution than they were allowed. Would-be substitute Milner Ayala was so incensed, he kicked English referee Richard Maddison and was banned from football for three years. Yet Paraguay remained in the tournament and went on to beat Brazil in the final – minus, of course, the disgraced Ayala.

ROTATING RIGHTS

The Campeonato Sudamericano de Selecciones was rebaptized the Copa America from 1975. Between then and 1983 there was no host nation, before CONMEBOL adopted the policy of rotating the right to host the Copa America among the ten member confederations. The first rotation was complete after Venezuela hosted the 2007 edition, with Argentina lined up to play host for the ninth time in 2011.

HISTORY MEN

The Copa America is the world's oldest surviving international football tournament, having been launched in 1916 when the participating nations were Argentina, Bolivia, Brazil, Chile, Colombia, Ecuador, Paraguay, Peru, Uruguay and Venezuela. In 1910, an unofficial South American championship had been won by Argentina, who beat Uruguay 4-1 in the decider – though the final match had been delayed a day after rioting fans burnt down a stand at the Gimnasia stadium in Buenos Aires.

HIGH FLIER

In 1975, Peru and Brazil drew their two-legged semi-final 3-3 on aggregate, before Peru were awarded a place in the final only through the drawing of lots. They needed three games to settle their final against Colombia, losing the first 1-0, winning the second 2-0 and then finally triumphing thanks to Hugo Sotil's single goal in a final playoff. That match was Sotil's only appearance of the tournament, having been barred from taking part beforehand by his Spanish club employers Barcelona. He only made it just in time for the final playoff, after flying into Venezuelan capital Caracas from Spain.

MORE FROM MORENO

Argentina were not only responsible for the Copa America's biggest win, but also the tournament's highest-scoring game, when they put 12 past Ecuador in 1942 – to no reply. Jose Manuel Moreno's five strikes in that game included the 500th goal in the competition's history. Moreno, born in Buenos Aires on 3 August 1916, ended that tournament as joint top-scorer with team-mate Herminio Masantonio – hitting seven goals. Both men ended their international careers with 19 goals for their country, though Moreno did so in 34 appearances – compared to Masantonio's 21. Masantonio scored four in the Ecuador thrashing.

BIGGEST WINS

1942: **Argentina 12 Ecuador 0**
1975: **Argentina 11 Venezuela 0**
1949: **Brazil 10 Bolivia 1**
1927: **Uruguay 9 Bolivia 0**
1957: **Brazil 9 Colombia 0**
1945: **Argentina 9 Colombia 1**
1949: **Brazil 9 Ecuador 1**
1945: **Brazil 9 Ecuador 2**
1926: **Argentina 8 Paraguay 0**
1957: **Argentina 8 Colombia 2**
1953: **Brazil 8 Bolivia 1**

FALLEN ANGELS

Argentina's 1957 Copa America-winning forward line of Humberto Maschio, Omar Sivori and Antonio Valentin Angelillo became known by the nickname "the angels with dirty faces". At least one of them scored in each of the side's six matches – Maschio finished with nine, Angelillo eight and Sivori three. Argentina's most convincing performance was an opening 8-2 win over Colombia, in which Argentina had scored four goals and missed a penalty within the first 25 minutes. The dazzling displays made Argentina, not eventual winners Brazil, favourites for the following year's FIFA World Cup. Before then, however, Maschio, Sivori and Angelillo had all been lured away to Europe by Italian clubs and the Argentine federation subsequently refused to pick them for the trip to Sweden for the FIFA World Cup. Sivori and Maschio ultimately made it to the FIFA World Cup, in 1962. However, to fury back home, they did so wearing not the light blue-and-white stripes of Argentina, but the Azzurri blue of their newly adopted Italy.

HEAVEN ELEVEN

Some 33 years after crushing Ecuador 12-0 in 1942, Argentina came closest to emulating that record, by beating Venezuela 11-0. The only other game to witness 11 goals was Brazil's 10-1 win over Bolivia in 1949.

AWAY THE LADS

In 1947, Uruguay not only scored the most goals by any team not on home turf, but also achieved the biggest away win in Copa America history, when they thrashed hosts Ecuador 6-1 – ten days earlier they had beaten Chile 6-0.

JAIR PLAY

The most prolific scoring team to take part in the Copa America was the 1949 Brazilian side, who managed 46 goals in their eight fixtures – inspired by nine-goal top scorer Jair, and Ademir and Tesourinha with seven goals. One of Brazil's goals was an own goal.

CONSISTENT COLOMBIANS

In 2001, Colombia, who went on to win the trophy for the first and only time in their history, became the only country to go through an entire Copa America campaign without conceding a single goal. They scored 11 goals themselves, more than half of them from six-goal tournament top scorer Victor Aristazabal. Keeping the clean sheets was goalkeeper Oscar Cordoba, who had previously spent much of his international career as back-up to the eccentric Rene Higuita. Just a month earlier, Cordoba had won the South American club championship, the Copa Libertadores, with Argentine side Boca Juniors.

FIRING BLANKS

In 1917, Chile became the first team to end a Copa America campaign without scoring a single goal. It would be another 50 years before any side was unfortunate enough to repeat the feat, when, in 1967, Bolivia endured five matches without scoring while conceding nine. Bolivia also finished the 1987, 1989 and 2001 tournaments without beating an opposing goalkeeper. Their goalless misery was shared in 1987 by Paraguay and in 1997 and 2001 by Venezuela.

FOUR DRAW

In 1963, in the opening game of the tournament, Bolivia and Ecuador played out the highest-scoring draw in Copa America history, hitting four goals apiece. Each side managed to squander a two-goal lead – Bolivia were 2-0 ahead, before Ecuador raced into a 4-2 lead.

LITTLE NAPOLEON

In 1942, Ecuador and their goalkeeper Napoleon Medina conceded more goals in one tournament than any other team, when they let in 31 goals across six games – and six defeats. Three years later he and his team-mates finally managed to keep a clean sheet, in a goalless draw against Bolivia – but still managed to let in another 27 goals in their five other matches.

TOP-SCORING TEAMS

1	Brazil	46 (1949)
2	Argentina	28 (1947)
3	Argentina	25 (1957)
4	Argentina	22 (1945)
=	Brazil	22 (1997)
6	Argentina	21 (1942)
=	Uruguay	21 (1942)
=	Uruguay	21 (1947)
8	Chile	19 (1955)
=	Argentina	19 (1959)
=	Bolivia	19 (1963)

SECONDS OUT

Chile were the top-scoring team at the 1955 tournament, scoring 19 goals in their five matches, including a 5-4 win over Peru – yet they still had to settle for only second place. They finished two points behind champions Argentina, who managed just 18 goals overall – eight of them from tournament leading scorer Rodolfi Micheli – in the final league table. Micheli hit the only goal of Argentina's crucial match against Chile.

COLLECTIVE RESPONSIBILITY

Brazil's players shared the goalscoring duties on their way to the 1997 Copa America title, finishing with a record ten scorers: Ronaldo (five goals), Leonardo and Romario (three apiece), Denilson, Djalminha and Edmundo (two each) and Aldair, Dunga, Flavio Conceicao and Ze Roberto (one each).

COPA AMERICA GOALSCORING

PELE'S INSPIRATION

Brazilian forward Zizinho jointly holds the all-time goalscoring record for the Copa America, along with Argentina's Norberto Mendez. Both men struck 17 goals, Zizinho across six tournaments and Mendez three – including the 1945 and 1946 tournaments, which featured both men. Mendez was top scorer once and runner-up twice and won championship medals on all three occasions, while Zizinho's goals only helped Brazil take the title once, in 1949. Zizinho, Pele's footballing idol, would emerge from the 1950 FIFA World Cup as Brazil's top scorer and was also voted the tournament's best player – but was forever traumatized by the hosts' surprise defeat to Uruguay that cost Brazil the title. On 16 July every year, the anniversary of the match, Zizinho would take his phone off the hook, because people would still call asking him how Brazil lost. He missed out on a place in Brazil's 1958 FIFA World Cup squad, when selectors instead opted for a promising 17-year-old striker – that childhood fan, Pele. The following year, Pele finished as Copa America top scorer for the first and only time, with eight goals.

FANTASTIC FIVES

Four players have scored five goals in one Copa America game: Hector Scarone in Uruguay's 6-0 win over Bolivia in 1926; Juan Marvezzi in Argentina's 6-1 win over Ecuador in 1941; Jose Manuel Moreno in Argentina's 12-0 win over Ecuador in 1942; and Evaristo de Macedo in Brazil's 9-0 win over Colombia in 1957.

CHILE'S ILL FORTUNE

The first Copa America own goal was scored by Chile's Luis Garcia, giving Argentina a 1-0 win in 1917, in the second edition of the tournament. Even more unfortunately for Chile, Garcia's strike was the only goal by one of their players throughout the tournament – making Chile the first team to fail to score a single goal in a Copa America competition.

HIGHS AND LOWS

The most prolific Copa America tournament, in terms of goals scored, was the 1949 event in Brazil. Then again, this competition did host the most matches in Copa America history – 29, spread across 39 days. They yielded 135 goals, an average of 4.66 per match. The Copa America with the greatest goals per game average came in 1927, when 37 were scored in six fixtures – an average of 6.17 goals per game. Since then, the highest was an average of 4.87 in 1955 – 73 goals across the 15 games, though the highest-scoring team, 19-goal Chile, only finished as runners-up. The meanest defences were those playing in the 1922 Copa America when only 22 goals were scored in 11 games. The lowest tally since then was in 1993, when only 54 goals were racked up in 26 attempts – a goal average of 2.08.

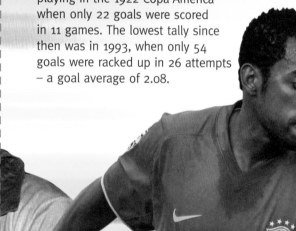

REPEATING THE FEAT

Uruguay's Pedro Petrone (in 1923 and 1924) and Argentina's Gabriel Batistuta (in 1991 and 1995) are the only players to finish as top scorers in the Copa America on two occasions. Batistuta made his Argentina debut just a few days before the 1991 Copa America, in which his starring performances – including a decisive goal in the final – helped him win a transfer from Boca Juniors to Italy's Fiorentina.

QUICK OFF THE MARK

in 1921, Julio Libonatti became the first player in Copa America history to score inside the first minute of a match, helping Argentina to a 3-0 win over Paraguay – a week before Uruguay's Angel Romano repeated the feat, in a 2-1 win over Brazil.

NO ONE BEATS NINE

No footballer has yet hit double figures at a single Copa America – and only three players have ended the tournament with nine goals to their name: Brazil's Jair Rosa Pinto in 1949; and Argentina's Humberto Maschio and Uruguay's Javier Ambrois eight years later. Two of Pinto's goals came in a 7-0 final victory over Paraguay, the biggest win recorded in any Copa America final.

LOW-KEY JOSE

The first-ever Copa America goal, in 1916, was scored by Jose Piendibene – setting Uruguay on the way to a 4-0 triumph over Chile. But he is not thought to have marked the moment with any great extravagance – Piendibene, renowned for his sense of fair play, made a point of not celebrating goals, to avoid offending his opponents.

MILESTONE GOALS

Antonio Urdinaran struck the landmark 100th Copa America goal, when he opened the scoring for Uruguay in their 2-0 defeat of Chile in 1922. The 1,000th strike came courtesy of Chile's Enrique Hormazabal as they beat Ecuador 7-1 in 1955. Luis Hernandez's only goal for Mexico against Costa Rica in 1997 broke the tournament's 2,000-goal barrier.

RECENT TOURNAMENT TOP SCORERS

2007	Robinho (Brazil)	6
2004	Adriano (Brazil)	7
2001	Victor Aristizabal (Colombia)	6
1999	Rivaldo (Brazil)	5
	Ronaldo (Brazil)	5
1997	Luis Hernandez (Mexico)	6
1995	Gabriel Batistuta (Argentina)	4
	Luis Garcia Postigo (Mexico)	4
1993	Jose Luis Dolguetta (Venezuela)	4
1991	Gabriel Batistuta (Argentina)	6
1989	Bebeto (Brazil)	6
1987	Arnoldo Iguaran (Colombia)	4

OVERALL TOP SCORERS

1	Norberto Mendez (Argentina)	17
=	Zizinho (Brazil)	17
3	Teodoro Fernandez (Peru)	15
=	Severino Varela (Uruguay)	15
5	Ademir (Brazil)	13
=	Jair da Rosa Pinto (Brazil)	13
=	Gabriel Batistuta (Argentina)	13
=	Jose Manuel Moreno (Argentina)	13
=	Hector Scarone (Uruguay)	13

COPA AMERICA APPEARANCES

FROG PRINCE

Chilean goalkeeper Sergio Livingstone holds the record for most Copa America appearances, with 34 games, across the 1941, 1942, 1945, 1947, 1949 and 1953 tournaments. Livingstone, nicknamed "The Frog", was voted player of the tournament in 1941 – becoming the first goalkeeper to win the award – and might have played even more Copa America matches had he not missed out on the 1946 competition. Livingstone, born in Santiago on 26 March 1920, spent almost his entire career in his home country – save for a season with Argentina's Racing Club in 1943–44. Overall, he made 52 appearances for Chile between 1941 and 1954, before retiring and becoming a popular TV journalist and commentator.

MOST GAMES PLAYED

Sergio Livingstone (Chile)	34
Zizinho (Brazil)	33
Leonel Alvarez (Colombia)	27
Carlos Valderrama (Colombia)	27
Alex Aguinaga (Ecuador)	25
Claudio Taffarel (Brazil)	25
Teodoro Fernandez (Peru)	24
Angel Romano (Uruguay)	23
Djalma Santos (Brazil)	22
Claudio Suarez (Mexico)	22

REGULAR GUEST

Of the non-South Americans invited to take part in the Copa America, Mexico's Claudio Suarez has appeared the most – 22 games across five tournaments from 1993 to 2004. Suarez, the world's most-capped outfield footballer, was ever-present during Mexico's run to the 1993 final, but missed the 2001 event, when they finished runners-up, to rest before crucial FIFA World Cup qualifiers – only to break his leg just before the 2002 FIFA World Cup itself.

MAGIC ALEX

When Alex Aguinaga lined up for Ecuador against Uruguay in his country's opening game at the 2004 event, he became only the second man to take part in eight different Copa Americas – joining legendary Uruguayan goalscorer Angel Romano. Aguinaga, a midfielder born in Ibarra on 9 July 1969, played a total of 109 times for his country – 25 of them in the Copa America, a competition that yielded four of his 23 international goals. His Copa America career certainly began well: Ecuador went undefeated for his first four appearances, at the 1987 and 1989 events, but his luck had ran out by the time his Ecuador career was coming to an end: he lost his final seven Copa America matches.

ORLANDO GLOOM

It was third time unlucky for Brazilian defender Orlando, in his team's third game of the first tournament in 1916 – he limped off injured after just 16 minutes of the 2-1 defeat to Uruguay and never featured in a Copa America – or a Brazil shirt – again.

SAME OLD STORY

Argentina's Roberto Ayala and Javier Zanetti have been among the most consistent performers in recent Copa America history, with Ayala making 19 appearances since 1995 and Zanetti 18. Unfortunately for both, all four tournaments in which they took part had a persistent theme: defeat to Brazil, who eliminated Argentina in 1995, 1999, 2004 and 2007. Ayala suffered most when favourites Argentina lost the 2007 final 3-0 to their arch-rivals: he scored an own goal in what turned out to be his 115th and final game for his country.

⚽ TAFF ACT TO FOLLOW

After Sergio Livingstone, Brazil's Claudio Taffarel has made the most Copa America appearances as a goalkeeper, keeping clean sheets in 15 of his 25 matches, conceding 15 goals. He was the penalty shoot-out hero against Argentina in a 1995 quarter-final, saving from Diego Simeone and Nestor Fabbri, but was helpless to prevent Uruguay winning the final, six days later, also on spot-kicks. Taffarel was a member of Brazil's triumphant teams in 1989 and 1997 – both times alongside captain Dunga, who also lifted the trophy as Brazil's coach in 2007. Dunga attended his first Copa America in 1987, as a non-playing member of Brazil's squad, before making 18 appearances across the 1989, 1995 and 1997 tournaments.

START TO FINISH

Colombia playmaker Carlos Valderrama and defensive midfielder Leonel Alvarez played in all 27 of their country's Copa America matches between 1987 and 1995, winning ten, drawing ten and losing seven – including third-place finishes in 1987, 1993 and 1995. Valderrama's two Copa America goals came in his first and final appearances in the competition – in a 2-0 victory over Bolivia in 1987 and a 4-1 thrashing of the United States eight years later.

⚽ LOLO'S HIGHS

Teodoro "Lolo" Fernandez, on his way to becoming Peru's most regular performer at the Copa America, finished the 1939 contest not only as a member of the championship-winning team, but also as top scorer and player of the tournament. His seven goals helped Peru to their first Copa America triumph – and eased the disappointment of their disqualification from the 1936 Olympics, after a quarter-final victory over Austria was annulled. Fernandez had scored one of Peru's goals in a 4-2 win that allegedly angered Adolf Hitler – though a pitch invasion was given as the official reason Peru were thrown out. At the 1939 Copa, hosts Peru made the most of the absence of both Brazil and Argentina to beat Uruguay to the title, Fernandez top-scoring with seven overall. He ended his career with 15 Copa America goals in 24 matches, across six tournaments between 1935 and 1947.

SOLAR POWER

Peruvian midfielder Jose Del Solar played at six different Copa America competitions from 1987 to 2001, scoring six goals in 19 games. Despite retiring from the game in 2002, he is aiming to make it to a seventh Copa America, this time as his country's coach – he took over in July 2007, after a poor Copa America that summer put paid to predecessor Julio Cesar Uribe.

MOST TOURNAMENTS

Alex Aguinaga (Ecuador) 8 (1987, 1989, 1991, 1993, 1995, 1999, 2001, 2004)
Angel Romano (Uruguay) 8 (1916, 1917, 1919, 1920, 1921, 1922, 1924, 1926)
Hector Scarone (Uruguay) 7 (1917, 1919, 1923, 1924, 1926, 1927, 1929)
Jose Del Solar (Peru) 6 (1987, 1989, 1991, 1993, 1995, 2001)
Teodoro Fernandez (Peru) 6 (1935, 1937, 1939, 1941, 1943, 1947)
Ivan Hurtado (Ecuador) 6 (1993, 1995, 1999, 2001, 2004, 2007)
Sergio Livingstone (Chile) 6 (1941, 1942, 1945, 1947, 1949, 1953)
Zizinho (Brazil) 6 (1942, 1945, 1946, 1949, 1953, 1957)
Leonel Alvarez (Colombia) 5 (1987, 1989, 1991, 1993, 1995)
Julio Cesar Baldivieso (Bolivia) 5 (1991, 1993, 1995, 1997, 2001)
Luis Cristaldo (Bolivia) 5 (1993, 1995, 1997, 1999, 2004)
Carlos Gamarra (Paraguay) 5 (1993, 1995, 1997, 1999, 2004)
Jose Manuel Rey (Venezuela) 5 (1997, 1999, 2001, 2004, 2007)
Marco Sandy (Bolivia) 5 (1993, 1995, 1997, 1999, 2001)
Estanislao Struway (Paraguay) 5 (1991, 1993, 1995, 1997, 2001)
Claudio Suarez (Mexico) 5 (1993, 1995, 1997, 1999, 2004)
Claudio Taffarel (Brazil) 5 (1989, 1991, 1993, 1995, 1997)
Carlos Valderrama (Colombia) 5 (1987, 1989, 1991, 1993, 1995)

COPA AMERICA OTHER RECORDS

HOME COMFORTS

Uruguay have a unique record in remaining unbeaten in 38 Copa America games on home turf, all played in the country's capital Montevideo – comprising 31 wins, seven draws. The last tournament match they hosted was both a draw and a win – 1-1 against Brazil in 1995, with Uruguay emerging as champions, 5-3 on penalties after Fernando Alvez saved Tulio's penalty.

SUCCESSFUL INVADERS

Only two foreign coaches have led a country to Copa America glory – Brazilian Danilo Alvim, whose Bolivian side won in 1963, and Englishman Jack Greenwell, Peru coach in 1939. Alvim, who won the tournament as a centre-half with Brazil in 1949, not only coached Bolivia to their one and only Copa America triumph – he did it by beating his native land 5-4 in the final match.

POINTS WIN PRIZES

If every Copa America win were awarded three points, with one for a draw, Argentina would emerge from the tournament's history with the most per game – an average 2.1 points per match, ahead of Brazil's 1.89 and Uruguay's 1.82. The only country to still go without a single Copa America match victory is Japan, who failed to triumph in three matches when invited to take part – for the first and, so far, only time – in the 1999 competition.

TROPHY-WINNING COACHES

6 Guillermo Stabile (Argentina 1941, 1945, 1946, 1947, 1955, 1957)

2 Alfio Basile (Argentina 1991, 1993)
Juan Carlos Corazzo (Uruguay 1959, 1967)
Ernesto Figoli (Uruguay 1920, 1926)

1 Jorge Pacheco and Alfredo Foglino (Uruguay 1916)
Ramon Platero (Uruguay 1917)
Pedro Calomino (Argentina 1921)
Lais (Brazil 1922)
Leonardo De Lucca (Uruguay 1923)
Ernesto Meliante (Uruguay 1924)
Americo Tesoriere (Argentina 1925)
Jose Lago Millon (Argentina 1927)
Francisco Olazar (Argentina 1929)
Raul V Blanco (Uruguay 1935)
Manuel Seoane (Argentina 1937)
Jack Greenwell (Peru 1939)
Pedro Cea (Uruguay 1942)
Flavio Costa (Brazil 1949)
Manuel Fleitas Solich (Paraguay 1953)
Hugo Bagnulo (Uruguay 1956)
Victorio Spinetto (Argentina 1959)
Danilo Alvim (Bolivia 1963)
Marcos Calderon (Peru 1975)
Ranulfo Miranda (Paraguay 1979)
Omar Borras (Uruguay 1983)
Roberto Fleitas (Uruguay 1987)
Sebastiao Lazaroni (Brazil 1989)
Hector Nunez (Uruguay 1995)
Mario Zagallo (Brazil 1997)
Wanderlei Luxemburgo (Brazil 1999)
Francisco Maturana (Colombia 2001)
Carlos Alberto Parreira (Brazil 2004)
Dunga (Brazil 2007)

MULTI-TASKING

Argentina's Guillermo Stabile not only holds the record for most Copa America triumphs as coach – he trounces all opposition. He led his country to the title on no fewer than six occasions – in 1941, 1945, 1946, 1947, 1955 and 1957. No other coach has lifted the trophy more than twice. Stabile coached Argentina from 1939 to 1960, having been appointed at the age of just 34. He lasted for 123 games in charge, winning 83 of them – and still managed to coach three clubs on the side at different times throughout his reign. His remained as Red Star Paris manager during his first year in the Argentina role, then led Argentine club Huracan for the next nine years – before leading domestic rivals Racing Club from 1949 to 1960. Stabile's Argentina may have, unusually, missed out on Copa America success in 1949, but that year brought the first of three Argentina league championships in a row for Stabile's Racing Club.

INVITED GUESTS

1993 Mexico (runners-up),
      United States
1995 Mexico, United States (fourth)
1997 Costa Rica, Mexico (third)
1999 Japan, Mexico (third)
2001 Costa Rica, Honduras (third),
      Mexico (second)
2004 Costa Rica, Mexico
2007 Mexico (third), United States

WRONG JUAN

It took 21 years, but Uruguay's Juan Emilio Piriz became the first Copa America player sent off, against Chile in 1937 – the first of 170 dismissals so far. Some 127 of those disgraced players have had a red card flourished in their face, since FIFA introduced the card system for referees in 1970.

SEEING RED

Argentina may have the worst World Cup disciplinary record, but neighbours Uruguay assume that unenviable position in the Copa America. Uruguayan players have been sent off 30 times, followed by Argentina and Peru on 22 dismissals apiece, Brazil (19), Venezuela (18), Chile (15), Bolivia and Paraguay (11 each), Colombia, Ecuador and Mexico (nine each), and Honduras and Japan (one each). Only Costa Rica and the US have, so far, made their way through Copa America participations with eleven men on the field throughout.

ONE-NIL TO THE ANYONE

Perhaps predictably, the most common scoreline in Copa America history is the 1-0 win – the result on no fewer than 106 occasions, most recently when Javier Mascherano's first goal for Argentina saw off Paraguay in the 2007 group stage.

FINE HOST

Argentina has hosted more tournaments than any other South American country, followed by Uruguay (seven), Chile (six) and Peru (also six). Despite hosting the final play-off game in 1975, Venezuela remained the last South American country not to host a full tournament until 2007.

CAPTAIN CONSISTENT

Uruguay's 1930 World Cup-winning captain Jose Nasazzi is the only footballer to be voted player of the tournament at two different Copa America tournaments. Even more impressively, he achieved the feat 12 years apart – first taking the prize in 1923, then again in 1935. He was a Cup winner in 1923, 1924, 1926 and 1935. Nasazzi also captained Uruguay to victory in the 1924 and 1928 Olympic Games and in the 1930 World Cup.

PART 5:
OTHER FIFA TOURNAMENTS

FOOTBALL at the highest level is not only about the most high-profile superstars, but also about the working investment of a myriad of enthusiasts at grassroots level across the world. Regional confederations organize international championships for players in a wide range of age groups. In 1977, FIFA extended its own worldwide development programme with the launch of the FIFA World Youth Cup. The first finals were hosted by Tunisia and the Soviet Union beat Mexico in the final. Later, in 1985, came the FIFA U-17 World Cup. Simultaneously, the Olympic Games football tournament was converted into an Under-23 event with, initially, an exception for teams in the finals to field up to three over-age players.

The establishment of such events at the pinnacle of the world game encouraged all the regional confederations to create matching tournaments of their own so that their teams could qualify for a place on the big stage. A flood of outstanding players first made headlines in the age-group system. Most notable among these players was Diego Maradona, who led Argentina to victory in Japan in the FIFA World Youth Cup in 1979. Seven years later, in 1986 in Mexico, he was his country's winning captain and inspiration at the FIFA World Cup. Women's championships were organized in response to the rapid acceleration of interest in the game and, in 2000, FIFA stepped into the club sphere with the launch of what is now the established, annual FIFA Club World Cup.

Pablo Zabaleta of Argentina hails his team's gold-medal victory over Nigeria in the final of the 2008 Olympic Games football tournament in the Bird's Nest Stadium in Beijing.

FIFA U-20 WORLD CUP

First staged in 1977 in Tunisia and known as the FIFA Youth World Championship until 2005, the FIFA U-20 World Cup is the world championship of football for players under the age of 20 and has featured some of the game's most notable names. Staged on a bi-annual basis, the tournament's most successful team has been Argentina, who have lifted the trophy on six occasions.

CAPTAIN MARVELS

Two men have lifted both the FIFA Under-20 World Cup and the FIFA World Cup as captain: Brazil's Dunga (in 1983 and 1994) and Argentina's Diego Maradona (in 1979 and 1986). Many had expected Maradona to make Argentina's full squad for the 1978 FIFA World Cup but he missed out on selection. He showed his potential by being voted best player at the 1979 youth tournament in Japan.

SIX APPEAL

Argentina have won the FIFA Under-20 World Cup the most times, winning six times, including the two most recent – in 2005 and 2007. Brazil have won four times, Portugal twice, with one success apiece for Germany, Spain, the Soviet Union and Yugoslavia. The only final Argentina have contested, but lost, came against arch-rivals Brazil, in 1983, when Geovani struck the only goal.

WHAT A MESSI

Lionel Messi was the star of the show for Argentina in 2005, and not just for scoring both his country's goals in the final – both from the penalty spot. He achieved a hat-trick by not only winning the Golden Boot for top scorer and Golden Shoe for best player, but also by captaining his side to the title. This feat was emulated two years later by compatriot Sergio Aguero, who scored once in the final against the Czech Republic, before team-mate Mauro Zarate struck a late winner. Two other men have finished as both top scorer and as the tournament's best player (as voted by journalists) – Brazil's Geovani in 1983 and Argentina's Javier Saviola.

SAVIOUR SAVIOLA

Javier Saviola has scored more goals in one FIFA Under-20 World Cup than any other player – he managed 11 in seven games at the 2001 competition, as his side Argentina went on to beat Ghana in the final, with Saviola scoring his team's three unanswered goals. Saviola, born on 11 December 1981 in Buenos Aires, was playing for River Plate at the time but joined Barcelona for £15 million not long afterwards – before later signing for the Spanish side's arch-rivals Real Madrid. When Pele picked his 125 "greatest living footballers" for FIFA in March 2004, 22-year-old Saviola was the youngest player on the list.

EVERY LOOSE WINS

Despite mainly playing as sweeper, Ralf Loose was West Germany's goalscoring hero during their only FIFA Under-20 World Cup triumph in 1981, with four strikes – including two in the final.

LISBON LIONS

In 1991, Portugal became the first hosts to win the tournament with a team that became known as the country's "Golden Generation", featuring the likes of Luis Figo, Rui Costa, Joao Pinto, Abel Xavier and Jorge Costa. Portugal's winning squad was coached by Carlos Queiroz, who would later manage the full national side twice, with spells in charge at Real Madrid and as assistant at Manchester United in between. Their penalty shoot-out win over Brazil in the final was played at Benfica's iconic Estádio da Luz in the capital Lisbon. In 2001, Argentina became the second team to lift the trophy on home territory.

WAITING GAME

Nigeria were originally scheduled to host the 1995 tournament, but were replaced by Qatar due to concerns about human rights issues – and Nigeria did not even get to take part in the competition. The country finally hosted the event, four years later. The 2009 edition of the FIFA Under-20 World Cup will be held in Egypt, with Colombia set to host the competition two years later.

TOURNAMENT HOSTS AND FINAL RESULTS

1977 (Host: Tunisia) USSR 2 Mexico 2 (aet: USSR win 9-8 on penalties)
1979 (Japan) Argentina 3 USSR 1
1981 (Australia) West Germany 4 Qatar 0
1983 (Mexico) Brazil 1 Argentina 0
1985 (USSR) Brazil 1 Spain 0 (aet)
1987 (Chile) Yugoslavia 1 West Germany 1 (aet: Yugoslavia win 5-4 on penalties)
1989 (Saudi Arabia) Portugal 2 Nigeria 0
1991 (Portugal) Portugal 0 Brazil 0 (aet: Portugal win 4-2 on penalties)
1993 (Australia) Brazil 2 Ghana 1
1995 (Qatar) Argentina 2 Brazil 0
1997 (Malaysia) Argentina 2 Uruguay 1
1999 (Nigeria) Spain 4 Japan 0
2001 (Argentina) Argentina 3 Ghana 0
2003 (United Arab Emirates) Brazil 1 Spain 0
2005 (Holland) Argentina 2 Nigeria 1
2007 (Canada) Argentina 2 Czech Republic 1

TOURNAMENT TOP SCORERS

1977 Guina (Brazil) 4
1979 Ramon Diaz (Argentina) 8
1981 Ralf Loose (West Germany), Roland Wohlfarth (West Germany), Taher Amer (Egypt), Mark Koussas (Argentina) 4
1983 Geovani (Brazil) 6
1985 Gerson (Brazil), Balalo (Brazil), Muller (Brazil), Alberto Garcia Aspe (Mexico), Monday Odiaka (Nigeria), Fernando Gomez (Spain), Sebastian Losada (Spain) 3
1987 Marcel Witeczek (West Germany) 7
1989 Oleg Salenko (USSR) 5
1991 Sergei Sherbakov (USSR) 5
1993 Ante Milicic (Australia), Adriano (Brazil), Gian (Brazil), Henry Zambrano (Colombia), Vicente Nieto (Mexico), Chris Faklaris (USA) 3
1995 Joseba Etxeberria (Spain) 7
1997 Adailton Martins Bolzan (Brazil) 10
1999 Mahamadou Dissa (Mali), Pablo (Spain) 5
2001 Javier Saviola (Argentina) 11
2003 Fernando Cavenaghi (Argentina), Dudu (Brazil), Daisuke Sakata (Japan), Eddie Johnson (USA) 4
2005 Lionel Messi (Argentina) 6
2007 Sergio Aguero (Argentina) 7

SUPER SUB

The Soviet Union became the first winners of the FIFA Under-20 World Cup when they beat hosts Mexico 9-8 on penalties after a 2-2 draw in the 1977 final. Their shoot-out hero was substitute goalkeeper Yuri Sivuha, who had replaced Aleksandre Novikov during extra-time. It remains the only time the Soviet Union won the event, though their striker Oleg Salenko, a future 1994 FIFA World Cup Golden Boot winner, took the top scorer award in 1989, with five goals. Two years later, fellow Soviet Sergei Sherbakov also finished top scorer, also with five goals, although his full international career was less successful. He only played twice for Ukraine before injuries suffered in a car accident in 1993 left him in a wheelchair.

CHILE RECEPTION

Members of Chile's team fought with police both inside and outside the Toronto stadium after their 2007 semi-final against Argentina, when German referee Wolfgang Stark showed them two red cards. Ten Chilean players were held in custody for ten hours and Jaime Grondona was later banned for nine months for hitting match officials.

FIFA U-17 WORLD CUP

First staged in China in 1985, when it was known as the FIFA Under-16 World Championship, the age limit was raised from 16 to 17 in 1991 and the competition became known as the FIFA U-17 World Cup from 2007. Staged on a bi-annual basis, the 2009 edition of the event is due to be staged in Nigeria, the defending champions, who, along with Brazil, are the tournament's most successful side, with three wins.

GOLDEN HAUL

West Germany's Marcel Witeczek is the only person to finish top scorer at both a FIFA Under-17 World Cup and the Under-20 version of the event. The Polish-born striker hit eight goals at the 1985 Under-17 tournament, followed by seven more at the Under-20 championship two years later. Brazil's Adriano – a different Adriano to the one who later played for the senior side and Serie A club Internazionale – came closest to equalling the feat: he won the Golden Shoe, for top scorer, after scoring four goals at the 1991 FIFA Under-17 World Cup, then the Golden Ball, for best player, at the Under-20 event in 1993.

EVER-PRESENT AMERICA

While Brazil and Nigeria have enjoyed the most success in the FIFA U-17 World Cup, with three triumphs each, the only country to take part in all 12 competitions is the United States – their best finish was fourth in 1999.

FAB FABREGAS

Spain's Cesc Fabregas is one of only two players to win both the Golden Ball, for top scorer, and the Golden Shoe, for best player, at a FIFA Under-17 World Cup. He took both prizes after scoring five goals at the 2003 tournament, despite losing the final to Brazil. He and team-mate David Silva would later be part of the senior Spanish team that won the 2008 European Championships. Fabregas left Barcelona for Arsenal a month after the 2003 tournament, where he later became club captain. At the 2004 Under-17 European Championships, Fabregas, born in Arenys de Mar on 4 May 1987, again won the best player award – and again finished on the losing side in the final.

TOURNAMENT TOP SCORERS

1985	Marcel Witeczek (West Germany)	8
1987	Moussa Traore (Côte d'Ivoire)	5
	Yuri Nikiforov (USSR)	5
1989	Khaled Jasem (Bahrain)	3
	Fode Camara (Guinea)	3
	Gil (Portugal)	3
	Tulipa (Portugal)	3
	Khalid Al Roaihi (Saudi Arabia)	3
1991	Adriano (Brazil)	4
1993	Wilson Oruma (Nigeria)	6
1995	Daniel Allsopp (Australia)	5
	Mohamed Al Kathiri (Oman)	5
1997	David (Spain)	7
1999	Ishmael Addo (Ghana)	7
2001	Florent Sinama-Pongolle (France)	9
2003	Carlos Hidalgo (Colombia)	5
	Manuel Curto (Portugal)	5
	Cesc Fabregas (Spain)	5
2005	Carlos Vela (Mexico)	5
2007	Macauley Chrisantus (Nigeria)	7

TAKING WING

Nigeria's youth side side, the "Golden Eaglets", became the first African nation to win a FIFA tournament when they triumphed at the inaugural Under-16 FIFA World Cup in 1985 (it became an Under-17 event in 1991). Their opening goal in the final against West Germany was scored by striker Jonathan Akpoborie, who would go on to play for German clubs Stuttgart and Wolfsburg.

LITTLE ITALY

The 1991 tournament was originally scheduled to take place in Ecuador, but a cholera outbreak in the country meant it was switched to Italy instead – though played in much smaller venues than those that had been used for the previous year's senior FIFA World Cup in the country. The 1991 tournament was the first to be open to Under-17s – the first three had been known as the FIFA U-16 World Cup.

HOSTS AND FINAL RESULTS

(Host country)

1985 (China) Nigeria 2 West Germany 0

1987 (Canada) USSR 1 Nigeria 1
(aet: USSR win 4-2 on penalties)

1989 (Scotland) Saudi Arabia 2 Scotland 2
(aet: Saudi Arabia win 5-4 on penalties)

1991 (Italy) Ghana 1 Spain 0

1993 (Japan) Nigeria 2 Ghana 1

1995 (Ecuador) Ghana 3 Brazil 2

1997 (Egypt) Brazil 2 Ghana 1

1999 (New Zealand) Brazil 0 Australia 0
(aet: Brazil win 8-7 on penalties)

2001 (Trinidad and Tobago) France 3 Nigeria 0

2003 (Finland) Brazil 1 Spain 0

2005 (Peru) Mexico 3 Brazil 0

2007 (South Korea) Nigeria 0 Spain 0
(aet: Nigeria win 3-0 on penalties)

2009 (Nigeria)

SEOUL SURVIVOR

The final of the 2007 tournament was the first to be hosted by a former FIFA World Cup venue – the 68,476-capacity Seoul FIFA World Cup Stadium in South Korea's capital, which had been built for the 2002 FIFA World Cup. The game was watched by a crowd of 36,125, a tournament record. The 2007 event was the first to feature 24 teams instead of 16, and was won by Nigeria – after Spain missed all three of their spot-kicks in a penalty shoot-out.

GOOD AND BAD BOY BOJAN

Barcelona star Bojan Krkic quickly went from hero to villain in the final moments of Spain's semi-final victory over Ghana in 2007 – he scored his team's winner with four minutes of extra-time remaining, but was then sent off for a second yellow-card offence just before the final whistle. His expulsion meant he was suspended for the final, which Spain lost on penalties to Nigeria.

GOALS FLO

Apart from Cesc Fabregas, the only other man to have won both the Golden Ball and the Golden Shoe is France's Florent Sinama-Pongolle, whose nine goals in 2001 set a tournament record for one player. His tally included two hat-tricks in the opening round. Unlike Fabregas, Sinama-Pongolle also ended the final on the winning side. The team goalscoring record is held by Spain, who struck 22 times on their way to third place in 1997.

FIFA CONFEDERATIONS CUP

The FIFA Confederations Cup has assumed numerous guises over the years. In 1992 and 1995 it was played in Saudi Arabia and featured a collection of continental champions. From 1997 to 2003 FIFA staged a tournament every two years. The tournament was played in its current format for the first time in Germany in 2005. It is now celebrated throughout the football world as the Championship of Champions.

KING FAHD CUP FINALS

1992 (Host country: Saudi Arabia) Argentina 3 Saudi Arabia 1;
1994 (Saudi Arabia) Denmark 2 Argentina 0

FIT FOR A KING

Before being rebranded as the FIFA Confederations Cup, a tournament bringing together the continental champions of the world was known as the King Fahd Cup and was hosted in Saudi Arabia. Copa America holders Argentina reached both finals, beating their hosts in the first in 1992 thanks to goals by Leonardo Rodriguez, Claudio Caniggia and Diego Simeone. Only four teams took part in the 1992 event, with the United States and the Ivory Coast also represented, but world champions Germany and European champions Holland did not participate. In 1995, a six-team version was won by European champions Denmark, when goals from Michael Laudrup and Peter Rasmussen were enough to see off Argentina in the final in Riyadh.

THREE APIECE

Brazil's Romario holds the record for the most goals scored in a single FIFA Confederations Cup – seven, in five games, as his country took the title for the first time in 1997. His tally included three in the 6-0 final win over Australia – but he had to share the hat-trick glory: the rest of the goals were claimed by his strike-partner Ronaldo.

UNEVEN DISTRIBUTION

Both Saudi Arabia's Marzouk Al-Otaibi and Brazil's Ronaldinho were on the scoresheet in their sides' 1999 semi-final, when Brazil won 8-2 – the most goals ever scored in one FIFA Confederations Cup match. Al-Otaibi got two and Ronaldinho hit three, in a match that was even at 2-2 after half an hour.

SIX-SHOOTERS

Brazilian playmaker Ronaldinho and Mexico's Cuauhtemoc Blanco share the record for most goals scored overall in FIFA Confederations Cup history, with nine each – including six apiece at the 1999 event. Perhaps the most significant of those goals was Blanco's strike in the final, his country's fourth in a 4-3 win over defending champions Brazil. In his country's semi-final against the United States, he had ensured Mexico's passage to the final with the first-ever FIFA Confederations Cup golden goal, seven minutes into extra-time. However, both Ronaldinho and Blanco had to share the glory of finishing top scorer at that tournament with Saudi Arabia striker Marzouq Al-Otaibi, who also hit six – including four in a 5-1 victory over Egypt. The rest of the Saudi team only managed to score two more goals between them.

TRIPLE CROWNS

Two countries have held a clean sweep hat-trick of titles at one time. Brazil's FIFA Confederations Cup triumph in December 1997 came six months after they were crowned South American champions, in the Copa America – and while still reigning world champions, after winning the 1994 FIFA World Cup. Patrick Vieira's golden-goal winner for France in the 2001 FIFA Confederations Cup final meant they emulated Brazil's feat, having won the FIFA World Cup in 1998 and the European Championship in 2000.

MEXICAN WAVES

The 1999 tournament in Mexico, won by the hosts, was the best-attended in FIFA Confederations Cup history, attracting a total of 970,000 spectators – an average 60,625 per match. The final was watched in the Estadio Azteca, in Mexico City, by a FIFA Confederations Cup-record crowd of 110,000. The most sparsely attended tournament was the 1995 version of the King Fahd Cup in Saudi Arabia, with crowds averaging 20,625 in Riyadh's 67,000-capacity King Fahd Stadium.

MISSING OUT

Two countries have refused invitations to take part in the tournament since it became known as the FIFA Confederations Cup – Germany and France. Germany were entitled to play in 1997, after winning the previous year's European Championships, but were replaced by European runners-up, the Czech Republic, who finished third. They were also invited in 2003, having lost the 2002 FIFA World Cup final to Brazil – who were already representing South America as Copa America winners. But Germany allowed FIFA World Cup third-placed side Turkey to enter instead. The Turks also finished third. In 1999, France became the only FIFA World Cup winners to stay away from the tournament. Brazil took their place.

FIFA CONFEDERATIONS CUP HOSTS AND FINAL RESULTS

1997   (Host country: Saudi Arabia) Brazil 6 Argentina 0
1999   (Mexico) Mexico 4 Brazil 3
2001   (South Korea and Japan) France 1 Japan 0
2003   (France) France 1 Cameroon 0
        (aet: France win on golden goal)
2005   (Germany) Brazil 4 Argentina 1

TOURNAMENT TOP SCORERS

1992	Gabriel Batistuta (Argentina), Bruce Murray (USA)	2
1995	Luis Garcia (Mexico)	3
1997	Romario (Brazil)	7
1999	Ronaldinho (Brazil), Cuauhtemoc Blanco (Mexico), Marzouq Al-Otaibi (Saudi Arabia)	6
2001	Shaun Murphy (Australia), Eric Carriere (France), Robert Pires (France), Patrick Vieira (France), Sylvain Wiltord (France), Takayuki Suzuki (Japan), Hwang Sun-Hong (South Korea)	2
2003	Thierry Henry (France)	4
2005	Adriano (Brazil)	5

OVERALL TOP SCORERS

1	Cuauhtemoc Blanco (Mexico)	9
=	Ronaldinho (Brazil)	9
3	Romario (Brazil)	7
=	Adriano (Brazil)	7
5	Marzouq Al-Otaibi	6
6	Alex (Brazil)	5
=	John Aloisi (Australia)	5
=	Vladimir Smicer (Czech Rep.)	5
=	Robert Pires (France)	5

SHARED SADNESS

The 2003 tournament was overshadowed by the tragic death of Cameroon's 28-year-old midfielder Marc-Vivien Foe, who collapsed on the Lyon pitch after suffering a heart attack 73 minutes into his country's semi-final win against Colombia. After Thierry Henry scored France's golden-goal winner against Cameroon in the final, he dedicated his goal to Foe, who played much of his club career in the French championship. When the trophy was presented at the Stade de France in Paris, it was jointly lifted by the captains of both teams – Marcel Desailly for France and Rigobert Song for Cameroon.

FIFA CLUB WORLD CUP

As is the case with the FIFA Confederations Cup, the FIFA Club World Cup has been played in many different formats since 1960, when Real Madrid defeated Penarol. In its current guise, the competition pits the champion clubs from all six continents against each other and has been staged on an annual basis, in Japan, since 2005. In 2009 and 2010, the tournament will be staged in Abu Dhabi for the first time.

LONG-DISTANCE, LONG-RUNNING RIVALRY

The precursor to the modern FIFA Club World Cup was the Intercontinental Cup, also known informally as the World Club Cup and/or the Europe–South America Cup, which pitted the champions of Europe and South America against each other. Representatives of UEFA and CONMEBOL contested the event from 1960 to 2004, but now all continental federations send at least one club to an expanded Club World Cup organized and endorsed by the world federation, FIFA. The original final, in 1960, was between Spain's Real Madrid and Uruguay's Penarol. After a goalless draw in the rain in Montevideo, Real triumphed 5-1 at their own stadium in Madrid – including three goals scored in the first eight minutes, two of them by Ferenc Puskas. The two clubs are among five sharing the record for Intercontinental Cup triumphs, with three victories apiece – the others being Argentina's Boca Juniors, Uruguay's Nacional and AC Milan of Italy. Milan are the only one of these clubs to have added a FIFA Club World Cup to their tally, as the championship was first contested in 2000 (in Brazil) before it was swallowed up by the Intercontinental Cup and was instituted on an annual basis.

SUCCESS IN PHASES

Since FIFA introduced its own, expanded Club World Cup in 2000, with representatives from all the world's continental football federations, Brazilian sides have the best overall record – with Corinthians the first winners. Carlo Ancelotti's AC Milan finally broke the Brazilian stranglehold in 2007, when the trophy was lifted by club captain Paolo Maldini, who had appeared for Milan – alongside Alessandro Costacurta – in five Intercontinental Cup showdowns between 1989 and 2003.

COACHING CONSISTENCY

Carlos Bianchi is the only man to have won the world club title three times as coach – lifting the Intercontinental Cup with Velez Sarsfield in 1994 and Boca Juniors in 2000 and 2003. Two Uruguayans have won the world title both as player and coach – Luis Cubilla and Juan Mugica, who were team-mates when Nacional beat Greek side Panathinaikos in the 1971 final. Midfielder Cubilla had already won the trophy with Penarol in 1961, and coached Paraguay's Olimpia Asuncion to glory in 1979. Mugica was the winning manager the following year, again with Nacional.

FIFA CLUB WORLD CUP FINALS (2000–)

2000	Corinthians (Brazil) 0 Vasco da Gama (Brazil) 0 (aet: Corinthians win 4-3 on penalties)
2005	Sao Paulo (Brazil) 1 Liverpool (England) 0
2006	Internacional (Brazil) 1 Barcelona (Spain) 0
2007	AC Milan (Italy) 4 Boca Juniors (Argentina) 2
2008	Manchester United (England) 1 LDU Quito (Ecuador) 0

OVERALL NATIONAL RECORD

9	Argentina
7	Italy
6	Brazil, Uruguay
4	Spain
3	Germany, Netherlands
2	Portugal
1	England, Paraguay, Yugoslavia

INTERCONTINENTAL CUP TRIUMPHS (1960–2004)

3 wins: Real Madrid, Spain (1960, 1998, 2002); Penarol, Uruguay (1961, 1966, 1982); AC Milan, Italy (1969, 1989, 1990); Nacional, Uruguay (1971, 1988, 1988); Boca Juniors, Argentina (1977, 2000, 2003).

2 wins: Santos, Brazil (1962, 1963); Internazionale, Italy (1964, 1965); Ajax, Netherlands (1972, 1995); Independiente, Argentina (1973, 1984); Bayern Munich, West Germany/Germany (1976, 2001); Juventus, Italy (1985, 1996); Porto, Portugal (1987, 2004); Sao Paulo, Brazil (1992, 1993).

1 win: Racing Club, Argentina (1967); Estudiantes, Argentina (1968); Feyenoord, Netherlands (1970); Atletico Madrid, Spain (1974); Olimpia Asuncion, Paraguay (1979); Flamengo, Brazil (1981); Gremio, Brazil (1983); River Plate, Argentina (1986); Red Star Belgrade, Yugoslavia (1991); Velez Sarsfield, Argentina (1994); Borussia Dortmund, Germany (1997); Manchester United, England (1999).

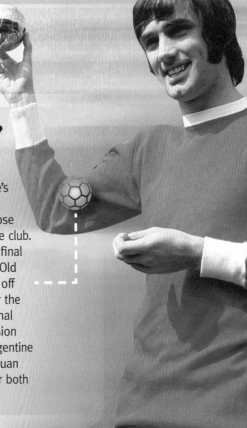

SWITCHING SYSTEMS

From 1960 until 1968, the Intercontinental Cup was settled, not on aggregate scores, but by using a system of two points for a win and one for a draw. This meant a third, deciding match was needed in 1961, 1963, 1964 and 1967. No team that had not been worse off on aggregate after the first two legs had gone on to win the third match, though before losing their playoff 1-0 to Argentina's Racing Club in 1967, Celtic would have won the two-legged tie if aggregate scores and away goals counted. The Scottish side won their home leg 1-0, before losing 2-1 away. From 1980 onwards, the annual event was a one-off match staged in Japan.

BIG IN JAPAN

From 1980 to 2008, every Intercontinental Cup or FIFA Club World Cup took place in Japan, apart from FIFA's 2000 tournament in Brazil – which was then followed by a five-year gap. Spain was scheduled to host a 12-team Club World Cup in 2001, but the tournament was cancelled. The 2009 and 2010 events are due to be staged in the United Arab Emirates.

FIGHTING BACK

Manchester United's Nobby Stiles and George Best were both sent off during their side's 1968 Intercontinental Cup tie against Estudiantes, as was Jose Hugo Medina for the Argentine club. After punching Medina in the final minutes of the second leg at Old Trafford, Best walked straight off the field, not even waiting for the referee to dismiss him. The final was a more memorable occasion for Juan Ramon Veron, the Argentine club's goalscorer, whose son Juan Sebastian would later play for both Estudiantes and United.

WAYNE REIGNS

In December 2008, Wayne Rooney was the hero as Manchester United became the first English club to win the new FIFA Club World Cup. The England international striker scored the only goal of the final, 17 minutes before the final whistle in United's fixture against Ecuador's LDU Quito. Rooney had taken just two minutes to get on the scoresheet in the semi-final, after coming on as a 73rd-minute substitute against Japan's Gamba Osaka and ended the game with a brace, adding his second goal in the 79th minute as Manchester United ran out 5-3 winners. He finished up in Japan not only as top scorer, with three goals, but also voted outstanding performer of the tournament to become the first player to win both the Golden Boot and Golden Shoe since FIFA began the competition in 2000. No player has scored more than three goals in one FIFA Club World Cup, though Rooney now shares the tournament record with Brazil's Romario and France's Nicolas Anelka, Egypt's Mohamed Aboutrika and Brazil's Washington.

FIGURE OF EIGHT

Manchester United's 5-3 win over Gamba Osaka in the semi-final of the FIFA Club World Cup was the highest-scoring single game in the history of the competition in all its forms – bettering the 5-2 victory over Benfica by a Santos team featuring Pele in 1962. Even more amazingly, all but two of the goals in the Manchester United–Gamba game were scored in the final 16 minutes, plus stoppage-time. United were leading 2-0 with 74 minutes gone, before a burst of goals – including two by substitute Wayne Rooney – at both ends. Manchester United became the first team to score five goals in the FIFA Club World Cup's revised format.

MANCHESTER REUNITED

Aside from manager Sir Alex Ferguson, three members of Manchester United's 2008 FIFA Club World Cup-winning squad survived from the club's only previous world club title triumph, in the 1999 Intercontinental Cup: defender Gary Neville and midfielders Paul Scholes and Ryan Giggs. All three started the semi-final against Gamba Osaka, though only Neville made it on to the field in the final – as an 85th-minute substitute for young defender Rafael.

THIRD TIME UNLUCKY

Egypt's Al-Ahly became the first side to compete in three separate FIFA Club World Cups, though they failed to emulate their best performance – when they finished third in 2006. This time they came sixth out of seven. Their first attempt, in 2005, saw them finish six out of six teams.

AGES APART

The oldest and youngest scorers of the 2008 FIFA Club World Cup hit the net within five minutes of each other, in the competition's opening game. Waitakere United were given a 34th-minute lead by 33-year-old midfielder Paul Seaman, only for Adelaide United's 20-year-old right-back, Daniel Mullen, to equalize five minutes later.

RED CARDS FOR RED DEVILS

Manchester United won the 2008 FIFA Club World Cup final despite playing for much of the second half with ten men, after Serbia centre-back Nemanja Vidic was sent off for a 49th-minute elbow on Claudio Bieler. Four months earlier, United midfielder Paul Scholes had been sent off in another showpiece match – the European Supercup defeat to UEFA Cup winners Zenit St Petersburg of Russia. Going into the final two games of the 2008 FIFA Club World Cup, there were high hopes that the tournament would become only the second, after the 2006 event, to pass without a single red card.

FAMILIAR FACES

Australia's Adelaide United suffered a sad case of deja vu when beaten in their quarter-final by Japan's Gamba Osaka. Just a month earlier, the sides had met over two legs in the final of the Asian Champions League, with Gamba winning both games to triumph 5-0 on aggregate. Gamba made it three in a row with a 1-0 victory, in only the third time a FIFA Club World Cup fixture has featured two teams from the same continental federation. Corinthians' win over Vasco in the 2000 final was an all-Brazilian affair, not just a meeting of two sides from South America, while the 2007 quarter-final saw Japan's Urawa Red Diamonds knock out Asian rivals Sepahan, from Iran.

FIFA CLUB WORLD CUP 2008 (RESULTS)

PLAYOFF FOR QUARTER-FINALS:
Adelaide United (Australia) 2 Waitakere United (New Zealand) 1
QUARTER-FINALS: Pachuca (Mexico) 4 Al-Ahly (Egypt) 2 (aet);
Gamba Osaka (Japan) 1 Adelaide United 0
SEMI-FINALS: LDU Quito (Ecuador) 2 Pachuca 0
Manchester United (England) 5 Gamba Osaka 3
FIFTH-PLACE PLAYOFF: Adelaide United 1 Al-Ahly 0
THIRD-PLACE PLAYOFF: Gamba Osaka 1 Pachuca 0
FINAL: Manchester United 1 LDU Quito 0

FINAL POSITIONS AND PRIZES

1st	Manchester United	$5 million
2nd	LDU Quito	$4 million
3rd	Gamba Osaka	$2.5 million
4th	Pachuca	$2 million
5th	Adelaide United	$1.5 million
6th	Al-Ahly	$1 million
7th	Waitakere United	$500,000

Top scorer: Wayne Rooney (Manchester United), 3 goals
Golden Ball for best player: Wayne Rooney (Manchester United)
Silver Ball: Cristiano Ronaldo (Manchester United)
Bronze Ball: Damian Manso (LDU Quito)
Fair Play Award: Adelaide United
Referee for the final: Ravshan Irmatov (Uzbekistan)

SEVEN UP

Despite Al-Ahly's defeat to Adelaide United in the fifth-place playoff, the game was a landmark for four of the Egyptian club's players: Wael Gomaa, Mohamed Aboutrika, Shady Mohamed and Hossam Ashour were all playing in a FIFA Club World Cup match for a seventh time. They passed the six-match record previously held by Brazilian goalkeeper Dida, who played in the tournament for Corinthians (2000) and AC Milan (2007).

MEN'S OLYMPIC FOOTBALL TOURNAMENT

First played at the 1900 Olympic Games in Paris, although not recognized by FIFA as an official tournament until the 1908 Games in London, the men's Olympic football tournament was played strictly in accordance with the Games' strong amateur tradition until 1984, when professionals were allowed to play for the first time. Since then, the competition has provided countries with an opportunity to hand their rising young stars an invaluable taste of tournament football under the glare of the world media spotlight.

RETROSPECTIVE MEDALS

Football was not played at the very first modern Summer Olympics, in Athens in 1896, and the football tournaments played at the 1900 and 1904 events are not officially recognized by FIFA. Medals were not handed out to the winning teams at the time – with Great Britain represented in 1900 by the Upton Park club from East London – though the International Olympic Committee has since allocated first, second and third place to the countries taking part.

NOT A HIT

German dictator Adolf Hitler was reputedly among the VIP guests watching his country's players lose 2-0 to Norway in a second-round game at the 1936 Olympics in Berlin. He stormed out of the Olympic Stadium in a rage at the German team's performance, having been assured by officials that they could not lose.

SWEDES BEAT BRUSSELS

Defending champions Belgium suffered one of the biggest Olympics upsets in history in their opening game at the 1924 Games, going down 8-1 to eventual bronze medal winners Sweden.

BLOC PARTY

Eastern European countries dominated the Olympic Games football competitions from 1948 to 1980, when professional players were officially banned from taking part. Teams comprising so-called "state amateurs" from the Eastern Bloc took 23 of the 27 medals available during those years. Only Sweden, in 1948, brought gold medals west of the Iron Curtain. Sweden also collected bronze four years later, before Denmark claimed silver in 1960 and Japan bronze in 1968.

CZECH OUT

The climax of the 1920 Olympic Games tournament is the only time a major international football final has been abandoned. Czechoslovakia's players walked off the pitch minutes before half-time, in protest at the decisions made by 65-year-old English referee John Lewis – including the dismissal of Czech player Karel Steiner. Belgium, who were 2-0 up at the time, were awarded the victory, before Spain beat the Netherlands 3-1 in a playoff for silver.

AFRICAN AMBITION

Ghana became the first African country to win an Olympic football medal, picking up bronze in 1992, but Nigeria went even better four years later by claiming the continent's first Olympic football gold medal – thanks to Emmanuel Amunike's stoppage-time winner against Argentina. Nigeria's triumph came as a huge surprise to many – especially as their rival teams included such future world stars as Brazil's Ronaldo and Roberto Carlos, Argentina's Hernan Crespo and Roberto Ayala, Italy's Fabio Cannavaro and Gianluigi Buffon, and France's Robert Pires and Patrick Vieira (above). Future FIFA World Cup or European Championships winners to have played at Summer Olympics include France's Michel Platini and Patrick Battiston (at the Montreal Games in 1976), West Germany's Andreas Brehme and Brazil's Dunga (Los Angeles, 1984), and Brazil's Taffarel, Bebeto and Romario and West Germany's Jurgen Klinsmann (Seoul, 1988).

HOW REFRESHING

Argentina's 1-0 victory over Nigeria in the 2008 final at Beijing's Bird's Nest Stadium had to be interrupted twice, so both sets of players – including Lionel Messi, Juan Roman Riquelme, Javier Mascherano and Sergio Aguero – could be offered water to help them cope with the oppressive 42°C (107°F) midday heat. Messi set up Angel Di Maria for the only goal of the game in the 58th minute.

AWAY FROM HOME

Olympic football matches often take place outside, even far from, the Games' host cities. The furthest afield came at the 1984 Los Angeles Olympics in the US, when two of the venues used were more than 3,200km away – the Navy-Marine Corps Memorial Stadium in Annapolis, Maryland, and the Harvard Stadium in Boston, Massachusetts. Not a single minute of football was played in Atlanta during that city's 1996 Games, with the closest action taking place 105km away in Athens, Georgia.

SHARE AND SHARE ALIKE

The bronze medal was shared at the 1972 Olympic Games in Munich, when the playoff between defeated semi-finalists East Germany and the Soviet Union ended 2-2 after extra-time. East Germany had been 2-0 down after half an hour.

MEN'S OLYMPIC FOOTBALL FINALS

1896 Not played
1900 (Paris, France)
Gold: Upton Park FC (GB) Silver: USFSA XI (France) Bronze: Université Libre de Bruxelles (Belgium) (only two exhibition matches played)
1904 (St Louis, US)
Gold: Galt FC (Canada) Silver: Christian Brothers College (US) Bronze: St Rose Parish (US) (only five exhibition matches played)
1908 (London, England)
Great Britain 2 Denmark 0 (Bronze: Netherlands)
1912 (Stockholm, Sweden)
Great Britain 4 Denmark 2 (Bronze: Netherlands)
1916 Not played
1920 (Antwerp, Belgium)
Belgium 2 Czechoslovakia 0 (Silver: Spain, Bronze: Netherlands)
1924 (Paris, France)
Uruguay 3 Switzerland 0 (Bronze: Sweden)
1928 (Amsterdam, Netherlands)
Uruguay 1 Argentina 1; Uruguay 2 Argentina 1 (Bronze: Italy)
1932 Not played
1936 (Berlin, Germany) Italy 2 Austria 1 (aet) (Bronze: Norway)
1940 Not played
1944 Not played
1948 (London, England) Sweden 3 Yugoslavia 1 (Bronze: Denmark)
1952 (Helsinki, Finland) Hungary 2 Yugoslavia 0 (Bronze: Sweden)
1956 (Melbourne, Australia) USSR 1 Yugoslavia 0 (Bronze: Bulgaria)
1960 (Rome, Italy) Yugoslavia 3 Denmark 1 (Bronze: Hungary)
1964 (Tokyo, Japan) Hungary 2 Czechoslovakia 1 (Bronze: Germany)
1968 (Mexico City, Mexico) Hungary 4 Bulgaria 1 (Bronze: Japan)
1972 (Munich, West Germany) Poland 2 Hungary 1 (Bronze: USSR/East Germany)
1976 (Montreal, Canada) East Germany 3 Poland 1 (Bronze: USSR)
1980 (Moscow, USSR) Czechoslovakia 1 East Germany 0 (Bronze: USSR)
1984 (Los Angeles, USA) France 2 Brazil 0 (Bronze: Yugoslavia)
1988 (Seoul, South Korea) USSR 2 Brazil 1 (Bronze: West Germany)
1992 (Barcelona, Spain) Spain 3 Poland 2 (Bronze: Ghana)
1996 (Atlanta, USA) Nigeria 3 Argentina 2 (Bronze: Brazil)
2000 (Sydney, Australia) Cameroon 2 Spain 2 (Cameroon win 5-3 on penalties) (Bronze: Chile)
2004 (Athens, Greece) Argentina 1 Paraguay 0 (Bronze: Italy)
2008 (Beijing, China) Argentina 1 Nigeria 0 (Bronze: Brazil)

LAPPING IT UP

Uruguay have a perfect Olympic football record, winning gold on the two occasions they took part (1924 and 1928). Those Olympics were seen as a quasi-world championship and helped prompt FIFA into organizing the first World Cup in 1930. This was also won by Uruguay, who included 1924 and 1948 Olympic gold medallists Jose Nasazzi, Jose Andrade and Hector Scarone in their squad. Uruguay's triumphant 1924 team are thought to have pioneered the lap of honour.

WELL DONE, PEDRO

Uruguay's Pedro Petrone not only finished top scorer at the 1924 tournament (with seven goals), he also became the youngest footballer to win a gold medal – a record that remains. He was just 18 years and 363 days old when Uruguay won the final, his opening goal setting them on their way to success. Although he did not finish top scorer four years later, he again claimed gold in the only Olympic final to be settled by a replay. Ghana's Samuel Kuffour is the youngest footballer to have won a medal, claiming bronze at the 1992 Olympic Games in Barcelona despite being only 15 years 11 months and four days old.

JUST SEVENTEEN

Carlos Tevez was the top-scoring hero as Argentina won their first FIFA Olympic gold in 2004 – including the only goal of the final. But his team-mates in defence could claim plenty of the credit: they completed the tournament without conceding a single goal.

HARD AS NILS

In 1908, Denmark's Nils Middelboe became the first man to score at an officially recognized FIFA Olympic football tournament, against France. He went on to spearhead his country to consecutive silver-medal placings. In 1913, he became the first non-British footballer to play for Chelsea.

SPECS APPEAL

Italy's Annibale Frossi, top scorer and gold medallist at the 1936 Olympic Games, certainly had an eye for goal – and was notable as a footballer who wore his glasses throughout games. His seven goals at the Berlin Games included a 92nd-minute winner against Austria in the final. His performances won him a transfer from Italian club L'Aquila to Internazionale, the club he would later go on to manage.

BARCELONA BOUND

Future Barcelona team-mates Samuel Eto'o and Xavi (right) scored penalties for opposing sides in 2000, when Cameroon and Spain contested the first Olympic final to be settled by a shoot-out. Ivan Amaya was the only player to miss, handing Cameroon gold.

HAPPY HARRY

Harold Walden, who scored nine goals at the 1912 tournament for gold medallists Great Britain, went on to become a successful music-hall variety singer and performer, on stage, silver screen and record.

HUNGARY FOR SUCCESS

Hungary's 1964 gold medallists may not be as legendary as their 1952 counterparts – the famous Mighty Magyars – but Ferenc Bene's 12-goal haul, in five games, remains a record for one Olympic football tournament. Six of those came in Hungary's opening 6-0 win over Morocco. He also scored the winner in the final against Czechoslovakia.

VIVA VIV

Vivian Woodward was the first football captain to receive a gold medal, representing Britain in 1908 at the London Olympics – and repeating the achievement four years later, after a victory over Denmark in the final. Army officer Woodward, who played for Tottenham Hotspur and Chelsea, also served in World War One as part of the 17th Battalion of the Middlesex Regiment – known as the "Footballers' Battalion" on account of the large number of professional footballers among its ranks.

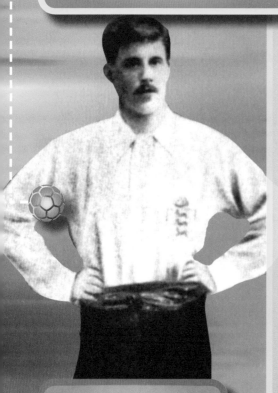

ROSSI CROSSES OVER

In 2008, Giuseppe Rossi became the first Italian since Annibale Frossi (in 1936) to finish an Olympics as top scorer, with four goals. Rossi was born in New Jersey, to Italian immigrants living in the US, but refused an invitation from the American squad ahead of the 2006 FIFA World Cup – he made his debut for the senior Italian side in 2008.

COUNT TO TEN

Two players have managed to score ten goals each in a single match at the Olympics, sharing a record that stood for all internationals until almost a century later. Denmark's Sophus Nielsen hit double figures in his team's 17-1 trouncing of France at the 1908 Games, including a hat-trick within the first six minutes. The French were so traumatized by the semi-final defeat, they forfeited the right to contest a playoff for the bronze medal. Nielsen, however, had to be content with silver-medal finishes, both in 1908 and 1912. His ten-goal feat was emulated in 1912 by Germany's Gottfried Fuchs, against Russia. Fuchs, who was Jewish, later fled Nazi Germany to live the rest of his life in Canada.

TOURNAMENT TOP SCORERS

1896 n/a
1900 Unknown
1904 Alexander Hall (Canada) 3, Tom Taylor (Canada) 3
1908 Sophus Nielsen (Denmark) 11
1912 Gottfried Fuchs (Germany) 10
1916 n/a
1920 Herbert Karlsson (Sweden) 7
1924 Pedro Petrone (Uruguay) 8
1928 Domingo Tarasconi (Argentina) 9
1932 no competition
1936 Annibale Frossi (Italy) 7
1948 John Hansen (Denmark) 7, Gunnar Nordahl (Sweden) 7
1952 Rajko Mitic (Yugoslavia) 7, Branko Zebec (Yugoslavia) 7
1956 Neville D'Souza (India) 4, Dimitar Milanov (Bulgaria) 4, Todor Veselinovic (Yugoslavia) 4
1960 Hans Nielsen (Denmark) 8
1964 Ferenc Bene (Hungary) 12
1968 Kunishige Kamamoto (Japan) 7
1972 Kazimierz Deyna (Poland) 9
1976 Andrzej Szarmach (Poland) 6
1980 Sergei Andreev (USSR) 5
1984 Daniel Xuereb (France) 5, Borislav Cvetkovic (Yugoslavia) 5, Stjepan Deveric (Yugoslavia) 5
1988 Romario (Brazil) 7
1992 Andrzej Juskowiak (Poland) 7
1996 Hernan Crespo (Argentina) 6, Bebeto (Brazil) 6
2000 Ivan Zamorano (Chile) 6
2004 Carlos Tevez (Argentina) 8
2008 Giuseppe Rossi (Italy) 4

BLUE STARS FIFA
YOUTH CUP

Staged on an annual basis by Zurich club FC Blue Stars since 1939, and granted FIFA's patronage since 1991, the Blue Stars/FIFA Youth Cup tournament has become football's premier youth event and features many teams from around the globe. Several of the game's greatest names – from Bobby Charlton to David Beckham – gained their first taste of international football competition at the event.

BAD FELLOWS

Swiss club Young Fellows suffered an even more agonizing defeat than those who lose penalty shoot-outs, when they were denied the 1941 title after an extra-time draw with FC Lugano. Instead of a shoot-out, the match, and the championship, was settled by drawing lots.

WANDERING FREE

In 1951, Wolverhampton Wanderers (who were managed by Stan Cullis at the time) became the first English team to take part. Cullis's senior team would soon claim to be champions of Europe, after defeating Hungarian champions Honved: the match inspired Gabriel Hanot to organize the first European Cup in 1955.

BRAZIL FORTUNE

It took until 1999 before the tournament was first won by a club from outside Europe, when Brazil's Sao Paulo beat FC Zurich on penalties, at the Swiss side's Letzigrund stadium. Sao Paulo, having added Kaka to their line-up, retained their title the following year.

BLUE STARS CHAMPIONSHIPS

Manchester United 18
(1954, 1957, 1959, 1960, 1961, 1962, 1965, 1966, 1968, 1969, 1975, 1976, 1978, 1979, 1981, 1982, 2004, 2005)

Grasshoppers 6
(1939, 1956, 1971, 1987, 1998, 2006)

Barcelona 3
(1993, 1994, 1995)

FC Zurich 3
(1946, 1949, 2008)

FC Young Fellows 3
(1941, 1942, 1953)

AC Milan 2
(1958, 1977)

Arsenal 2
(1963, 1964)

AS Roma 2
(1980, 2003)

FK Austria Vienna 2
(1947, 1948)

Sao Paulo 2
(1999, 2000)

Spartak Moscow 2
(1991, 1992)

MOST APPEARANCES: SWITZERLAND

FC Blue Stars (Switzerland)	70
Grasshoppers (Switzerland)	70
FC Zurich (Switzerland)	69
FC Young Fellows (Switzerland)	42
FC Red Star (Switzerland)	29

HEART OF THE BLATTER

Long before he was elected FIFA president in 1998, Sepp Blatter was a keen amateur footballer who played centre-forward for Swiss club FC Sierre in the Blue Stars tournament in the early 1950s. He is now an honorary member of FC Blue Stars.

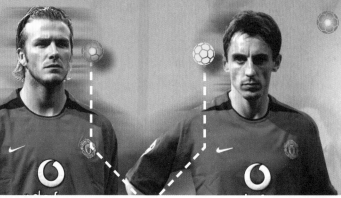

RAISING THE BARÇA

No Spanish side took part until Barcelona's involvement in 1988, with a team featuring midfielder Josep Guardiola and right-back Albert Ferrer – both of whom would help the club to their first European Cup triumph in 1992.

BLUE STARS, RED DEVILS

Manchester United's first-team squad may have been enduring a rare barren season, as Arsene Wenger's Arsenal took the 2003–04 Premier League title without a single defeat – but the Old Trafford club did win the Blue Stars trophy that year and then retained the title in 2005, to complete a record 18th triumph. Players who have represented United in the tournament include David Beckham, Paul Scholes, Ryan Giggs, Nicky Butt, Gary Neville and Philip Neville – all of whom would go on to collect Champions League winners' medals with the club in 1999. Former captain Roy Keane, who missed the 1999 final through suspension, had played in the 1990 Blue Stars tournament for Nottingham Forest. Beckham played in the 1992, 1993, 1994 and 1995 contests for United.

PLAYING THE FULVIO

Another future FIFA World Cup winner to have taken part in the Blue Stars tournament is defender Fulvio Collovati, a member of Italy's 1982 squad, who had won the Blue Stars tournament with AC Milan in 1977. Collovati, 20 that year, also won the 1977 Italian Cup and would win the Serie A title with Milan in 1979, before later joining city rivals Internazionale.

ATHLETIC CHARLTON

Bobby Charlton, who would go on to win the FIFA World Cup in 1966 and the European Cup two years later, is one of the most illustrious names to have featured in the Blue Stars tournament. He represented United in the Blue Stars tournament every year from 1954 to 1958 – alongside future FIFA World Cup-winning colleague Nobby Stiles in 1954. Also taking part in 1956 was West German forward Helmut Haller, playing for Augsburg. Ten years later, he and Charlton would face each other in the FIFA World Cup final between England and West Germany, which Charlton's England won 4-2.

SWISS ARTISTS

The club after which the competition is named, FC Blue Stars, are based in the Swiss capital and have been running the contest for Under-18s teams since 1939. Blue Stars, founded in 1898, were one of the first clubs in the world to set up a dedicated youth section – doing so in 1921. FIFA has officially recognized the youth tournament since 1991.

MOST APPEARANCES: NON-SWITZERLAND

Manchester United (England) 39, Bayern Munich (Germany) 8, Internazionale (Italy) 7, Barcelona (Spain) 6

FIFA FUTSAL WORLD CUP

Developed in South America in the 1930s, Futsal – a variant of five-a-side indoor football – has enjoyed a huge surge in popularity, and participation numbers, in recent years. The first FIFA Futsal World Cup was staged in the Netherlands in 1989 and has been contested on a four-yearly basis since 1992. Two teams have dominated the event: Spain (with two wins) and, above all, Brazil (with four).

PENALTY APPEAL

Three of Spain's goals in their 4-3 win over Brazil in the 2000 final came from penalties – which are taken six metres from goal in Futsal. These included a dramatic last-minute winner by Javi Rodriguez, who was appearing in his second of four consecutive finals.

WHAT'S IN A WORD?

The word "Futsal" is thought to come from the Portuguese "futebol de salão" and/or the Spanish "fútbol sala" or "fútbol de salón" – translated as "indoor football".

THE FIRST MANOEL

Brazilian Manoel Tobias can claim to be the FIFA Futsal World Cup's most prolific goalscorer, with 43 in 32 appearances. Tobias, born in Salgueiro on 19 April 1971, represented his country in the 1992, 1996, 2000 and 2004 tournaments – only once ending up on the losing side within normal time. He ended both the 1996 and 2000 competitions with the prizes for both best player and top scorer.

DRUGS DISGRACE

Two players failed drugs tests at the 2008 FIFA Futsal World Cup: Eduardo Carlos Morgado Oliveira of third-placed Italy was suspended for two years, while Liberia's Melvin King was handed a five-month suspension.

CUBAN EMBARGO

Cuba hold the record for the fewest goals scored in a single tournament. They managed only one goal in their three games at the 2000 FIFA Futsal World Cup, while conceding 20 in defeats to Iran, Argentina and eventual champions Spain.

NINE'S ENOUGH

Russia's Pula may have pipped Falcao to the top scorer prize in 2008 (with 16 goals to 15), but the Brazilian, who had already won both the Golden Ball and Golden Shoe awards four years earlier, was voted player of the tournament. Pula's 16 goals across the 2008 event included nine in one game – an all-time FIFA Futsal World Cup record – as the Solomon Islands were thrashed 31-2.

DIVIDED FAMILY FOCUS

While Futsal is increasingly being seen as a discipline with its own individual quirks and demands, several players have tried their hand – that is, feet – at the more mainstream, 11-a-side version of the outdoor game, especially in the MLS in America. One member of the US team at the 2008 FIFA Futsal World Cup was Jamar Beasley, older brother of PSV Eindhoven, Manchester City and Rangers midfielder DaMarcus Beasley – who had represented the United States at the rather more high-profile 2006 FIFA World Cup.

TOURNAMENT AWARDS AND RECORDS

1989
Golden Ball (for best player): Victor Hermans (Netherlands)
Golden Shoe (for top scorer): Laszlo Zsadanyi (Hungary), 7
Top-scoring team: Brazil 33 goals, 8 games (4.1 per game)
Red cards: 4
Goals: 221 goals, 40 games (5.5 per game)
Total attendance: 86,500 (2,162 per game)

1992
Golden Ball: Jorginho (Brazil)
Golden Shoe: Saeid Rajabi Shirazi (Iran), 16
Top-scoring team: Brazil 44 goals, 8 games (5.5 per game)
Red cards: 5
Goals: 307 goals, 40 games (7.7 per game)
Total attendance: 50,300 (1,257 per game)

1996
Golden Ball: Manoel Tobias (Brazil)
Golden Shoe: Manoel Tobias (Brazil), 14
Top-scoring team: Brazil 55 goals, 8 games (6.9 per game)
Red cards: 2
Goals: 290 goals, 40 games (7.3 per game)
Total attendance: 116,400 (2,910 per game)

2000
Golden Ball: Manoel Tobias (Brazil)
Golden Shoe: Manoel Tobias (Brazil), 19
Top-scoring team: Brazil 78 goals, 8 games (9.8 per game)
Red cards: 7
Goals: 300 goals, 40 games (7.5 per game)
Total attendance: 224,038 (5,600 per game)

2004
Golden Ball: Falcao (Brazil)
Golden Shoe: Falcao (Brazil), 13
Top-scoring team: Brazil 48 goals, 8 games (6 per game)
Red cards: 5
Goals: 237 goals, 40 games (5.93 per game)
Total attendance: 50,923 (1,273 per game)

2008
Golden Ball: Falcao (Brazil)
Golden Shoe: Pula (Russia), 16
Top-scoring team: Brazil 64 goals, 9 games (7.1 per game)
Red cards: 7
Goals: 387 goals, 56 games (6.91 per game)
Total attendance: 292,161 (5,217 per game)

FIFA FUTSAL WORLD CUP FINALS (AND HOSTS)
1989 (Host country: Netherlands) Brazil 2 Netherlands 1
1992 (Hong Kong) Brazil 4 United States 1
1996 (Spain) Brazil 6 Spain 4
2000 (Guatemala) Spain 4 Brazil 3
2004 (Chinese Taipei) Spain 2 Italy 1
2008 (Brazil) Brazil 2 Spain 2 (aet: Brazil win 4-3 on penalties)

SAMBA SUPREMACY
Predictably for a game relying heavily on swift, deft passing and nimble footwork, Brazilians have excelled at Futsal – an indoor, five-a-side, 40-minute version of the 11-a-side game. Since FIFA inaugurated its Futsal World Cup in 1989, Brazil have won the trophy four times out of a possible six – finishing runners-up to Spain in 2000 and third behind Spain and Italy four years later. Brazil have ended every tournament as the top-scoring team, hitting the back of the net a record 78 times during eight games in 2000 – at a staggering rate of 9.3 goals per match. Their largest FIFA Futsal World Cup win was a 29-2 trouncing of Guatemala in 2000 – though their best-ever scoreline, an overall record for Futsal, came when they beat East Timor 76-0 in October 2006. Strangely enough, though, their first-ever FIFA Futsal World Cup match ended in defeat – 3-2 to Hungary in the first-round group stage in 1989.

SHIFT SWAP
After losing a 2004 semi-final to Spain on penalties, 2008 hosts Brazil redeemed themselves by winning the first-ever final to go to extra-time and then spot-kicks. The penalty-saving hero of the shoot-out was Brazil's substitute goalkeeper Franklin (right). But the man Franklin replaced at the end of extra-time, Tiago, was nevertheless chosen by judges as the tournament's best goalkeeper.

FIFA BEACH SOCCER WORLD CUP

Another variant of the game that can trace its roots to South America, beach soccer is a high-octane, all-action, made-for-TV, goal-crazy version of the game that has enjoyed a rapid surge in popularity in recent years. First contested in 1995 at its spiritual home on Copacabana Beach in Rio de Janeiro, Brazil, the FIFA Beach Soccer World Cup is set to become a biannual event after the 2009 tournament.

TOP OF THE WORLD

To be a success for Brazil at world level possibly demands a nickname like… Jorginho. Jorge de Amorim Oliveira Campos (born August 17, 1964) played right back for Brazil between 1987 and 1996 and was a FIFA World Cup-winner in the United States in 1994 when he was also named in the official FIFA Team of the Tournament. Jorge Augusto Gabriel (born on October 19, 1974), also nicknamed Jorginho, went one better – being twice a winner with Brazil of the FIFA Beach Soccer World Cup in 1999 and 2004. He was voted player of the tournament on both occasions. Brazil have won the FIFA Beach Soccer World Cup a record 12 times, most recently in 2008 when they defeated Italy in the final.

82 NOT OUT

The Brazilian team at the 1982 FIFA World Cup is often described as the finest never to win football's highest prize, but various members of that talented team have since done rather well in the beach version of the game. Former team-mates such as Zico, Junior and Eder were among those contributing to Brazil's earliest FIFA Beach Soccer World Cup triumphs. In 1995, former FIFA World Player of the Year Zico was top scorer with 12 goals, winning the trophy in 1995 and 1996. Junior was part of the Brazil squad that won in 1995, 1996, 1997, 1998, 1999 and 2000, finishing as top scorer in the final four of those events.

GOAL GLUT

The 2003 tournament was the most prolific, with an average of 9.4 goals per game – 150 in total. Two years earlier had brought the lowest average – 7.2 per match, 144 in total.

FRENCH SELECTION

The 2008 tournament, on the beaches of Marseille in the south of France, was the first to take place outside Brazil. Hosting rights for the 2009 tournament were awarded to Dubai, in the United Arab Emirates.

ERIC THE KING

Footballer, actor and wannabe poet and philosopher Eric Cantona coached the French team that won the 2005 FIFA Beach Soccer World Cup – the first tournament to be staged under the FIFA banner, having previously been known as the Beach Soccer World Championship. However, the former Manchester United striker only allowed himself limited playing time and ended the tournament with a solitary goal to his name – in a 7-4 quarter-final victory over Spain.

MADJER FOR IT

In 2006, Angolan-born Portuguese star Madjer set a record for goals in one tournament when he put the ball in the net 21 times – his fifth tournament as top scorer.

EUROPEAN REUNION

Hernani Neves, a FIFA Beach Soccer World Cup scorer in 2001, is the only man to have taken part in a tournament after having played in a European Cup final. As a Benfica midfielder, he was on the losing side against AC Milan in 1990.

PORT IN A STORM

After winning the first six FIFA Beach Soccer World Cup titles, Brazil fell back down to earth with a bump in 2001 and finished "only" fourth, as Portugal swept to the title by beating France in the final.

FIFA BEACH SOCCER WORLD CUP FINALS

1995 (Host beach and city/country: Copacabana, Rio de Janeiro/Brazil) Brazil 8 USA 1
1996 (Copacabana) Brazil 3 Uruguay 0
1997 (Copacabana) Brazil 5 Uruguay 2
1998 (Copacabana) Brazil 9 France 2
1999 (Copacabana) Brazil 5 France 2
2000 (Marina da Gloria, Rio de Janeiro) Brazil 6 Peru 2
2001 (Costa do Sauipe, Rio de Janeiro) Portugal 9 France 3
2002 (Vitoria/Brazil) Brazil 6 Portugal 5
2003 (Copacabana) Brazil 8 Spain 2
2004 (Copacabana) Brazil 6 Spain 4
2005 (Copacabana) France 3 Portugal 3 (France win 1-0 on penalties)
2006 (Copacabana) Brazil 4 Uruguay 1
2007 (Copacabana) Brazil 8 Mexico 2
2008 (Plage du Pardo, Marseille/France) Brazil 5 Italy 3

SCORE BLIMEY

Brazil's 16-2 victory over the Netherlands, in the first tournament in 1995, remains the biggest FIFA Beach Soccer World Cup win – while Brazil's 15-5 triumph over France four years later is still the highest-scoring game. Two matches have ended a tight 1-0: Germany's win over Argentina in 1995 and Peru's victory over Venezuela five years later.

MAGIC ALEX

Alessandro Altobelli is the only man to score in a FIFA World Cup final and play and score in a FIFA Beach Soccer World Cup. Having struck Italy's third goal in their 3-1 victory over West Germany in 1982, 13 years later he finished the 1995 FIFA Beach Soccer World Cup as joint top scorer with Zico – and then was sole top scorer in 1996. Romario may have failed to break the deadlock when Brazil beat Italy on penalties in the 1994 FIFA World Cup final, but he did manage six goals – including two hat-tricks – in Brazil's march to third place at the 2005 FIFA Beach Soccer World Cup.

LIFE SAVING

Brazil's Paulo Sergio was voted best goalkeeper for the first four FIFA Beach Soccer World Cups, but since then the award has been shared between Portugal's Pedro Crespo (1999), Japan's Kato (2000), France's Pascal Olmeta (2001), Thailand's Normcharoen (2002), Brazil's Robertinho (2003) and Spain's Roberto (2004) and Roberto Valeiro (2008).

DIEGO AGAIN

A name even more famous in football than that of Altobelli, Zico or Cantona made it on to the scoresheet in the 2008 FIFA Beach Soccer World Cup final: Diego Maradona. But this was not Argentina's 1986 FIFA World Cup-winning captain, but his son Diego Maradona Jr – playing for Italy.

FIFA INTERACTIVE WORLD CUP

The EA SPORTS FIFA Interactive World Cup, the world's largest football video game tournament, made its debut in 2004 with participants from around the world battling it out on the virtual pitch in FIFA 2005. The inaugural event showcased an eight-player finals tournament in Zurich, Switzerland, with the winner earning a trip to the FIFA World Player Gala in Amsterdam. Since then, the FIWC has expanded its reach into more than 50 countries with an average of 400,000 players per year. The 2009 FIWC grand finals were held in Barcelona, Spain, with players battling for the cup on EA Sports™ FIFA 09 on the PlayStation®3.

GRAND CHAMPIONS

There are five grand champions in FIFA Interactive World Cup history, beginning with Brazil's Thiago Carrico de Azevado, winner of the inaugural tournament in 2004 held in Zurich, Switzerland. Chris Bullard of the United Kingdom captured the second FIWC title after rolling through the championship field in London. In 2006, Andries Smit of the Netherlands captured the championship on his home soil, besting the field of finalists in Amsterdam. Smit, then 17, is the youngest competitor to capture the FIWC title. Spain's Alfonso Ramos won the 2008 FIWC held in Berlin, and France's Bruce Grannec is the reigning champion after capturing the 2009 title in Barcelona.

500K AND COUNTING

The total number of participants in the 2009 FIFA Interactive World Cup "online" tournament was 515,000 players.

UK PRIDE

Approximately one-fifth of the 2009 FIFA Interactive World Cup participants were from the United Kingdom.

HOW TO QUALIFY

There are two routes to qualify for the FIFA Interactive World Cup grand final: either via online qualification on the PlayStation® network, or by participating in one of the many live qualifying events staged around the world every year – numerous prizes are on offer for those talented enough to qualify.

A GLOBAL TURNOUT

500,000-plus 2009 FIFA Interactive World Cup players represented more than 50 countries around the world. Nearly half were represented in the FIWC grand finals.

OVER SIX MILLION SERVED

The total number of games played climbed to an unprecedented 6.87 million during the 2009 FIFA Interactive World Cup.

PRACTICE MAKES PERFECT

Putting in a countless number of gaming hours, the player best known as "floera64" led all participants in 2009 with 1,875 total tournament wins.

CLASH OF THE RED DEVILS

Bruce Grannec of France captured the 2009 FIFA Interactive World Cup championship with an impressive 3-1 victory over Mexico's Ruben Zerecero at the grand finals in Barcelona. In a unique matchup that featured Manchester United vs. Manchester United, Grannec took command of the match by breaking a 1-1 tie with two second-half goals. Grannec, who earned a grand prize of $20,000 and a Kia Soul, will be a guest at the FIFA World Player Gala in 2010. Runner-up Zerecero was awarded a second-place prize of $5,000. The 2009 FIWC featured 32 finalists representing countries around the world, including England, Australia, Brazil, Mexico, France, Germany, Italy, India, New Zealand, Saudi Arabia, South Africa, Spain, the United States and more competing for the chance to become the FIWC 2009 champion.

QUALIFYING EVENTS

The FIWC hosted 21 live tournament events around the world, with tour stops in Australia, New Zealand, Brazil, the United States, India, South Africa, Italy, Portugal, Spain, the United Kingdom, Austria, France, Germany, Denmark, the Czech Republic, Hungary, Poland and Switzerland.

BEST OF THE BEST

The top-ten gamers with the most points in the 2009 FIFA Interactive World Cup include: Legend_Never_Die, 9,074 pts; Mikaeel, 8,854; dannytaylor, 8,625; undercover_king, 8,544; herzex, 8,526; AdamW, 8,514; MuStiLinHo, 8,507; SeNSaTIoN9, 8,393; Nunogomesscp, 8,383; and floera64, 7,956.

A GLOBAL APPEAL

More than 20 countries were represented at the 2009 FIFA Interactive World Cup grand finals: England, Australia, Brazil, Mexico, Austria, Czech Republic, Denmark, Egypt, France, Germany, Netherlands, Hungary, Italy, India, Switzerland, New Zealand, Poland, Portugal, Saudi Arabia, South Africa, Spain, Singapore, Turkey, and the United States.

WORLD LEADERS

Four of the five countries with the most participants were in Europe, with the United Kingdom leading all territories with more than 172,000 players. France had the second-most players (67,000), followed by Germany (51,000), the United States (50,000), and Spain (with 40,000).

PART 6:
WOMEN'S FOOTBALL

UP to 30 million women are playing football around the world and participation has more than doubled over the past ten years. Those simple statistics demonstrate better than perhaps any others how successfully football has managed to break down the old prejudices of bygone eras with greater success than many other sports disciplines. International women's competitions now pull in significant crowds, whose enthusiasm and support has spilled over into national domestic leagues and domestic cup competitions around the world. In fact, women's football is recorded as having been organized in England in the early years of the last century, but it was banned by the Football Association in 1921. That led to the creation of an independent women's association with a cup competition of its own. Women's football developed simultaneously elsewhere and the surge of interest ultimately led, in the early 1980s, to the first formal European Championships and, in 1988, to a FIFA invitational tournament in Chinese Taipei.

FIFA then launched an inaugural world championship in 1991, which was won by the United States to establish their claim to primacy in the game. The Americans duly hosted the next FIFA Women's World Cup, which saw a record crowd of 90,185 celebrate their shoot-out victory over China in the final in Pasadena. They underlined their No.1 status by winning the first women's football gold medal at the Olympic Games in 1996, taking silver in 2000 and gold again in 2004 and 2008. Meanwhile FIFA set up a world youth championship in 2002, initially for players aged Under-19, later amended to Under-20, and added an Under-17 event to the international calendar in 2008. An initial attempt to create a professional league in the United States to build on the momentum created by the FIFA Women's World Cup and Olympic successes proved unsuccessful, but a second attempt was launched in 2009. Clubs in Women's Professional Soccer signed some of the world's finest players, including Brazil's Marta and England's Kelly Smith.

Captain Birgit Prinz leads Germany's celebrations after their victory over Brazil in the final of the FIFA Women's World Cup 2007 in Shanghai.

FIFA WOMEN'S WORLD CUP™

FINALS FORMAT

The first FIFA Women's World Cup finals were held in China in 1991. Twelve teams, divided into three groups of four, took part, with the top two in each group, plus the two "best losers" going through to the knock-out quarter-finals. The tournament was expanded in 1999 to include 16 teams, divided into four groups of four, with the top two in each group progressing to the quarter-finals. That is the current format, although an expansion of the tournament to 24 teams is still under consideration.

HAVELANGE'S DREAM COMES TRUE

The FIFA Women's World Cup was the brainchild of former FIFA president Joao Havelange. The tournament began as an experimental competition in 1991 and has expanded in size and importance ever since. The success of the 1999 finals in the United States was a turning point for the tournament, which now attracts big crowds and worldwide TV coverage. The US and Norway – countries in which football (soccer) is one of the most popular girls' sports – dominated the early competitions. The Americans won the inaugural competition and the 1999 tournament. Norway lifted the trophy in 1995. Germany became the dominant force in the new century, winning the trophy in 2003 and retaining it in 2007. The recent emergence of challengers such as Brazil, China and Sweden underlined the worldwide spread and appeal of the women's game.

FINALS SHOOT-OUT DRAMA

The 1999 clash between the US and China was the only final in FIFA Women's World Cup history settled by a shoot-out. The losing Chinese had previously been involved in the first shoot-out – in the quarter-finals in 1995, when they beat Sweden 4-3 on penalties after a 0-0 draw. The 1999 third-place game was also settled by a shoot-out, with Brazil pipping Norway 5-4 after a 0-0 draw. These are the only three shoot-outs since the tournament began in 1991.

US LEAD GAMES TALLY

The US have played the most games in the finals – 30. They have also recorded the most wins – 24. They have drawn three games and lost three. Germany are the next most successful team. They have played 28, won 20, drawn three and lost five. Norway have also played 28 matches, won 19, drawn two and lost seven.

LA FINALE BEATS THEM ALL

The 1999 finals in the US were the best attended of the five tournaments to date. A total of 3,687,069 spectators watched the matches, at an average of 24,913 per game. The final, between hosts US and China – at the Rose Bowl, Los Angeles on 10 July – drew 90,185 spectators, a world record for a women's match. The programme that day also included the third-place playoff between Brazil and Norway.

FIFA WOMEN'S WORLD CUP™ FINALS

Year	Venue	Winners	Runners-up	Score
1991	Ghuangzhou	US	Norway	2-1
1995	Stockholm	Norway	Germany	2-0
1999	Los Angeles	US	China	0-0
	US won 5-4 in penalty shoot-out			
2003	Los Angeles	Germany	Sweden	2-1 (aet)
2007	Shanghai	Germany	Brazil	2-0

THIRD-PLACE PLAYOFF MATCHES

Year	Venue	Winners	Losers	Score
1991	Guangzhou	Sweden	Germany	4-0
1995	Gavle	US	China	2-0
1999	Los Angeles	Brazil	Norway	0-0
	Brazil won 5-4 in penalty shoot-out			
2003	Los Angeles	US	Canada	3-1
2007	Shanghai	US	Norway	4-1

US CELEBRATE FIRST ACHIEVEMENT

The US's victory in the inaugural FIFA Women's World Cup in 1991 made them the first US team to win a world football title. The US men's best performance came when they reached the quarter-finals in 2002, losing 1-0 to Germany.

FOUR GAIN DOUBLE MEDALS

Four of the US's 1991 winners were in the team that beat China on penalties in the 1999 final: Mia Hamm (right), Michelle Akers, Kristine Lilly and Julie Foudy.

WINNERS KEEP SQUAD TOGETHER

Six Germany players appeared in their 2003 and 2007 final wins: Kerstin Stegemann, Birgit Prinz, Renate Lingor, Ariane Hingst and Kerstin Garefrekes started both games, while Martina Muller came on as a substitute both times.

AUSTRALIA, GHANA LEAD ON REDS

Only two teams have had more than one player sent off in the finals: Australia's Sonia Gegenhuber was red-carded in their 5-0 defeat by Denmark in 1995; and Alicia Ferguson was sent off in 1999, in the second minute of Australia's 3-1 defeat by China. Ghana are the other side to have two players dismissed. Both came at the 1999 finals: Barikisu Tettey-Quao was red-carded in the 1-1 draw against Australia; and Regina Ansah was sent off in the 7-0 defeat by China.

GERMANS SET DEFENSIVE RECORD

In 2007, Germany became the first team to make a successful defence of the FIFA Women's World Cup. They also set another record. They went through the tournament – six games and 540 minutes – without conceding a single goal. As a result, their goalkeeper Nadine Angerer overhauled Italy keeper Walter Zenga's record of 517 minutes unbeaten in the 1990 men's finals. The last player to score against the Germans was Sweden's Hanna Ljungberg, who scored in the 41st minute of the 2003 final.

THE LOWEST CROWD...

The lowest attendance for any match at the finals came on 8 June 1995, when only 250 spectators watched the 3-3 draw between Canada and Nigeria at Helsingborg.

TOP TEAMS

Country	Winners	Runners-up	Third
Germany	2	1	-
US	2	-	3
Norway	1	1	-
Brazil	-	1	1
Sweden	-	1	1
China	-	1	1

TOP TEAM SCORERS

1991:	US	25
1995:	Norway	23
1999:	China	19
2003:	Germany	25
2007:	Germany	21

TOP ALL-TIME TEAM SCORERS

1	US	85
2	Germany	84
3	Norway	75
4	China	48
5	Brazil	46

THE FIRST GAME

The first-ever game in the FIFA Women's World Cup finals was hosts China's 4-0 win over Norway at Guangzhou on 16 November 1991. A 65,000 crowd watched the game.

THE REGULAR EIGHT

Eight teams have played in all five finals tournaments – the US, Germany, Norway, Brazil, China, Japan, Nigeria and Sweden.

NORWAY POST LONGEST WIN RUN

Norway, winners in 1995, hold the record for the most consecutive matchtime wins in the finals – ten. Their run started with an 8-0 win over Nigeria on 6 June 1995 and continued until 30 June 1999 when they beat Sweden 3-1 in the quarter-finals. It ended when they lost 5-0 to China in the semi-finals on 4 July.

UNBEATEN CHINA SENT HOME

In 1999, China became the only team to go through the finals without losing a match, yet go home empty-handed. The Chinese won their group games, 2-1 against Sweden, 7-0 against Ghana and 3-1 against Australia. They beat Russia 2-0 in the quarter-finals and Norway 5-0 in the semi-finals, but they lost on penalties to the US in the final after a 0-0 draw.

FIFTEEN ON TARGET FOR NORWAY

Norway hold the record for scoring in the most consecutive games – 15. They began their sequence with a 4-0 win over New Zealand on 19 November 1991 and ended it with a 3-1 win over Sweden in the quarter-finals on 30 June 1999.

CHAMPIONS RUN UP 11

The biggest victory margin in the finals was Germany's 11-0 win over Argentina in Shanghai on 10 September 2007. Argentina keeper Vanina Correa punched a Melanie Behringer corner into her own net after 12 minutes. Birgit Prinz and Sandra Smisek scored hat-tricks, with Germany's other goals coming from Renate Lingor (2), Behringer and Kerstin Garefrekes.

LILLY KEEPS SETTING RECORDS

Kristine Lilly is the only player to have appeared in five finals tournaments. She has played a record 340 games for the US and scored 129 goals. She is also the oldest scorer in finals history – she was 36 years, 62 days when she netted the third in the US's 3-0 quarter-final win over England at Tianjin on 22 September 2007.

QUICKEST RED AND YELLOW

The record for the fastest red card is held by Australia's Alicia Ferguson, who was sent off in the second minute of their 3-1 defeat by China in New York on 26 June 1999. North Korea's Ri Hyang Ok received the quickest yellow card, in the first minute of their 2-1 defeat by Nigeria in Los Angeles on 20 June 1999.

NORDBY THE LONG-DISTANCE KEEPER

Norway goalkeeper Bente Nordby is the only other player to have gone to five FIFA Women's World Cup tournaments. She was a squad member in 1991, but did not play any games. Four years later, she conceded only one goal in six matches as Norway won the trophy. She retired from the national team in January 2008, after making 172 appearances.

DANILOVA THE YOUNGEST SCORER

The youngest scorer at the finals was Russia's Elena Danilova. She was 16 years 96 days when she scored her country's only goal in the 2003 quarter-final against Germany at Portland on 2 October. The Germans scored seven in reply.

MORACE HITS FIRST HAT-TRICK

Carolina Morace of Italy scored the first hat-trick in finals history when she netted the last three goals in Italy's 5-0 win over Taiwan at Jiangmen on 17 November 1991.

HOT SHOT AKERS SETS THE STANDARD

US forward Michelle Akers (born in Santa Clara on 1 February 1966) hold the record for the most goals scored in a single finals tournament – ten in 1991. She also set a record for the most goals scored in one match, with five in the US's 7-0 quarter-final win over Taiwan at Foshan on 24 November 1991. Akers grabbed both goals in the US's 2-1 victory in the final, including their 78th-minute winner. Judges voted her as FIFA's Women's Player of the 20th Century.

THE FASTEST GOAL

Lena Videkull of Sweden netted the fastest goal in finals history when she scored after 30 seconds in their 8-0 win over Japan at Foshan on 19 November 1991. Canada's Melissa Tancredi struck the second-fastest goal – after 37 seconds – in their 2-2 draw with Australia in Chengdu on 20 September 2007.

THE FASTEST SUBSTITIONS

The fastest substitutions in finals history were both timed at six minutes. Taiwan's defender Liu Hsiu Mei was subbed by reserve goalkeeper Li Chyn Hong in their 2-0 win over Nigeria in Jiangmen on 21 November 1991. Li replaced number one keeper Lin Hui Fang, who had been sent off. Therese Lundin subbed for the injured Hanna Lungberg, also after six minutes, in Sweden's 2-0 win over Ghana at Chicago on 26 June 1999.

NEW STARS DOMINATE THE FINALS

The FIFA Women's World Cup has been dominated by a series of great players. American attackers Michelle Akers and Carin Jennings starred in the opening tournament in 1991. Playmaker Hege Riise and top scorer Ann-Kristin led Norway to victory four years later. Another American great, Mia Hamm, was at the top of her form when the US triumphed for a second time in 1999. That tournament marked the emergence of the best-ever Chinese player, Sun Wen, who finished joint top scorer and won the Player of the Tournament award. Birgit Prinz of Germany was Player of the Tournament and top scorer when Germany won for the first time in 2003. The Brazilian forward, Marta, matched that feat in 2007, though, unlike Prinz, she found herself on the losing side in the final. Hamm, Prinz and Marta are the only winners of FIFA's Woman Player of the Year award, introduced in 2001. Hamm took the prize in 2001 and 2002. Prinz won it in 2003, 2004 and 2005. Marta came top of the voting list in 2006, 2007 and 2008.

MOST FINALS APPEARANCES (BY TOURNAMENTS)

5   Kristine Lilly (US – 1991, 1995, 1999, 2003, 2007)
4   Bente Nordby (Norway – 1995, 1999, 2003, 2007)
    Joy Fawcett (US – 1991, 1995, 1999, 2003)
    Julie Foudy (US – 1991, 1995, 1999, 2003)
    Mia Hamm (US – 1991, 1995, 1999, 2003)
    Hege Riise (Norway – 1991, 1995, 1999, 2003)
    Sun Wen (China – 1991, 1995, 1999, 2003)
    Bettina Wiegmann (Germany – 1991, 1995, 1999, 2003)
    Formiga (Brazil – 1995, 1999, 2003, 2007)
    Katia (Brazil – 1995, 1999, 2003, 2007)
    Tania (Brazil – 1995, 1999, 2003, 2007)
    Sandra Minnert (Germany – 1995, 1999, 2003, 2007)
    Birgit Prinz (Germany – 1995, 1999, 2003, 2007)
    Sandra Smisek (Germany – 1995, 1999, 2003, 2007)
    Maureen Mmadu (Nigeria – 1995, 1999, 2003, 2007)
    Andrea Neil (Canada – 1995, 1999, 2003, 2007)
    Cheryl Salisbury (Australia – 1995, 1999, 2003, 2007)
    Homare Sawa (Japan – 1995, 1999, 2003, 2007)
    Briana Scurry (US – 1995, 1999, 2003, 2007)

SUN RATTLES THE MEN

In 1999, Shanghai-born Sun Wen became the first woman player ever to be nominated for the Asian Footballer of the Year award, following her performances in China's run to the 1999 FIFA Women's World Cup final. Three years later, she won the Internet poll for FIFA's Women's Player of the 20th Century.

PRINZ SEIZES FINALS CHANCE

In 2007, Birgit Prinz became the first player to appear in three FIFA Women's World Cup finals. She was also the youngest player to appear in a FIFA Women's World Cup final. The Germany forward was 17 years 336 days when she started in the 2-0 defeat by Norway in 1995. Team-mate Sandra Smisek was just 14 days older. The oldest finalist was Sweden's Kristin Bengtsson, who was 33 years 273 days when her side lost to Germany in the 2003 final.

MARTA'S FINAL AGONY

Brazil's Marta may have been the star of the 2007 tournament, but she was heartbroken in the final after Germany goalkeeper Nadine Angerer saved her penalty that would have put Brazil level. Germany won the match 2-0.

FIFA WOMEN'S WORLD CUP™ PLAYER OF THE TOURNAMENT

Year	Venue	Winner
1991	China	Carin Jennings (US)
1995	Sweden	Hege Riise (Norway)
1999	US	Sun Wen (China)
2003	US	Birgit Prinz (Germany)
2007	China	Marta (Brazil)

FIFA WOMEN'S WORLD CUP™ FINALS TOP SCORER

1991	Michelle Akers (US)	10
1995	Ann-Kristin Aarones (Norway)	6
1999	Sissi (Brazil)	7
2003	Birgit Prinz (Germany)	7
2007	Marta (Brazil)	7

ALL-TIME TOP SCORERS

1	Birgit Prinz (Germany)	14
2	Michelle Akers (US)	12
3	Sun Wen (China)	11
=	Bettina Wiegmann (Germany)	
5	Ann Kristin Aarones (Norway)	10
=	Marta (Brazil)	
=	Heidi Mohr (Germany)	
8	Linda Medalen (Norway)	9
=	Hege Riise (Norway)	
=	Abby Wambach (US)	

FIFA WOMEN'S WORLD CUP™-WINNING CAPTAINS

1991	April Heinrichs (US)
1995	Heidi Store (Norway)
1999	Carla Overbeck (US)
2003	Bettina Wiegmann (Germany)
2007	Birgit Prinz (Germany)

MOST FINALS APPEARANCES (BY GAMES)

30	Kristine Lilly (US)
24	Julie Foudy (US)
23	Mia Hamm (US)
22	Bente Nordby (Norway)
	Birgit Prinz (Germany)
	Hege Riise (Norway)
	Bettina Wiegmann (Germany)

THE FIRST SENDING OFF

Taiwan goalkeeper Lin Hui Fang was the first player to be sent off in finals history. She was red-carded after six minutes of Taiwan's 2-0 win over Nigeria in Jiangmen on 21 November 1991.

OTHER FIFA WOMEN'S TOURNAMENTS

"GOLDEN GOAL" NORWAY

Norway are the only team to have won Olympic gold thanks to a "golden goal". In the 2000 final, Dagny Melgren scored their winner 12 minutes into extra-time, to beat the US 3-2. That came as sweet revenge for the Norwegians, who had lost their 1996 semi-final to the Americans after Shannon MacMillan's golden goal.

CRISTIANE'S TREBLE DOUBLE

Brazil striker Cristiane is the only player to score two hat-tricks in FIFA Olympic history. She netted three in a 7-0 win over hosts Greece in 2004 and added another treble in a 3-1 win over Nigeria in Beijing four years later. Birgit Prinz is the only other hat-trick scorer, with four goals against China in 2004.

WOMEN'S OLYMPIC FINALS

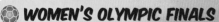

Year	Venue	Winners	Runners-up	Score
1996	Atlanta	US	China	2-1
2000	Sydney	Norway	US	3-2
	Norway won with a golden goal			
2004	Athens	US	Brazil	2-1 (aet)
2008	Beijing	US	Brazil	1-0 (aet)

THIRD-PLACE PLAYOFFS

Year	Venue	Winners	Losers	Score
1996	Atlanta	Norway	Brazil	2-0
2000	Sydney	Germany	Brazil	2-0
2004	Athens	Germany	Sweden	1-0
2008	Beijing	Germany	Japan	2-0

MEDALLISTS

Country	Gold	Silver	Bronze
US	3	1	-
Norway	1	-	1
Brazil	-	2	-
China	-	1	-
Germany	-	-	3

WOMEN'S OLYMPIC TEAM TOP SCORERS

1996:	Norway	12
2000:	US	9
2004:	Brazil	15
2008:	US	12

WOMEN'S OLYMPIC INDIVIDUAL TOP SCORERS

1996:	Ann Kristin Aarones (Norway)	
	Linda Medalen (Norway)	
	Pretinha (Brazil)	4
2000:	Sun Wen (China)	4
2004:	Cristiane (Brazil)	
	Birgit Prinz (Germany)	5
2008:	Cristiane (Brazil)	5

US DOMINATE OLYMPIC GOLDS

The US have dominated the Olympic football tournament since it was introduced at the 1996 Games in Atlanta. They have won three gold medals and finished runners-up in the other final. Norway and China were the Americans' early challengers, with Brazil and FIFA Women's World Cup holders Germany proving their toughest rivals in the past two Olympics (2004 and 2008). The tournament has rapidly grown in popularity, attracting record crowds at the 2008 Olympic Games in Beijing. FIFA have added two worldwide competitions for younger teams, too. The FIFA U-20 Women's World Cup was staged for the first time in 2000 and the first edition of the Under-17 event followed in 2008. Once more, the US have been prominent, though they have faced a strong challenge from North Korea in recent years.

GERMANS CHALK UP BIGGEST WIN

Germany hold the record for the biggest win in the Olympic finals. They beat China 8-0 at Patras on 11 August 2004, with Birgit Prinz scoring four times. The Germans' other goals came from Pia Wunderlich, Renate Lingor, Conny Pohlers and Martina Muller.

PRINZ ALWAYS ON TARGET

Germany forward Birgit Prinz is the only player to have scored in all four Olympic finals tournaments. Prinz is the joint overall leading scorer, along with Brazil's Cristiane. Both have ten goals. Next in the scoring list are two Brazilians, Pretinha (8) and Marta (6).

A LOSING RECORD

No team has ever won all of its matches in a finals tournament. However, Denmark and Japan (1996), Nigeria (2000 and 2008), Greece (2004) and Argentina (2008) lost all their games.

TOP CROWD FOR FIRST FINAL

The record crowd for an Olympic tournament match was the 76,489 who watched the US beat China 2-1 in the 1996 final at Athens, Georgia, on 1 August. The highest overall attendance was 740,014 for the 2008 finals in China.

EDMONTON FINAL SETS RECORD

The record attendance for an Under-20 match was 47,784 for the first final, at Edmonton on 1 September 2002. The US beat hosts Canada 1-0 with an extra-time winner by Lindsay Tarpley.

YOUNGEST, OLDEST GOLD MEDALLISTS

Cindy Parlow became the youngest gold medal winner – at 18 years 85 days – when she helped the US win in 1996. Joy Fawcett was the oldest – at 36 years 199 days – when she played in the winning US team in the 2004 final.

O'REILLY NETS QUICKEST GOAL

The fastest goal in Olympic finals history was scored by Heather O'Reilly of the US. She scored after just 42 seconds in their 4-0 win over New Zealand at Shenyang on 12 August 2008.

OLDEST, YOUNGEST PLAYERS

The oldest player in Olympic women's finals history was the Brazil goalkeeper Meg, when she appeared in the third-place playoff against Norway on 1 August 1996, aged 40 years 212 days. The youngest was also a Brazilian, Daniela, who made her finals debut against Sweden on 13 September 2000, aged 16 years 244 days.

FORMIGA LEADS THE WAY

Brazil midfielder Formiga has made most appearances in the Olympic finals – 21. Team-mate Tania has played 20 games. Birgit Prinz of Germany has made 19 appearances. Three other players have featured in each of the four Olympic tournaments – Tania of Brazil and the German pair, Renate Lingor and Kerstin Stegemann.

KRAHN SCORES FOR BOTH

Germany's Annike Krahn was the first player to score for both sides in the Under-20 tournament. She gave Germany an 11th-minute lead in their 2004 semi-final against the US, then conceded an own goal five minutes later. The Germans won 3-1 with goals by Melanie Behringer and Patricia Hanebeck. Simone Laudehr and Behringer netted in their 2-0 final win over China.

FIFA U-20 WOMEN'S WORLD CUP

FINALS

Year	Venue	Winner	Runners-up	Score
2002	Edmonton	US	Canada	1-0 (aet)
2004	Bangkok	Germany	Chile	2-0
2006	Moscow	N Korea	China	5-0
2008	Santiago	US	N. Korea	2-1

TOP SCORERS

Year	Player	
2002	Christine Sinclair (Canada)	10
2004	Brittany Timko (Canadad)	7
2006	Ma Xiaoxu (China),	
	Kim Song Hui (North Korea)	5
2008	Sydney LeRoux (US)	5

FIFA U-17 WOMEN'S WORLD CUP

FINAL

Year	Venue	Winners	Runners-up	Score
2008	Auckland	N. Korea	US	2-1 (aet)

TOP SCORERS

- 6 Dzsenifer Marozsan (Germany)
- 5 Vicki Di Martino (US)
- 4 Jon Myong Hwa (North Korea)
-   Courtney Verloop (US)
-   Chinatsu Kira (Japan)
-   Natsuki Kishikawa (Japan)

US SUNK BY KOREAN SUB

Substitute Jang Hyon Sun hit North Korea's 113th-minute winner to beat the US in the first Under-17 final, in Auckland, on 16 November 2008. The US went ahead in the second minute when Korean keeper Hong Myong Hui deflected a long throw into her own net. Kim Un Hyang headed a 76th-minute equalizer to force extra-time. Germany beat England 3-0 in the third place playoff, with goals by Inka Wesely, Turid Knaak and Lynn Mester.

KIM GRABS ONLY HAT-TRICK

North Korea's Kim Song Hui netted the only hat-trick in the history of the FIFA U-20 Women's World Cup finals, in their 5-0 win over China on 3 September 2006. Jo Yun Mi and Kil Son Hui scored the other goals.

SINCLAIR HITS FIVE

Christine Sinclair of Canada holds the record for the most goals scored in the Under-20 finals (ten). She also holds the record for the most goals in one game. She netted five in Canada's 6-2 quarter-final win over England at Edmonton on 25 August 2002.

Awarded on an annual basis since 2001, and run along the same lines as the men's award, only three players have been elected as the FIFA Women's World Player of the Year – Mia Hamm (in 2001 and 2002), Birgit Prinz (in 2003, 2004 and 2005) and Marta (in 2006, 2007 and 2008).

MARTA!

Marta of Brazil, FIFA Woman Player of the Year three times in a row and previously placed third and second, is one of the greatest women players of all time. Born on 19 February 1986, Marta Vieira da Silva has won a string of team awards and personal prizes. She won the Golden Ball as best player and the Golden Boot as seven-goal top scorer at the 2007 Women's FIFA World Cup and was a silver medal winner with Brazil at both the 2004 and 2008 Olympic Games in Athens and Beijing respectively. Marta has been twice a winner at the Pan-American Games and was voted the best player at the 2004 FIFA Under-19 Women's World Championships in which she scored six goals. Born and brought up in Dois Riachos, Alagoas, at the age of 14 Marta's teenaged footballing talents took her 1,200 miles south to Rio de Janeiro, where she startled coaches and other players with her attacking skill for Vasco da Gama and Sao Martins. In 2004, she transferred to Swedish club Umea, with whom she won four league titles and one domestic cup before transferring to Los Angeles Sol in the new Women's Professional Soccer championship in the United States in early 2009.

⚽ WINNERS

2001
1. Mia Hamm (United States)
2. Wen Lirong (China)
3. Tiffeny Milbrett (US)

2002
1. Mia Hamm (United States)
2. Birgit Prinz (Germany)
3. Wen Lirong (China)

2003
1. Birgit Prinz (Germany)
2. Mia Hamm (United States)
3. Hanna Ljungberg (Sweden)

2004
1. Birgit Prinz (Germany)
2. Mia Hamm (United States)
3. Marta (Brazil)

2005
1. Birgit Prinz (Germany)
2. Marta (Brazil)
3. Shannon Boxx (United States)

2006
1. Marta (Brazil)
2. Kristine Lilly (United States)
3. Renate Lingor (Germany)

2007
1. Marta (Brazil)
2. Birgit Prinz (Germany)
3. Cristiane (Brazil)

2008
1. Marta (Brazil)
2. Birgit Prinz (Germany)
3. Cristiane (Brazil)

One of football's biggest social events is the FIFA World Player Gala at which FIFA rewards a range of achievements in the international game over the previous 12 months. Pride of place, of course, goes to the World Player of the Year awards – presented in 2008 by president Sepp Blatter to top woman Marta of Brazil and to top men's player Cristiano Ronaldo.

FIFA PLAYER OF THE YEAR

The game's most prestigious individual prize, as voted by coaches and captains of international teams (who are given three votes each), the FIFA World Player of the Year award was started in 1991 (and was won by Germany's Lothar Matthaus). The award has been dominated by European-based Brazilians, who have won eight of the 18 editions of the prize. In 2008, Manchester United and Portugal star Cristiano Ronaldo became the first Premier League-based player to win the accolade.

CRISTIANO RONALDO

Cristiano Ronaldo crowned a sensational 2008 season when he was hailed as FIFA's World Player of the Year at a star-studded gala in the world federation's home city of Zurich. The Portugal forward was a clear winner ahead of Lionel Messi (Argentina and Barcelona) and Fernando Torres (Spain and Liverpool).

Remarkably, it was the first time a player from the English Premier League had lifted the award since its inception in 1991 (when Germany's Lothar Matthaus became the first winner). FIFA polls its votes from the managers and captains of the world's national teams. They are asked to vote for their top three players, but cannot vote for anyone from the national association under whose jurisdiction they operate. Cristiano Ronaldo dos Santos Aveiro was born on 5 February 1985 on the island of Madeira and began playing in the youth sections of his local club, Nacional of Funchal. Soon, however, he was playing in the Portuguese capital, Lisbon, for Sporting Clube – from whom Manchester United bought him for £13m in 2001 after he had starred against them in a friendly. A year later, Ronaldo was winning the first of a hoard of trophies as Manchester United beat Millwall to win the 2004 FA Cup. Honours since then have included three Premier League titles, two League Cups, the UEFA Champions League and the FIFA Club World Cup. In 2008, Ronaldo was the Premier League's top scorer with 31 goals and has twice won both the Footballer of the Year prize in England and the Players' Player of the Year award. In 2008, he was also voted European Footballer of the Year six months ahead of his world record £80m move to Real Madrid.

WINNERS

1991
1. Lothar Matthaus (Germany)
2. Jean-Pierre Papin (France)
3. Gary Lineker (England)

1992
1. Marco Van Basten (Netherlands)
2. Hristo Stoichkov (Bulgaria)
3. Thomas Hassler (Germany)

1993
1. Roberto Baggio (Italy)
2. Romario (Brazil)
3. Dennis Bergkamp (Netherlands)

1994
1. Romario (Brazil)
2. Hristo Stoichkov (Bulgaria)
3. Roberto Baggio (Italy)

1995
1. George Weah (Liberia)
2. Paolo Maldini (Italy)
3. Jurgen Klinsmann (Germany)

1996
1. Ronaldo (Brazil)
2. George Weah (Liberia)
3. Alan Shearer (England)

1997
1. Ronaldo (Brazil)
2. Roberto Carlos (Brazil)
3. Dennis Bergkamp (Netherlands)
= Zinedine Zidane (France)

1998
1. Zinedine Zidane (France)
2. Ronaldo (Brazil)
3. Davor Suker (Croatia)

1999
1. Rivaldo (Brazil)
2. David Beckham (England)
3. Gabriel Batistuta (Argentina)

2000
1. Zinedine Zidane (France)
2. Luis Figo (Portugal)
3. Rivaldo (Brazil)

2001
1. Luis Figo (Portugal)
2. Zinedine Zidane (France)
3. Rivaldo (Brazil)

2002
1. Ronaldo (Brazil)
2. Oliver Kahn (Germany)
3. Zinedine Zidane (France)

2003
1. Zinedine Zidane (France)
2. Thierry Henry (France)
3. Ronaldo (Brazil)

2004
1. Ronaldinho (Brazil)
2. Thierry Henry (France)
3. Andriy Shevchenko (Ukraine)

2005
1. Ronaldinho (Brazil)
2. Frank Lampard (England)
3. Samuel Eto'o (Cameroon)

2006
1. Fabio Cannavaro (Italy)
2. Zinedine Zidane (France)
3. Ronaldinho (Brazil)

2007
1. Kaka (Brazil)
2. Lionel Messi (Argentina)
3. Cristiano Ronaldo (Portugal)

2008
1. Cristiano Ronaldo (Portugal)
2. Lionel Messi (Argentina)
3. Fernando Torres (Spain)

OTHER FIFA AWARDS

In conjunction with the FIFA World Player of the Year awards (for both men and women), and tournament-specific prizes for best player, top scorer and top goalkeeper, in recent years the game's governing body has handed out other prizes at its end-of-year gala: the presidential award, the fair play award, a development prize, and recognition to the best rankings mover of the year and the team of the year.

1991
Fair Play award: Real Federacion Espanola de Futbol (Spanish FA), Jorginho (Brazil)

1992
Fair Play award: Union Royale Belge des Societes de Football Association

1993
Fair Play award: Nandor Hidgekuti (Hungary)*, Football Association of Zambia
Top Team of the Year: Germany
Best Mover of the Year: Colombia

1994
Top Team of the Year: Brazil
Best Mover of the Year: Croatia

1995
Fair Play award: Jacques Glassmann (France)
Top Team of the Year: Brazil
Best Mover of the Year: Jamaica

1996
Fair Play award: George Weah (Liberia)
Top Team of the Year: Brazil
Best Mover of the Year: South Africa

1997
Fair Play award: Irish spectators at the FIFA World Cup preliminary match versus Belgium, Jozef Zovinec (Slovak amateur player), Julie Foudy (United States)

Top Team of the Year: Brazil
Best Mover of the Year: Yugoslavia

1998
Fair Play award: National associations of Iran, the United States and Northern Ireland
Top Team of the Year: Brazil
Best Mover of the Year: Croatia

1999
Fair Play award: New Zealand football community
Top Team of the Year: Brazil
Best Mover of the Year: Slovenia

2000
Fair Play award: Lucas Radebe (South Africa)
Top Team of the Year: Netherlands
Best Mover of the Year: Nigeria

2001
Presidential award Marvin Lee (Trinidad)*
Fair Play award: Paolo Di Canio (Italy)
Top Team of the Year: Honduras
Best Mover of the Year: Costa Rica

*award presented posthumously

2002
Presidential award: Parminder Nagra (England)
Fair Play award: Football communities of Japan and Korea Republic
Top Team of the Year: Brazil
Best Mover of the Year: Senegal

2003
Presidential award: Iraqi football community
Fair Play award: Fans of Celtic (Scotland)
Top Team of the Year: Brazil
Best Mover of the Year: Bahrain

2004
Presidential award: Haiti
Fair Play award: Confederacao Brasileira de Futebol
Top Team of the Year: Brazil
Best Mover of the Year: China PR
Interactive World Player: Thiago Carrico de Azevedo (Brazil)

2005
Presidential award: Anders Frisk (Sweden)
Fair Play award: Football community of Iquitos (Peru)
Top Team of the Year: Brazil
Best Mover of the Year: Ghana
Interactive World Player: Chris Bullard (England)

2006
Presidential award: Giacinto Facchetti (Italy)*
Fair Play award: Fans of the 2006 FIFA World Cup
Top Team of the Year: Brazil
Best Mover of the Year: Italy
Interactive World Player: Andries Smit (Netherlands)

2007
Presidential award: Pele (Brazil)
Fair Play award: FC Barcelona (Spain)
Top Team of the Year: Argentina
Best Mover of the Year: Mozambique

2008
Presidential award: Women's football (presented to the United States women's team)
Fair Play award: Armenia, Turkey
Development award: Palestine
Interactive World Player: Alfonso Ramos (Spain)
Top Team of the Year: Spain
Best Mover of the Year: Spain

Note: The FIFA Fair Play award was instituted in 1987 and, before its inauguration into the annual gala, was made as follows:
1987: Fans of Dundee United (Scotland)
1988: Frank Ordenewitz (Germany) and spectators at the Olympic football tournament in Seoul
1989: Spectators of Trinidad and Tobago
1990: Gary Lineker (England)

*award presented posthumously

FIFA's world rankings paint a regular statistical picture of the rise and fall of the fortunes of both world football's mightiest nations and its minnows. Spain dominated the rankings in the wake of their triumph over Germany in the final of the 2008 European Championship co-hosted in Austria and Switzerland.

FIFA/COCA-COLA
WORLD RANKINGS 2009

FIFA launched its monthly world-ranking system in August 1993. The system, revised and simplified in 2005–06, computes national teams' results according to a formula based on the results of international A matches. Relevant data concern whether the match was competitive or friendly, home or away, goals for and against, strength of opposition (based on the world ranking) and regional strength (as derived from results at the previous three FIFA World Cups™). A decline in the value of past results, over the previous four years, is also taken into account.

RANKINGS (MAY 2009)

Pos.	Country	Points
1	Spain	1729
2	Germany	1362
3	Netherlands	1360
4	Brazil	1281
5	Italy	1271
6	Argentina	1195
7	England	1173
8	Croatia	1151
9	Russia	1117
10	France	1074
11	Portugal	1013
12	Czech Republic	968
13	Greece	927
14	Turkey	923
15	United States	919
16	Uruguay	909
17	Paraguay	906
18	Switzerland	883
19	Cameroon	871
20	Bulgaria	840
21	Israel	836
22	Ukraine	832
23	Serbia	819
24	Scotland	815
25	Mexico	803
26	Chile	796
27	Northern Ireland	795
28	Romania	792
29	Denmark	790
30	Nigeria	781
31	Ghana	779
32	Australia	776
33	Sweden	769
34	Rep. of Ireland	761

Pos.	Country	Points
35	Japan	749
36	Cote d'Ivoire	743
37	Egypt	742
38	Bosnia-Herzegovina	737
39	Honduras	736
40	Poland	724
41	Costa Rica	721
42	Ecuador	695
43	Hungary	662
44	Colombia	660
45	Norway	642
46	Korea Republic	641
47	Slovakia	626
48	Gabon	616
49	Mali	604
50	Morocco	593
51	Finland	591
52	Tunisia	585
53	Iran	582
53	Guinea	582
55	Saudi Arabia	577
56	Venezuela	565
57	Burkina Faso	559
58	Bolivia	554
59	Lithuania	550
60	Panama	547
61	Latvia	541
62	Belgium	534
63	Slovenia	510
64	FYR Macedonia	507
65	Togo	506
66	Senegal	497
67	Congo	493
68	Uganda	492

Pos.	Country	Points
69	Gambia	491
70	Jamaica	480
71	Bahrain	476
72	Algeria	475
73	Wales	468
74	Trinidad and Tobago	463
75	Cyprus	460
76	Uzbekistan	455
77	South Africa	453
78	New Zealand	450
79	Austria	446
80	Mozambique	436
81	Oman	432
82	Belarus	431
83	Libya	419
84	Rwanda	417
85	Sudan	412
86	Iraq	408
87	Peru	397
88	Congo DR	395
89	Canada	394
90	Zambia	393
91	Angola	392
92	Albania	390
93	Moldova	387
94	Iceland	386
94	Benin	386
96	Qatar	376
97	China PR	370
98	Sierra Leone	359
99	Syria	358
100	Cuba	355
101	Ethiopia	347
102	El Salvador	345

Pos.	Country	Points
103	Grenada	344
104	Tanzania	342
105	Cape Verde Islands	335
106	Korea DPR	334
106	Zimbabwe	334
108	Fiji	333
109	Kenya	327
110	Georgia	322
111	Guatemala	309
112	Malawi	302
113	Thailand	298
113	Estonia	298
115	Bermuda	296
116	Antigua and Barbuda	293
117	Montenegro	284
118	Kuwait	282
119	Equatorial Guinea	279
120	UAE	278
120	Barbados	278
122	Haiti	276
123	Botswana	274
124	Namibia	270
125	Armenia	268
126	Luxembourg	259
127	Jordan	255
127	Guyana	255
129	Suriname	253
130	Chad	251
131	Madagascar	231
132	New Caledonia	229
133	Burundi	224
134	Singapore	220
135	Swaziland	217
136	Vietnam	216
137	Kazakhstan	214
138	Liberia	207
139	Indonesia	206
140	Vanuatu	201
141	Nicaragua	195
142	Azerbaijan	193
143	Hong Kong	183
144	Niger	168
145	Yemen	162
146	India	156
147	Netherlands Antilles	152
147	Tajikistan	152
149	Maldives	142
150	Malta	141
150	St Vincent/Grenadines	141
150	Kyrgyzstan	141
153	Turkmenistan	140
154	St. Kitts and Nevis	139
154	Puerto Rico	139

Pos.	Country	Points
156	Liechtenstein	134
157	Mauritania	130
158	Myanmar	129
159	Lebanon	121
160	Eritrea	114
161	Lesotho	109
162	Sri Lanka	107
163	Malaysia	105
164	Solomon Islands	100
165	Faroe Islands	96
166	Philippines	90
167	Pakistan	88
168	Chinese Taipei	86
169	Somalia	82
170	Cayman Islands	76
171	Mauritius	74
172	Laos	73
173	Nepal	72
174	Bangladesh	70
175	Palestine	69
176	Mongolia	68
177	Samoa	64
178	Seychelles	61
179	Cambodia	60
179	Belize	60
181	Bahamas	53
182	Turks & Caicos Islands	51
183	Afghanistan	44
184	Djibouti	40
184	Dominican Republic	40
186	Brunei Darussalam	38
186	Guinea-Bissau	38
188	Guam	34
189	St Lucia	32
189	Tahiti	32
189	Tonga	32
192	British Virgin Islands	30
193	Macau	26
194	Bhutan	23
195	Aruba	22
196	Andorra	18
197	Dominica	12
198	Timor-Leste	9
199	Comoros	8
199	US Virgin Islands	8
201	Central African Republic	4
202	San Marino	0
202	Anguilla	0
202	Montserrat	0
202	American Samoa	0
202	Cook Islands	0
202	Papua New Guinea	0

REP. OF IRELAND
34th Position
761 Points

ITALY
5th Position
1271 Points

INDEX

PICTURE CREDITS

The publishers would like to thank the following sources for their kind permission to reproduce the pictures in this book:

(Abbreviations: T-top, B-bottom, L-left, R-right, C-centre, BKG-background)

Action Images: /Matthew Childs: 230, 231TL, 231TR, 231B

Getty Images: 102BR, 153C; /AFP: 66BR, 92BR, 107TR, 129BL, 152BL, 153TR, 155BL, 159C, 160BL, 161BL, 173BR, 174BR, 176, 187TR, 193BR, 201T, 201BL, 203BR, 206; /Allsport: 61BR; /Odd Andersen/AFP: 48BR, 51TR, 101TR; /Mladen Antonov/AFP: 96R, 194TR; /Brian Bahr: 135BL, 135BR; /Dennis Barnard/Fox Photos: 105C; /Robyn Beck/AFP: 171TR; /Sandra Behne/Bongarts: 166R; /Bentley Archive/Popperfoto: 23BR, 158B; /Gunnar Berning/Bongarts: 166BL; /Torsten Blackwood/AFP: 171BL; /Bagu Blanco: 247BR; /Bongarts: 42, 156C; /Shaun Botterill: 20L, 33R, 73TR, 78BC, 78BR, 110TR, 157R, 169R, 177, 190TR, 245BL, 247TR; /Clive Brunskill: 77TR, 189R; /Simon Bruty: 83BR; /Eric Cabanis/AFP: 149C; /Jose Cabezas/AFP: 147TR; /David Cannon: 31BL, 105B; /Ben Borg Cardona/AFP: 94BL; /Nico Casamassima/AFP: 173BL; /Ron Case/Keystone: 118B; /Central Press: 80BC; /Robert Cianflone: 122L; /Tim Clary/AFP: 178BL; /Fabrice Coffrini/AFP: 146TL, 240B; /Chris Cole: 169TR; /Phil Cole: 17L, 82L; /Yuri Cortez/AFP: 109BL, 136L; /Adrian Dennis/AFP: 190TL, 209; /Philippe Desmazes/AFP: 248-249; /Dimitar Dilkov/AFP: 89TR; /Denis Doyle: Front Endpaper, 54, 57BR, 245BR; /Allen Einstein/Time & Life Pictures: 178L; /Darren England: 148TL, 149BR; /Tony Feder: 148BR; /Franck Fife/AFP: 4BL, 32BL, 115BR; /Julian Finney: 96BL; /Stu Forster: 14C, 23TR, 25BL, 45BL, 67T, 88C, 103BR, 128TL, 187BR, 247BL; /Stuart Franklin: 184BL; /Romeo Gacad/AFP: 69BR; /Gallo Images/Foto24: 140-141; /Paul Gilham: 24C; /Georges Gobet/AFP: 69R; /Laurence Griffiths: 65L, 73TL; /Valery Hache/AFP: 126BR, 166BR, 192BR; /Ronny Hartmann/AFP: 65BR, 89C, 185BL; /Alexander Hassenstein/Bongarts: 34BL, 90R; /Haynes Archive/Popperfoto: 124BR, 151TR, 151BR, 200BL; /Patrick Hertzog/AFP: 43R, 46, 91TC, 151BL, 153BL; /Boris Horvat/AFP: 44TR, 191TL; /Hulton Archive: 16TC, 70BR, 151L, 159BL; /Karim Jaafar/AFP: 114BL; /Jasper Juinen: 16TL, 17TR; /Yeon-Je Jung/AFP: 125BL; /Burak Kara: 194BL; /Keystone: 30BL, 71BL, 80BL, 137BR; /Keystone/Hulton Archive: 48BL, 97BR; /Saeed Khan/AFP: 147BL; /Matt King: 127L; /Michael King: 159TR; /Ian Kington/AFP: 67L; /Ross Kinnaird: 15BL, 29BR, 163TL; /Glyn Kirk/AFP: 14R; /Toshifumi Kitamura/AFP: 148BL; /Joe Klamar/AFP: 66BL, 244B; /Christof Koepsel/Bongarts: 5BR, 55C, 68R, 69BL, 73C; /Mark Kolbe: 123B; /Jean-Philippe Ksiazek/AFP: 109TR; /Jimin Lai/AFP: 120-121; /David Leah: 165TR; /Bryn Lennon: 71L; /Francisco Leong/AFP: 76BR; /Alex Livesey: 144-145, 172L, 195TL; /John MacDougall/AFP: 41B; /Pierre-Philippe Marcou/AFP: 55BL, 57TR; /Clive Mason: 59R, 75BR, 88BL; /Jamie McDonald: 67BR; /Philippe Merle/AFP: 111TR; /Douglas Miller/Keystone: 15BR; /Jeff J. Mitchell: 22BL; /Filippo Monteforte/AFP: 93TR; /Don Morley: 15BC; /John Mottern/AFP: 133BC; /Beate Mueller/Bongarts: 62BL; /Peter Muhly/AFP: 95T, 184BR; /Kazuhiro Nogi/AFP: 218R; /Ryan Pierse: 68L; /Vincenzo Pinto/AFP: 181TR; /Jan Pitman/Bongarts: 175T; /Hrvoje Polan/AFP: 64BC, 75T; /Paul Popper/Popperfoto: 25TR; /Popperfoto: 20BC, 20BR, 24BL, 32C, 39TR, 40, 41TR, 50BR, 62BR, 65BC, 96BR, 104, 106TR, 106BR, 127B, 128BR, 129TR, 137BL, 155BC, 156BR, 159BR, 161TL, 161BR, 168L, 185BR, 186B, 188TR, 189TR, 189B, 192T, 195BR, 202L, 207BR; /Craig Prentis: 132BC; /Adam Pretty: 122R; /Gary M. Prior: 165B, 251TR; /Tony Quinn/MLS: 135TR; /Ben Radford: 56BR, 164, 246BL; /Roslan Rahman/AFP: 128TR; /Aizar Raldes/AFP: 108BL; /Chris Roberts: 179T; /Graeme Robertson: 187BL; /Rolls Press/Popperfoto: 16BL, 50BL; /Clive Rose: 15TR, 63TL; /Martin Rose/Bongarts: 44BR, 73B, 181BR; /Karim Sahib/AFP: 124C; /Mark Sandten/Bongarts: 30BR, 173TR; /Issouf Sanogo/AFP: 116T; /Wesley Santos/Fotoarena/Latin Content: 245BC; /Roberto Schmidt/AFP: 163BL; /Antonio Scorza/AFP: 33BL, 34C; /Torsten Silz/AFP: 39L, 160TL; /Javier Soriano/AFP: 58L; /Cameron Spencer: 241BR; /Michael Steele: 103TR; /Patrik Stollarz/AFP: 154BR, 180TL; /Koen Suyk/AFP: 43BC; /Henri Szwarc/Bongarts: 51BL, 109L, 116BL, 169BC, 186TR; /Bob Thomas: 11, 21C, 23TL, 24BR, 25R, 26L, 27BL, 27R, 37T, 47, 51BC, 53B, 56TR, 57TL, 58BR, 60BL, 75BL, 94BR, 100, 103BL, 107L, 109BR, 110BR, 111BL, 117TC, 125TR, 126T, 146BR, 153BR, 154BL, 155TR, 155BR, 158R, 161TC, 162R, 172R, 174BL, 175BL, 175BR, 179B, 180BL, 180R, 185TR, 188BL, 189TL, 190B, 191BL, 193BL, 195BL, 203L, 241TR, 246BC; /Bob Thomas/Popperfoto: 59L, 146BL, 150B, 152BL, 157TR; /Mark Thompson: 61R; /Omar Torres/AFP: 65TR, 125TC, 132BR; /Robert Van Den Brugge/AFP: 61BL; /Jean-Christophe Verhaegen/AFP: 92BL; /Ian Walton: 25BR, 70BL; /Koji Watanabe: 240TR; /World Sport Group: 123TR; /Andrew Yates/AFP: 244C; /John Zich/AFP: 241BC

Press Association Images: /AP: 52BL, 134, 150R, 157B; /Bernat Armangue/AP: 183; /Matthew Ashton/Empics Sport: 29L, 91TR, 107C, 117TR, 123L, 136R, 205BL, 214B, 222L, 236B; /Greg Baker/AP: 235BL; /Gavin Barker/Sports Inc: 117BL; /Fabian Bimmer/AP: 133L; /Gero Breloer/DPA: 2, 143C, 143BR; /Luca Bruno/AP: 9, 251BR; /Jon Buckle/Empics Sport: 237BL; /Adam Butler: 19TR; /Felice Calabro/AP: 171BR; /Lynne Cameron/Rangers FC: 64BR, 72BL; /Roberto Candia/AP: 197, 235TL; /Mario Castillo: 198TR; /Barry Coombs/Empics Sport: 60R, 220; /Malcolm Croft: 149TR; /Claudio Cruz/AP: 215R; /Ben Curtis/AP: 115L; /DPA: 35, 38TR, 43TL, 64BL, 71R, 107R, 158L, 171BC; /Adam Davy/Empics Sport: 5BL, 112-113, 117BR, 225TL, 234R; /Jerome Delay/AP: 143BL; /Alessandro Della Bella/AP: 224, 225BL; /Sean Dempsey: 36; /Digital Sports Archive: 238TL; /Pablo Duarte/AP: 76R, 77L, 211L; /Mike Egerton/Empics Sport: 6-7, 84R, 85BL, 137TC; /Paul Ellis/AP: 81BR; /Empics Sport: 83BL, 102BL, 162BL, 221BR, 223L; /Fred Ernst/AP: 210R; /Paul Faith: 26R; /Chen Fei/Landov: 237BC; /Carlo Fumagalli/AP: 84BL; /Vadim Ghirda/AP: 87BL; /Renzo Gostoli/AP: 228L; /Gouhier-Hahn-Orban/ABACA: 87R; /Michel Gouverneur/Reporter: 213L; /Frank Gunn/AP: 212R; /Zhang Guojun/Landov: 234L; /David Guttenfelder/AP: 219TL; /Themba Hadebe/AP: 142BR; /Nam Y. Huh/AP: 130-131, 204L; /Itsuo Inouye/AP: 217TR, 218BL; /Silvia Izquierdo/AP: 207BL, 227BR, 228R, 229T, 229BL; /Julie Jacobson/AP: 236TL, 239BR; /Shuji Kajiyama/AP: 219TR; /Shizuo Kambayashi/AP: 218BR; /Thomas Kienzle/AP: 97TR; /Ross Kinnaird/Empics Sport: 119T, 205TL; /Kai-Uwe Knoth/AP: 90L; /Junji Kurokawa/AP: 219B; /Jin-Man Lee/AP: 236TR; /Tony Marshall/Empics Sport: 12-13, 19TL, 44BL, 52BR, 77TL, 82B, 88BC, 89BR, 93BR, 95BR, 107TC, 108BR, 111BR, 119R, 123TL, 126BC, 127T, 135R, 149TL, 156TR, 200BR, 201BR, 210L, 215TR, 215BR, 221TL, 225TR; /Ricardo Mazalan/AP: 202R, 205BR, 214R; /John McConnico/AP: 87BC; /Cathal McNaughton: 14L; /Martin Meissner/AP: 4R, 38C, Back Endpaper; /Ricardo Moraes/AP: 226BL, 227TR, 227BL; /Peter Morrison/AP: 28BR; /Anja Niedringhaus/AP: 233; /Jussi Nukari/Lehtikuva: 212L; /Phil O'Brien/Empics Sport: 49, 102TC; /PA Archive: 19B, 26BL, 37B, 60BC, 74R, 167B, 216BR, 217BR; /Panoramic: 213R; /Claude Paris/AP: 229BR; /Eraldo Peres/AP: 226BKG, 226R, 226BR; /Gabriel Piko/Empics Sport: 198BL, 216BC; /Pinnace/Empics Sport: 69T; /Natacha Pisarenko/AP: 204B, 207TC, 221TR; /Sergey Ponomarev/AP: 80R; /Nick Potts/Empics Sport: 31BR; /Michael Probst/AP: 139; /Peter Robinson/Empics Sport: 16BR, 22TR, 27C, 38TL, 39TC, 45BR, 53T, 61TR, 63BL, 74BL, 83TR, 91L, 101BL, 110BL, 168R, 199BR, 211C, 225BR; /S&G and Barratts: 16R, 17BR, 18, 28BL, 56L, 77BR, 118R, 133BR, 142BL, 167TR; /SMG: 21BR, 23BL; /Marcio Jose Sanchez/AP: 211R; /Patricia Santos/AP: 98-99; /Steffen Schmidt/AP: 242-243; /Mary Schwalm/AP: 135L; /Ivan Sekretarev/AP: 80C; /Murad Sezer/AP: 4BR, 34R; /Sven Simon: 106BL; /Neal Simpson/Empics Sport: 63BR, 78BL, 79TR, 81BL, 84BR, 86B, 86R, 114BR, 133TL, 169BL, 203T; /Michael Sohn/AP: 5TL, 137TR, 238TR; /Thanassis Stavrakis/AP: 223R; /Jon Super/AP: 217TL, 235TR; /Alessandra Tarantino/AP: 79BR; /Topham Picturepoint: 76BL, 85BL, 95BL; /Fernando Vergara/AP: 198BR, 199BC; /John Walton/Empics Sport: 5BC, 45TR, 102TR, 125BR, 207TR; /Aubrey Washington/Empics Sport: 67BL, 72BR; /Paul White/AP: 222R; /Kirsty Wigglesworth: 29TR; /Witters: 170; /Ren Yong/Landov: 238BR; /Vincent Yu/AP: 239BC

Every effort has been made to acknowledge correctly and contact the source and/copyright holder of each picture, and Carlton Books Limited apologises for any unintentional errors or omissions, which will be corrected in future editions of this book.

ABOUT THE AUTHOR

Keir Radnedge has been covering football for more than 40 years. He has written countless books on the subject, from tournament guides to comprehensive encyclopedias, aimed at all ages. His journalism career included *The Daily Mail* for 20 years, as well as *The Guardian* and other national newspapers and magazines in the UK and abroad. He is a former editor of *World Soccer,* generally recognized as the premier English language magazine on global football. In addition to his writing, Keir has been a regular analyst for BBC radio and television, Sky Sports and the American cable news channel CNN. He also edited a tournament newspaper at the FIFA World Cup tournaments of 1982, 1986 and 1990. He has also scripted video reviews of numerous international football tournaments. He is also the London-based editor of SportsFeatures.com, the football and Olympic news website.